Advanced Sciences and Technologies for Security Applications

Indexed by SCOPUS

The series Advanced Sciences and Technologies for Security Applications comprises interdisciplinary research covering the theory, foundations and domain-specific topics pertaining to security. Publications within the series are peer-reviewed monographs and edited works in the areas of:

- biological and chemical threat recognition and detection (e.g., biosensors, aerosols, forensics)
- crisis and disaster management
- terrorism
- cyber security and secure information systems (e.g., encryption, optical and photonic systems)
- traditional and non-traditional security
- energy, food and resource security
- economic security and securitization (including associated infrastructures)
- transnational crime
- human security and health security
- social, political and psychological aspects of security
- recognition and identification (e.g., optical imaging, biometrics, authentication and verification)
- smart surveillance systems
- applications of theoretical frameworks and methodologies (e.g., grounded theory, complexity, network sciences, modelling and simulation)

Together, the high-quality contributions to this series provide a cross-disciplinary overview of forefront research endeavours aiming to make the world a safer place.

The editors encourage prospective authors to correspond with them in advance of submitting a manuscript. Submission of manuscripts should be made to the Editor-in-Chief or one of the Editors.

Hamid Jahankhani · Arshad Jamal · Guy Brown ·
Eustathios Sainidis · Rose Fong · Usman J. Butt
Editors

AI, Blockchain and Self-Sovereign Identity in Higher Education

Springer

Editors
Hamid Jahankhani
Northumbria University London
London, UK

Guy Brown
Northumbria University London
London, UK

Rose Fong
Northumbria University London
London, UK

Arshad Jamal
Northumbria University London
London, UK

Eustathios Sainidis
Northumbria University London
London, UK

Usman J. Butt
Northumbria University London
London, UK

ISSN 1613-5113   ISSN 2363-9466 (electronic)
Advanced Sciences and Technologies for Security Applications
ISBN 978-3-031-33629-4   ISBN 978-3-031-33627-0 (eBook)
https://doi.org/10.1007/978-3-031-33627-0

This Springer imprint is published by the registered company Springer Nature Switzerland AG
The registered company address is: Gewerbestrasse 11, 6330 Cham, Switzerland

Contents

The Role of Blockchain with a Cybersecurity Maturity Model in the Governance of Higher Education Supply Chains

Stefan Kendzierskyj, Hamid Jahankhani, Arshad Jamal, Osama Hussien, and Longzhi Yang

Abstract The world of Higher Education has become ever more complex with the expansion of global supply chains with numerous connected organisations, technological advancements, the recent demands of educational hybrid learning, and the growing importance attached to individuals' data and its security. In many ways the pandemic has accelerated the acceptance of remote learning and faster technological advancements but in other ways it has exposed areas of weakness with respect to the data security/privacy in education and its supply chains. Artificial intelligence (AI) can fundamentally support Higher Education objectives to enhance teaching efficacy and solve the future necessary skills essential in the twenty-first century. Multiple ways are being harnessed for AI to help solution Higher Education needs, even in helping to shape future employment requirements but comes with a heavy risk of infringing individuals' data privacy and more malicious scenarios when data is leaked through cyberattacks/breaches or through potential AI bias issues. The technology growth has added more complexity to education supply chains and there is more pressure being applied to have a higher degree of governance to minimise the risks. This chapter will focus on Higher Education supply chain issues and a suggested hybrid framework is presented that details the benefits of a Cyber Security Maturity Model (CSMM).

Keywords Education · Blockchain · Cyberattacks · IoT · Supply chain · Smart contracts · CSMM · AI · SSI · DID

S. Kendzierskyj (✉) · H. Jahankhani · A. Jamal · O. Hussien · L. Yang
Northumbria University London, London, UK
e-mail: stefan@cyfortis.co.uk

© The Author(s), under exclusive license to Springer Nature Switzerland AG 2023
H. Jahankhani et al. (eds.), *AI, Blockchain and Self-Sovereign Identity in Higher Education*, Advanced Sciences and Technologies for Security Applications,
https://doi.org/10.1007/978-3-031-33627-0_1

1 Evolution of Education and Its Supply Chain Relationship

Education has travelled a long way from its earliest beginnings. The history of organised education dates back to ancient civilizations such as the Egyptians, Greeks, and Romans [16, 26]. These ancient civilizations were the centre of learning and research that attracted scholars from all over the world. In the beginning, education was often reserved for the elite and was focused on practical skills such as reading, writing, and arithmetic. It was also closely tied to religion, with education often being provided by religious institutions. As societies developed and became more complex, education began to expand beyond these practical skills and began to include more diverse subjects such as science, history, and literature.

One of the earliest known universities was the University of Alexandria, which was founded in the third century BCE in Alexandria, Egypt. The University of Alexandria was a research and teaching institution that attracted scholars from all over the ancient world [20]. It was known for its impressive library, which contained over 700,000 scrolls and was considered one of the greatest libraries of the ancient world [21]. The teaching methods used in ancient education establishments and universities were similar to those used in modern universities, with professors delivering lectures and students engaging in discussions and debates [13, 24].

In the modern era, education has continued to evolve with the incorporation of innovative technologies, and as societies developed and became more complex, education began to expand beyond these practical skills and began to include more diverse subjects such as science, history, and literature. The development of the printing press in the fifteenth century played a significant role in the expansion of education, as it revolutionized education by allowing for the mass production of books and other educational materials. This made it possible for more people to access educational resources and contributed to the spread of knowledge and ideas.

During the nineteenth and twentieth centuries, education underwent further transformation with the development of public education and the increasing emphasis on higher education. The growth of the industrial revolution also led to the development of vocational and technical education to meet the needs of a changing workforce, new manufacturing technologies dramatically changed peoples working conditions and lives. The changes wrought by industrialization brought Europe, the United States of America, and most of the world into the modern age. The Industrial Revolution unleashed sustained, rising rates of productivity, first in the British economy, and later, throughout Continental Europe, northern America, and Upper Canada. The latter decade of the twentieth century saw the emergence of the words "higher education" and "higher education system" [43].

1.1 Technology Advancements in Education

The onset of technology and specifically the development of the internet has made significant impacts in how education is delivered and its interaction with all. The development of online learning platforms has made it easier for students to access a wealth of information and resources with clear advantages of platform freedom/access and independence from the classroom. When an application is deployed and maintained through one location, it may be accessed by numerous students who have internet connection as well as any type of computer. This era also brought the foundation of the intelligent tutoring systems and computer assisted learning and the use of Artificial Intelligence (AI) in education systems [4].

According to [25] there were three benefits of the computer assisted learning:

- speed of which content could be accessed and its ease of storage
- control that was given to the learner according to their objectives and goals
- improvement that could be achieved from the new ways of interaction between the learner and the teacher.

The University of Phoenix began offering an online instructional programme in 1989 [22]. Throughout the late 1990s through the 2000s, more educational institutions jumped on board the trend and started offering online tutorials and classes to those who could not join the on-campus classes. Many educational and training institutions now have a form of distance learning and the rise of popularity of the Massive Open Online Courses (MOOC's) have grown increasingly popular and widely available in offering university teaching [23].

Another type of emerging style of education in the twenty-first century is blended learning, which combines traditional face-to-face instruction with distance learning and has become increasingly popular in recent years [30]. Particularly, in the COVID-19 pandemic where many colleges were impacted, resulting in concerns regarding how to manage facilitating an education programme. Since the outbreak of the COVID-19 pandemic, universities across the globe have been scrambling to transition their courses to online, and offer blended options. While some institutions were already offering online courses before the pandemic, many were not prepared for the sudden switch. As a result, the quality of online courses has been highly variable, with some students praising the flexible format and others struggling to adapt. There are a number of reasons why the transition to online learning has been challenging for universities, as follows:

- **Access**: reliable internet connections, plus online access issues is more evident in the developing world and rural areas.
- **Quality**: Online courses can be exceedingly difficult to design well in terms of user experience/interaction, and many instructors are not well versed in this type of teaching format; resulting with some online courses being poor substitutes for in-person classes.

- **Engagement**: It can be difficult to keep students engaged using online courses, especially if the motivation is low due to quality/level of interaction. Also, potentially compounded with many students taking multiple online courses at the same time.
- **Support**: Students taking online courses often need more support than those using traditional courses, both in terms of academic and technical. Universities may not have the staff or resources to sufficiently cope with providing adequate support for their online students.

1.1.1 Education and Its Relationship with Emerging Technologies

Artificial intelligence (AI), has also started to play an increasing role in education, which has been used to develop personalised learning and AI-powered learning platforms. Although education needs the active engagement of human to human interactions, AI can work alongside the instructors in boosting education quality, particularly through personalisation/behavioural based learning. Another new emerging technology in the education sector is the rise of the Virtual Reality (VR) and Augmented Reality (AR) which enables many learners to apply whatever concepts and theories they have learned, inside a simulated physical scenario, making teaching approaches increasingly compelling. This does not imply that the current education system and materials, such as books and documents, would become obsolete but that AR and VR technology will make the course materials more accessible in a new interactive fashion [29].

The concept of the metaverse, and digital twins, has also gained attention in recent years as a potential tool for education and as a platform for virtual classrooms and online learning. The metaverse is a virtual reality in which people can interact with each other and with digital objects and environments. It has the potential to revolutionise education by providing a more immersive and interactive learning experience and enable more flexible and personalised learning; as students could access course materials and participate in class activities from any location. Students could participate in virtual simulations or role-playing exercises that allow them to experience real-world situations and concepts in a controlled environment. Students will have a more hands-on and interactive learning experience and learn through trial and error, without the risk of real-world consequences.

Digital twins has also gained increasing attention in recent years and is a virtual representation of a physical object, system, or process that can be used for a variety of purposes, including simulation, analysis, and control [35, 42].

A novel idea, which has gained attention in recent years, is subscription-based, Netflix-like education [36]. This model involves offering educational content on a subscription basis, similar to the way Netflix offers movies and TV shows, and provide a wide range of educational materials and experiences at a lower cost than traditional on-campus programs [35]. One example of an education company using this model is MasterClass (MasterClass n.d). The company offers online courses taught by experts in various fields, such as cooking, writing, and music. Students can access the courses on a subscription basis, and the company has attracted over 4 million subscribers since its launch in 2015.

1.2 Education Supply Chain

In the education sector, the supply chain's main goal is to increase the educational value by engaging students to collaborate with the instructors to satisfy the job market's ever changing demands and requirements. The educational supply chain has many stakeholders such as parents, students, faculty members, regulatory agencies, the government, employers and employees such as lecturers, admission officers and many more who are involved with education institution [1]. The mission of higher education institutions is typically stated in terms of their obligations to teach, research, and serve communities. Cooperation and opportunities for shared leadership extend beyond employees, including students, families, community members, and leaders from community-based organizations, local government agencies, and university partners. When educators and other school personnel collaborate with community members and families, they can ensure that the extra services and programs that they deliver are appropriate for, and responsive to, community needs and cultural practices (Community Schools Strategy). Before getting into the specifics of education and its supply chain it is worth looking at the fundamentals to all supply chains.

1.2.1 The Importance of Supply Chain

Supply chain has a much broader meaning than logistics [17], other than just the movement of the product as it involves the traditional logistics element plus other functions such as product development, marketing, customer service and finances and there tends to be an integrated relationship looping into many ecosystems since it can involve everything from gathering of raw materials to manufacturing, distribution and retail or end users. Globalization is a cause for supply chains to be more complex nowadays. Due to this element, Ribeiro and Ana [37] claim that supply chains suffer more risks and vulnerability as a consequence of the prominent level of uncertainty that has to be handled along the chain. Therefore, appropriate risk management is vital in the organisation and should normally include the identification, assessment, analysis, mitigation as well as contingency plans to control those risks. Ribeiro and Ana [37] agree that consciousness in terms of supply chain risk management as well as the ability to foresee the occurrence of disruption is vital, since underestimation of this aspect can cause severe impacts to the organization.

1.2.2 Understanding Supply Chain Risk

In recent years, activities such as global outsourcing, has contributed to generate a higher degree of risk in supply chain management, due to customer's demands, economic cycles, geographic locations and similar aspects [2]. Furthermore, natural events, crisis in different economies and illegal activities have also extrapolated those risks. As a consequence, the necessity to study and generate control over those risks has become almost mandatory and different risk models have been developed in order to implement mitigation strategies and control [41]. Nonetheless, some of those risks are inevitable and sometimes the cause of their occurrence is hard to establish due to the numerous amount of people involved within the supply chain [44]. Many logistics' companies understand the importance of risk assessments and use some quantitative models to assess supply chain risks nonetheless, little attention has been taken to mitigate certain risks, especially if it is assumed that the occurrence of those risks is rather unlikely [2]. As supply chain has become more complex, so too is the management of it and having supply chain working inefficiently can be an expensive cost and legal risk to organisations.

1.2.3 Key Reasons of Supply Chain Vulnerability

There are numerous moving parts to supply chains and outsourcing companies, which often run on disparate and outdated network infrastructures, making them easy prey to cyber threat actors. According to Duncan [11] some of the reasons why supply chain organisations are vulnerable to cyber risk are as follows:

- Organisations often disregard supply chain security as their problem
- Smaller organisations may lack the means and incentive to invest in security
- Supply chains expand the potential number of user targets, who can be undereducated about security
- Services organisations in particular have access to the information of multiple businesses thereby which make them a lucrative target for cyber threats
- Lack of visibility and inability to extend and control cyber security related policies of organisations across the supply chains.

Most security implementations fail because organisations do not implement proper processes and user education alongside security technology. The right balance is difficult to strike, especially for large, security mature companies—and smaller businesses often do not give it as much thought [11]. Many supply chain attacks use malware as their preferred weapon, which often relies on user error to activate it inside a company (phishing and spear-phishing attacks as the most common entry method). User orientated malware such as trojans remains the steadfast favourite of criminals, while the rise of enterprise ransomware has grown by over 340% from 2.8 million in the first quarter of 2018 to 9.5 million in the first quarter of 2019, [34]. WannaCry was the first successful large-scale ransomware attack, designed to inflict maximum disruption and it can be seen why the enterprise sector gained the attraction for ransomware.

1.3   Relationships in the Education Supply Chain

For supply chain management concepts to be implemented and used to their full potential, the qualities mentioned so far, necessitate a special strategy. A well-designed change management programme and agreement between the administration of Higher Education Institutions (HEIs) and the faculty should be part of the approach [1].

What is noticeable is the lengthy period between enrolment and graduation. As a result, the preparation of students for the employment market spans approximately four to five years. Academic independence and discipline are part of the educational institutions' moral code, which represents the most important distinction between them and business institutions [1]. There are significant relationships between several factors in education supply chain management; see Fig. 1. In addition to the facilitation of interaction activities with stakeholders, the supply chain sustainability efforts require higher education institutions to determine, manage, and develop their own internal expertise, skills, and knowledge [15, 31].

The current educational system is a complex system that is made up of a variety of stakeholders who are all interconnected, and all play a role in the supply chain. These stakeholders include General Education Institutions (GEIs), Higher Education Institutions (HEIs), the labour market, and professional development and retraining

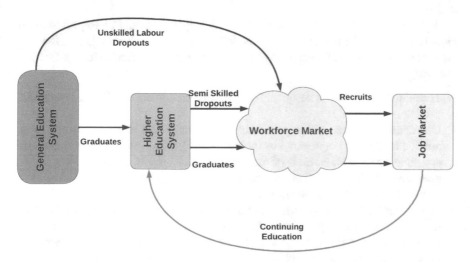

Fig. 1 Centre of the educational supply chain (workforce market)

providers. Each of these stakeholders has a different role to play in the overall system, and they are all connected to each other through a supply chain.

It was also stated in, Al-Turki et al. [1], that the interactions between all these parts as a chain of suppliers and clients. The flow of labour through educational institutions to higher education institutions to the labour market, where it finishes, is depicted in Fig. 1 and is at the core of the supply chain. For professional development and retraining, a return of workforce again from the employment market to HEIs is displayed. To help further explain these key components of the supply chain and their significant role that they carry, are as follows.

Labour market—is the most important stakeholder in the education system and at the heart of the supply chain and one that all stakeholders are connected to. It is where the flow of labour starts and ends and is made up of several different stakeholders including employers, employees, and job seekers.

General education institutions—are the first link in the supply chain, and they are responsible for providing education to children and young adults. These institutions include primary schools, secondary schools, and tertiary institutions. The general education institutions play a vital role in the education system, and they are responsible for preparing students for the next step in the supply chain.

Higher education institutions—are the next link in the supply chain, and they are responsible for providing further education to students who have completed their general education. These institutions include universities and colleges. The higher education institutions play a vital role in the education system, and they are responsible for preparing students for the next step in the supply chain, the next link in the supply chain is the labour market, and this is where the flow of labour starts and ends.

As mentioned, the main aim of the education system should be to provide individuals with the skills and knowledge needed to succeed in the workforce. However, there are various issues that prevents the education system from achieving this goal such as:

- The education system is designed for mass production not specific and individual needs.
- Universities are designed to pump out large numbers of graduates with specific qualifications that employers are looking for. However, this approach does not consider the individual needs of each student. As a result, many students end up graduating with degrees that they are not interested in and do not have the skills needed to succeed in the workforce.
- The current education system is outdated and does not reflect the needs of the modern workplace. With the ever-changing landscape of the workforce, employers are looking for employees who are adaptable and have a range of skills. However, the education system is not producing graduates with these skills.

- Managing the system is too expensive. The rising cost of tuition fees and living costs means that many individuals are unable to access education. This is particularly true for lower-income individuals who cannot afford to take on debt in order to pay for their education.
- Requirements and needs are not meeting the expectations of students, employers or the economy.

It is essential that reform takes place in order to ensure that the education system is fit for purpose and satisfies not only current demands but has futureproofing. The push production system is equivalent to the flow in the labour supply chain [1]. To fill the labour market with people who possess a variety of abilities that companies could need to hire in the employment market, HEI push specific qualifications along the chain in the push production process and Fig. 2 outlines this process. People serve as both customers and providers in the labour supply chain, while institutions act as service providers [1]. Students who have completed high school seek admission to universities, which is part of the supply end of the workforce supply chain. Universities enrol a sizeable number of individuals after putting them throughout many formalities, such as admission examinations and interviewing, and then put them into various pre-made academic programmes [1].

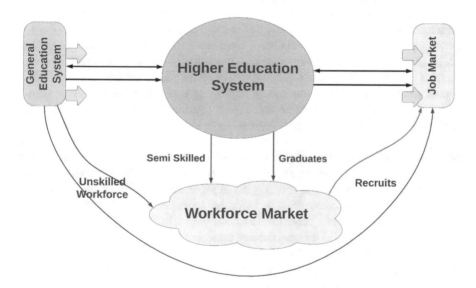

Fig. 2 Higher educational institutions in the centre of the supply chain

1.4   Increasing Risks to Education in Cyberattacks

The education sector is no stranger to data breaches and cyberattacks. In recent years, there have been a number of high-profile attacks that have led to the leak of sensitive and personal data of students and staff. While the education sector is working hard to improve its cybersecurity posture, the reality is that it remains an attractive target for cybercriminals.

One of the biggest challenges facing the education sector when it comes to data security is the fact that there are so many disparate silos of information. This can make it extremely difficult to implement a comprehensive and cohesive security strategy. Another problem is the lack of governance and information governance around data security. It can leave individuals vulnerable to having their personal data leaked. Data breaches in the education sector are becoming more common, as the number of cyberattacks and the amount of personal data being stored by educational institutions continues to grow. It is a major concern for both students and staff, as the consequences of a data breach can be extremely damaging.

There are a number of ways in which data breaches can occur, but some of the most common include hacking, malware, phishing, and social engineering. Hacking is when an unauthorised person gains access to a system or database, usually by exploiting a security vulnerability. This can be done remotely, or by physically gaining access to a system. Malware is software that is designed to damage or disable a system and can be used to steal data or gain access to systems. Phishing, a type of social engineering attack, where attackers send emails/text messages that appear to be from a legitimate source in order to trick the recipient into clicking on a malicious link or attachment and is an immensely popular type of cyberattack.

The consequences of a data breach can be significant, and can include identity theft, monetary loss, and damage to reputation. In the case of educational institutions, a data breach can also lead to a loss of accreditation or legal action. There are a number of steps that educational institutions can take to prevent data breaches, including implementing strong security measures, training staff and students in cybersecurity, and having a robust incident response plan in place. However, the most crucial step is to ensure that there is an effective information governance framework in place for managing and protecting core information, and includes everything from setting policies and procedures to destruction and retention of data.

With the technological advances of the twenty-first century, data breaches and cyberattacks have become all too common. Educational institutions are not immune to these threats and have been the target of data breaches and attacks in recent years. As more educational institutions adopt digital technologies, the risk of data breaches and cyberattacks increase. This is due to the fact that digital technologies are often not properly secured, leaving educational institutions vulnerable to attack. There have been a number of high-profile data breaches and cyberattacks on educational institutions in recent years.

Lincoln College was targeted by a ransomware assault in May 2022 [14], that unfortunately they were unable to recover from. While the pandemic had a role in the closure, with students electing to postpone enrolment or take a leave of absence, the institution was the first to collapse due to a ransomware assault. The cyberattack left vital systems unworkable, including those utilised for fundraising, recruiting, retention, and enrolment, and barred institutional data.

In 2014, the University of Maryland was the victim of a data breach that affected more than 300,000 students and staff. The breach, which was the result of a phishing attack, exposed a range of personal and financial data, including Social Security numbers, dates of birth, and credit card information [39]. Also in 2014, Iowa State University was the target of a cyberattack that resulted in the theft of personal data belonging to more than 30,000 students and staff. The attack exposed a range of sensitive data, including Social Security numbers and the students university ID, the main intention behind this hack was to use the university's servers for cryptocurrency mining operations.

Ransomware has also played a significant role in cyberattacks on educational institutions. The threat actor usually seeks a ransom charge in return for releasing access (via decryption to the locked files) to the afflicted organisation and in the UK, institutions such as Newcastle University, Queen's University in Belfast, Hertfordshire University, Oxford University and Sunderland University, have been affected. According to [8] approximately, one-third of UK institutions have been hit by ransomware. The UK's National Cyber Security Centre issued a warning to all the universities and educational sectors that as the number of ransomware attacks are increasing in the UK, the educational institution shall always prepare their security to safeguard the students from this types of attacks [18, 32].

In addition to the financial and reputational damage that can result from a breach, these incidents can also have a profound impact on the individuals whose data is exposed. This is why it is so important for educational institutions to have proper security measures in place to protect their systems and the personal data of their students.

2   Managing Data Security Using Blockchain, DID and SSI

In recent years, there has been an explosion of interest in blockchain technology.

Blockchain is said to be one of the most disruptive computing paradigms after the Internet; [40]. The technology has advanced more than just a means of financial and economic trading and looks to provide a consensus of trust which can be where transactions require storing by multiple parties who may be unknown and untrusted. Over recent years different arms of industry are starting to harness the technology to take advantage of its benefits, attributes and methods of application and provide a more auditable supply chain.

Blockchain technology has been quoted as allowing records to be 'shared by all network nodes, updated by miners, monitored by everyone, and owned and controlled by no one,' [40], p. 1]. Blockchain is based on a decentralised system, a distributed ledger database where sequential inventory of transactions has identical copies shared and maintained by numerous individuals over network nodes. The multiple parties hold the consensus over the data and its validity rather than one individual.

2.1 Blockchain Variations

There are several types of blockchain, and supply chain organisations need to evaluate, not just technology requirements, but also the business model requirements which can have a host of questions to decide what type of blockchain framework to setup. Understanding these types will help organisations decide on deployment and how should they allow permissions/authentication, depending on what type of data and other circumstances. These generally can be classified into three main types of Public, Private and Consortium (or hybrid) blockchains but can have options of many consensus mechanisms; these are the algorithms that set in place how the network will operate.

- **Permissionless Blockchains**: Also referred to as public blockchains and allow anyone to participate with no restrictions on reading/submitting transactions. All network nodes are unknown but take part in the consensus process. Examples of these are Bitcoin and Ethereum. However, public permissioned blockchains are restricted to those allowed to enter but anyone can read/submit transactions.
- **Permissioned Blockchains**: These private blockchains will restrict access and who may enter the network of nodes and transactions are only validated by those recognised as authenticated on the ledger; essentially the network belongs to an entity or organisation. Private permissioned are usually totally restricted such as Bluemix by IBM or Rubix by Deloitte as example.
- **Consortium Blockchains**: Approved entities validate requirements. An ecosystem would find this type blockchain more suited since all parties will have a common aim in deciding what process of data workflow should be included, etc., and so only where a particular group participates in the consensus process.

In terms of differences, it will mostly have impact in the aspect of decentralisation and how the technology handles the data considerations. For public blockchains, these offer complete decentralisation whereas hybrid or consortium blockchains will be partly decentralised. For private blockchains, as they are mostly controlled by one entity or organisation that set the 'rules,' can be a similar concept to centralisation as the group of users are a closed group.

For transaction processing purposes, organisations need to evaluate on blockchain's technical and confidential considerations. They need look at how best to execute access to data and can be dependent on what type of data it is, if it is sensitive, etc. The data storage methods can be as follows:

(1) **On-chain**: data is stored on the blockchain structure
(2) **Off-chain**: access links are saved on blockchain and function as authenticated indicators to data stored in other centralised networks/databases.

(3) **Hybrid**: having a mixture of the above with some standard data sets stored directly on the blockchain (beneficial for immediate permissioned use) and other access to off-chain data links.

(4) **InterPlanetary File System (IPFS)**: A protocol/network that allows peer-to-peer hypermedia storing and sharing of content, held across a distributed file system (such as BitTorrent). Network nodes store content it is interested in but with indexing information so it can be intuitive as to where content is stored. When requests are made to look up/search content, the network will request the nodes storing the content behind a unique hash to provide it. Mentioned by many to be the replacement to HTTP and the web of tomorrow.

2.2 Beneficial Attributes Common Across Blockchain

If content and data are held in silos there is more chance of corruption, fraud, traceability, audit trail failures and so on. Some of the benefits blockchain can offer are as follows:

- **Immutability**: Used for its authentication mechanism to allow permissions to stored data, and provides a fingerprint of all activities, held in chronological order (smart contracts) and cannot be tampered. Depending on the types of blockchain, then parties can make use of its smart contracts feature to help provide greater efficiency and integration, all time-stamped and ordered to give the immutability factor.
- **Smart contracts**: It can be observed as a method to ensure products/data in the supply chain are audited and records untampered. Using smart contract relieves a lot of the complex processes, negotiations and supply chain issues by streamlining it, to provide efficiency and reduce cost. This can support automated supplier contracts and provide analytics to maximise productivity and control.
- **Interoperability and transparency**: Traditionally, a lot of data is still held in silos and managed under a centralised or trusted third party (TTP) and the current challenges are the accountability in those silos. Lack of interoperability is an issue that makes it inefficient with a potential for tampering and loss of data. There is also limited control of data ownership whilst the individual, whom is the centre of all, has the least ownership or control. Blockchain can eliminate these data silos and provide a more coherent and seamless integrated data model that can control access through cryptographic methods, but where authenticated, make encounters between disparate parties more accessible.
- **Privacy and security**: The confidentiality, integrity, availability and audit (CIAA) is subject to a lot of pressurised issues both internally through non-malicious behaviours as, for example, accidental loss of data and to outside vectors such as targeted malicious behaviours for the purpose of identity and data theft. Industry is trying to tackle this with the day to day traditional structures (the typical network security, compliance, Intrusion Prevention and Detection Systems, training, etc.,) that help mitigate risk and have a continual cycle of lessons learned. But through an

additional layer of blockchain, it can offer enhanced security with encryption and would increase the integrity with the use of a decentralised and distributed ledger system. With data encrypted, more complex permission settings and the most suited consensus mechanism, will offer good controls for a secure authenticated data interchange.

- **Logistics and chain of custody transparency**: Supply chain logistics has become increasingly complex over the years and depending on the type of product can involve hundreds of stages spread across a global geography where multitudes of paperwork should correspond accurately to all stages and payments made. It is this securing of the supply chain and knowing it is completely accurate and non-tampered with that blockchain gives its appeal to. Applying technology to improve supply chain efficiencies is nothing new, considering the complexities around freight logistics, or computing systems to manage the manual processes. Blockchain can be observed as just a technology mechanism to provide confidence of knowing the data is maintained at 100% accuracy, is secure and validates the sequence of events from start to the end. As well as all the entities that engage in the supply chain process it is also an important aspect for the end user of the products to know that all is as it is supposed to be and transparent. It becomes exceedingly difficult to know if there are counterfeit issues, malpractice, criminality, etc., involved at any stage of the supply chain. Merely looking at documents that state the case is as factual and accurate is not enough to know it has not been tampered with, or if it is of unethical practices/origins.

2.3   Decentralised Digital Identities (DID)

A major application of blockchain is decentralised digital identities (DID). In the education sector, digital identity can be used for various purposes such as verifying academic qualifications, authenticating students and staff, and managing educational resources. There are many benefits of using blockchain for digital identity in education. First, blockchain is tamper-proof and thus provides an elevated level of security. Second, blockchain enables different institutions to share data securely and efficiently. Finally, blockchain gives individuals more control over their own data.

However, there are also some challenges associated with using blockchain for digital identity in education. For example, it can be difficult to change data once it has been committed to the blockchain. Additionally, there is a risk that confidential data could be exposed if the blockchain is not properly secured. Despite these challenges, blockchain is a promising technology for digital identity in education. By carefully addressing the challenges, blockchain can provide a secure, efficient and decentralised solution for managing educational data. With the development of internet technologies, the education sector has been under pressure to move away from the traditional way of handling data and information. The old system is seen as insecure and time-consuming. The new system, on the other hand, is seen as more efficient and secure.

The traditional way of handling data and information in the education sector is through the use of centralised systems. These systems are managed by a single entity. The problem with this is that it is easy for the entity to manipulate the data to their benefit. This is because they have total control over the system. Another problem with the traditional system is that it is slow. This is because the entity has to go through a lot of bureaucracy to get the data. This can take weeks or even months. The education sector is under pressure to move away from the traditional way of handling data and information. The old system is seen as insecure and time-consuming. The new system using blockchain, on the other hand, is seen as more efficient and secure.

The education sector is a fundamental sector in society with the span covering from the start of educating students to managing individuals and its requirements in the general labour force. The sector is responsible for imparting knowledge and skills to the future generations who will lead the societies of tomorrow. In recent years, the education sector has undergone a digital transformation. A number of institutions have started to use digital technologies to improve the quality of education. The use of digital technologies has also made it possible for institutions to offer more personalised and customised education experiences to students.

One of the most important aspects of the education sector is the issue of identity. Every student has a unique identity which is used to identify them within the education system. This identity is used to track their educational progress and to access their academic records. In the past, the education sector has relied on physical documents to store and manage student identities. However, this system is no longer feasible in the digital age.

The use of blockchain technology can help to solve the identity problem in the education sector. As it is a distributed database it can be used to store and manage digital identities and is secure and tamper-proof, which makes it an ideal platform for storing sensitive data. It can also be used to manage the issuing and verification of digital identities. The potential for blockchain to help solve many of the world's current education problems is very encouraging for all involved in the education ecosystem. Blockchain technology could provide a way to securely store and share data, to verify academic credentials, and to manage the digital identities of students, educators, and institutions.

The problem of identity management in education is a common one. In the traditional educational system, students' academic records are maintained by their schools or universities. These records are then used by other institutions to verify the student's identity and credential when they move on to further their education. The process is often slow and cumbersome, and there is no guarantee that the records are accurate or up to date. With blockchain, each student could have a secure, digital identity that is stored on a decentralized network. This would allow them to share their academic records easily and quickly with any institution they wish to attend. The records would be verified by the network, so there would be no need for slow and expensive background checks. In Fig. 3, the student has their decentralised digital identifier (DID) stored on blockchain. In this case the issuer (University) and Verifier (Examination entity) can use blockchain to check the DID of the student and be confident they have

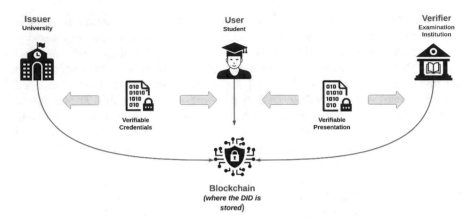

Fig. 3 Using blockchain as the mechanism to verify the DID of the student

verified what data needed checking, all with no risk to the student and in a secure and private method.

Another advantage of using blockchain for identity management is that it would allow for the creation of "self-sovereign" identities (SSI). This is expanding up from the use case of having a DID just for verifying education related data, as it can relate to wider and more practical uses outside of education but connected to everything in the education ecosystem (if we think of smart devices, IoT, banks, social media, etc.). This means that the student would be in control of their own data and would be able to allow or revoke permission for others to access it. Figure 4, explains the SSI model and digital attributes associated with each 'channel'. Students would have a much higher level of control over their personal data, and it would certainly support strengthening protecting their privacy. There are many other potential uses for blockchain in education. For example, blockchain could be used to create a secure, decentralised system for storing and sharing academic research. This would make it easier for researchers to find and access the data they need, and would help to prevent fraud. There are many ways in which the use of blockchain technology can help to solve the identity problem in the education sector and supply chain.

A number of institutions have already started to experiment with blockchain-based digital identity systems. The University of Nicosia in Cyprus was one of the first institutions to start using blockchain for student identities and has developed a digital identity system that uses blockchain to store and manage student data. The system is used to verify the identity of students when they apply for academic positions or when they need to access their academic records.

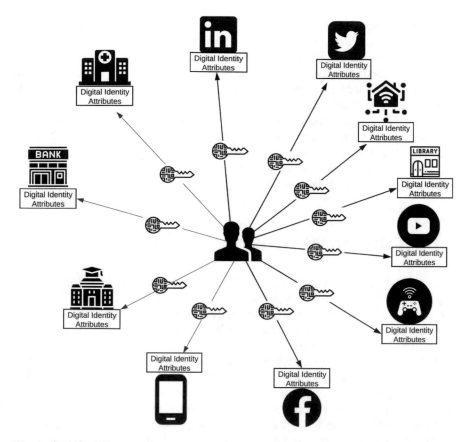

Fig. 4 SSI in multiple use cases to strengthen and protect individual data privacy and security

2.4 Self-Sovereign Identity and Internet of Things

There are concerns about the security and privacy of the data collected by IoT sensors, as this data is often transmitted over the internet and stored in cloud-based servers that may not have the same level of security as more traditional data storage systems. This can make the data vulnerable to cyberattacks and other forms of data theft. Within the education sector, IoT is increasingly becoming more common and utilised and therefore a potential weak spot for individual data loss/theft.

In response to these risks, the concept of self-sovereign identity (SSI) may be a solution to help mitigate these risks. In an SSI system, individuals have the ability to create, manage, and revoke digital identities without the need for a central authority or third-party verifier [38]. This helps to ensure that the data collected by the sensors is only used for the purposes for which it was intended and that individuals are not subjected to unauthorized use of their data.

One way that SSI can be used to secure IoT devices is by incorporating digital identity solutions into the device's authentication process. For example, an IoT device may require the user to present a digital credential in order to access the device or certain features of the device. This ensures that only authorised users are able to access the device and its data, helping to prevent unauthorized access and tampering, users can then easily and securely access their devices without having to remember multiple usernames and passwords. Overall, SSI and digital identity solutions offer a powerful tool for securing IoT devices and protecting against unauthorized access and tampering. By incorporating these solutions into their authentication processes, IoT device manufacturers and users can help to ensure the security and integrity of their devices and the data they collect.

3   The Role of Artificial Intelligence in Education

Artificial intelligence (AI) has the potential to revolutionize the education sector and generally any business or institution, but it also poses significant risks, if it is left unchecked [10]. One of the primary concerns is that AI could end up delivering what it thinks the job market requires, rather than what students need to thrive in their personal and professional lives.

There are several ways in which AI in education could pose a threat if left unchecked. First, AI algorithms may be biased, replicating and amplifying existing inequalities [10]. For example, if an AI system is trained on data that is predominantly from one gender or racial group, it may end up perpetuating biased outcomes. This could lead to a further widening of the already existing gap between underrepresented groups and the majority population. This is particularly concerning in the education sector, as AI is increasingly being used to make decisions that have significant consequences for students, such as selecting candidates for scholarships, admissions, or job placements. An AI system that is trained on data from predominantly male students may be more likely to recommend male students for certain scholarships or job placements, even if there are equally or more qualified female candidates. This could lead to a further widening of the already existing gap between underrepresented groups and the majority population, rather than promoting equity and diversity.

Another potential risk is that AI could displace human teachers and lead to a loss of personalisation and interactions in education [48]. While AI may be able to provide efficient and cost-effective education, it may lack the ability to understand and respond to the unique needs and learning styles of individual students. This could lead to a one-size-fits-all approach that does not consider the diverse needs and abilities of students. For example, AI may be able to provide students with customized learning plans based on their strengths and weaknesses, but it may not be able to provide the same level of support and guidance as a human teacher. AI may not be able to understand and respond to the emotional and social needs of students, or to foster critical thinking skills in the same way that a human teacher can. This may lead to a loss of personalisation and individualised attention, which are important for student learning and development. It is important to recognise the limitations of AI in education and to ensure that it is used in a way that complements and enhances, rather than replaces, the role of human teachers. This can be achieved through the development of clear guidelines and standards for the use of AI in education, as well as the establishment of mechanisms for monitoring and evaluating its impact. It is also essential to involve all stakeholders, including students, teachers, parents, and policymakers, in the development and implementation of AI in education.

That being said, AI is poised to offer a new level of personalised education, enable a revolution in ease and personalisation of university courses, and provide much-needed support to the professors by automating menial tasks in classrooms. AI technologies are well suited to achieving crucial education objectives, such as enhancing teaching efficiency and effectiveness, providing education for all, and developing the skills that will be essential in the twenty-first century [28]. Studies undertaken in survey's across ten countries, show that there are significant skills mismatches of the education system to reflect employers demands and frictions in the labour market, preventing matching individuals to jobs [27]. The survey indicated only 50% of students thought their education studies improved employment opportunities and approximately one third of employers thought skills shortages were a leading reason for entry-level vacancies. It is thought that AI can help to bridge this skills gap.

Using machine learning (ML) and AI data sets on potential employees may enable hiring companies to pinpoint precise skills sets and personal traits to increase success for individuals being placed in very suited roles and thus shorten the current skills gap. Fundamentally, AI can also help governments to make crucial decisions on forecasting job to market demand and steer educational institutions in an extremely focused manner. This is already being undertaken in Saudi Arabia, as their current exploration of machine learning as a tool to reduce unemployment. The administration hopes to leverage substantial amounts of past and forecasted economic and social information about the country to possibly guide students toward an education best matched to their abilities [28].

Another example of how AI can enhance the academic sphere is by automatic essay scoring. The University of California Berkeley has experimented with such solutions for years now. The idea behind it is that teachers will no longer have to manually read or grade lengthy course assignments. By accessing the tool's artificial intelligence engine, parameters are setup, so that all essays will be scored on categories such as organisation, content/ideas, language use and conventions as well as plagiarism detection.

Artificial intelligence has multiple uses in the education sector, mainly to take over heavy-weight tasks. It can also provide a more bespoke and individual learning experience with artificial produced one-to-one content that can help make it a more interactive and engaging experience for all students.

Some other AI education benefits are:

(1) **Automation of assessment tasks**: This can now be achieved by developing tools which automatically assess without connecting a human being's opinion manually.
(2) **Microcredentials**: where the course result is assessed by artificial intelligence based on its input on whether it assessed they had reached the particular goal(s), and so providing micro ranks.

AI also has the potential to transform the education sector by providing innovative solutions to a wide range of challenges faced by universities and include:

Personalised learning: AI can be used to create personalised learning experiences for students by analysing their learning patterns and adapting the course content to their individual needs and preferences. AI can help students learn at their own pace and improve their retention of the material and in the following ways:

- **Tutoring and mentoring**: used to provide one-on-one tutoring and mentoring to students through virtual assistants or chatbots. These AI-powered tools can help students with their coursework, provide feedback on their assignments, and answer their questions in real-time.
- **Grading and assessment**: used to grade assignments, quizzes, and exams, freeing up instructors to focus on more high-level tasks such as lesson planning and student engagement. AI can also be used to assess student progress and provide feedback to help students improve their learning outcomes.
- **Course creation and management**: used to create and manage online courses, including generating and organizing course content, tracking student progress, and providing feedback. This can help universities scale their education offerings and reach a wider audience.
- **Adaptive testing**: used to create adaptive tests that adjust to a student's level of understanding and provide more targeted feedback and create bespoke learning pathways. This can help students learn more efficiently and effectively.

As mentioned, AI has the potential to create course content tailored to the job market requirements in the education sector, helping universities prepare students for success in their careers.

Some of the detailed ways in which AI can be used to create job-specific course content in the education sector include:

- **Analysing job market data**: used to analyse job market data to identify in-demand skills and knowledge areas which would support universities to design courses and curriculum and meet the needs of employers. It will also provide students with the skills and knowledge they need to succeed in the job market.
- **Curating relevant course materials**: used to curate relevant course materials from a wide range of sources, including academic journals, industry publications, and online resources and help universities create course content that is up-to-date and relevant to the job market.

- **Generating customized learning paths**: AI has the ability to generate customised learning paths for students based on their career goals and the job market requirements in their field. This can help students stay focused and motivated as they work towards their career aspirations.
- **Providing personalised feedback**: AI can be used to provide personalised feedback to students based on their learning progress and the job market requirements in their field. This will help students to identify areas where they need to improve and focus their efforts on developing the skills and knowledge they need to succeed in their careers.

Overall, the use of AI to create job-specific course content in the education sector can help universities prepare students for success in the job market and meet the needs of employers. However, it is important for universities to carefully consider the ethical implications of using AI in education and ensure that they are transparent about their use of the technology.

One potential risk is that AI could lead to a shift towards standardised, test-based learning, rather than a focus on creativity and critical thinking [46]. AI systems may prioritize efficiency and the ability to quickly assess and grade large numbers of students, leading to a narrow focus on rote learning and memorisation. This could discourage students from pursuing higher-level thinking skills and stifle creativity, as students may feel pressure to focus solely on achieving good grades rather than exploring and engaging with latest ideas and concepts. Standardised testing and rote learning may be effective for assessing certain types of knowledge, but they do not necessarily promote deep learning or the development of critical thinking skills.

It is essential to ensure that AI in education is transparent, accountable, and ethically responsible. This can be achieved through the development of clear guidelines and standards for the use of AI in education, as well as the establishment of mechanisms for monitoring and evaluating its impact. It is also essential to involve all stakeholders, including students, teachers, parents, and policymakers, in the development and implementation of AI in education.

To ensure that AI in education is transparent, accountable, and ethically responsible, there are several steps that can be taken. First, it is important to develop clear guidelines and standards for the use of AI in education. These guidelines should address issues such as bias, data privacy, and the ethical use of AI. It is also essential to establish mechanisms for monitoring and evaluating the impact of AI in education, to ensure that it is being used in a way that is consistent with these guidelines and standards. Involving all stakeholders in the development and implementation of AI in education is also essential and includes students, teachers, parents, and policymakers. By engaging these stakeholders, it is possible to ensure that the needs and concerns of all parties are considered, and that AI is used in a way that benefits all students. It is also important to recognise the limitations of AI in education and to ensure that it is used in a way that complements and enhances, rather than replaces, the role of human teachers. This can be achieved through the development of clear guidelines and standards for the use of AI in education, as well as the establishment of mechanisms for monitoring and evaluating its impact. Governance is needed in

AI because it is a complex and rapidly evolving technology that can have significant impacts on society and individuals. Without proper governance, AI could be used to perpetuate biases, undermine privacy and security, or make decisions that are not in the best interests of society. Governments have a significant role to play in the governance of AI. They can set policies and regulations that ensure that AI is used in a way that is consistent with their values and laws. They can also provide funding and support for research and development of AI governance frameworks.

There are clear opportunities for AI to greatly increase education quality, job market strategy, direction and student fulfilment in matching job skills to education achievements. However, the education supply chain is complex and fragmented and needs a more joined up methodology. The key question to address is data privacy and how AI may raise legitimate concerns regarding how the educational data is collated, mixed with personal data and how/where it is used. It is clear the education sector is no different in suffering from cyberattacks and data breaches; so, the question is how to ensure and improve the current solutions in place. Good intentions of AI measuring a student's longitudinal performance data (intended for teachers to help in assessments) could become public or other scenarios of poor performing students denied employment [28].

Hence, the focus on discussions around self-sovereign identity and the importance on mechanisms to protect individuals' data privacy is gaining momentum. AI is clearly a 'game changer' to help bridge the skills gap but with some caveats to consider regarding data privacy, governance of AI with frameworks and mechanisms to monitor AI bias.

4   Higher Education Cyber Security Maturity Model with Blockchain

Essentially, devising a blockchain framework to suit the education supply chain revolves around the environment and what the data interchange requirements are and other parameters that may go beyond just security aspects. This is why a combination of methodologies is needed.

In this section, a theoretical framework is presented where blockchain is supported with a Cyber Security Maturity Model (CSMM) that is the underlying structure supporting all education organisations that would sign up to the requirements of such a supply chain framework. The framework allows mechanisms such as blockchain/SSI to be more securely supported and further information governance procedures will be applied to give direction that is specific to the education supply chain and can be documented under the Statement of Applicability (SoA), explained later in this chapter. Within the supply chain the SoA mandatory controls needs be respected, followed and audited and also selecting those optional controls that enhance the model more directly and to their environment. What should also be considered is to ensure the continual review and amendment of the framework, as the supply chain evolves, using a methodology to monitor the SoA and organisations through perhaps models of Capability Maturity Model Integration (CMMi), Information Technology Information Library (ITiL), and other such type methodologies.

4.1 Cyber Security Maturity Model (CSMM) Framework

Taking a deeper dive in CSMM, is the following explanation of its use case applied to the education supply chain. According to [6], the cyber security model can be categorised in 5 distinct levels (see Fig. 5).

Chapman [6] employed the following 8 key characteristics to distinguish between the 5 levels of maturity:

(1) Senior Management Attitude
(2) Project personnel attitude to risk management
(3) Policy, plans and processes
(4) Terminology
(5) Risk appetite
(6) Engagement with the supply chain

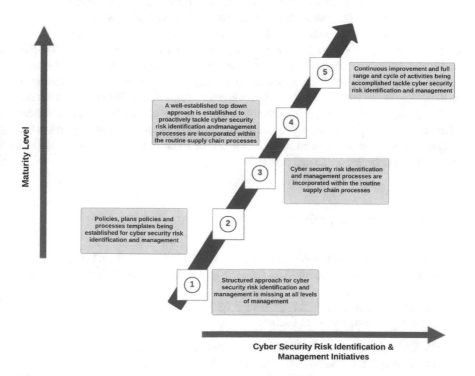

Fig. 5 Cyber security maturity model levels (Adopted from Chapman [6])

(7) Risk management integration and
(8) Meeting attendance.

The details are provided in Table 1.

4.1.1 End-to-End Education Framework Combined with CSMM

In Fig. 6, a framework is suggested for the end-to-end education supply chain using blockchain and SSI as the underpinning mechanism to control the transparency, tracking and audit trail. The model will help position typical current areas of concern and how this framework may help position and protect these points of the chain of custody where problems are encountered, and numbered points explained in Table 1.

The underlying framework that all organisations sign up to and agree to its requirements is the Cyber Security Maturity Model (CSMM) that ensures compliance, diligence and process is adhered to. The end-to-end supply chain can then be secured with blockchain and its attributes, complimented by a methodology that will monitor, audit and check compliance through CMMi or a similar type of industry standard. This framework fits in with earlier explained end-to-end verification models undertaken in Ireland and similar Euro models but goes further than just a means of verification. It applies a framework that encompasses that cyber risk identification, how to plan and facilitate policies to match and incorporate it across the supply chain; then the approach top-down to tackle risk treatment and of course the especially important continuous cycle of improvement. Tied into this is the monitoring and ongoing training that each organisation in the supply chain should be undertaking to compliment the complete process and ensure to limit its identified risks. Interestingly, although this proposed framework focuses on the education industry it could also be applied to practically any industry where there are many moving parts in the supply chain, where it could be subject to forms of fraud or similar and where ethics are misaligned or danger to end users.

4.2 Cyber Risk Standards

A key part of understanding the Cyber Security risks and issues facing supply chains in the industry 4.0 context, involves reflecting on the 7 standards. Table 2 explains these.

According to Radanlieve et al., findings for the cyber risks standards reviewed in Table 3 can be summarized as follows:

- **The FAIR (Factor Analysis of Information Risk)** promotes a quantitative, risk based, acceptable level of loss exposure. In practice, FAIR represents a framework for understanding, measuring and analysing information risk in financial terms. The FAIR model is complementary to existing risk frameworks and applies

Table 1 Key characteristics of cyber security maturity model levels (Adopted from Chapman [6])

S. No.	Attributes	Level 1	Level 2	Level 3	Level 4	Level 5
1	Senior management attitude	Unsupportive, unaccommodating, obstructive, hostile	Passive support	Support the concept but not directly engaged	Directly engaged in risk management	Actively champion risk management and call to task individuals or teams that do not adhere to published practices
2	Project personnel attitude to risk management	Disciplines address risk matters if all other activities are complete	Disciplines pay lip service to risk management and treat it as a chore	Visible improvement over time	Value-add of risk management understood but not yet second nature	The value-add of risk management is understood, the ramifications or poor implementation accepted and recognised and participation 'second nature'
3	Policy, plans and processes	Not prepared, signed-off, disseminated or briefed-out	Under development and not yet put into practice	Revised and updated as required	Prepared, signed-off, disseminated, briefed-out to the project and updated as required	Completed, regularly reviewed and being implemented
4	Terminology	No common vocabulary leading to different interpretation of the same terms and confusion	Common vocabulary starting to evolve	Common vocabulary starting to evolve	Terms and definitions complete and being augmented as required	Mutual understanding of the terms and definitions and are in everyday use. Additional terms added as required

(continued)

Table 1 (continued)

S. No.	Attributes	Level 1	Level 2	Level 3	Level 4	Level 5
5	Risk appetite	No common understanding of risk appetite, capacity, tolerance or target	Evolving comprehension of appetite, capacity, tolerance and target	The terms appetite, capacity, tolerance and target defined as they relate to the organisation	Appreciation of appetite, capacity and tolerance and reflected in approaches to procurement	Limitations of appetite and capacity reflected in the assessment of threats and the approach adopted towards the supply chain
6	Engagement with the supply chain	Lack of integration of risk management with the supply chain and procurement processes	Emerging awareness of the need for risk management to be integrated with the procurement processes	Being improved over time	Engagement being refined	Clear understanding of the transfer and retention of risk and contract documents prepared on the basis of the agreed ownership of risk
7	Risk management integration	Not commenced	Emergence of the recognition of the need to integrate risk management with the other disciplines	Integration commenced but not completed with the other core project disciples	Almost completely integrated with the other core project disciples	Fully integrated with other project disciplines such as estimating, scheduling and change control
8	Meeting attendance	Need for meetings challenged or project personnel decline to attend	Poor, inconsistent, late, ill prepared	Improved attendance but preparation for meetings inadequate diminishing effectiveness	Standing meeting agenda refined as required	Scheduled meetings regularly attended and absences challenged and not tolerated

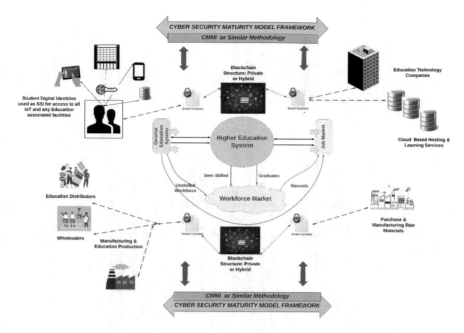

Fig. 6 Education CSMM/blockchain framework to manage the supply chain through whole education lifecycle

knowledge from existing quantitative models, such as RiskLens, and Cyber VaR [12].

- **The CMMI (Capability Maturity Model Integrated)** integrates five levels of the original Capability Maturity Model (CMM) [45]. However, this model does not provide guidance on disaster and recovery planning [7].
- **CVSS (Common Vulnerability Scoring System)** provides 'Modified Base Metrics' for assigning metric values to real vulnerabilities. The 'Modified Base Metrics' represent a severity group (low, medium, high, critical), associated with a mathematical approximation of metric combinations ranked in order of severity. CVSS works on assembling standards, guidelines, and practices that are working effectively in industry. However, like CMMI, CVSS also does not discuss disaster and recovery planning [9].
- **The ISO (International Organisation for Standardisation)** promotes a standard for disaster recovery. The ISO 27032 is a framework for collaboration that provides specific recommendations for cyber security. ISO 27001 sets requirements for organisations to establish an Information Security Management System (ISMS). ISO 27031 provides recommendations for disaster recovery [19].
- **NIST (National Institute of Standards and Technology's Cyber Security Framework)** organises cyber security activities in five categories: Identify, Protect, Detect, Respond, and Recover. The recovery category differentiates this framework from all other frameworks [33]. The NIST framework recognises the

Table 2 Leading cyber risk standards and frameworks

Cyber risk frameworks	FAIR	CMMI	CVSS	ISO	NIST	Octave	TARA
How to measure risk	Financial model	Combine/integrate capability maturity models	Modified base metrics	ISO 27032	Categorising risk	Workshops	Threat matrix
How to standardise risk	Complementary	Reflected in ISO 15504-SPICE	Mathematical approximation	ISO 27001	Assembling standards, guidelines, and practices	Encouraging institutionalisation and repeatability	Using standard template to record system threats
How to compute risk	Quantitative	Staged representation with five maturity level	Qualitative severity rating scale	Compliance based	Compliance based	Guide and training qualitative	Qualitative analytical
Disaster and recovery planning	Acceptable level of exposure	NA	NA	ISO 27031	Recovery planning; improvements; and communications	Recovery impact areas	Promotes and facilitates system recovery

Table 3 Example of statement of applicability (SoA)

A.5 Information securities policies

A.5.1 Management direction for information security

Control	Description	Adopted	Justification	Owner
A.5.1.1	Policies for Information Security	Y	Mission critical to the Company	Information Security Officer
A.5.1.2	Review of the Policies for Information Security	Y	Regular review is an objective as the SoA is dynamic document. It has senior management backing and approval from CEO	Information Security Officer

A.8 Asset management

A.8.1 Responsibility of assets

Control	Description	Adopted	Justification	Owner
A.8.1.1	Inventory of assets	Y	Inventory of assets are to be maintained and held secure. Transfer from 3rd party must be by secure FTP only	IT Director
A.8.1.2	Ownership of assets	Y	Clear ownership is identified	Data Content Manager
A.8.1.3	Acceptable use of assets	Y	Must be within the scope of contracts and legal as to the use	Data Content Manager
A.8.1.4	Return of assets	Y	Upon any client termination of contract, all content assets shall be loaded onto secure FTP and time advised to client before complete deletion	IT Director

A.10 Cryptography

A.10.1 Cryptographic controls

Control	Description	Adopted	Justification	Owner
A.10.1.1	Policy on the use of cryptographic controls	Y	Cryptographic controls are in place with military grade DRM protection	Information Security Officer
A.10.1.2	Key management	Y	AES 256-bit encryption in place protecting all assets and content and continually reviewed	Information Security Officer

(continued)

Table 3 (continued)

A.13 Communications security

A.13.2 Information transfer

Control	Description	Adopted	Justification	Owner
A.13.2.1	Information transfer policies and procedures	Y	Transfer of information is done securely as per IT Policy terms	CTO
A.13.2.2	Agreements on information transfer	Y	• Content assets must be transferred via secure FTP • Agreements with external hosting providers must be audited and assurances given from the 3rd party on data cloud security	IT Director
A.13.2.3	Electronic messaging	Y	Protected by normal use cases	IT Director
A.13.2.4	Confidentiality or non-disclosure agreements	Y	NDA's are in place	Legal Dept. and Regional Heads

A.14 System acquisition, development and maintenance

A.14.1. Security requirements of information systems

Control	Description	Adopted	Justification	Owner
A.14.1.1	Information security requirements analysis and specification	Y	New applications or enhancements must go through approval checks and signed off by IT Director	IT Director
A.14.1.2	Securing application services on public networks	Y	Fraud is covered by IT Policy. This control applies to applications are subject to unauthorized disclosure. Mainly the CRM system (Salesforce can only have authorized large data extractions	IT Director
A.14.1.3	Protecting application services transactions	Y	Handled within the IT Policy to safeguard transmission issues where software tools are used to alert and detect	Network Operations Centre Mgr

Not specified to any exact requirements and only as guidance example

importance of recovery planning and suggest the development, implementation and maintenance of plans for timely recovering and restoring any capabilities or services that were impaired by a cyberattack. NIST is the most advanced framework in terms of disaster and recovery planning, and it provides recommendations on recovery planning, improvements and communications [33].
- **The OCTAVE (Operationally Critical Threat, Asset, and Vulnerability Evaluation)** developed a standardised questionnaire to investigate and categorise

recovery impact areas. This is a qualitative method for measuring cyber risk through workshops. The OCTAVE method recommends three levels of recovery (low, medium, high), but fails to provide a quantification method for calculating the required level of recovery. Hence, one way to regard OCTAVE is as a guide for researchers measuring cyber risks [5].

- **TARA (Threat Assessment and Remediation Analysis)** is a qualitative analytical model that applies threat matrix and standardised template to record system threats. TARA promotes and somewhat facilitates the identification of appropriate recovery options, but fails to quantify the impact of cyber risks, which is crucial for deciding on appropriate recovery planning [47].

4.3 Statement of Applicability (SoA)

The Statement of Applicability (SoA) is an important basis for the treatment of the risks and direction of the Controls to deploy and covers the 10 clauses in ISO/IEC 27001:2013 [3]. It provides clear guidance on how to manage the risks and vulnerabilities and forms a basis of the monitoring and auditing process. A particularly important benchmark that all organisations in the supply chain can follow and adopt. It also means any new parties wanting to join the supply chain would need to have some level of understanding of these practises plus be willing to undergo constant monitoring and evaluation of a cycle of continuous improvement.

Table 3 is an example snapshot of a few identified important Controls as example as per BS ISO/IEC 27001:2013 [3]: Annex A 27001 controls.

The SoA will also allow flexibility to select optional controls that would benefit organisations within the supply chain that want to adapt more specific items to monitor.

4.4 Governance of the CSMM Supply Chain Framework

A strong Information Governance (IG) policy would be set in place for the supply chain that had a clear purpose and scope as to what the policy should cover and defined roles and responsibilities. The Information Security Management System (ISMS) sets in place the policies and procedures to secure sensitive data and ensure risks are minimised. Included within the SoA, part of ISO 27001 procedures can be a number of controls that manage risk areas. Likely there needs to be many simulations and pilots that could be run over a number of supply chains and accumulate enough understanding to know optimal configurations.

Identifying risks will be key and one of the biggest dangers of Internet of Things (IoT) and Enterprise Internet of Things (eIoT) is that these devices are often poorly secured, making them easy targets for hackers. In many cases, the data collected by IoT devices is sensitive, such as location, health information or financial data.

Potentially, with data falling into the wrong hands, it could be used to commit fraud, identity theft or other crimes.

With the increase of sensors, IoT devices and AI software across the education supply chain means a lot more structure and conformity are needed to ensure not just an end-to-end verification model as used by some examples described, but the method and framework to manage those that participate in the supply chain and new entrants understanding what they are signing up to. What is probably the most important consideration in the end-to-end supply chain will be the individual and safety of their personal data. If the student is taken as an example, they touch point across many parts of the supply chain from the basics of student personal identifiable information (so typically sensitive information such as name, address, date of birth, certifications, personalised learning, etc.) to eLearning systems, IoT sensors for tracking, entry and permissions, academic progress/qualifications, and so on. Tools and mechanisms such as blockchain/digital identities all enhance the capability to offer better security, tracking, audit and transparency. In combination with the student having a decentralised digital identity (DID) makes the model far more secure in terms of who is accessing sensitive information (is in allow or revoke permission) and mitigating any potential data loss, in the event of a data breach or cyberattack.

There is a definite synergy and link between blockchain and IoT devices/sensors towards helping to increase the efficiency, transparency and reduce the negative effects that criminality brings. The devices can behave autonomously and be attached to the network and collect data and coordinate data based on their location, identity, behaviour, etc. Other IoT sensors collect extrinsic data based on their behavioural and environmental surroundings. It is understandable, how IoT is harmonious to blockchain since these sensors and devices do exactly what blockchain wants to enforce in its benefits of immutability, non-tampering, transparency, etc. There is also the question of how artificial intelligence (AI) can also bring enhancements and benefits to blockchain operations. AI is being explored with operating with algorithms that can operate with data while it is in an encrypted state. Working in an encrypted state is always more secure than unencrypted.

Or perhaps AI data simulations on supply chain attacks and vulnerabilities or further explore data mining supply chain interactions.

5   Conclusions

Education has evolved significantly over the years as the supply chain became more complex with the fast changing landscape of market requirements, globalisation and technological advancements. At any point, tampering, misuse, malpractice, criminality and multitude of other negative factors, can all impact on education organisations and users who are trying to behave in a legitimate way and have unfettered access to the education ecosystem. The severity can depend on what and where the supply chain is impacted, all the way to damaging individuals, as we have seen in Higher Education supply chains and the numerous cyberattacks that have taken place over recent years. Blockchain can heavily influence how a supply chain community can behave and adhere to the conditions that all legitimate businesses require. Furthermore, blockchain/SSI and AI are complimentary to each other as AI can analyse data and make predications to help blockchain be more efficient and secure, operating in encrypted mode. As well as producing immense calculations on performance and better ways to enhance the model. However, AI needs its own governance framework to check on bias, corruption and other factors mentioned.

Lastly, the combination of a Cyber Security Maturity Model and blockchain/SSI gives an alternative method that various industries using supply chain can review to optimise a solution that minimises the criminality risk and dangers of individuals' data being stolen. It ensures all are agreed to the CSMM requirements, when approved to be part of the supply chain, and all are working towards efficiency, safety and reducing the risk of harm to end users. The framework can be applied in a comparable way, as shown in this education case study and model, to other industries with a complex chain of custody.

References

1. Al-Turki UM, Duffuaa S, Ayar T, Demirel O (2008) Stakeholders integration in higher education: supply chain approach. Euro J Eng Educ 33(2):211–219. https://doi.org/10.1080/030437 90801980136
2. Behzadia G, Michael O, Tavera L, Zhang A (2018) Agribusiness supply chain risk management: a review of quantitative decision models. Omega 79:21–42
3. BS ISO/IEC 27001:2013—Information Technology—Security techniques—Information Security Management Systems
4. Burns HL, Capps CG (2013) Intelligent tutoring systems: an introduction. Foundations of intelligent tutoring systems, pp 1–19
5. Caralli RA, Stevens JF, Young LR, Wilson WR (2007) Introducing OCTAVE Allegro: improving the information security risk assessment process. Hansom AFB, MA
6. Chapman RJ (2019) Exploring the value of risk management for projects: improving capability through the deployment of a maturity model. IEEE Eng Manage Rev 47(1):126–143 (First Quarter)
7. CMMI (2017) What is capability maturity model integration (CMMI)®? CMMI Institute. CMMI Institute [online]. Available http://cmmiinstitute.com/capability-maturity-modelintegra tion. Accessed 15 Dec 2022
8. Coker J (2020) A third of UK unis hit by ransomware in last 10 years. Infosecurity. https://www.infosecurity-magazine.com/news/third-uk-universities-ransomware/. Accessed 15 Dec 2022
9. CVSS (2017) Common vulnerability scoring system SIG. FIRST.org [online]. Available https://www.first.org/cvss/. Accessed 15 Dec 2022
10. DeBrusk C (2018) The risk of machine-learning bias (and how to prevent it). MIT Sloan Manage Rev
11. Duncan R, Data D (2019) How to secure your supply chain. Netw Secur: 18–19
12. FAIR (2017) Quantitative information risk management. The FAIR Institute. Factor analysis of information risk [online]. Available http://www.fairinstitute.org/. Accessed 15 Dec 2022
13. Garland R (2020, Aug 8) The education system in Ancient Greece. https://www.wondriumd aily.com/the-education-system-in-ancient-greece. Accessed 15 Dec 2022

14. Gibson K (2022) Ransomware attack shutters 157-year-old Lincoln College. Money-watch. https://www.cbsnews.com/news/lincoln-college-closes-ransomware-hackers-illinois/. Accessed 2 Jan 2023
15. Habib M, Jungthirapanich C (2008) An empirical study of educational supply chain management for the universities. In: 2010 international conference on industrial engineering and operations management Dhaka, Bangladesh, 9–10 Jan 2010. https://www.academia.edu/303521/Int egrated_Educational_Supply_Chain_Management_IESCM_for_the_Universities. Accessed 2 Jan 2023
16. Harris WV (1989) Ancient literacy. Harvard University Press
17. Hugos MH (2011) Essentials of supply chain management. Wiley, New Jersey, Hoboken, pp 2–39
18. Irwin L (2020) Victims of Blackbaud ransomware attack to take legal action. IT Governance. https://www.itgovernance.co.uk/blog/victims-of-blackbaud-ransomware-attack-to-take-legal-action. Accessed 2 Jan 2023
19. ISO (2017) ISO—International Organization for Standardization [online]. Available https://www.iso.org/news/ref2451.html. Accessed 2 Jan 2023
20. Joshi A (2021, Jan 31) The institutions of ancient history. Medium. https://medium.com/crypt-of-introspection/the-institutions-of-ancient-history-a4ab332a1303. Accessed 2 Jan 2023
21. Karlin S (2019, Oct 25) Oldest University unearthed in Egypt. Discover Magazine. https://www.discovermagazine.com/the-sciences/oldest-university-unearthed-in-egypt. Accessed 2 Jan 2023
22. Kentnor HE (2015) Distance education and the evolution of online learning in the United States. Curriculum Teach Dialogue 17(1):21–34
23. Kurzman PA (2013) The evolution of distance learning and online education. J Teach Soc Work 33(4–5):331–338
24. Lambert T (2022, Dec 2) A history of education. https://localhistories.org/a-history-of-educat ion/. Accessed 2 Jan 2023
25. Marchionini G (1988)Hypermedia and learning: freedom and chaos.Educ Technol 28(11):8–12. http://www.jstor.org/stable/44426153. Accessed 2 Jan 2023
26. Marrou HI, Marrou HI (1982) A history of education in antiquity. University of Wisconsin Press
27. McKinsey & Company (2013) Education to employment: designing a system that works
28. McKinsey & Company (2017) Artificial intelligence: the next digital frontier. https://www.mckinsey.com/~/media/mckinsey/industries/advanced%20electronics/our%20insights/how%20artificial%20intelligence%20can%20deliver%20real%20value%20to%20companies/mgi-artificial-intelligence-discussion-paper.ashx. Accessed 2 Jan 2023
29. Mentsiev AU, Almurzaeva PH, Ashakhanova MZ, Anzorova AI, Dauletukaeva KD (2019, Dec) The impact of digital technology on the study of languages and the development of digital education. J Phys Conf Ser 1399(3):033085
30. Moskal P, Dziuban C, Hartman J (2013) Blended learning: a dangerous idea? Internet Higher Educ 18:15–23
31. Muhonen T, Puhakka H, Timonen L (2022) INVEST4EXCELLENCE builds human capacity for more sustainable supply chains. Karelia University of Applied Sciences. https://karelia.fi/en/2022/11/invest4excellence-builds-human-capacity-for-more-sustainable-supply-chains/. Accessed 2 Jan 2023
32. National Cyber Security Centre (2020) Cyber security alert issued following rising attacks on UK academia. NCSC. https://www.ncsc.gov.uk/news/alert-issued-following-rising-attacks-on-uk-academia. Accessed 2 Jan 2023
33. NIST (2014) Framework for improving critical infrastructure cybersecurity
34. Posey B (2019) Why enterprise ransomware attacks are on the rise. ITPro Today. https://www.itprotoday.com/security/why-enterprise-ransomware-attacks-are-rise. Accessed 2 Jan 2023
35. Parmar R, Leiponen A, Thomas LD (2020) Building an organizational digital twin. Bus Horiz 63(6):725–736

36. Kumar PM, Asjola V, Chaudhary P, Shashikumara AA (2019) E-learning platforms for transforming higher education through distance learning. In: Librarianship development through internet of things and customer service, 61
37. Ribeiro JP, Ana B (2018) Supply chain resilience: definitions and quantitative modelling approaches—a literature review. J Comput Industr Eng 15:109–122
38. Satybaldy A, Nowostawski M, Ellingsen J (2020) Self-sovereign identity systems. privacy and identity management. Data for better living: AI and privacy. Privacy and identity 2019. In: IFIP advances in information and communication technology, vol 576. Springer, Cham. https://doi.org/10.1007/978-3-030-42504-3_28
39. Svitek P, Anderson N (2014) University of Maryland computer security breach exposes 300,000 records. Washington Post. https://www.washingtonpost.com/local/college-park-shady-grove-campuses-affected-by-university-of-maryland-security-breach/2014/02/19/ce438108-99bd-11e3-80ac-63a8ba7f7942_story.html. Accessed 2 Jan 2023
40. Swan M (2015) Blockchain: blueprint for a new economy, USA, O'Reily Media Inc.
41. Tang C (2016) Perspectives in supply chain risk management. Int J Prod Econ 103:451–488
42. Tao F, Zhang M, Nee AYC (2019) Digital twin driven smart manufacturing. Academic Press
43. Teichler U (2001) Higher education. In: Smelser NJ, Baltes PB (eds) International encyclopaedia of the social and behavioural sciences. Elsevier, Amsterdam, pp 6700–6705
44. Trkman P, McCormack K (2009) Supply chain risk in turbulent environments—a conceptual model for managing supply chain network risk. Int J Prod Econ 119(2):247–258
45. U.S. Department of Energy (2014) Cybersecurity capability maturity model (C2M2). Department of Energy, Washington, DC
46. Vincent-Lancrin S, van der Vlies R (2020) Trustworthy artificial intelligence (AI) in education: promises and challenges
47. Wynn J, Whitmore G, Upton L, Spriggs D, McKinnon R, McInnes R, Graubart L, Clausen J (2011) Threat assessment and remediation analysis (TARA) methodology description version 1.0. Bedford, MA
48. Yildirim Y et al (2021) Reimagining education with artificial intelligence. Eurasian J Higher Educ 2(4):32–46

Fighting the Tide—GPT and an Alarming Sense of Déjà Vu

Andy Phippen and Emma Bond

Abstract The emergence of Large Language Models such as GPT3 have caused ripples through academia around the impact of such tools on plagiarism and student assessment. There are claims that these tools will make the traditional assessment approaches obsolete and there has been something of a moral panic across the sector, with some universities already threatening students with academic misconduct hearings should they use these tools. However, we can see if we consider historical literature, that the same concerns were levelled at the widespread advent of search engines and, even further into history, electronic calculators. Rather than panic or try to ban the inevitable, we propose the approaches will have to adapt, but this is not the end of assessment as some have proposed.

Keywords GPT · Artificial intelligence · Moral panic · Assessment · Technology adoption

1 Introduction

> You are subject to me, as the land on which I am sitting is mine, and no one has resisted my overlordship with impunity. I command you, therefore, not to rise on to my land, nor to presume to wet the clothing or limbs of your master.
>
> Let all men know how empty and worthless is the power of kings, for there is none worthy of the name, but He whom heaven, earth, and sea obey by eternal laws. [1]

This famous quotation, documented supposedly over a century from the death of the individual purported to have spoken it, in Historia Anglorum—the History of

A. Phippen (✉)
Professor of Digital Rights, Bournemouth University, Poole, UK
e-mail: Aphippen1@bournemouth.ac.uk

E. Bond
Professor of Socio-Technical Research, University of Suffolk, Ipswich, UK
e-mail: e.bond@uos.ac.uk

the English People—relates to King Cnut (colloquially King Canute)—a tale that is well known in contemporary folklore and whose evolution of the tale suggests an English king who believed himself so powerful he could command the tides not to rise. The reality in the original source (with the second paragraph amended to the often quoted first) is a little different and suggests the King was showing his subject that no monarch is powerful enough to challenge natural law other than God himself.

Regardless, due to the communication and retelling of the story over the centuries, with embellishment and adornment with folklore, King Canute is now synonymous with the arrogance of man in wishing to control that which is impossible to command.

Perhaps this in, in itself, a useful tale in itself for authors to check original sources, rather than expressing colloquial wisdom as fact. But nevertheless, a worthy introduction to an exploration of the impact of Large Language Models and Natural Language Processing [2]. software, specifically the rising moral panic around Generative Pre-trained Transformer software (GPT) [3] and its use by students in producing articles, essays and report, as well as more subject specific issues such as code generation for computer science students.

More generally, the concerns arising at the current time in higher education centre on the use of these types of software in plagiarism among the student body (and also the wider academic corpus). The focus in context of this software is the widely available GPT-3, the third iteration of the GPT approach, and the one that has gained the most widespread adoption. However, we are also mindful that, at the time of writing (March 2023), GPT-4, an even more powerful and tested version of the tool has become available, predicting even greater use in generating text and other forms of content. And we are equally mindful that there are other tools emerging (such as Google's Bard[1]) and other platforms that existed prior to GPT which adopted a similar, less powerful, approach to content generation that have their roots in Natural Language Processing and Deep Learning (ibid.).

In this chapter, which is not by any means intended to provide a detailed exploration of the GPT-3 software tool, but instead a reflection upon how it has become the latest moral panic in the context of alleged academic misconduct and plagiarism, and if some of the rhetoric from the media was to be believed (see below), a platform the challenges the academy in the emergence of sinister technology that will shake the very foundations of academic integrity and change the very fabric of the student learning experience.

We explore the impact of GPT-3 current thinking in higher education both as academics who has explored disruptive technology throughout our academic careers (both of which began in the late 1990s), and as participants in the current higher education responses to the emergence of these tools. In our roles as senior academics within our institutions, we have seen a great deal of debate around the emergence of GPT-3 and have witnessed policy responses and questions from colleagues in other institutions. We remain active participants in the higher education sector and draw upon this experience with some of the observations we make. We also draw heavily upon previous academic debates around disruptive technologies and their

---

[1] https://bard.google.com/.

impact upon the academy and suggest that the current panic around GPT has failed to learn from history and adapt academic practice because of the emergence of new technology.

In the opening discussions in this article, we have referred already to the "moral panic" around the emergence of these software tools. While this language might be provocative, we will, in a later section argue that these current sectoral response to the emergence of these tools fits exactly into [4] seminal work ethnographically exploring the concept of the moral panic, how they emerge, and how they subside. By way of evidence of these panics, there is already a growing body of literature which specifically aligns the use of the tools with cheating [5, 6] and plagiarism [7, 8].

This is something we will explore in far more detail below. However, prior to exploring these issues, it is worthwhile to reflect upon the operation of GPT-3 as a tool.

1.1 A Brief Review of GPT-3

As we have stated above, it is not the intention of this article to be a technical exploration of GPT-3. There are other articles that do an excellent job of this (see for example, [9, 10]). Furthermore, there is a growing body of literature that considers the application of GPT-3 to specific text processing tasks, such as generating academic articles [11], and fictional stories [12]. It has been noted that the platform has potential to remove some of the early information collection and structuring tasks in the production of copy [13] and there are already a number of articles that raise concerns around deception [14] and its potential to be used to propagate misinformation [9]. Put simply, since its widespread availability, it has attracted the attention of a lot of academic communities.

Nevertheless, while we do not wish to present the reader with a review of reviews of the performance of GPT3, it is useful to understand its performance and its limitations, to be in a better to place to understand its potential impact upon the student body. Perhaps a useful starting place for this, given the nature of this article, is to allow ChatGPT (a chatbot interface that allows users to interact with the GPT-3 platform via a simple chat interface, such that the user can ask a question and the response appears via a simple browser/app interface presenting results as a conversational response) to explain what GPT-3 is. We simply asked it "What is GPT-3":

GPT-3 (Generative Pre-trained Transformer 3) is a state-of-the-art language model developed by OpenAI. It is the largest and most powerful language model to date, with 175 billion parameters. GPT-3 is based on the Transformer architecture and is trained on a massive amount of data using unsupervised learning.

GPT-3 is capable of performing a wide range of natural language processing tasks, including language translation, language generation, question answering, and text summarization. It can also be fine-tuned on specific tasks with supervised learning.

GPT-3 has received a lot of attention in the AI community for its impressive performance on various natural language tasks and its ability to generate coherent and human-like text.

Even with this simple answer, we are immediately faced with a few challenges should a student use this as an authoritative answer in, for example, an essay on GPT-3. Firstly, there are no sources—the response makes claims that are not supported with sources and do not allow the reader to seek other information for clarification. The jargon is somewhat technical in nature and does not elaborate on what a "parameter" is, the nature of the "massive amount of data" or what unsupervised learning might be. Admittedly, we might pursue these answers by following up the chat response with other questions (for example, "What is unsupervised learning?"). While we will not replicate the answers to these follow up questions within this article, we can assure the reader that these responses were equally devoid of referencing, and further steeped in technical jargon.

Perhaps most telling, in understanding the potential of this platform and its impact upon academic processes, is if you ask ChatGPT about the successor to GPT-3, the previously mentioned GPT-4. When asked about this, we obtained the following response:

> As of my knowledge cutoff date of September 2021, GPT-4 does not exist yet. However, it is expected to be the successor to GPT-3, a language processing model developed by OpenAI. GPT-3 has made significant advances in natural language processing, generating human-like text in a variety of tasks, such as language translation, question-answering, and content creation.
>
> GPT-4 is anticipated to be even more advanced than its predecessor, with potentially billions of parameters, allowing it to perform even more complex language tasks. However, as of now, there is no official announcement regarding the release or development of GPT-4.

What is certainly clear from this response is that the platform is only as informed as the data available to it. While there have been some concerns that this magical back box will be able to answer any question and replace the need for research, inquiry and the chasing of sources to support arguments in an academic text, even with this small and trivial experiment of its functionality, it is clear that while there are some impressive elements, such as the nature of the discourse presented and the speed of retrieval of factual information, as an academic scribe, it can easily be found lacking. Far better, it would seem, to take a definition from a peer review academic article written by a human which presents similar information in a more rigorous, accurately sourced manner [9]:

> GPT-3 (Generative Pre-trained Transformer) is a third-generation, autoregressive language model that uses deep learning to produce human-like text. Or to put it more simply, it is a computational system designed to generate sequences of words, code or other data, starting from a source input, called the prompt. It is used, for example, in machine translation to predict word sequences statistically. The language model is trained on an unlabelled dataset that is made up of texts, such as Wikipedia and many other sites, primarily in English, but also in other languages. These statistical models need to be trained with large amounts of data to produce relevant results. The first iteration of GPT in 2018 used 110 million learning parameters (i.e., the values that a neural network tries to optimize during training). A year later, GPT-2 used 1.5 billion of them. Today, GPT-3 uses 175 billion parameters. It is trained on Microsoft's Azure's AI supercomputer [15]. It is a very expensive training, estimated to have costed $ 12 million [16]. This computational approach works for a wide range of use cases, including summarization, translation, grammar correction, question answering, chatbots, composing emails, and much more.

While we can see similarities with this quotation and that generated from the platform itself, the above quote is written with supporting evidence, and elaborates on the points it is making, giving the reader far greater understanding on the nature of the platform, its source data, and its operation. Highlighting, perhaps, that these models still have some way to go in order to produce convincing academic writing. Nevertheless, it is worth noting that the generate text does at least provide a place to start, should one wish to write a more detailed article about the technical nature of the platform, reiterating the points made by [13] about its usefulness as a tool to reduce some of the repetitive and early stage tasks in the production of articles.

By further exploring the nature of the platform, we also took the liberty of asking ChatGPT about ourselves. Firstly, for Prof Phippen:

> Professor Andy Phippen is a well-known academic in the field of digital rights, particularly in relation to online privacy, cybersecurity, and child protection. He is currently a Professor of Digital Rights at Bournemouth University in the UK, where he also leads the Digital Society Research Theme.
>
> Prof. Phippen has published numerous academic articles, book chapters, and reports on digital rights, and has contributed to various policy debates and consultations on topics such as online safety, data protection, and internet regulation. He has also provided expert commentary on these issues to the media, including BBC News, The Guardian, and The Independent.
>
> In addition to his academic work, Prof. Phippen has been involved in various initiatives to promote digital literacy and online safety for young people, including the UK Safer Internet Centre and the European Commission's Better Internet for Kids project.

Most of the information presented by ChatGPT here is accurate. This should come as no surprise—the majority seems to be taken from a biography frequently circulated (for example for conference or seminar participation) that undoubtedly exists online in many places. However, there are also some elements in this short description that are not accurate. For example, Prof Phippen does not lead the Digital Society Research Theme at his University, and, to his knowledge, has not been involved in the European Commission's Better Internet for Kids project. However, given the small community around online safety across Europe, one can see how this inference might have been made, given stakeholder with whom I have worked. Nevertheless, the Digital Society Research Theme is entirely false, a completely incorrect inference by the platform.

However, for Prof Bond, the response is far less accurate:

> Professor Emma Bond is a well-known academic in the field of education. She is currently the Head of Research in the School of Education at the University of Winchester, UK. Her research interests include online learning, digital technologies, and teacher education. She has published numerous articles and book chapters on these topics and has presented her work at conferences around the world. In addition to her research, Professor Bond is also involved in teaching and supervising doctoral students.

The platform is incorrect about institution, research field and while there are hints that link to their actual discipline and the nature of their work, this is certainly extremely imprecise and also quite generic in nature, using language that could be applied to any profile of a senior and well established academic.

2   Don't Understand This, Lets Ban It!

The above exploration and review go some way to considering the potential for this particular technical innovation and its impact upon academic, but also very quickly highlights the flaws in its approach. A little knowledge, it would seem, is very useful in understanding the nature of an innovation and perhaps calming knee jerk reactions to its emergence into a particular field (in this a case academia) and society in general.

Which does beg the question why institutions are so key to prevent the use of this tool by students. Certainly, from the small experiments conducted above, we have quickly shown this is not a perfect or convincing solution, it is, at best, a starting point for the development of a discussion or an argument. However, should an individual not have tested the platform themselves, but instead reacted to reactions from others in the sector, we can see how this panic around the emergence of this technology has gathered pace. While the academic literature around the technology grows at a rapid rate (and will undoubtedly be absorbed into the training data of subsequent, larger, implementations of the GPT model) we can also see mass media keen to be seen to be engaging in the debates around the tool and, as is typical with mass media, trying to produce an attention grabbing headline that will lead to click throughs and article views. A brief, simple sample of recent headlines include:

- ChatGPT and AI writers: a threat to student agency and free will?[2]
- Universities warn against using ChatGPT for assignments.[3]
- Top French university bans use of ChatGPT to prevent plagiarism.[4]
- Cheating after ChatGPT – will AI destroy academic integrity?[5]
- AI breakthrough ChatGPT raises alarm over student cheating.[6]
- Cheating by students using ChatGPT is already on the rise, surveys suggest.[7]

All of above headlines have been taken from the last six months, and clearly show a groundswell of concern around the use of this new, disruptive technology. And also, undoubtedly contribute to concerns in the sector around the use of the tool for plagiarism and cheating by students.

We have, through this article, hinted at the response to GPT-3 having the hallmarks of a moral panic, rather than a measured response to an emerging technology that

---

[2] https://www.timeshighereducation.com/campus/chatgpt-and-ai-writers-threat-student-agency-and-free-will [Accessed March 2023].

[3] https://www.bbc.co.uk/news/uk-england-bristol-64785020 [Accessed March 2023].

[4] https://www.reuters.com/technology/top-french-university-bans-use-chatgpt-prevent-plagiarism-2023-01-27/ [Accessed March 2023].

[5] https://capx.co/cheating-after-chatgpt-will-ai-destroy-academic-integrity/ [Accessed March 2023].

[6] https://www.ft.com/content/2e97b7ce-8223-431e-a61d-1e462b6893c3 [Accessed March 2023].

[7] https://uk.finance.yahoo.com/news/cheating-students-using-chatgpt-already-104950384.html?guccounter=1&guce_referrer=aHR0cHM6Ly93d3cuZ29vZ2xlLmNvbS8&guce_referrer_sig=AQAAAK-QvrZuDc8skrFVETP91aBMn5pU75OuqLSRnZjg1qnUmkgTUP0fJ3fa-7sC6V-adoyWIY4fDXjED9CbAVTelTRKVS6V418wwwPbf2PwcqktrlWM54jV1pKXlMb9pUNCdN5kY_HL1o5atQAS1tNCfNfeKSOCxvfyp9sbBuhcAbxs [Accessed March 2023].

might cause some disruption to the status quo. If we consider this in more detail, an effective starting point to this is always Cohen's work in this area [4]. Cohen defines a moral panic as:

> a condition, episode, person or group of persons emerges to become defined as a threat to societal values and interests

And describes, through significant ethnographic field work, the evolving nature and stages of a moral panic.

1. **Something or someone is defined as a threat to values or interests**—something happens that is new, that has to potential to change things or threaten the status quo
2. **This threat is depicted in an easily recognisable form by the media**—if the media pick up on such a concern, and can distil this concern into simple messages distributed in mass media
3. **There is a rapid build-up of public concern**—as a result of simple interpretations of the threat, and the mass media communication, it is far more likely that concern will grow rapidly, and stakeholders will feel like they need to respond to "control" the threat
4. **There is a response from authorities or opinion makers**—the "gatekeepers of morality" have to respond to the threat and bring in "experts" who propose how the threat might be tackled or mitigated, which might result in new policies or laws
5. **The panic recedes or results in social changes**—it becomes the status quo. The fundamental aspects of this is that something emerges that could be viewed as a threat to the status quo, and therefore "something" needs to be done about it.

Unpicking this from the emergence of GPT-3 (and beyond) as a tool that might be used for plagiarism and how Cohen's model might be applied, we can see a clear fit if we break it down into the five stages:

1. GPT-3 is "new" to most within higher education. While it has its roots in the established academic disciplines of deep learning and natural language process, its scale and accessibility have now exposed the potential for these technologies, and it is a threat to the academic norms around assessment, particularly those who assess using essays and reports. If we cannot control this, it will significantly disrupt the status quo.
2. Broadly, artificial intelligence attracts the attention of the media, it is steeped in science fiction and while the technical understanding of the capabilities of artificial intelligence is not well understood, there is a great deal of fear and paranoia about "algorithms taking over" that is propagated by the media. This is a story the media can sell.
3. Certainly, there has been a swift build up of concern across the sector, resulting in many institutions, fearful of the use of the tools for plagiarising, compounded by a media narrative of students cheating and "destroying academic integrity", implement poorly thought about policies of a punitive nature

4. Which reflects the response of the gatekeepers (academics, academic administrators)—plagiarism is wrong, and academic integrity is paramount. Therefore,
   the gatekeepers have decided this is a technology that cannot be allowed to be
   adopted, it must be stopped!

In considering the response from gatekeepers, we are mindful that many institutions are already defining policies that "outlaw" the use of such tools and align their
use with academic misconduct. While we are privy to a number of these policies, it
is unfair to single out a specific institution by reproducing their policy here. We will,
instead, paraphrase the typical rhetoric and threats within:

- Staff are directed to remind students of plagiarism and academic offence policies
  within their institutions.
- Staff are directed to make clear in any assignment brief expectations in the use of
  these tools within the undertaking of the assessment task.
- Unauthorised use of such tools can give students an improper advantage and be
  guilty of plagiarism by not declaring the source of the work (should that source
  be a generative transformer such as GPT-3).
- Students caught using these tools will be subject to academic misconduct
  investigations and could risk a failed module or expulsion.
- They should only ever be used with the express permission of the module leader,
  who will provide clear guidance on permitted parameters for using such tools.

Within the nature of discourse in these policy statements, we can't help reflecting
upon the Canutian mindset of fighting the elements and the march of time.

And what of stage 5—acceptance or change? We would suggest that we are not
there yet, however, we are already seeing an emergence of literature, of which this
article makes a contribution, that is suggesting that, perhaps, that rather than blocking
the use of this tool, we should understand it and incorporate it into student learning
and assessment. For example, in Elkins and Chun [14]'s exploration of the potential
of GPT-3 to pass the Turing test, the often quoted test of a software's capability to
behave and converse in a human manner [17], they propose an adoption of these
tools which evolve digital literacy and practices from "copy and paste" to "prompt
and collate" [14].

3   An Alarming Sense of Deja Vu

A few words typed into a Web search engine can lead a student to hundreds, sometimes
thousands, of relevant documents, making it easy to "cut and paste" a few paragraphs from
here and a few more from there until the student has an entire paper-length collection. Or a
student can find a research paper published in one of the hundreds of new journals that have
gone online over the past few years, copy the entire text, turn it into a new document, and
then offer it up as an original work without having to type anything but a cover page. [18]

Stories about papers stored in the basements of fraternity houses and available for students to plagiarize have circulated among composition teachers for quite some time, but the virtual space of the Web and the download and cutting-and-pasting techniques available pose new questions related to issues of plagiarism, questions that we, as composition instructors, must address to be best equipped to better understand plagiarism, deter students from plagiarism, and encourage students to be thoughtful and critical researchers. [19]

PLAGIARISM, once known as "cut and paste" cheating, has morphed into "select, copy, and paste" cheating because of the Internet. Plagiarism continues to plague all disciplines in secondary and higher education because of easy online access to source documents. More worrisome, studies show that students not only plagiarize regularly but also believe that it is okay to do so. [20]

The above quotations are presented here as a means to highlight what we mean by a sense of déjà vu in the intuitional responses to a previous emergent technology that was going to shake the foundation of academia as well know it. Almost twenty five years ago, parallel debates to the ones we are having now around tools such as GPT-3 were being applied to concerns around the menace of the search engine, with its functionality that allowed students to access information easily and copy and paste it into essays, rather than the until then traditional approach of accessing articles in libraries and spending much of their hard earned grants on photocopies so they could take the information home and construct essays and analyses with information only readily accessible in printed form. While library systems provided indexes to the printed media, such that a student might perform a basic keyword search to locate articles germane to their need, it was rare that full text access would be available, so a fundamental academic literacy skill for those students (and we were both in this cohort) was obtaining information from print literature.

So, one can imagine the concern and surprise when early search engines, alongside an adoption of online methods and word processing, such that it was now far easier for a student to copy and paste information in electronic form and present it as their own which, in turn, resulted in much literature and academic debate around how we might prevent the use of these tools as they were eroding the foundations of academic credibility. Resulting in calls for anti-plagiarism policies and articles (for example [21–23]) defining technical approaches and methods academic could use to detect whether a student had fraudulently been using internet searches to compose their essays.

There were, of course, counter arguments, with some (such as [24]), suggesting that the adoption of the search engine should result in universities should rethink the concept of plagiarism as a negative just because it disrupts our processes and assessment approaches entirely, and that the internet challenges the very concept of authorship and the modernist notion of the author as an individual. Or, to phrase it another way, perhaps there are alternatives to how we might go about something?

It might seem, to the younger reader, that the idea a university wished to ban the use of search engines is an utterly ridiculous one. Nevertheless, these debates were taking place twenty-five years ago and the above quotes are but a tiny snippet of the fears of the impact of search engines on academic processes.

However, it we are to reflect upon Cohen's stages of a moral panic, we can clearly see that we are now well past stage five with search engines. The panic has receded and while there have been changes in academic process and how we monitor student plagiarism, change has occurred and been integrated into the mainstream. Indeed, it would seem ridiculous now for an academic to set an assignment saying that if students make use of search engines they will be failed or charged with an academic offence.

Around the same time as search engines became a concern for academia, the emergence, facilitated through online means, of essay mills, or contract cheating, also raised concerns and a panic in how we might stop their use [25]. Essay mills were online services that would provide essays for a student at a cost. Immediately responses emerged about how to stop their use, how to detect them in a student's work, and, in some cases incredulity that a student would use such a service in the first place [26].

Indeed, there have been serious legal analyses to consider whether the use of essay mills would be prosecutable under the UK's Fraud Act 2006 [27] resulting, in this particular article, in a:

> call for a new offence to be created in UK law which specifically targets the undesirable behaviours of these companies in the UK.

Which ultimately came to fruition in 2022, when the UK government passed the Skills and Post-16 Education Act[8] that makes it illegal to provide such services for financial gain, and also prohibits the advertising of contract cheating services and calls on Internet Service Providers to block access to these services. It is interesting to consider whether such legislation will be considered against the use of services such as GPT, given the statement in the statute in section 26 of the statue that:

```
26 Meaning of "relevant service" and other key expressions
(1) This section applies for the purposes of this Chapter.
(2) "Relevant service" means a service of completing all or part of
an assignment on behalf of a student where the assignment completed
in that way could not reasonably be considered to have been completed
personally by the student.
```

While one might level this accusation on a student using a GPT service, further narrative in the legislation goes on to define contract cheating as being a commercial service. Therefore, given the free use of some of the services offered by these platforms, it is unlikely that any use of the legislation would be successful. However, it remains to be seen whether it might be attempted, given the current appetite in the technology policy landscape (for example, with the much delay Online Safety Bill, 2023[9]) to place the burden of responsibility to prevent harm or illegal practice upon the platform itself. As we have explored in more detail in debates related to online harms [28], it seems a typical policy response to any emergent or disruptive technology is more like to align with the view "We don't understand this, lets ban it", rather than "Lets understand it, appreciate its capabilities and limitations, and how we might best adopt it into practice".

---

[8] https://www.legislation.gov.uk/ukpga/2022/21/enacted [Accessed March 2023].

[9] See https://bills.parliament.uk/bills/3137 (Accessed March 2023).

Again, returning to the fable, if not the accurate interpretation of the quotes attributed to King Cnut, the prevailing policy perspective is one where a view the technology can be controlled. Far easier, it seems, to try to stop things from being used that embark on a journey of developing digital literacies and embracing culture change.

For it seems we are failing to learn from history. While we have already provided evidence of moral panic around the use of search engines, now such an integral aspect of any student' digital literacy, there are other examples too from the education literature that show how disruptive technology will be rarely welcomed.

> Classroom use of calculators is so new that determination of long-range effects and the question of lasting increases of pupil achievement await extensive research. One early study [29] with calculators used only to verify answers to whole number operations found no improvement in computational skills or attitudes toward mathematics. [30]

When the electronic calculator became something that is easily accessible in shops, there immediately arose debate around whether such tools should play any part in the learning of mathematics, and there was much debate about the impact of electronic calculators on the arithmetic skills of young people was debate [31–34]. Again, it seems somewhat strange in 2023 that a calculator would not be part of the set of tools a student might use to perform mathematical problems. However, when they first became a mainstream technology, there were many opposed to their use and some (such as 34) who argued that using calculators would have a negative impact upon the development of critical thinking skills in mathematics and that handwritten approaches were more effective.

While we have, in this section, explored the nature of moral panics around emergent and disruptive educational technologies, we conclude with a simple message—you can't fight progress. We are minded of the observations of the author Adams [35], who, in an essay around the impact of technology on society, observed:

> I've come up with a set of rules that describe our reactions to technologies:
>
> 1. Anything that is in the world when you're born is normal and ordinary and is just a natural part of the way the world works.
>
> 2. Anything that's invented between when you're fifteen and thirty-five is new and exciting and revolutionary and you can probably get a career in it.
>
> 3. Anything invented after you're thirty-five is against the natural order of things

While Cohen's stages of moral panic align very closely with the frequent cycles of response to emerging technology, we feel this comment also sums things up very well—this wasn't the way we did it, so its not right.

4 A Post GPT Academia

So, perhaps we need to look backwards more, before looking forward. We have been here before, we have tried to stop the tide, and we have failed. And while the mainstream acceptance of search engines and calculators has now occurred, it is not still without some challenges along the way.

Alongside the use of search engines, we now have an environment where "Plagiarism detection systems" are implemented by universities to identify when a student might be copying and pasting without attribution, which, in some cases, is a useful tool to support academics in determining whether something is a student's own work. However, as is typical with any use of technology, it seems, there is now a culture of the application of the technology in a punitive manner, with the tools used in a threatening manner to scare students. We have both observed, in our roles as academics in our own institutions and external examiners in others, the presentation of the tool as some sort of surveillance device, reminiscent of the Docile Bodies theory claimed by [36], whereby an individual being told there are being monitored will become docile against the threat of discovery of wrongdoing. We have certainly seen some policies where tools would be used with blunt metrics, such that a score above a certain percentage would result in misconduct accusation. Which again would suggest a lack of appreciation of the capabilities and function of the innovation by those making use of it, rather than its intended use as a supportive tool to help students develop their academic writing skills. It would seem that, in a lot cases, we just can't help use technology badly.

As we have discussed above, surely a better approach is not to assume knowledge of emerging technology, but to endeavour to develop a better understanding to the tools that are becoming mainstream, in order to make informed choices about how they might be used. While academics might use many digital technologies in both work and social lives, this does not immediately mean that any new technology is immediately understood. The rapid change in the delivery of education from the classroom to online during the COVID pandemic resulted in many discussions around the literacy of teaching staff tasked, suddenly, with using new technology where it was assumed they might simply adapt their pedagogy through an osmosis type knowledge development process [37–39].

What is clear is that these tools will not go away. While there are certainly concerns around the ethics of artificial intelligence and the need for greater regulation, most of the debates in this space centre upon the abuse of personal data, bias in data sets and the problematic application of techniques to illegal activities (for example see [40, 41]). There are few political spotlights being cast on tools that will produce text that could be used in fraudulent ways. Far better, it seems, that institutions tackle these tools, consider their use and policing, and how they might develop education approaches around them rather than hoping they will go away. In the same way that search engines were once seen as a threat to academic integrity, we may, in twenty years, reflect upon the panic that ensued because of the introduction of these generative transformers when, once adopted, they became useful tools for academic writing.

Academia changes and adapts, and tools are adopted, and assessment strategies are modified as we progress.

If it could have been documented would we have seen articles in the fifteenth century where scholars expressed their anxieties at the introduction of the printing press and how it would erode the oral traditions of academics to impart knowledge through speech and debate, rather than the printed word and how widespread access to the printed word meant that learning by rote was being eliminated? As somewhat facetious example, perhaps, but certainly an illustration that we adapt.

That is not to say that we should simply accept their use and tell students they are free to use them with impunity. We will undoubtedly see the emergence of GPT plagiarism detection systems, they are already being discussed in the literature (for example [7, 42]), and we are sure they will be offered to universities at a premium.

It is certainly that these technologies will improve over time, and it would be better to be pre-emptive than reactive. We need to teach our students how to use the tools wisely and in the correct context, how they can be useful to help develop work, but do not provide the answer without their application with a critical mind. And if we are going to start to teach something, we also need to find ways of assessing it.

Clearly, there are opportunities to develop assessments where students are given generated text in answer to a question, and tasked with critically evaluating it and improving it, to identify the incorrect aspects of the answer and to enhance, and underpin with evidence, the information provided. Of course, the reintroduction of examination as a predominant form of assessment would significantly reduce the impact of these sort of tools on assessment performance. As would the use of vivas rather than written submissions in order to test knowledge and understanding. However, these are not idea solutions given the resource intensive nature of these approaches (particularly were we to viva on individual modules for single assessments).

In some disciplines the tool could become invaluable in the development of interesting approaches to assessment. Given that the tool can be used to generate software code, there is potential to expand the understanding of the student away from the simple process of writing the code, to understand whether the generated code is fit for requirements, and how one might verify its efficacy. And we should not exclude the potential power in learning support for those with, for example, dyslexia, and overseas students whose English language skills might hold back their potential to articulate their ideas and thinking. In these cases, a skeleton article produced by a GPT type tool might allow them to better construct their articles and build upon, rather than worrying about whether their grammar is correct.

Fundamentally, the tools will undoubtedly result in change, but great assessment diversity might not necessarily be a bad thing. We need to adapt, and trying to prevent the advancement of technology will never be successful. Which arrives us at a final thought around how we might incorporate these tools into assessment practice. If academics have a better understanding of the functioning of these tools, their potential and also their limitations, they will be in a better position to be able to work with, rather than against, them, rather than seeing them as magic boxes that use that artificial intelligence thing the media is always talking about which sounds quite scary.

If we refer back to the excellent description of ChatGPT by [9], we can see how having information about the tool is useful in understanding what it is, and is not, capable of. They clearly set out that, rather than being magic, above, this is not magic, it is a statistical model trained with extremely large amounts of data which it can then use to fulfil queries, and, because of its design and processing power, it does so in a convincing manner. Nevertheless, it is still a statistical engine that can only ever be as good as the data with which it has been trained.

The well-known computer scientist Grady Booch, posted on twitter in 2020 a quote that "GPT-3 has learned the statistics of English", referring to its struggle to produce answers in other languages and therefore still far removed from any form of general intelligence. It has learned a great deal about its training data, and it produced conversational English very well. But it has no way of understanding what it is doing, it is merely following instructions to draw data in a manner most suited to address the query it has been asked to answer. It is not magic—it is a tool. And the better we understand its function, the more effectively we can use it in the development of teaching, learning, and assessment. Because it is clear, just like the rising tide, this is not something we can prevent. We should work with it, rather than against it.

References

1. Greenway DE (ed) (2002) The history of the English people, 1000–1154. Oxford University Press, USA
2. Chowdhary K, Chowdhary KR (2020) Natural language processing. Fundamentals of artificial intelligence, 603–649
3. Brown T, Mann B, Ryder N, Subbiah M, Kaplan JD, Dhariwal P, Neelakantan A, Shyam P, Sastry G, Askell A, Agarwal S (2020) Language models are few-shot learners. Adv Neural Inf Process Syst 33:1877–1901
4. Cohen S (2011) Folk devils and moral panics. Routledge
5. Cotton DR, Cotton PA, Shipway JR (2023) Chatting and cheating: ensuring academic integrity in the era of ChatGPT. Innov Educ Teaching Int: 1–12
6. Fyfe P (2022) How to cheat on your final paper: assigning AI for student writing. AI & Society, 1–11
7. Dehouche N (2021) Plagiarism in the age of massive generative pre-trained transformers (GPT-3). Ethics Sci Environ Politics 21:17–23
8. Xiao Y, Chatterjee S, Gehringer E (2022) A new era of plagiarism the danger of cheating using AI. In: 2022 20th international conference on information technology based higher education and training (ITHET). IEEE, pp 1–6
9. Floridi L, Chiriatti M (2020) GPT-3: its nature, scope, limits, and consequences. Mind Mach 30:681–694
10. Shen Y, Heacock L, Elias J, Hentel KD, Reig B, Shih G, Moy L (2023) ChatGPT and other large language models are double-edged swords. Radiology: 230163
11. Gpt Generative Pretrained Transformer, Almira Osmanovic Thunström, Steinn Steingrimsson (2022) Can GPT-3 write an academic paper on itself, with minimal human input? ffhal-03701250f
12. Lucy L, Bamman D (2021, June) Gender and representation bias in GPT-3 generated stories. In: Proceedings of the third workshop on narrative understanding, pp 48–55

13. Jaimovitch-López G, Ferri C, Hernández-Orallo J, Martínez-Plumed F, Ramírez-Quintana MJ (2022) Can language models automate data wrangling? Machine Learn: 1–30
14. Elkins K, Chun J (2020) Can GPT-3 pass a Writer's turing test? J Cult Anal 5(2)
15. Scott K (2020) Microsoft teams up with OpenAI to exclusively license GPT-3 language model. Official Microsoft Blog
16. Wiggers K (2020) OpenAI's massive GPT-3 model is impressive, but size isn't everything. VentureBeat. June
17. French RM (2000) The Turing test: the first 50 years. Trends Cogn Sci 4(3):115–122
18. Ryan JJ (1998) Student plagiarism in an online world. ASEE Prism 8(4):20
19. DeVoss D, Rosati AC (2002) "It wasn't me, was it?" Plagiarism and the Web. Comput Compos 19(2):191–203
20. Bugeja M (2004) Don't let students" overlook" internet plagiarism. Educ Digest 70(2):37
21. McLafferty CL, Foust KM (2004) Electronic plagiarism as a college instructor's nightmare—prevention and detection. J Educ Bus 79(3):186–190
22. Neill CJ, Shanmuganthan G (2004) A web-enabled plagiarism detection tool. IT Profess 6(5):19–23
23. Vernon RF, Bigna S, Smith ML (2001) Plagiarism and the Web. J Soc Work Educ 37(1):193–196
24. Austin M, Brown L (1999) Internet plagiarism: developing strategies to curb student academic dishonesty. Internet Higher Educ 2(1):21–33
25. Medway D, Roper S, Gillooly L (2018) Contract cheating in UK higher education: a covert investigation of essay mills. Br Edu Res J 44(3):393–418
26. Naughton M (2020) Why do university students in the UK buy assignments from essay mills? Critical Educ 11(10)
27. Draper MJ, Ibezim V, Newton PM (2017) Are essay mills committing fraud? An analysis of their behaviours vs the 2006 fraud act (UK). Int J Educ Integr 13(1):1–14
28. Phippen A, Street L (2022) Online resilience and wellbeing in young people. Springer International Publishing
29. Cech JP (1972) The effect of the use of desk calculators on attitude and achievement with low-achieving ninth graders. Math Teacher 65(2):183–186
30. Rudnick JA, Krulik S (1976) The minicalculator: friend or foe? Arith Teach 1976(23):654–656
31. Bryant PE (1985) The distinction between knowing when to do a sum and knowing how to do it. Educ Psychol 5(3–4):207–215
32. Hembree R, Dessart DJ (1986) Effects of hand-held calculators in precollege mathematics education: a meta-analysis. J Res Math Educ 17(2):83–99
33. Roberts DM (1980) The impact of electronic calculators on educational performance. Rev Educ Res 50(1):71–98
34. Shuch ML (1975) The use of calculators versus hand computations in teaching business arithmetic and the effects on the critical thinking ability of community college students. New York University
35. Adams D (2005) The salmon of doubt: hitchhiking the galaxy one last time. Del Rey Books mass market ed. Ballantine Books, New York
36. Foucault M (1975) Discipline and punish. A. Sheridan, Tr., Paris, FR, Gallimard
37. Sánchez-Cruzado C, Santiago Campión R, Sánchez-Compaña MT (2021) Teacher digital literacy: the indisputable challenge after COVID-19. Sustainability 13(4):1858
38. Tejedor S, Cervi L, Pérez-Escoda A, Jumbo FT (2020) Digital literacy and higher education during COVID-19 lockdown: Spain, Italy, and Ecuador. Publications 8(4):48
39. Martzoukou K (2021) Academic libraries in COVID-19: a renewed mission for digital literacy. Libr Manage 42(4/5):266–276
40. Buiten MC (2019) Towards intelligent regulation of artificial intelligence. Euro J Risk Regul 10(1):41–59
41. Smuha NA (2021) From a 'race to AI' to a 'race to AI regulation': regulatory competition for artificial intelligence. Law Innov Technol 13(1):57–84
42. Gao CA, Howard FM, Markov NS, Dyer EC, Ramesh S, Luo Y, Pearson AT (2022) Comparing scientific abstracts generated by ChatGPT to original abstracts using an artificial intelligence output detector, plagiarism detector, and blinded human reviewers. bioRxiv, 2022-12

Embedding AI in Higher Education: A Call for a Service Design Approach

Carly Foster

Abstract This chapter discusses the opportunities for service design as a methodology for embedding artificial intelligence (AI) and analytics approaches in university settings for enhanced inclusivity, accessibility, and student experience. It explores the literature on service design for improving inclusivity, health, and wellbeing, as well as the application of service design for AI and analytics projects in university settings. Additionally, the paper reviews the literature on AI for improved student support at scale and discusses the potential benefits of combining service design with AI in university settings. The authors suggest that a co-creative service design approach could have multiple benefits, including identifying problems and designing solutions to improve the student experience. Ultimately, the authors argue that utilising service design in AI implementations could improve student outcomes in university settings.

Keywords Artificial intelligence · Service design · Student experience · Student support

1 Introduction

Recently published data shows that the rate of students declaring health issues such as disabilities, specific learning differences and mental health illnesses are on the rise [23]. Equity rather than equality within a 'whole university' framework [48, 49] is now a key focus of policy for student health in higher education. More specifically there is a drive towards student-centricity both in the classroom and wider campus

C. Foster (✉)
Northumbria University, London, UK
e-mail: carly.foster@northumbria.ac.uk

© The Author(s), under exclusive license to Springer Nature Switzerland AG 2023   53
H. Jahankhani et al. (eds.), *AI, Blockchain and Self-Sovereign Identity in Higher Education*, Advanced Sciences and Technologies for Security Applications,
https://doi.org/10.1007/978-3-031-33627-0_3

services [9] however, with the average UK university recording over 18,000 enrolments in 2021/2,[1] a personalised approach is difficult to achieve in practice. Consequentially, there is increased research investigation into the potential for advanced digital technologies such as artificial intelligence (AI) and analytics to enable flexible and personalised learning and support experiences by mining and processing data at scale (see [57], for a systematic review of research on AI applications in higher education).

Such trends evidence that the lived experiences of UK students are increasingly diverse and emphasise the importance of understanding students' needs to consciously design accessibility into all aspects of university encounters. The relationship between service experience and wellbeing is critical [2] and when organisations fail to design their services for users this leads to 'service exclusion' [11].

Given evidence of the challenges faced by UK students, service exclusion is a risk to the student experience that universities must work innovatively to mitigate. Pressure to evidence improved student outcomes for all demographics and student groups continues, underpinned by a transparent yet firm metrification of the student journey. Those who 'measure' university performance such as the regulatory bodies or the compilers of league tables all include a variety of metrics such as student satisfaction, retention, completion, good honours and employability. Student satisfaction often commands a higher weighting (e.g. see the methodologies for the recent Complete University Guide, Guardian University Guide and Times Good University Guide) and whilst the potential for service design is argued to extend further than customer satisfaction [24], a student-orientated approach is a good place to start and thus acts as the premise for the application of service design in higher education.

Service design is a human- centred approach to developing quality end-to-end service interactions; in a university setting it has already been deployed in projects looking to enhance the student experience [3, 16]. Specifically, the approach looks to augment and improve the transactions between 'the service encounter triad' [6] which comprises of:

(i)   the service organisation (here, the university or education provider)
(ii) the customer (whilst universities have many customers, here the focus of the current chapter is on student) and
(iii) the contact personnel.

In a university setting the 'contact personnel' represents a student-facing member of staff, whether that is a faculty academic, a technician or professional services employee. However this may also represent the algorithms which underpin the increasingly digitised and automated services with which students interact. This has been described as 'a new type of stakeholder i.e. a service provider on its own acting to some extent independently' [16], 1071.

---

[1] Data from https://www.hesa.ac.uk/data-and-analysis/students/where-study, table 'HE student enrolments by HE provider', downloaded dataset filtered to providers with 'university' in the title (n = 148).

This chapter explores the opportunities for utilising a service design approach in a university setting with the purpose of assessing its applicability to AI and analytics projects seeking to improve student success via more accessible and inclusive support journeys.

2   Digital Tools to Address Student Success Challenges

Understanding the specific needs of their populations means universities can personalise support for all students, thus abandoning the traditional deficit models of higher education ('they're not cut out for this') in favour of a growth mindset which sees the onus of removing barriers to success placed on the institution. Yet, universities are complex organisational structures and their populations are large, diverse and heterogenous. Therefore, strategically identifying the barriers to student success is not enough; there are then significant operational challenges which require innovative solutions in order to meet students' needs [29]. Approaches which are 'one size fits all' are problematic due to scale, complexity and a lack of specificity and in the context of designing solutions which promote accessibility, evidence that population level approaches are effective is inconclusive [32] (Newton et al. 2016). This is further compounded by the fact that navigating university structures to connect with an appropriate support resource is something students often find challenging [32] with ableism a particular threat to accessibility [52].

To address issues of accessibility, many universities have restructured and consolidated their services for ease of use (UUK 2015) and an important aspect of this is the use of digital tools to better present support options and streamline referral via crossteam data sharing for personalised triage [32]. Yet, as technology replaces humans on the frontline of service, issues emerge of communication quality, privacy and the need for some to engage with human presence [42]. Advancements in artificial intelligence are proving effective in the acceleration of enhanced student support at scale, particularly in the realm of chatbots [33, 56] however a recent systematic review found that less than a third were capable of personalized learning or localized to the particular university setting [26]. This is crucial given that students themselves perceive the level of tailoring to correlate with their perceived benefit of an AI chatbot [46] and thus the impacts of interactions between humans and non-humans therefore should take account of the wellbeing impact for those involved [36]. Yet, despite AI technology rapidly growing in maturity, it's too easy to suggest that AI alone has the answers to delivering accessible services to students at scale. Yet with student numbers rising, populations diversifying and the increased focus on 'proactivity', AI and analytics can at least take on a lot of the "heavy lifting" of repetitive tasks which are automatable thus freeing up more time for humans to invest in improving service flows and designing for more diverse student needs.

However, it's worth mentioning that AI chatbots are not without drawbacks and limitations that need to be addressed before they can be fully integrated into higher education. Some of these challenges include ensuring the quality and accuracy of the chatbot responses, maintaining the privacy and security of the student data, ensuring the ethical and responsible use of the chatbot technology as well as evaluating the effectiveness and impact of the chatbot interventions on student outcomes [41]. Moreover, AI chatbots need to be designed with user-centric principles that consider the needs, preferences and expectations of the students as well as the context and culture of the university setting [30, 41]. AI chatbots and Education systems also need to be adaptive and responsive to the changing needs and situations of the students as well as the evolving trends and developments in higher education [45]. Therefore, AI chatbots require constant monitoring, evaluation and improvement to ensure their relevance, usefulness and quality in supporting student success.

As technology develops, it is argued that the 'next level' of personalization in public services is unlocked: proactivity [40]. Proactive approaches are gaining traction such as Universal Design for Learning (UDL) [35] which aims to design accessibility for *all* students and learning analytics,[2] which aims to ensure students receive personalised support [14]. These examples of holistic approaches to student success innovation are part of the overarching theme 'technology and the student performance in higher education' [5], but are they effective? A systematic review of 34 learning analytics intervention programmes found that in the majority of cases it was effective at improving student outcomes including continuation, attainment and engagement [12].

Architected attempts to close attainment gaps introduce the idea that student success can be *designed* and those designs, like any service encounter, can have 'the same depth and rigor found in goods production' ([6], 159). The Educational Analytics framework [15] covers a range of analytics activities within a university setting including learner analytics (where the student engages directly with data), learning and academic analytics (where data is mediated by professional or faculty staff respectively), institutional analytics (representing improved service allocation and evaluation) and finally adaptive analytics which facilitates a customised learning environment including materials and support. Such approaches evolved from educational data mining where the crunching of the data took some time to give way to the action-taking and intervention stage as noted by the transition from collection, measurement and analysis of data [27] to sensemaking and evidence-based action [34, 39]. However, returning to that systematic review, it found that despite this evolvement, an inarticulation of causality or any theory of change was pervasive throughout the literature therefore the blueprint, crucial to architect service flows to meet student need, remains elusive.

---

[2] See Volume 45 Issue 6 of Assessment and Evaluation for a special edition on a variety of critical thinking articles related to learning analytics.

3   Adopting a Service Design Approach

Design is evolving; with a focus on human experience it is rendered "a natural tool for service innovation" [17]. It is no longer solely product focussed (if ever it was) but it is now invisibly located at the heart of innovation in all sectors including those which focus on delivering services and experiences such as Higher Education. In HE it can be evaluated as the extent to which students are able to effectively navigate institutional (i) behaviour, (ii) expertise, (iii) processes, (iv) and systems in order to (v) access the core educational offering (see [44] for a diagrammatic representation of this process in business). Traditionally service design offers a framework for change management and innovation [53], yet its real value proposition relies on the fact that consumers care more about the *experience* of consumption rather than the actual core offering. For example, [44] use the example of a hospital and argue that the patient ratings are based more on interactions with staff and the environment than the medical outcome. Translating this to marketized Higher Education suggests that students care more about the ease by which they can extend their deadline rather than the content (or outcome) of their assessment. Treating students as customers is complex and many in the sector are reluctant to make the conceptual switch [19] due to expectations that such an approach will have a detrimental impact on the value of education (ibid.). In such circumstances it feels as much that the apprehension exists not around the student as a customer but that education is a service. In the current context, both binaries are problematic; service design is rooted in our understanding of and ability to manipulate human behaviours land that in any context customers are people first [6] therefore in Higher Education it should be embraced as a route, not only to more accessible learning experience for students, but a richer teaching and support environment for staff.

> One of the common methods for initiating projects is problem reframing in which product design problems of the past are reframed as service design problems of the present. This method is often accompanied by qualitative research. [22]

Service design has evolved and is now an established approach, though whether it is a standalone discipline is contested (contrast, for example, the standpoints of [11] with [43]. Nevertheless, there are many examples where it is deployed to achieve new ways of thinking and delivering services by using or repurposing traditional, interdisciplinary research methods (see Stickdorn, 2018 for a comprehensive list of research methods with respect to a service design approach). For example an online banking company deployed "human–computer interaction (HCI), usability design methods, qualitative research, and ethnographic customer studies as well as more traditional focus groups for customer propositions and marketing campaigns" [37], 16. Similarly, Agent-Oriented Modeling (AOM) was used as part of an Action Design Research methodology to visualise how service design thinking may be applied to a family benefit public service [40]. Whilst the output of the latter is useful to visualise a GOAL model, it lacks the specificity and detail to act as a blueprint for how to achieve these goals by design.

As service design is a methodology to achieve kaizen or 'continuous improve-ment' (see [47]), the gains made through service enhancement may be incremental and are part of a strategic investment in the student experience. 'Blue sky thinking approaches' would suggest that knowing what outcomes you want to achieve from a new process can operate outside of collective operational habitus, generating multiple possible future versions and overlooking constraints in the current model [54]. But understanding what actually needs to change (or be created) in current practice to achieve those outcomes involves a forensic consideration of what is happening currently and with what effect. As such, and in addition to traditional empirical research approaches, bespoke methods are emerging within the service designer toolkit [21] which facilitate more forensic enquiry [11] including' customer scripting' and 'event flows' [6], 'journey mapping' and 'persona development' [43, 44], and Multilevel Service Design (MSD) [31] which includes diagrammatising the service concept, service system and service encounter.

Not only do these methods support the requirements gathering and design phase, but as service design has a fundamentally practical application, it may also aid in the prototyping and iteration phases as in the case of Wang et al. [50] where multiple research methodologies were integrated (Theory of Inventive Problem Solving, Quality Function Deployment and service blueprinting) to facilitate improved and scalable hospitality services.

In a case study from Derby University, an institution with a widening participa-tion agenda and diverse student body, utilised service design techniques including service blueprinting [3] which involves creating a detailed service map. A further Derby University case study in *Study on Innovation in Higher Education* [5] details service design for analytics processes to successfully improve their operations (see [5], 94–95). Service blueprinting was also used in a project developing an AI-based library solution called 'James' at the University of Oslo [16]. This project usefully published visual records of the methods for mapping the student journey and AI 'touchpoints',yet despite the level of service mapping detail it concluded that, in the case of AI, more fundamental ontological decisions were required in order to comfortably navigate student expectations of an AI based service.

The educational analytics framework (see Fig. 1, [15]) is a diagrammatised series of outcomes-based statements which starts at the high level 'strategic outcome' and drills down through levels of granularity to the tactical inputs of the model. Between the strategic outcome and the tactical input the framework explores the value of each analytical approach and has been used to implement several projects including learner analytics [13] and learning analytics [15]. Ultimately the framework ends with the 'tactical inputs' to the model: data, systems, processes, policies and people. It is at this level of granularity that encounters occur between the university, the student and the contact personnel.

Five years on this framework requires some notable updates including level 1 acknowledgement of the current challenges in the sector, most notably student health and wellbeing, and more articulation at level 3 of the specific opportunities of artificial intelligence. Using the framework for AI currently would see an exploration and elaboration of the adaptive analytics concept, described as driving a 'customised

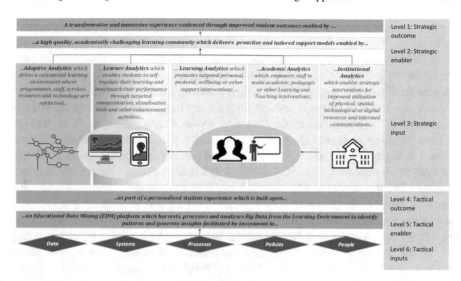

Fig. 1 Educational analytics [15]

learning environment where programmes, staff, services, resources and technology are optimised' [15]. It is defined as "the latent application of educational data mining and associated techniques to provide a real-time personalised learning environment" [12, 3] where the emphasis on 'real time' highlights the speed at which AI can operate without mediation.

A commonality present in the Oslo and Derby service design case studies as well as the Educational Analytics framework is that they each start at a holistic level, what some may consider 'the service concept' yet it's argued that, to date, HE service design has been focussed with student support services at the expense of using it to advance a more holistic university-wide experience [22]. Whilst service design is capable of operation at the minutia of a transaction or encounter, what may often be missed is the original 'concept'. The service concept links institutional strategy to operational delivery and 'kickstarts' the design process by setting out the outcomes which are sought from the service [18]. In the current context then it is therefore crucial to articulate what outcomes can be attempted (and later evaluated) by embedding adaptive analytics and AI into higher education.

Responsibly designing quality touchpoints *for* students inevitably involves designing *with* students. Often called *co-creation* [8], the action of bringing service users into the service design process is essential as services are consumed longitudinally and in ways in which the designer may not be able to predict [28]. The way in which customers influence the realisation of a service design is acknowledged in the 'service encounter triad' [6] however there is also research on co-creation for improved accessibility (particularly wellbeing and health services) which suggests that there can be benefits for designer wellbeing as well as the service user [51]; in this sense having students as part of the design process may be doubly impactful.

At the end of the day, 'while students are not disciplinary experts, they are experts at being students, and therefore have the ability and knowledge frame necessary to contribute meaningfully to advancement of practice' [8].

Given the evidence for a relationship between levels of satisfaction and propensity to give feedback [10] and the fact that service design aims to improve satisfaction, there is a circular relationship which may render the process either exponentially successful (if the institution already has high levels of satisfaction) or difficult to get started (if, conversely, the university has typically low levels of satisfaction). It is therefore important to have a good baseline of student satisfaction (with a process or holistic experience) a the beginning of the design phase to not only measure impact after the design is implemented but also to manage expectations of what may be achieved in phase 1. In this sense, I argue that service design within a university setting should consider the rate of 'Student Voluntary Performance', the higher education equivalent to Consumer Voluntary Performance (CVP) as a key metric not only to establish a baseline from which improvements can be measured, but also as an index which should inform the level of resources required to adopt a service design approach e.g. a university with negatively trending NSS scores.

4   Ethical Implication of Using AI in University's Settings

The implementation of Artificial Intelligence (AI) in university settings raises several ethical considerations that must be carefully addressed. AI technologies are increasingly being integrated into student support systems, such as adaptive learning platforms, chatbots, and learning analytics. These technologies have the potential to enhance student learning outcomes and experiences, but they also pose significant risks of exacerbating existing inequalities or biases in higher education. For instance, biased algorithms could negatively impact students from underrepresented groups, such as women, ethnic minorities, or low-income students, by providing them with inaccurate or unfair feedback, recommendations, or assessments. This could perpetuate existing gaps in access, participation, and achievement in higher education. Therefore, it is essential to establish ethical guidelines for the design, development, and deployment of AI in student support systems, as well as mechanisms for ongoing evaluation and accountability, [38]. This will require collaboration between universities, policymakers, and experts in AI ethics to ensure that these technologies are used in a way that is both effective and equitable. Moreover, it will require a critical reflection on the pedagogical choices and values that underpin the use of AI in education, as well as the potential unintended consequences that may arise from its application. As [20] argue, there is a need to differentiate between doing ethical things and doing things ethically in the context of AI in education [20]. This implies that ethical considerations must be at the forefront of any implementation of AI in university settings, not only as an afterthought or a compliance issue.

Another ethical consideration that is worth noting is the impact of AI on the roles and responsibilities of educators and students. Since AI can augment and complement the work of educators by providing them with data-driven insights, personalized feedback, and automated tasks. However, they can also challenge and undermine the professional autonomy and authority of educators by replacing or delegating some of their functions to AI systems. For example, AI systems can generate and grade assignments, monitor and evaluate student performance, and recommend learning paths and resources, [1]. This may raise questions about the quality and validity of AI-generated or AI-assessed outputs, as well as the accountability and transparency of AI decision-making processes. Furthermore, it may affect the relationship and interaction between educators and students, as well as among students themselves. For example, AI systems can mediate or facilitate communication, collaboration, and socialization among learners, but they can also create distance, isolation, or dependence on AI agents, [55] and killing the human-to-human communication which is a key factor in the education system itself. Therefore, it is important to consider how AI can enhance rather than replace or diminish the human aspects of education, such as creativity, critical thinking, empathy, and ethics, which will require a careful balance between the benefits and risks of AI applications in higher education, as well as a clear definition of the roles and responsibilities of educators and students in relation to AI systems. As [38] argue, there is a need for AI ethics in higher education to address the socio-technical nature of AI systems, [38]. which implies that ethical considerations must take into account not only the technical features of AI systems, but also the social context and purpose of their use in university settings.

A final ethical consideration that is worth noting is the impact of AI on the privacy and security of data in higher education. AI applications rely on large amounts of data to train, test, and improve their algorithms and models. This data often includes sensitive and personal information about students, such as their academic records, learning behaviours, preferences, interests, emotions, and biometrics. The collection, storage, analysis, and sharing of this data poses significant risks of data breaches, misuse, or abuse by unauthorized or malicious parties. For example, hackers could access and expose students' data for identity theft, blackmail, or harassment, [7]. Alternatively, third-party vendors could use students' data for commercial purposes, such as targeted advertising or profiling, [4]. Moreover, students may not be fully aware of or consent to how their data is used by AI systems or who has access to it. This may violate their rights to privacy and data protection, as well as their autonomy and agency over their own data [4]. Therefore, it is essential to ensure that AI applications in higher education adhere to ethical principles and standards of data governance, such as transparency, accountability, security, and privacy by design, [25]. This will require collaboration between stakeholders, such as universities, developers, regulators, and students, to establish clear policies and protocols for data collection, storage, analysis, and sharing. It will also require educating students about their rights and responsibilities regarding their data and how to protect it from potential threats. As [57] argue, there is a need for a data culture in higher education that fosters trust and responsibility among all actors involved in AI applications.

5   Conclusions

This chapter has explored the opportunities of service design as a methodology for embedding AI and analytics approaches in university settings for enhanced inclusivity, accessibility and student experience. It has reviewed literature on the application of service design for improving inclusivity, health and wellbeing (refs) and similarly the application of service design for AI and analytics projects in university settings (refs). However an area for future research is to combine these two agendas to implement the service design approach for improved inclusivity and accessibility in the student population to address the rising rates of disabilities, specific learning differences and mental health illnesses [23]. Chatbots have been deployed to varying degrees of success already however, without the level of personalisation required to confront the diversity agenda.

It's also necessary to consider the ethical implications of AI as it requires careful consideration of bias, educator-student roles, and data privacy. Collaborative efforts are necessary to establish ethical guidelines and protocols to ensure the responsible use of AI in higher education.

University managers and policymakers must also understand the key operational components impacting their students' success and be prepared to embrace a constant cycle of product consolidation, evaluation and innovation. A co-creative service design approach may have multiple benefits not only in identifying problems, but also designing solutions and an improved student experience from the cocreation process alone. Given the emergence of new bespoke service design methods, a thorough evaluation of which may be most applicable for embedding AI into university student support systems should be conducted with a specific focus on how it may enable co-creative practice.

Service design is certainly a vehicle by which we may realise the opportunity to use advanced technologies such as educational analytics and artificial intelligence to support students, but also support staff to support students including a reconceptualization of university service delivery agents as not always human. In this sense we may learn from the lessons of learning analytics and establish at an early stage in sector-wide development, a service concept and theory of change which understands how and why AI and adaptive technologies can improve student outcomes.

References

1. Al Ka'bi A (2023) Proposed artificial intelligence algorithm and deep learning techniques for development of higher education. Int J Intell Netw
2. Anderson L, Ostrom AL (2015) Transformative service research: advancing our knowledge about service and well-being. J Serv Res 18(3):243–249
3. Baranova P, Morrison S, Mutton J (2011) Enhancing the student experience through service design: the University of Derby approach. Perspect Policy Pract Higher Educ 15(4):122–128
4. Bostrom N, Yudkowsky E (2018) The ethics of artificial intelligence. In: Artificial intelligence safety and security. Chapman and Hall/CRC, pp 57–69

5. Brennan J, Broek S, Durazzi N, Kamphuis B, Ranga M, Ryan S (2014) Study on innovation in higher education. Publications Office of the European Union, Luxembourg
6. Cooke R, Barkham M, Audin K, Bradley M, Davy J (2004) Student debt and its relation to student mental health. J Further Higher Educ 28(1):53–66. doi: https://doi.org/10.1080/030987 7032000161814
7. Daries JP, Reich J, Waldo J, Young EM, Whittinghill J, Ho AD, Seaton DT, Chuang I (2014) Privacy, anonymity, and big data in the social sciences. Commun ACM 57(9):56–63
8. Dollinger M, Lodge J, Coates H (2018) Co-creation in higher education: towards a conceptual model. J Mark High Educ 28(2):210–231
9. ESG (2015) Standards and guidelines for quality assurance in the European higher education area (ESG). Brussels, Belgium. Accessed 13 Mar 2023. http://www.eua.be/Libraries/quality-assurance/esg_2015.pdf?sfvrsn=0
10. Eisingerich AB, Auh S, Merlo O (2013) Acta non verba? The role of customer participation and word of mouth in the relationship between service firms' customer satisfaction and sales performance. J Serv Res 17(1):40–53
11. Fisk RP, Dean AM, Alkire L, Joubert A, Previte J, Robertson N, Rosenbaum MS (2018) Design for service inclusion: creating inclusive service systems by 2050. J Serv Manag 29(5):834–858
12. Foster C, Francis P (2020) A systematic review on the deployment and effectiveness of data analytics in higher education to improve student outcomes. Assess Eval High Educ 45(6):822–841
13. Foster C (2020) Students' adoption of learner analytics. https://doi.org/10.1007/978-3-030-473 92-1_8
14. Francis P, Broughan C, Foster C, Wilson C (2020) Thinking critically about learning analytics, student outcomes, and equity of attainment. Assess Eval High Educ 45(6):811–821
15. Francis P, Foster C (2018) Educational analytics: a systematic review of empirical studies. Paper presented to advance HE surveys conference, Leeds, 9th May 2018
16. Gasparini A, Mohammed AA, Oropallo G (2018) Service design for artificial intelligence. In: Linköping electronic conference proceedings. Linköping University Electronic Press, pp 1064–1073
17. Gobble MM (2014) Design thinking. Res Technol Manag 57(3):59–62
18. Goldstein SM, Johnston R, Duffy J, Rao J (2002) The service concept: the missing link in service design research?. J Oper Manag 20(2):121–134
19. Guilbault M (2016) Students as customers in higher education: reframing the debate. J Market Higher Educ 26(2):132–142
20. Holmes W, Porayska-Pomsta K, Holstein K et al (2022) Ethics of AI in education: towards a community-wide framework. Int J Artif Intell Educ 32:504–526. https://doi.org/10.1007/s40 593-021-00239-1
21. Holmlid S, Evenson S (2008) Bringing service design to service sciences, management and engineering. In: Service science, management and engineering education for the 21st century, 341–345
22. Huang Y, Hands D (2022) Design thinking for new business contexts. Springer Books
23. Hubble S, Bolton P (2021) House of commons library: briefing paper number 8716, 22 February 2021: support for disabled students in higher education in England. House of commons library briefing paper
24. Iriarte I, Alberdi A, Urrutia E, Justel D (2017) Beyond customer satisfaction. Supporting organisational change through Service Design. A case study in the insurance industry. Des J 20(1):424–434
25. Kotsiantis S, Patriarcheas K, Xenos M (2010) A combinational incremental ensemble of classifiers as a technique for predicting students' performance in distance education. Knowl-Based Syst 23(6):529–535
26. Kuhail MA, Alturki N, Alramlawi S, Alhejori K (2023) Interacting with educational chatbots: a systematic review. Educ Inf Technol 28(1):973–1018
27. Long P, Siemens G (2011). Penetrating the fog: analytics in learning and education. Educause Rev 46(5):31–40

28. Mager B, Sung TJD (2011) Special issue editorial: designing for services. Int J Design 5(2)
29. Mowbray CT, Mandiberg JM, Stein CH, Kopels S, Curlin C, Megivern D, Lett R (2006). Campus mental health services: recommendations for change. Am J Orthopsych 76(2):226–237
30. Okonkwo CW, Ade-Ibijola A (2021) Chatbots applications in education: a systematic review. Comput Educ Artif Intell 2:100033
31. Patrício L, Fisk RP, Falcão e Cunha J, Constantine L (2011) Multilevel service design: from customer value constellation to service experience blueprinting. J Service Res 14(2):180–200
32. Priestley M, Broglia E, Hughes G, Spanner L (2021) Student Perspectives on improving mental health support Services at university. Counsell Psych Res 22(1). https://doi.org/10.1002/capr.12391
33. Ralston K, Chen Y, Isah H, Zulkernine F (2019) A voice interactive multilingual student support system using IBM Watson. In: 2019 18th IEEE international conference on machine learning and applications (ICMLA). IEEE, pp 1924–1929
34. Reimann P (2016) Connecting learning analytics with learning research: the role of design-based research. Learn Res Pract 2(2):130–142
35. Rose D (2000) Universal design for learning. J Spec Educ Technol 15(4):47–51
36. Russo-Spena T, Mele C, Marzullo M (2019) Practising value innovation through artificial intelligence: the IBM Watson case. J Creating Value 5(1):11–24
37. Saco RM, Goncalves AP (2008) Service design: an appraisal. Design Manage Rev 19(1):10
38. Sam AK, Olbrich P (2023) The need for AI ethics in higher education. In: Corrigan CC, Asakipaam SA, Kponyo JJ, Luetge C (eds) AI ethics in higher education: insights from Africa and beyond. SpringerBriefs in Ethics. Springer, Cham. https://doi.org/10.1007/978-3-031-230 35-6_1
39. Siemens G (2013) Learning analytics: the emergence of a discipline. Am Behav Sci 57(10):1380–1400
40. Sirendi R, Taveter K (2016) Bringing service design thinking into the public sector to create proactive and user-friendly public services. In: HCI in business, government, and organizations: information systems: third international conference, HCIBGO 2016, held as part of HCI international 2016, Toronto, Canada, July 17–22, 2016, proceedings, part II 3 (221–230). Springer International Publishing
41. Smutny P, Schreiberova P (2020) Chatbots for learning: a review of educational chatbots for the Facebook Messenger. Comput Educ 151:103862
42. Song M, Xing X, Duan Y, Cohen J, Mou J (2022) Will artificial intelligence replace human customer service? The impact of communication quality and privacy risks on adoption intention. J Retail Consum Serv 66:102900
43. Stickdorn M, Schneider J (2011) This is service design thinking. Wiley
44. Stickdorn M, Hormess ME, Lawrence A, Schneider J (2018) This is service design doing: applying service design thinking in the real world., O'Reilly Media, Inc.
45. Stock L (2023, Jan 24) Chatgpt is changing education, AI experts say—but how? dw.com. Retrieved March 27, 2023, from https://www.dw.com/en/chatgpt-is-changing-education-ai-experts-say-but-how/a-64454752
46. Sáiz-Manzanares MC, Marticorena-Sánchez R, Martín-Antón LJ, Díez IG, Almeida L (2023) Perceived satisfaction of university students with the use of chatbots as a tool for self-regulated learning. Heliyon: e12843
47. Temponi C (2005). Continuous improvement framework: implications for academia. Qual Assur Educ 13(1):17–36
48. Thomas L (2002) Student retention in higher education: the role of institutional habitus. J Educ Policy 17(4): 423–442. https://doi.org/10.1080/02680930210140257
49. Universities UK (2020) Step change: mentally healthy Universities. Universities UK, from https://www.universitiesuk.ac.uk/policy-and-analysis/reports/Documents/2020/uuk-ste pchange-mhu.pdf Accessed on 12/07/22
50. Wang YH, Lee CH, Trappey AJ (2017) Service design blueprint approach incorporating TRIZ and service QFD for a meal ordering system: a case study. Comput Ind Eng 107: 388–400

51. Warwick L, Tinning A, Smith N, Young R (2018) Co-designing Wellbeing: the commonality of needs between co-designers and mental health service users. Proceedings of DRS 2018 catalyst
52. Wertans E, Burch L (2022) 'It's backdoor accessibility': disabled students' navigation of university campus. J Disability Stud Educ 1(aop):1–22
53. Wolfe K (2020) Service design in higher education: a literature review. Perspect Policy Pract High Educ 24(4):121–125
54. Wrigley C, Bucolo S, Straker K (2016) Designing new business models: blue sky thinking and testing. J Bus Strategy
55. Xu W, Ouyang FA (2022) Systematic review of AI role in the educational system based on a proposed conceptual framework. Educ Inf Technol 27:4195–4223. https://doi.org/10.1007/s10639-021-10774-y
56. Yang S, Evans C (2019) Opportunities and challenges in using AI chatbots in higher education. In: Proceedings of the 2019 3rd international conference on education and e-learning, pp 79–83
57. Zawacki-Richter O, Marín VI, Bond M, Gouverneur F (2019) Systematic review of research on artificial intelligence applications in higher education—where are the educators? Int J Educ Technol High Educ 16(1):1–27

An Empirical Study into Ransomware Campaigns Against the Education Sector and Adopting the Cybersecurity Maturity Model Certification Framework

Mauricio Alexander Nieto Acosta and Hamid Jahankhani

Abstract The global pandemic forced many education establishments around the world to move to remotely learning. Criminals, have taken this opportunity to target vulnerable education institutions and carry out State-of-the-Art Cyber Attacks, exploiting flaws in their security systems by using social engineering methods and carrying out sophisticated high-profile ransomware and distributed denial of service (DDoS) campaigns that are propagated through various email phishing techniques. Many Universities faced challenges with security involving personal data & intellectual property material theft. Bluevoyant carried out an analysis and concluded that the universities were targeted more frequently by ransomware campaigns. With data breaches resulting in sensitive data and credentials being exfiltrated and sold in Dark web marketplaces. This research recommends a Cybersecurity Maturity Model (CSMM) Framework that serves as a benchmark to assess and evaluate processes using industry best practices and standards. This study carried out a quantitative method to collect secondary datasets. These secondary datasets were gathered from two type of sources: Temple University and Hackmargeddon. Using the IBM SPSS Statistic Software to measure the collected datasets and find out the relation between the two variables.

Keywords Ransomware · Cyber extortion · High education · Cybersecurity · Maturity model

1 Introduction

The unprecedented pandemic in 2020 had a huge impact on the education sector many education institutions had to deploy remote systems to provide teleworking for its staff and students. During this time, financially motivated Cybercrime organizations have taken advantage to target vulnerable systems, hitting critical infrastructure and

M. A. N. Acosta · H. Jahankhani (✉)
Northumbria University London, London, UK
e-mail: Hamid.jahankhani@northumbria.ac.uk

© The Author(s), under exclusive license to Springer Nature Switzerland AG 2023
H. Jahankhani et al. (eds.), *AI, Blockchain and Self-Sovereign Identity in Higher Education*, Advanced Sciences and Technologies for Security Applications,
https://doi.org/10.1007/978-3-031-33627-0_4

compromising sensitive data. Cyber threat actors aim to generate profits and disrupt the teaching cycle activities.

A study from [1] found that the education sector has been the primary and a profitable target for cyber-attacks, resulting in several high impact incidents and becoming a lucrative business for Cyber criminals, hacktivists, and cyber espionage. Threat Actors are motivated to seek their own financial gains or are state affiliated looking to steal trade secrets [2], Cyber criminals often threaten to expose stolen data if the ramson is not paid. There have been cases that sensitive information has been leaked and exposed in public, often called name and shame websites residing in the dark web.

Ransomware campaigns are on the rise and continue to contribute to an intense financial burden to educational institutions, BlueVoyant [3] provides an analysis on open-source data which suggests that cyber incidents in universities have an increase of 100% amongst the years of 2019 and 2020. The cost for a ransomware attack in 2020 was of $447,000. Cyber criminals use different tactics, techniques, and procedures to disrupt business processes and have a financial impact on them.

2 Ransomware Attack

The meaning of ransomware is defined using the words "Ransom", which means a request of payment and "ware" which is a kind of a malware program [4] The term "Ransomware" is referred as a type of malware which stops users from gaining access to their computing systems, network resources and by encrypting files and sensitive. Data and Computing resources are held at ramson until the victim pays money [5]. To obtain a decryption key This ransom demands payment in bitcoin which is a type of cryptocurrency that cannot be traced. The crypto ransomware uses symmetric and asymmetric techniques for encryption [4].

In 1989 the first type of Ransomware used was the "PC Cyborg/AIDS Trojan", this type of malware was installed in systems using a floppy disk, where the program would change the autoexec.bat file into a file the counts the number of times of the system restart, when the system hits 90, the Trojan would hide directories and encrypt all files in the system root directory. A new form of ransomware took place in 2005 with a "GP Coder", that was improved using RSA encryption algorithms, this new method of ransomware would be entered through emailing system as spam, this trojan would look for predetermined file extensions and perform encryptions and display a ransom message on every file directory [6]. In 2007 a new malware called Locker Ransomware started to strike many victims in Russia by displaying pornographic footage on the victim's computer and requesting payment to remove it, the payment was done through text messages or a premium phone number at an expensive rate, soon after, the attacks propagated to Europe and USA [7]. 2013 saw the rise of CryptoLocker, this type of malware encrypted data and infected computers, then demanded a ramson to recover the files from their victims, normally the payment was requested in bitcoins, Dell SecureWorks explains that in the first 100 days of the CryptoLocker malware resulted in 250,000 infections with an estimated profit of $380,000 [8].

CryptoWall emerged as a clone of CryptoLocker with a GUI. In February 2014, a second variant appeared as CryptoDefense with bugs that resided in the cryptographic implementation which allowed the victim to restore the files encrypted, then in March 2014 CryptoWall was introduced, an updated version of CryptoDefense, having fixed bug errors and better attack capabilities. However, the Deletion functions used were weak enough that data could be retrieved using recovery software and digital forensics methods [5]. In February 2015, TeslaCrypt emerged and was propagated through spam campaigns and the Angler exploit Kits using compromised websites. TeslaCrypt Developers carried out campaigns using random notes which looked like CryptLocker. It targeted Office files as well as gaming files [9]. DMA Locker was launched in December 2015, it propagated over the Remote Desktop Connection Protocol, when it has penetrated the victim's system, it interrupts all applications that are used for backups and starts encrypting utilizing AES encryption [5].

Locky made its first appearance in February 2016, it targeted Windows Operating Systems using anti-analysis and sandboxing capabilities. An RSA 2048 + AES 128 cypher was used for encrypting hard drives, removable HD's, and accessible network shares. Encryption keys from victims were kept on the Server Side making it impossible for decrypting victim's files [5]. Cerber ransomware was first launched in July 2016, it infected 150,000 Windows OS using phishing methods and exploit kits as well as using malicious macro files to spread the infection. Cybercriminals netted with an estimate of $2.3 million in Ransom payments. Cerber propagates as a ransomware as a service model and contains over six types of variants [5]. Discovered in February 2017 WannaCry is a type of crypto ransomware that use worm capabilities targeting Windows Operating systems exploiting Windows Server Message Block (SMB), it gains popularity on May 12, 2017 when a large campaigns targeted health and telecommunications sectors [5].

NotPetya is a second variant from Petya and was launched in June 2017 with a dangerous effect as encryption keys are randomly generated and destroyed and as a result data becoming unrecoverable. Targeting Windows OS and infecting the Master boot Record (MBR). NotPetya propagated through emails as a ransomware as a service, using stolen exploits such as EternalBlue and EternalRomance from the NSA and targeting large organizations in Russia and Ukraine [5]. In May 2018 Samsam ransomware targeted high profile organizations such as U.S enterprises and large public sectors such as City of Atlanta and Colorado Dept of Transportation. Samsam used vulnerabilities in server applications such as JBoss and FTP servers and brute forcing weak passwords in accounts in the Remote Desktop protocols and gain entry to the corporate network [5].

There are three different kinds of ransomware attacks, [10]. The first type is "scareware" which is used in malicious advertising where pop ups advertisements, notifies the user that an infected malware has been identified on their system and provides instructions on how to pay through a website to remove the installed malware. "Screen lockers or locker ransomware" on the other hand are like encrypting ransomware [10], this third type of ransomware consists in freezing devices and displaying a message that they must pay a ransom, or face being investigated by an authority such as the FBI, its main intention is to scare the user to pay the ransom, but in most situations the data is safe. The third type "Encrypting Ransomware or Crypto Ransomware" is much more critical [10], as data and resources are encrypted the only way is paying a ransom, in this method the criminal will take copies the data and will expose it on the internet if the ransom is not paid.

Cybercriminals use a set of steps to carry out a Ransomware attack, these steps follow certain stages as follow:

- Deployment

The initial stage of a ransomware attack is to install components which are utilized to infect, encrypt and to lock a system, there are various techniques used in the attack to download files to the system, such as the Drive by download, this will normally happen when malware or software is installed without the user consent or knowledge. The Strategic web compromises also referred as to watering hole attacks, which is a subcategory of a drive by download to target a chosen target rely on strategic reconnaissance to target end users. Phishing emails that are contain spam or are designed to target an organization, these emails can contain attachments or have links to deceptive websites. Exploiting vulnerabilities are aimed in searching for networks through the Internet that contain vulnerabilities that can be exploited or a user interaction [11].

- Installation

When the malicious payload is delivered to the user's system, the infection is initiated. The delivery of this infection is done in various forms, regardless of the system that is targeted. One installation technique is to utilize the download dropper methodology, this file is a small component of coding that has been designed to avoid being detected and provide communication with the cyber extortionist's command and control channels, where the executable would get commands and download the ransomware and infect the system. The ransomware will then be installed on the operating system by setting keys in the registry that ensures that the coding of malware is executed every time the system is initiated [11]. The targeted attack involves a more proactive approach to installing obfuscating and code packing, its exploitation methods are forced to maximize ransom. The initial installation phase is used to slowly infect networks by installing itself into systems and opening files that are encrypted. The installation stage can vary and depends on the crypto ransomware variants, where a type of macro virus or an exploitable PDF is injected into the system. When malware is downloaded, the code will be executed to analyse whether a system is real or is a virtual environment and would be the first stage of Dopper. The second phase is initiated once it is determined that the host is worth infecting, the malware would hide under normal processes of windows using md5 hash of pc name or other identifiers such as MAC addresses, this will be useful for the Cyber extortionist to know which have been the compromised hosts. Then the malware runs several scripts that disable any protection and turn off shadow copy feature on files and volumes, turn off system recovery and terminating antivirus software and log functions on the systems., once this phase is terminated, the ransomware is attached to windows processes such as svchost.exe, then the command-and-control stage commences [11].

- Command and Control

When the malicious code is delivered and installed, it initiates communication with the command servers, where there will be a set of instructions or specific requests that involves identification of file types that requires to be targeted for encryption, waiting time to start with the process, and if infecting the system should be carried out before the process initiation. Ransomware variants can even send back system information, IP addresses, domain names, OS, browsers used and anti-malware software. This valuable information is used by Cybercriminals to determine which hosts have been infected and if a high value target has been compromised [11].

- Destruction

At this stage, the key that is utilized in encrypting files on the system is now ready to be used by the malware on the user's device. Files which have been located by the command-and-control processes can now be encrypted using the malicious coding. This includes Microsoft files documents, JPG's, Gif is and several other type of files. Other Ransomware variants also encrypt file names which makes it harder in assessing the loss of files and how much damage has been done [11].

- Extortion

Once all files are encrypted, the victim will be notified that the system has been compromised, the Cybercriminal utilize different methods to request payment. One type of Ransomware Variant allows one file to be decrypted for free, this is to prove that they contain the key to unlock the system. Other types of Ransomwares contain a payments scalation, where payment increases periodically if ransom is not paid in time before the key gets deleted [11].

3 The Impacts of Ransomware Attacks

Ransomware attacks have been devastating for many educational establishments around the globe, with an increase demand on payments, ransomware has become a lucrative business. Amongst those universities hit by ransomware are the Maastricht University in Netherlands paying a total of $220,000 in 2019 and the university of Utah paying $457,000, the university of California follows a pay-out of $1.14 million in 2020 [12]. Another educational institution hit by ransomware was West Coast University, the attack involved data from their medicine's dept. Once the University found out that research data had been encrypted, the university decided to pay cyber-criminals and estimate of $1.14 million in cryptocurrency to unlock all the encrypted data [12].

Educational Institutions have faced financial challenges due to the covid landscape and the ransomware demands. It has also had an impact on privacy, the unauthorized access to confidential and personally identifiable information (PII). These private and stolen data contained financial details, which included names, social security numbers and addresses. There are severe implications, if the compromised PII from students and the faculty falls into the wrong hands, it can result in PII being sold in the dark web and lead to identity theft and students can carry out a lawsuit against the educational establishment for failing to protect PII and comply with privacy laws and exercising due care of their information [13].

3.1 Security Landscape in Education

Many educational institutions experienced devastating cyber-attacks, disrupting their teaching cycle, and being affected for several days. Most educational institutions do not have appropriate security measures for protecting private information and end up risking the loss or exposure of intellectual property, academic research data, students, and staff personal information. This type of data is highly valuable for cyber organizations and cyber criminals that operate either domestically or internationally. With the number of successful cyber-attacks on the rise, educational institutions leaders must consider if their cyber protection governance is robust enough [14].

The education industry has been the primary target for cybercriminals, the lack of robust IT infrastructure. Also considering that budgets are limited and IT and cybersecurity falling short that leaves IT personnel to deal with limited resources and trying to secure an old infrastructure. With the rapid transition from physical classrooms to virtual learning during covid, IT personnel were left with no time to design security strategies or buy new IT infrastructure. Sophos carried out a survey in all sectors and found out that the highest ransomware attack belonged to the education sector with a staggering 44% that is levelled to the retail sector [15]. Figure 1 indicates the different sectors surveyed with education and retail being the primary target for ransomware attacks.

3.2 State-Sponsored Attacks

State-sponsored attacks have been carried out against universities targeting research data and Intellectual property. In many instances the exposure or theft of academic research and data is not publicly announced. There should be a better understanding and a greater awareness of General Data Protection Regulation (GDPR), as well as the responsibilities and actions that an education establishment or organization

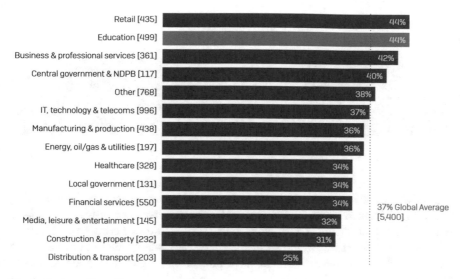

Fig. 1 Sectors affected by ransomware [15]

must take if a data breach occurs such as reporting data breaches to the information Commissioner. In a public story Greenwich University was fined £120.000 for having data on an unsecure server. Most Cyber incidents are not reported or do not seem to be big enough to be publicly disclosed, but any type of cyber incident could lead to sensitive data being leaked, exfiltrated personal information, financial loss and reputational harm [14].

According to a survey carried out by Sophos:

- 44% of educational establishments were hit by ransomware in 2020.
- 58% of Successful ransomware attacks were carried out, resulting in systems and data being encrypted.
- 35% of those institutions paid the ransom to decrypt the systems and data.
- Organizations that paid the ransom, only 68% obtained their data back, meaning that third of the data become inaccessible.
- 55% used backups to restore data.
- The bill for recovering from a ransomware attack was on average on US$2.73 million.

4 Cybercrime and Cyber Extortion

The cybercrime guidelines indicate and describes two types of criminal activity [16]. The government's National Cyber Security Strategy explains that Cyber-dependent crimes are "crimes that can be committed only through the use of Information and Communications Technology ('ICT') devices, where the devices are both the tool for

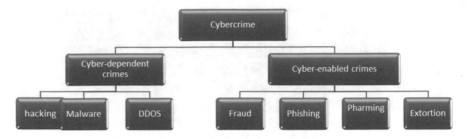

Fig. 2 Cybercrime subcategories

committing the crime, and the target of the crime (e.g., developing and propagating malware for financial gain, hacking to steal, damage, distort or destroy data and/or network or activity)" and "Cyber-enabled crimes—traditional crimes which can be increased in scale or reach by the use of computers, computer networks or other forms of ICT (such as cyber-enabled fraud and data" theft)". Figure 2 diagram illustrates the subcategories of Cybercrime.

When Cyber Extortion Campaigns are carried out, data is exfiltrated and encrypted. If an organization decides not to pay the ramson, the threat actors release sensitive data. Therefore, organizations suffer a reputational damage and end up paying massive compliance fines (2021, Ransomware Threat Report). There are currently 35 ransomware families that are used for double extortion, putting pressure on organizations that are demanded to pay the ransom, where ransomware attackers use extortion techniques like DDoS. There are four phases of ransomware cyber extortion, the single extorting begins by encrypting files and banning access to systems, the perpetrator normally requested payment from the victim to decrypt the files. In double extortion phase the perpetrators exfiltrate data and threatens the victim with publicize the collected data, the perpetrators use websites, forums, and blogs on the darknet to leak the information. The triple extortion use encryption on the files and threatens to leak data and carry out a DDoS attack on the network and servers and as a result disrupt business operations. With the Quadruple extortion all stages mentioned before are launched and the perpetrators contact the victim's clients and stakeholders, pressuring the victim to pay the ransom [17].

4.1 Motives Behind Cyber Extortion

Cyber criminals are motivated to monetize access through company's networks, DART carried out an investigation and concluded that a threat actor performs reconnaissance attacks to access sensitive information such as contractual documents, financial papers, and internal communications. Once access is gained, the data is copied and exfiltrated before ransomware is deployed. Having this information before ransomware is executed enables the threat actor to sell this data on the dark web, leak or simply demand a ransom by showing proof that the attacker accessed the network system and took the sensitive files.

5   An Overview of Cybersecurity Maturity Models

The purpose of a Cybersecurity Maturity model is to examine and measure the current state of an organization's readiness against cyberthreats and the desired state for that organization, using controls, processes, and assessments to evaluate the maturity level of an organization. Every level relies on a set of process. Every process relies on the organization infrastructure, operational functions, resources available and employee's knowledge [18]. Cybersecurity maturity models are created by a various experts in the field and to attempt to gather best practises, considering the dispersion in size, capabilities, knowledge, and the organizations experience that will eventually use the maturity model, enabling them to provide services effectively without disruption, safeguard private customer and proprietary information and at the same time comply with regulators laws which governs its operations. Cyber security maturity models offer a structure for organizations with a foundation capability in cybersecurity planning and creating a baseline for evaluating consistently and creating management tools where opportunities can be identified for growing and organization evolution.

5.1   Maturity Model Components

A Maturity model consists of a well-defined structure where every stage ensures its consistency. Its components include different stages, attributes, appraisals, scoring techniques and domain models. Levels illustrate the measurement characteristics of a maturity model. Therefore, if scaling is either incomplete or inaccurate, the model would not be validated, and its results would become either inaccurate or inconsistent. Attributes describes and illustrates a maturity model's content, these attributes are categorized by levels and domains, these attributes are determined at every domain intersection and maturity stage, which is normally based on observation practices, standards, and expert knowledge, that is illustrated with indicators, characteristics, best practices, and processes. In capability models, attributes describe and illustrate the qualities of an organization maturity model, such as measuring and planning, and which also supports process enhancement. Normally appraisal and scoring mechanisms are used to perform assessments. These can be either informal or formal or can also be carried out by an expert or self-applied. Scoring Techniques are standards for measurements, these scoring mechanisms are based on mathematical algorithms that ensures consistency of appraisals. The scoring techniques include weighting, which means that attributes can be valued depending on how relevant or important collected data is. Model domains describes the maturity model scope. Domains allows the grouping of attributes into area of importance for a particular subject or model characteristics. In capability models, domains are called process areas as these are a group of processes that creates a bigger process or discipline [19].

There are three types of maturity models such as capability models, progression models and hybrid models. The progression models illustrate how the progression or scaling of attributes, characteristics, patterns, or indicators move across the maturity stages indicating the progression of an attribute or attributes maturity. Progression models are concerned with the evolution of the model's core subject matter, instead of the attributes that determine maturity. The main goal of a progression model is to define a path of progressiveness and improvement such as better versions of attributes as the scale's progresses. A CMM is focuses on the organization capabilities. These capabilities reflect culture maturity and how capabilities are institutionalised within the culture. Hybrid models is divided into two types of abilities; ability in measuring maturity attributes and ability in measuring evolution within the progressive models [19].

5.2   Related Work on Maturity Models

In 1986 The Department of Defence developed the evaluation of maturity capability which was used for assessing maturity capabilities in software engineering processes. Later this model was adopted by various domains that included the cybersecurity domain. Cybersecurity maturity models were created suiting the requirement from organizations, including international standards such as ISO/IEC 27001, NIST. The ISO/IEC 27001 was created USING British standards BS7799 and ISO/IEC 17799 which offers all the requirements for maintaining and improving Information Security Management Systems. ISO/IEC 27001 describes ISMS as an integral component of a management system for establishing, implementing, operating, monitoring, reviewing, maintaining, and improving information security.

The Cyber security Maturity Model Certification, (CMMC) was published in January 2020, its framework verifies that implementation of processes and practices that are associated with achieving a cybersecurity maturity model. The CMMC was created to offer an increases assurance to the Department of Defence in which a Defence Industrial Base contractor can appropriately safeguard Controlled Unclassified Information at a stage corresponding to the risk and considering the information flow amongst its subcontractors in a multilevel supply chain [20]. CMMC also validates that those contractors have acquired NIST SP 800-171 framework and meet the basic cybersecurity requisites before being awarded for a contract. The CMMC Framework depend on other cybersecurity models, including the NIST cybersecurity framework and 27001 standards as well as the Payment Card Industry Data Security Standard [21]. The Cybersecurity maturity model Certificate uses a set of cybersecurity standards and best practises combined that are layered through various maturity levels starting from cyber hygiene to a more advanced practice. CMMC is composed of controls and processes that permits organizations to reduce risks such as cyber threats [22].

The following figure illustrates the stages of CMMC, practices and process.

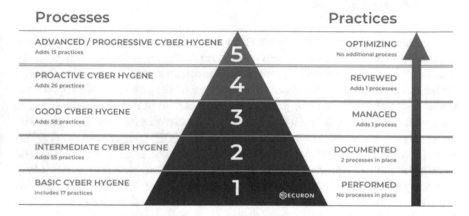

CMMC Certification Levels

Processes		Practices
ADVANCED / PROGRESSIVE CYBER HYGENE Adds 15 practices	5	**OPTIMIZING** No additional process
PROACTIVE CYBER HYGENE Adds 26 practices	4	**REVIEWED** Adds 1 processes
GOOD CYBER HYGENE Adds 58 practices	3	**MANAGED** Adds 1 process
INTERMEDIATE CYBER HYGENE Adds 55 practices	2	**DOCUMENTED** 2 processes in place
BASIC CYBER HYGENE Includes 17 practices	1	**PERFORMED** No processes in place

ECURON

6 Research Methodology

In this research study a systematic investigation is conducted, using a quantitative research methodology. The aim of this quantitative research is to collect information from the University of Temple and Hackmargeddon, using sampling methods such as a dataset, these gathered secondary datasets are based on publicly disclosed incidents in the media or security reports classified as "Critical Infrastructures Ransomware Attacks". The purpose of collecting these datasets is to measure the ransomware attacks on The University of Temple carried an investigation and reported the number of ransomware attacks against the education sector between 2017 and 2020 against education institutions between 2019 and 2020. Hackmargeddon also conducted a similar investigation and reported the number of ransomware attacks that affected education establishments between 2017 and 2020 and investigate whether there was an increase where data is evaluated and analysed using numerical comparisons and statistical references. The results of these analysis will provide the increasing evidence of the incidence and the impact reported by the education Sector. These structured datasets are also validated through data collections instruments.

The hypothesis testing is also an attempt to investigate the relationship amongst the two variables using Data collection techniques. To Develop a frame for analysis, IBM SPSS Statistic software will be used to measure the collected datasets. This Study also has the purpose of recommending a cybersecurity mature model to education institutions. Created by de Department of Defence the CMMC model aims to measure cybersecurity maturity using five levels and encompasses a set of processes and practises with the kind of sensitive information that is safeguarded as well as related threats. The CMMC model will promote a good cyber hygiene.

6.1 Research Design

The research design structure consists of several decisions made on what to research topic to use in the study, it uses various procedures of inquiry, collection data methods, data analysis and interpretation. The nature of the research problem should be the base for the research design, or the situation being assessed [23]. Selecting the appropriate research design structure is the primary main procedure in this study. The research statement for this study is based on the theory that there is an increase in ransomware attacks on the education sector during the pandemic 2020 compared to the previous year. To verify whether this is true, a quantitative research method approach is used to gather secondary datasets from two similar investigations used from two different sources (University of Temple and Hackmargeddon). The first case study for this investigation involves using the number of ransomware attacks reported by The University of Temple, compare these datasets to investigate if there was an increase of ransomware campaigns between 2019 and 2020. The second study also involves the use of datasets 2019 and 2020 collected from hackmargeddon.

These collected dataset samples will be statistically measured using The SPSS statistical tools to perform and analyse findings and results.

6.2 Quantitative Research

The primary purpose of quantitative research is to establish and describe the reality [24]. Quantitative research is described as the process of collecting and analysing numerical data to explain, describe or predict an event of interest. Quantitative research requires that the researcher identifies a hypothesis that is to be analysed and defines a research strategy that is required to conduct the study [25]. This investigation wants to determine if the supported hypothesis (The pandemic contributed to a rise of Ransomware against the education sector) is correct or to the contrary, accept the null hypothesis (The Pandemic did not influence the rise of Ransomware attacks against the education sector). To test this study's hypothesis, sample datasets from University of Temple and Hackmargeddon are used. The collected secondary sample datasets will be measured to provide results and indicate whether the increased ransomware attacks in 2020 compared to the previous year 2019 happened because the pandemic or the rising was expected to occur. The following dataset will be used for the hypothesis testing:

| Sample dataset 1 | University of Temple N of attacks | Jan 2019 | Dec 2019 |
| Sample dataset 2 | University of Temple N of attacks | Jan 2020 | Dec 2020 |

| Sample dataset a | Hackmargeddon N of attacks | Jan 2019 | Dec 2019 |
| Sample dataset b | Hackmargeddon N of attacks | Jan 2020 | Dec 2020 |

Descriptive research is used to explain various circumstances of a phenomenon, the main purpose of descriptive research is to explain a sample's behaviour or its properties. To conduct a descriptive research, the researcher can use a number of variables, where only one variable is used to conduct the study.

The purpose of hypothesis testing is to use data and determine if there are various probabilities that resolve an unknown factor or an uncertain situation. Hypothesis testing is used to provide a decision on which probabilities are likely to be correct, based on the collected data [26]. In this investigation, hypothesis testing will be used to determine if the proposed alternate hypothesis is correct based on the probabilities of the different datasets collected.

Steps in formulation of the study hypothesis:

- Study Hypothesis development
- Formulate the alternative hypothesis and null hypothesis
- Provide Level of significance
- Calculate the Test Statistic and Corresponding P-Value
- Interpreting results
- Hypothesis Development.

This initial process involves developing the alternate hypothesis based on the study theory and research questions and using collected data for hypothesis testing. The following 3 points provides a foundation for the proposed hypothesis.

- Theory formulation: An increase in ransomware attacks against education sector from 2019 and 2020.
- Research question: is there a significant increase in ransomware attacks against education sector from 2019 to 2020?
- Hypothesis: There is a significant increase in ransomware attacks against education sector in 2020 compared to 2019.

To begin formulating the hypothesis, there should be two types of competing hypothesis to be considered:

Ho—null hypothesis	Ha—alternative hypothesis
There isn't a significant increase of ransomware attacks against education sector in 2020 compared to 2019	There is a significant increase of ransomware attacks against education sector in 2020 compared to 2019

6.3   Significance Level

The significance level also denoted as (α) and normally set at 0.05 represents a 5% chance that the alternative hypothesis is accepted when the null hypothesis is true. For this hypothesis the significance level is set to 0.05, denoted as $a = 0.05$.

The following contingency table will be used to test the hypothesis.

Decision	In reality	
	H0 is TRUE	H0 is FALSE
Accept H0	Correct	Type II error β = probability of type II error
Reject H0	Type I error α = probability of type I error	Correct

6.4   Calculating the Statistic Test and Corresponding P-Value

To conduct the statistic test, two different datasets have been collected from two different organizations, where both entities carried out an investigation on ransomware attacks from 2019 to 2020. Statistic tests will be performed on the datasets collected by University of Temple as well as the datasets gathered by hackmargeddon. The results of each study will provide a decision to test the alternate hypothesis. The following datasets will be used in this study.

Sample dataset 1	University of Temple	Jan 2019	Dec 2019
Sample dataset 2	University of Temple	Jan 2020	Dec 2020

Sample dataset a	Hackmargeddon	Jan 2019	Dec 2019
Sample dataset b	Hackmargeddon	Jan 2020	Dec 2020

Study 1—University of Temple—Sample datasets.

Use SPSS to perform descriptive statistic tests on Sample dataset 1 to identify the mean, range, standard deviation, variance, minimum and maximum number value.

The goal of using SPSS descriptive statistics, is to obtain a summary of the dataset such as the following.

➡ **Descriptives**

Descriptive Statistics

	N	Minimum	Maximum	Sum	Mean	Std. Deviation	Variance	Skewness	
	Statistic	Statistic	Statistic	Statistic	Statistic	Statistic	Statistic	Statistic	Std. Error
University of temple	10	1	14	45	4.50	4.116	16.944	1.619	.687
Valid N (listwise)	10								

The theory which this investigation supports is referred to as alternative hypothesis (Ha) and is denoted as $\mu > 4.50$, where μ refers to the true mean level of ransomware attacks throughout the year of 2019. The theory that contradicts the alternative hypothesis, the null Hypothesis (H0) indicates that μ is equal or less than 4.50, this is denoted as $\mu = 4.50$. This investigation will attempt to support the alternative hypothesis that $\mu > 4.50$, using sample evidence that indicates that the null hypothesis is false. This investigation wants to test the following:

H0: $\mu = 4.50$ (The null hypothesis says that the mean for the dataset temple university in 2020 is the same as the previous year 2019).

Ha: $\mu > 4.50$ (The alternative hypothesis says the mean in the dataset temple university 2020 is bigger than the dataset in 2019).

By carrying out a test statistic, a decision can be made whether to accept or reject the null hypothesis. The study uses a sample n = 10.

6.5   Conducting a One Sample t Test

Using SPSS to compare the mean of the sample dataset previously collected (temple university 2019) against the sample dataset means collected (temple university 2020).

One-Sample Test

Test Value = 4.50

	t	df	Significance		Mean Difference	95% Confidence Interval of the Difference	
			One-Sided p	Two-Sided p		Lower	Upper
University of temple	.173	10	.433	.866	.136	-1.62	1.90

6.6   Interpreting Results

This section involves interpreting the outcome for the statistic tests performed on the two dataset samples. These two datasets are used for the purpose of comparing their means.

Sample dataset 1—University of temple 2019.

Sample dataset 2—University of temple 2020.

Sample dataset-1. Temple University 2019 Descriptive statistic test summary.

→ **Descriptives**

Descriptive Statistics

	N Statistic	Minimum Statistic	Maximum Statistic	Sum Statistic	Mean Statistic	Std. Deviation Statistic	Variance Statistic	Skewness Statistic	Std. Error
University of temple	10	1	14	45	4.50	4.116	16.944	1.619	.687
Valid N (listwise)	10								

- N Statistic: Refers to the numbers of valid observations, in this case 10 out of 12 months.
- Maximum statistic: This value represents the maximum number of ransomware attacks in 2019.
- Minimum statistic: This value indicates the minimum number of ransomware attacks in 2019.
- Sum statistic: This value is the total number of ransomware attacks in 2019.
- Mean statistic: also called the average is used to measure the central tendency, there is an average of 4.50 ransomware attacks.

Sample dataset—2. Temple University 2020 one sample test summary.

One-Sample Test

Test Value = 4.50

	t	df	Significance One-Sided p	Two-Sided p	Mean Difference	95% Confidence Interval of the Difference Lower	Upper
University of temple	.173	10	.433	.866	.136	-1.62	1.90

- T: represents the t value of 0.173
- DF: indicates there are 15 degrees of freedom.

Significance—one-sided p: Represents the level of significance of alpha level. The significance level is a primary value used in the statistic test to enable the interpretation of the t-test. A 95% of certainty has been used to interpret the statistics, this is to allow 5% of error.

Mean difference: indicates the difference in means amongst the two datasets, which is 1.36.

6.7 Drawing Conclusions

A sample t test was conducted to measure and compare the means of the sample dataset 1 against the means of dataset 2. Using the means of dataset 1 as test value 4.50, the sample t test is conducted on dataset 2, and found the following significant difference (t $(10) = 173, p = 0.433$) including the means difference of 0.136 between dataset 1 and dataset two.

Then the decision rule is:

Reject H0 if P-value $\leq \alpha$—(A small p value indicates strong evidence that the null hypothesis is incorrect).

Do not reject H0 if P-value $> \alpha$—(A large p value indicates strong evidence that the alternate hypothesis is weak, and that the null hypothesis cannot be rejected).

Results: $0.433 > 0.05$.

The results indicate that $p = 0.433$ is greater than 0.05, and that the null hypothesis cannot be rejected, even though, the null hypothesis has not been proven to be correct. It can't be stated that there was no difference in means between the two datasets because of the p value is 0.433. It has also not been demonstrated that the null hypothesis is true but have concluded that the evidence is not strong enough to disprove it.

Study 2—Hackmargeddon—Sample datasets.

Use SPSS to perform descriptive statistic tests on Sample datasets A and B to identify the mean, range, standard deviation, variance, minimum and maximum number value.

Using the mean value found from sample dataset—A and conduct a one sample t test to the sample dataset B, to determine the mean and significance level or alpha.

Interpret results.

Drawing conclusions.

Descriptive Statistics.

The main objective of descriptive statistics is to provide a summary a collected dataset. SPSS is commonly used when analysing datasets and finding out in detail information about those datasets, the output includes occurrences such as percentages, valid percentages. The following summary from dataset A has been obtained from Using a descriptive statistics approach.

Descriptive Statistics

	N	Range	Minimum	Maximum	Sum	Mean		Std. Deviation	Variance	Skewness		Kurtosis	
	Statistic	Statistic	Statistic	Statistic	Statistic	Statistic	Std. Error	Statistic	Statistic	Statistic	Std. Error	Statistic	Std. Error
Hackmargeddon	8	12	2	14	54	6.75	1.386	3.919	15.357	.781	.752	.337	1.481
Valid N (listwise)	8												

The theory which this investigation supports is referred to as alternative hypothesis (Ha) and is denoted as $\mu > 6.75$, where μ refers to the true mean level of ransomware attacks throughout the year of 2019. The theory that contradicts the alternative hypothesis, the null Hypothesis (H0) indicates that μ is equal or less than 6.75, this is denoted as $\mu = 6.75$. This investigation will attempt to support the alternative hypothesis that $\mu > 6.75$, using sample evidence that indicates that the null hypothesis is false. This investigation wants to test the following:

H0: $\mu = 6.75$ (The null hypothesis says that the mean for the dataset A is the same as the previous dataset B).

Ha: $\mu > 6.75$ (The alternative hypothesis says the mean in the dataset A is bigger than university dataset in B).

By carrying out a test statistic, a decision can be made whether to accept or reject the null hypothesis. The study uses a sample n $= 10$.

6.8 Conducting a One Sample t Test

The one-sample t-test is a type of statistical hypothesis testing that is used to determine if an unknown population mean is different from a specific value. SPSS will be used to compare and determine if the sample dataset means has changed. Using (Dataset A) against the sample dataset means collected (Dataset B). A test value of 6.75 is used to test the hypothesized mean against the test variable.

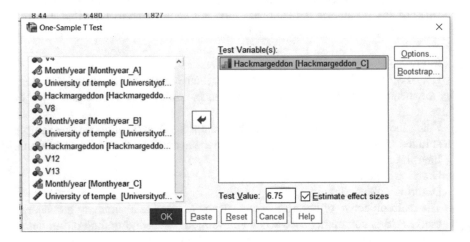

One-Sample Test Output

One-Sample Test

Test Value = 6.75

| | t | df | Significance | | Mean Difference | 95% Confidence Interval of the Difference | |
			One-Sided p	Two-Sided p		Lower	Upper
Hackmargeddon	.928	8	.190	.381	1.694	-2.52	5.91

This section involves interpreting the outcome for the statistic tests performed on the two dataset samples. These two datasets are used for the purpose of comparing their means.

Sample dataset A—Hackmargeddon 2019.

Sample dataset B—Hackmargeddon 2020.

Sample dataset-1. Temple University 2019 Descriptive statistic test summary.

Descriptive Statistics

| | N | Range | Minimum | Maximum | Sum | Mean | | Std. Deviation | Variance | Skewness | | Kurtosis | |
	Statistic	Statistic	Statistic	Statistic	Statistic	Statistic	Std. Error	Statistic	Statistic	Statistic	Std. Error	Statistic	Std. Error
Hackmargeddon	8	12	2	14	54	6.75	1.386	3.919	15.357	.781	.752	.337	1.481
Valid N (listwise)	8												

N Statistic: Refers to the numbers of valid observations, in this case 8 out of 12 months.

Maximum statistic: This value represents the maximum number of ransomware attacks in 2019.

Minimum statistic: This value indicates the minimum number of ransomware attacks in 2019.

Sum statistic: This value is the total number of ransomware attacks in 2019.

Mean statistic: also called the average is used to measure the central tendency, there is an average of 6.75 ransomware attacks.

One sample test summary

One-Sample Test

Test Value = 6.75

| | t | df | Significance | | Mean Difference | 95% Confidence Interval of the Difference | |
			One-Sided p	Two-Sided p		Lower	Upper
Hackmargeddon	.928	8	.190	.381	1.694	-2.52	5.91

T: represents the t value of 0.928.
DF: indicates there are 8 degrees of freedom.

Significance—one-sided p: Represents the level of significance of alpha level. The significance level is a primary value used in the statistic test to enable the interpretation of the t-test. A 95% of certainty has been used to interpret the statistics, this is to allow 5% of error.

Mean difference: indicates the difference in means amongst the two datasets, which is 1.694.

6.9   Drawing Conclusions

A sample t test was conducted to measure and compare the means of the sample dataset A against the means of dataset B. Using the means of dataset A as test value 4.50, the sample t test is conducted on dataset B, and found the following significant difference (t (8) = 0.928, p = 0.190) including the means difference of 0.136 between dataset 1 and dataset two.

Then the decision rule is:

- Reject H0 if P-value $\leq \alpha$—(A small p value indicates strong evidence that the null hypothesis is incorrect).
- Do not reject H0 if P-value $>$—(A large p value indicates strong evidence that the alternate hypothesis is weak, and that the null hypothesis cannot be rejected).

Results: 0.190 > 0.05.

The results indicate that $p = 0.190$ is greater than 0.05, and that the null hypothesis cannot be rejected, even though, the null hypothesis has not been proven to be correct.

It can't be stated that there was no difference in means between the two datasets because of the *p* value is 0.190. It has also not been demonstrated that the null hypothesis is true but have concluded that the evidence is not strong enough to disprove it.

6.9.1   Statistics Table and Data Visualization

Ransomware attacks in 2019 reported by University of Temple and Hackmargeddon.

Monthyear_C	Universityoft emple_C	Hackmarge ddon_C
Jan 20	4	2
Feb 20	7	10
Mar 20	5	2
Apr 20	1	.
May 20	3	.
Jun 20	2	.
Jul 20	6	7
Aug 20	8	17
Sep 20	9	15
Oct 20	.	11
Nov 20	4	9
Dec 20	2	3

Ransomware attacks in 2020 reported by University of Temple and Hack-margeddon.

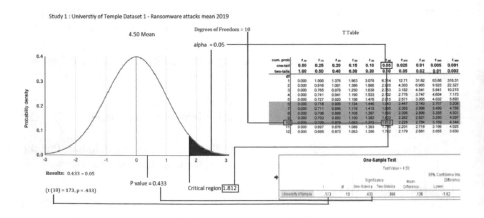

Study 1 University of Temple: Normal Distribution using the t table.

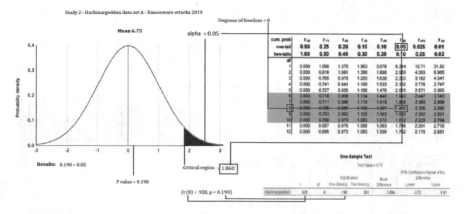

Study 2 Hackmargeddon: Normal Distribution using the t table.
Descriptive statistics Dataset 1.
The following table represents the output of University of Temple 2019 Dataset 1.

N	Valid	10
	Missing	2
Mean		4.50
Std. Error of Mean		1.302
Median		3.50
Mode		1
Std. Deviation		4.116
Variance		16.944
Range		13
Minimum		1
Maximum		14
Sum		45
Percentiles	25	1.00
	50	3.50
	75	6.00

Descriptive statistics Dataset 2 University of Temple

Descriptive Statistics

	N	Range	Minimum	Maximum	Sum	Mean		Std. Deviation	Variance
	Statistic	Statistic	Statistic	Statistic	Statistic	Statistic	Std. Error	Statistic	Statistic
University of temple	11	8	1	9	51	4.64	.789	2.618	6.855
Valid N (listwise)	11								

Descriptive statistics Dataset A Hackmargeddon

Descriptive Statistics

	N	Range	Minimum	Maximum	Sum	Mean		Std. Deviation	Variance
	Statistic	Statistic	Statistic	Statistic	Statistic	Statistic	Std. Error	Statistic	Statistic
Hackmargeddon	8	12	2	14	54	6.75	1.386	3.919	15.357
Valid N (listwise)	8								

Descriptive statistics Dataset B Hackmargeddon

Descriptive Statistics

	N	Range	Minimum	Maximum	Sum	Mean		Std. Deviation	Variance
	Statistic	Statistic	Statistic	Statistic	Statistic	Statistic	Std. Error	Statistic	Statistic
Hackmargeddon	9	15	2	17	76	8.44	1.827	5.480	30.028
Valid N (listwise)	9								

Histogram Dataset 1
The histogram below represents the frequency statistics, it provides the mean, standard deviation and Numbers used of the dataset 1.

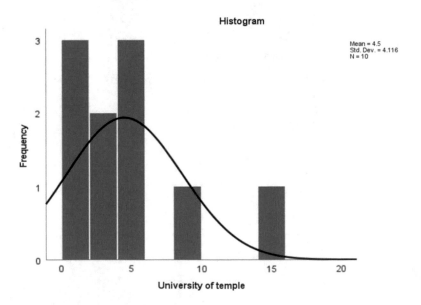

Histogram

Mean = 4.5
Std. Dev. = 4.116
N = 10

Histogram Dataset 2
The histogram below represents the frequency statistics, it provides the mean, standard deviation and Numbers used of the dataset A.

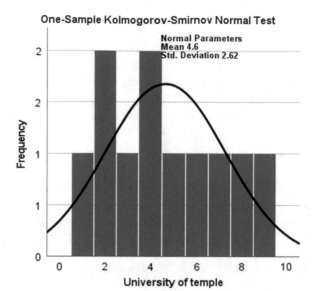

Hackmargeddon Study 2 Dataset A 2020

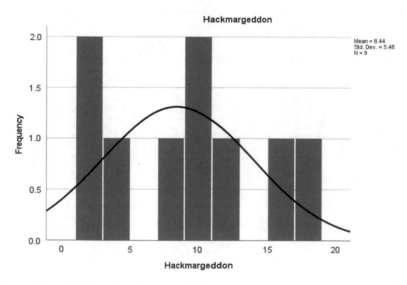

Mean Plot of University of temple 2019

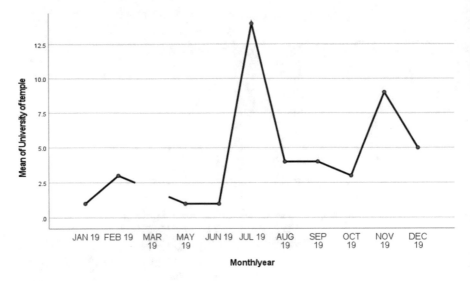

Mean Plot of Hackmargeddon

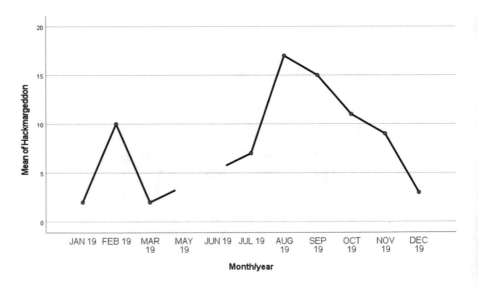

T table

cum. prob	$t_{.50}$	$t_{.75}$	$t_{.80}$	$t_{.85}$	$t_{.90}$	$t_{.95}$	$t_{.975}$	$t_{.99}$	$t_{.995}$	$t_{.999}$	$t_{.9995}$
one-tail	0.50	0.25	0.20	0.15	0.10	0.05	0.025	0.01	0.005	0.001	0.0005
two-tails	1.00	0.50	0.40	0.30	0.20	0.10	0.05	0.02	0.01	0.002	0.001
df											
1	0.000	1.000	1.376	1.963	3.078	6.314	12.71	31.82	63.66	318.31	636.62
2	0.000	0.816	1.061	1.386	1.886	2.920	4.303	6.965	9.925	22.327	31.599
3	0.000	0.765	0.978	1.250	1.638	2.353	3.182	4.541	5.841	10.215	12.924
4	0.000	0.741	0.941	1.190	1.533	2.132	2.776	3.747	4.604	7.173	8.610
5	0.000	0.727	0.920	1.156	1.476	2.015	2.571	3.365	4.032	5.893	6.869
6	0.000	0.718	0.906	1.134	1.440	1.943	2.447	3.143	3.707	5.208	5.959
7	0.000	0.711	0.896	1.119	1.415	1.895	2.365	2.998	3.499	4.785	5.408
8	0.000	0.706	0.889	1.108	1.397	1.860	2.306	2.896	3.355	4.501	5.041
9	0.000	0.703	0.883	1.100	1.383	1.833	2.262	2.821	3.250	4.297	4.781
10	0.000	0.700	0.879	1.093	1.372	1.812	2.228	2.764	3.169	4.144	4.587
11	0.000	0.697	0.876	1.088	1.363	1.796	2.201	2.718	3.106	4.025	4.437
12	0.000	0.695	0.873	1.083	1.356	1.782	2.179	2.681	3.055	3.930	4.318

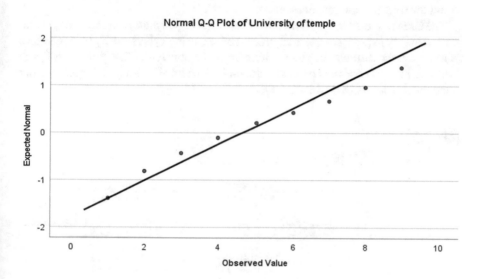

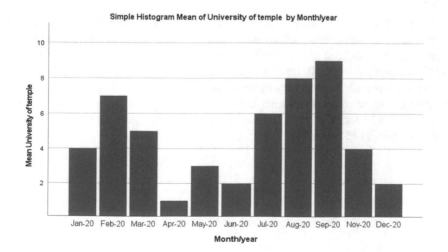

7 Cybersecurity Maturity Model Certification, CMMC

The CMMC framework should be used in the education sector, many institutions will find it beneficial to use a Cybersecurity Maturity model that can be used to assess all the internal and external processes of the organizations, based on the ISO 27001 NIST standards, the CMMC regulates these processes according to the policies and best practices. It is imperative to consider using a robust Cybersecurity Maturity Model that measures the organization Maturity to handle risks and provides levels for identifying risks or gaps for improvement. The following is the proposed framework that could be used in educational institutions, bearing in mind that the CMMC was designed for government contractors, nevertheless the CMMC can be accommodated to suit the organization requirements.

The CMMC model offers a benchmark where an organization can assess its current level of ability in processes, techniques, practises, using cybersecurity best practices from across the different cybersecurity standard frameworks The following figure describes how practices and processes are embedded into the domains mapping them along the five levels [27].CMMC Levels

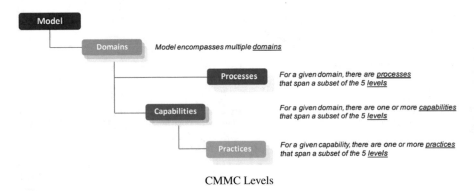

CMMC Levels

The CMMC model consists in measuring cybersecurity maturity with five levels. Every level contains a group of processes and practices. The processes start at level 1 performed to level 5 optimizing. The organization seeking certification and wanting to achieve a particular CMMC level is required to demonstrate that the lower levels have also been achieved. Additionally, the organization seeking certification is required to prove that the processes and the implementation of practises for a particular CMMC level and the lower levels have been achieved [27]. The figure bellow describes the set of practises and processes.

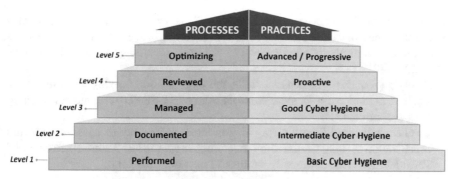

CMMC Specifications

The organization seeking certification must understand the requirements, specifications and mappings of practices and processes to a specific level, considering regulations, kind of information handled and its sensitivity, implementation process, implications in the assessments, costs, and threats. The Cybersecurity Maturity Model offers an improvement in maturity processes and a set of cybersecurity best practices that protects sensible information from an advanced persistent threats (APT) [27]. CMMC is focus on the following:

- Level 1: Safeguard Federal Contract information
- Level 2: Serve as transition step in cybersecurity maturity procession to protect CUI
- Level 3 Protect Controlled Unclassified Information CUI
- Level 4–5 Protect CUI and reduce risk of Advance Persistent Threats (APT
- Level 1: Basic Cyber Hygiene: this phase consists of any organizations seeking.

Certification to implement the 17 controls control that NIST SP 800-171 contain. This phase is designed to protect the Federal Classified Information and not for organizations that process Controlled Unclassified Information or CUI. As its practises are only concerned with the basic protection requirements which are specified in 48 CFR 52.204-2 and are thought to be the basic or minimum control for protecting FCI [21].

- Level 2: Intermediate Cyber Hygiene—For the Organization Seeking Certification there is a requirement to implement 48 controls more from the NIST 800-171, including the new controls. The organization must implement and document its practices, including the policies that will guide them through the implementation of CMMC. Documenting practises enables the organization to repeat them as often as they required. This is the lowest stage that organizations can process Controlled Unclassified Information, where controls are not only executed but also should documented [21].
- Level 3: Good Cyber Hygiene—The Organization Seeking Certification is required to implement the final 45 controls from NIST SP 800-171 Rev. 2, including another 14 new controls. The organization is responsible in establishing, maintaining, and resourcing a plan which demonstrates the activities

management for practise implementation. This level is concerned with safe-guarding the Controlled Unclassified Information and covers the specified security requirements by the NIST SP 800-171 controls, including practices in DFARS 252.204-7012 [21].

- Level 4: Proactive—To pass an audit, the Organisation seeking Certification is required to implement 13 more controls from NIST SP 800-171 and additionally 13 new controls [21].
- Level 5: Advanced/Progressive—In this level, to be able to pass an audit the Organization seeking Certification must implement the last 5 controls from NIST SP 800-17225 and additionally another 11 new controls [21].

7.1 Implementation

The Cybersecurity Maturity Model Certification contains 17 security families or domains, these domains belong to the NIST SP 800-171 framework and the FIPS, the Federal Information Processing Standards Publication 200. Additionally, The Cybersecurity Maturity Model Certification framework must include a set of three more domains, such as Recovery, Situation Awareness and Asset Management [27]. The following figure illustrates the 17 domains:

Access Control (AC)

Preserving the integrity, confidentiality and availability is vital in cybersecurity for organizations. The organizations seeking certification must establish methods in limiting access to information systems to users that have been authorised. Also the limiting of processes on devices are required. To achieve this, the organization must establish a process referred to as access control.

7.1.1 Awareness and Training (AT)

Organizations must conduct awareness training to their employees that make use of their organization systems. Users must be trained to be aware of potential security risks that are related to their job activities as well as the applicable laws, processes, policies, procedures and regulations or any type of activities that involves the organization security information systems. Conducting an adequate training for staff enables them to perform their security related activities.

7.1.2 Configuration Management (CM)

The Organizations are responsible for establishing and maintaining the configurations of information system such as documentation as well as the information systems inventory such as hardware, software, and firmware. Organizations are also responsible for enforcing and implementing security configurations to all the digital products used by the informational systems from the organization. Inventories are an essential part in the ISO 27001 process.

7.1.3 Identification and Authentication (IA)

Organization must use verification and authentication mechanisms to verify, identify and authenticate devices, users, or processes. This is a prerequisite to grant access to the information systems from the organization. ISO 27001 Annex A control set A.9 provides controls on Identification and authentication.

7.1.4 Incident Response (IR)

Organizations must plan an incident response, that deals with operational incidents from the information systems. The plan must include preparation, detection, analysis, and recovery, tracking, documenting, and reporting the operational incidents accordingly to the officials from the organization or the pertinent authorities. ISO 27001 Annex A control set A.16. considers the Information security incident management.

7.1.5 Maintenance (MA)

Organizations must carry out maintenance periodically on their information systems and implement controls that are effective on their tools, methods, and mechanisms and the users that carry out the maintenance the organization information system. ISO 27001 Annex A control A.11.2.4. covers maintenance.

7.1.6   Media Protection (MP)

Organizations are required to safeguard information system media, including paper and digital. Limiting access to only authorized users to information from information system media. They are also responsible for sanitizing or destroying of any information system media. ISO 27001 Annex A control set A.11. discusses Media safeguarding.

7.1.7   Personnel Security (PS)

Organizations are required to make sure that employees that have positions of responsibility are trustworthy, this includes individuals from services providers and third-party organizations. These individuals are subject to a security criterion for those positions of responsibility. The organization is also responsible for safeguarding their information and information systems when personnel leave the organization or gets a transfer. They must also establish and implement a set procedures and security policies for formally sanctioning personnel that fails in complying with the organization policies.

7.1.8   Physical and Environmental Protection (PE)

Organizations are required to restrict access to individuals and only allow authorized users accessing the physical information systems. They must safeguard the physical information system's infrastructure, offering information system support and safeguard the physical information systems from hazards from the environment. They are also responsible for implementing an adequate environment control where information systems reside.

7.1.9   Risk Assessment (RA)

Organizations are responsible in assessing the risk periodically to their operations, assets and users. They must also access risk to processes, storage and information that are transmitted. The risk assessment is a primary section of ISO 27001 in Information Security Management System.

7.1.10   Security Assessment (SA)

Organizations are required to provide the necessary resources to effectively safeguard their information systems. They must also implement a system development cycle framework that permits the incorporation of properties of information security. Make sure that third party providers are using the correct security mechanisms to safeguard organizations information.

7.1.11 System and Communications Protection (SC)

Organizations are responsible for monitoring, controlling, and protecting their transmitted information, The organization must, use architectural designs, software development methods and engineering principles to promote an adequate, effective information security system for their information systems.

7.1.12 System and Information Integrity (SI)

Organizations are responsible for identifying, reporting, and correcting the information and inconsistencies in the information system within a time frame. Offer safeguarding against malicious coding in adequate places. They are responsible for monitoring of the information system alerts taking the required steps to deal with them.

7.1.13 Extra Three Domains

Three more domains have been included to the 14 domains that belongs to NIST SP 800-171. This domain that has been included area requirement for higher certification levels, ranging from level two and to the upper levels. The following are the new controls.

- **Asset Management**

The Asset Management domain provides 14 more controls. These controls are concerned in creating, protecting, and reviewing of the logs. As the maturity level progresses from level two to level five, the controls expand in sophistication and log monitoring frequency. Organizations seeking certifications must review audit logs at level two, while in level four reviewing audit logs must be automated. There are mapping between these controls and the controls from the framework ISO 27001 Annex A, specially controls A.12.4 and including controls such as SI-11 and RA-5 in NIST SP 800-53 Rev.4.

- **Situation Awareness**

The situation awareness domain contains 3 controls, the first control is found at level 3 the other two controls are found at level 4. These controls are focused on hunting threats. They provide a control to share information in forums such as US-Cert found in level 3. In level 4, Hunting capabilities are required for detecting, tracking, and disrupting advanced persistent threats that evades controls. Even though, the

NIST SP 800-53 Rev.4 does not have a domain for Situation Awareness, there is one domain for system information and integrity that provides various controls referring to Situation Awareness.

- **Recovery**

The recovery domain is required to have 4 new controls that is focused on backup requirements. Requirements for backup at different stages are defined by the scope, availability and resiliency, those requirements are the same as the publications of NIST SP 800-53 Rev.4 CP-9 and ISO 27001 Annex A 12.3.

8 Ethical and Legal Aspects

One of the most important aspects of this research is to evaluate and identify how collected data from secondary sources are used and processed. It is a main concern for the researcher to comply with data protection principles by adhering to the data protection act 2018 (Data protection, 2018) which states that the information should be used fairly, lawfully, and transparently. The collected information must be used adequately, it should also be used for specific and explicit purposes and that it should be destroyed once it has served its purpose. This research also abides to GDPR guidelines [28] which relates to data protection principles, rights, and obligations to businesses and organizations.

Considerations must be made when performing quantitative research in an ethical form. In this research an ethical practise is carried out, following the code of conducts that also governs a professional practice. The ethical issues when carrying a research project involves the researcher and any participants involved. Research participants can pose a significant ethical issue in dealing with collecting data, obtaining consent for data use, seeking sensitive information, causing harm to participants, and maintaining confidentiality. The researcher can also pose an ethical concern if an appropriate research methodology is not used, inaccurate reporting, and incorrect use of information. It is then essential to examine that no unethical practise is performed while carrying out this research [29].

There are other ethical issues and the implications when collecting data form secondary sources such as plagiarism [29]. It would be unethical to claim someone else's work as being your own. In this research all data sources have been cited down correctly using the appropriate Harvard styling. Data Collection is a primary part used in this research as for understanding the raising of Ransomware attacks on education institutions, written consent was obtained from an institution which carried out research on ransomware attacks, as well as data gathered from hackmargeddon research site. This data will be presented using the same format and context without any changes, as modification would lead to a different interpretation of the original collected data and resulting in an unethical practise [29]. Ranjit [29] also explains that it is essential to avoid disclosing data sources. It can only be disclosed with the consent given by the author, this is to protect the identity of participants or institutions. Disclosing information about the source without permission is considered unethical.

9   Critical Discussions

This investigation intended to find out if there really was a significant change in the increasing ransomware attacks, by using 0.05 as the alpha, this study could determine that there isn't a significant change, even though there were small differences in means. An alternative procedure would be to use an alpha of 0.40, this percentage will provide better results allowing the rejection region to be larger and thus allowing the p-values fall into the critical region.

The result of this study reflects that even thought there were not significant, it does show that ransomware attacks have been on the rise already, and the pandemic did not contribute or caused an increase of ransomware attacks against the education sector, to the contrary ransomware attacks have been arising from 2017.

This study suggests that most of the education establishments that were hit by ransomware attacks did not have an effective information security, risk management and control programs, further to this the lack of user awareness programs and appropriate defence mechanisms to detect and deter threats. Poor IT governance and a low budged for IT resources have also been a major factor for education institutions that are already struggling to meet the criteria for data protection. After conducting the investigation of ransomware attacks against the education sector is evident that a Framework such as the CMMC must be implemented to benchmark the organization risk maturity, make improvements, and establish a basic cyber hygiene level and progressively continue to level 5.

This investigation concludes the following about the hypothesis testing conducted on the study 1 University of temple data set.

A sample t test was used to measure and compare the means of the sample dataset 1 against the means of dataset 2. Using the means of dataset 1 as test value 4.50, the sample t test is conducted on dataset 2, and found the following significant difference $(t\,(10) = 173, p = 0.433)$ including the means difference of 0.136 between dataset 1 and dataset two.

The results indicates that $p = 0.433$ is greater than 0.05, and that the null hypothesis cannot be rejected, even though, the null hypothesis has not been proven to be correct. It can't be stated that there was no difference in means between the two datasets because of the p value is 0.433. It has also not been demonstrated that the null hypothesis is true but have concluded that the evidence is not strong enough to disprove it. Using the Normal distribution in the study 1 of Temple University dataset 1, this study determines that the p value 0.433 does not fall into the rejection region, where the null hypothesis is rejected. This result means that $0.433 > 0.05$ and according to the hypothesis rule, (Reject H0 if P-value $\leq \alpha$ and do not reject H0 if P-value $> \alpha$) the study draws the conclusion that the null hypothesis is to be accepted because $0.433 > 0.05$.

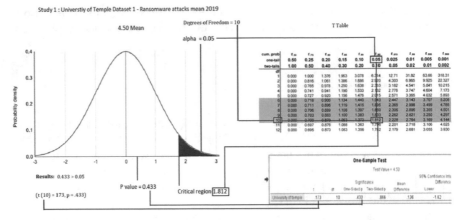

Conclusion on Study 1

Drawing Conclusions on Study 1

Study 1. University of temple dataset 1		
Ho null hypothesis	There isn't a significant increase of ransomware attacks against education sector in 2020 compared to 2019	Accepted
Ha alternative hypothesis	There is a significant increase of ransomware attacks against education sector in 2020 compared to 2019	Rejected

This investigation concludes the following about the hypothesis testing conducted on the study 2 Hackmargeddon datasets.

A sample t test was conducted for the hypothesis testing, its purpose was to measure and compare the means of the sample dataset A against the means of dataset B. Using the means of dataset 1 as test value 6.75, the sample t test is conducted on dataset B, and found the following significant difference ($t(8) = 0.928, p = 0.190$) including the means difference of 0.136 between dataset A and dataset B.

The results indicates that $p = 0.190$ is greater than 0.05, and that the null hypothesis cannot be rejected, even though the null hypothesis has not been proven to be correct. It can't be stated that there was no difference in means between the two datasets because of the p value is 0.190. It has also not been demonstrated that the null hypothesis is true but have concluded that the evidence is not strong enough to disprove it. Using the Normal distribution in the study 1 of Temple University dataset 1, this study determines that the p value 0.190 does not fall into the rejection region, where the null hypothesis is rejected. This result means that $0.190 > 0.05$ and according to the hypothesis rule, (Reject H0 if P-value $\leq \alpha$ and do not reject H0 if P-value $> \alpha$) the study draws the conclusion that the null hypothesis is to be accepted because $0.190 > 0.05$.

Conclusion on Study 1

Study 2. Hackmargeddon 1		
Ho null hypothesis	There isn't a significant increase of ransomware attacks against education sector in 2020 compared to 2019	Accepted
Ha alternative hypothesis	There is a significant increase of ransomware attacks against education sector in 2020 compared to 2019	Rejected

Summary of findings

- A 4.50 mean ransomware attacks in 2019 found in Study 1
- A 4.64 mean ransomware attacks in 2020 found in Study 1
- A maximum of 14 attacks were found in a year from study 1 in 2019
- A total of 45 ransomware attacks occurred in 2019 found in study 1
- A maximum of 9 attacks were found in a year from study 1 in 2020
- A total of 51 ransomware attacks occurred in 2020found in study 1
- A 6.75 mean ransomware attacks in 2019 found in Study 2
- A 8.44 mean ransomware attacks in 2020 found in Study 2
- A maximum of 14 attacks were found in a year from study 2 in 2019
- A maximum of 17 attacks were found in a year from study 2 in 2020
- A total of 54 ransomware attacks occurred in 2019 found in study 2
- A total of 76 ransomware attacks occurred in 2019 found in study 2.

The CMMC was designed for the supply chain contractors that have direct access to government intellectual property. The Cybersecurity Maturity Certifications Provides a framework for implementing policies and practises for organizations from the Defence Industry Base. A cybersecurity Maturity Model should be the cornerstone for any organization. Establishing a benchmark where an organization can assess internal or external processes using policies and using the ISO 27001 and NIST standards. As the CMMC is based on ISO 27001 and NIST frameworks, it has a rigorous implementation. Organizations must use basic cyber hygiene that includes system security, password hygiene, and antiviruses. As well as using security defence mechanisms for detecting and mitigating threats and carryout out audits to identify and fix possible risks or gaps.

Conclusions

Research studies on ransomware attacks against the education sector have been conducted and have shown that education industries are the primary target for cyber criminals, hacktivists, and cyber espionage. The global pandemic demanded that people remotely and education institutions had to deliver remote learning to students. Cyber organizations took this opportunity to hit Education establishments with ransomware attacks, encrypting systems demanding a ransom payment for decryption. Seeking to steal research material such as intellectual property (IP), sensitive information and trade secrets by exploiting the organization vulnerable systems and hitting critical infrastructure. Often, the organizations impacted by ransomware lacked a well-established Cybersecurity Maturity Framework and defence mechanisms. Cyber criminals often Extract and leak sensitive data over to the dark web. Cyber threat actors exploited fear and used the unstable economy and social conditions to perform Ransomware Campaigns to generate profits and disrupt business functions This ransomware cyber-attack had a huge impact on many public and private organizations, this is the main reason this investigation is conducted to find out the impacts of ransomware campaigns.

Organizations such as educational establishments should consider using a CMMC framework, even though the CMMC was developed for government contractors, they primary objective of CMMC is preserving and protecting Intellectual Property (IP). Similarly, education establishments contain Intellectual Property material that requires to be protected according to the data protection act 2018. The CMMC is the best framework for education institutions since its based in ISO and NIST standards, its policies provide guidance when developing their information security, risk management and control programs.

References

1. Ulven J, Wangen G (2021) A systematic review of cybersecurity risks in higher education. Future Internet 13(2):39
2. NCSC (2020) Alert: targeted ransomware attacks on the UK education sector by cyber criminals [online]. Crown. Available at https://www.ncsc.gov.uk/files/20200917-Alert-Academia-Ransomware.pdf. Accessed 1 Mar 2021
3. Cybersecurity in Higher Education (2021) [online] Bluevoyant. Available at https://www.bluevoyant.com/resources/cybersecurity-in-higher-education/. Accessed 28 Feb 2021
4. Humayun M, Jhanjhi N, Alsayat A, Ponnusamy V (2021) Internet of things and ransomware: evolution, mitigation, and prevention. Egypt Inform J 22(1):105–117 [online]. Available at https://doi.org/10.1016/j.eij.2020.05.003. Accessed 14 Mar 2021
5. Hassan N (2019) Ransomware revealed, 1st edn. A Press, New York, p 3
6. Shinde R, der Veeken P, Schooten S, den Berg J (2017) Ransomware: studying transfer and mitigation. IEEE [online]. Available at https://ieeexplore.ieee.org/document/7914946/authors#authors. Accessed 13 Mar 2021
7. Richardson R, North M (2017) Ransomware: evolution, mitigation and prevention. Int Manage Rev 13 [online]. Available at https://digitalcommons.kennesaw.edu/facpubs/4276. Accessed 15 Mar 2021
8. Network Security (2014) CryptoLocker success leads to more malware 2014(1):20 [online]. Available at https://www.sciencedirect.com/science/article/pii/S1353485814700121. Accessed 15 Mar 2021
9. Gallo T, Liska A (2016) Ransomware, 1st edn. O'Reilly Media Inc., United States of America
10. Calder A (2021) The ransomware threat landscape. IT Governance Ltd., Ely, pp 13, 15
11. Liska A, Gallo T (2017) Ransomware defending against digital extortion. 1st edn. O'Reilly Media, pp 6, 7, 8, 9, 10, 11, 12
12. Scholz S, Hagen W, Lee C (2022) The increasing threat of ransomware in higher education [online]. Educause Review. Available at https://er.educause.edu/articles/2021/6/the-increasing-threat-of-ransomware-in-higher-education. Accessed 13 Apr 2022
13. Koomson J (2022) Rise of ransomware attacks on the education sector during the COVID-19 pandemic [online]. ISACA. Available at https://www.isaca.org/resources/isaca-journal/issues/2021/volume-5/rise-of-ransomware-attacks-on-the-education-sector-during-the-covid-19-pandemic. Accessed 13 Apr 2022

14. Chapman J (2019) How safe is your data? Cyber-security in higher education
15. Sophos (2021) The state of ransomware in education [online]. Available at https://assets.sop hos.com/X24WTUEQ/at/g523b3nmgcfk5r5hc5sns6q/sophos-state-of-ransomware-in-educat ion-2021-wp.pdf. Accessed 13 Apr 2022
16. Cps.gov.uk. (2021) Cybercrime—prosecution guidance. The Crown Prosecution Service [online]. Available at https://www.cps.gov.uk/legal-guidance/cybercrime-prosecution-gui dance. Accessed 8 Mar 2021
17. Agcaoili J, Ang M, Earnshow E, Gelera B (2022) Ransomware double extortion and beyond: REvil, Clop, and Conti [online]. Trend MICRO. Available at https://www.trendmicro.com/ vinfo/us/security/news/cybercrime-and-digital-threats/ransomware-double-extortion-and-bey ond-revil-clop-and-conti. Accessed 20 Jan 2022
18. Al-Matari O, Helal I, Mazen S, Elhennawy S (2021) Adopting security maturity model to the organizations' capability model. Egypt Inform J 22(2):193–199
19. Aliyu A, Maglaras L, He Y, Yevseyeva I, Boiten E, Cook A, Janicke H (2020) A holistic cybersecurity maturity assessment framework for higher education institutions in the United Kingdom. Appl Sci 10(10):3660
20. Cybersecurity Maturity Model Certification (2021) [ebook]. Carnegie Mellon University and The Johns Hopkins University, USA. Available at https://www.acq.osd.mil/cmmc/docs/ CMMC_ModelMain_V1.02_20200318.pdf. Accessed 11 Apr 2021
21. Gamble W (2020) Cybersecurity maturity model certification (CMMC) [s.l.]. It Governance Ltd.
22. Ignite (2022) How can my organization obtain CMMC [ebook]. Ignati, Ignite. Available at https://ignyteplatform.com/wp-content/uploads/2020/05/How-Can-My-Organization-Obtain-CMMC_-1.pdf. Accessed 19 Jan 2022
23. Creswell J (2016) Research design, 3rd edn. SAGE Publications India Pvt. Ltd., Singapore, p 048763
24. Biddix J (2018) Research methods and applications for student affairs. Jossey-Bass, A Wiley Brand, San Francisco, California
25. Mills G, Gay L, Airasian P (2016) Educational research competencies for analysis and applications, 10th edn. Pearson Education
26. Baker L (2021) Hypothesis testing, 1st edn
27. Department of Defence (2020) Cybersecurity maturity model certification. Department of Defence
28. Information Commissioners Office (2021) Guide to the UK general data protection regulation (UK GDPR) [online]. Ico.org.uk. Available at https://ico.org.uk/for-organisations/guide-to-data-protection/guide-to-the-general-data-protection-regulation-gdpr/. Accessed 9 May 2021
29. Kumar R (2014) Research methodology: a step-by-step guide for beginners. SAGE Publications. ProQuest Ebook Central. https://ebookcentral.proquest.com/lib/northumbria/detail.act ion?docID=1619553

Strategic Decision-Making for Pedagogical Course Planning Using NLP in Social Media Data

Shahin Houshmand, Rose Fong, Eustathios Sainidis, and Hamid Jahankhani

Abstract A higher education system needs to ensure its teaching process and materials are aligned with the graduate employment market needs and expectations. If a university has built trust in the industry, it would be more likely to have its graduates to find suitable relevant jobs in the market. As a result, this will have positive feedback to absorb better students to select the desired university as their first choice to study; consequently, the university's reputation will improve. In this research, a novel prototype has been suggested to support strategic decision-making in academic curriculum planning based on the university's 'business-focus' vision. To achieve the aim, the CRISP-DM model was used, and different Python libraries were applied for scraping data, creating a dataset, data preparation, and weighting keyword technologies depending on the most demanded skills. A job dataset was created by scraping job descriptions from social media. In this research, the skills, gathered from Stack Overflow's survey, were counted in job descriptions and the most popular skills were identified. Finally, the job dataset was categorised based on the top-ranked skills.

Keywords NLP · CRISP-DM · Python · Decision support · Pedagogy · Social media · Higher education

S. Houshmand · R. Fong (✉) · E. Sainidis · H. Jahankhani
Northumbria University, London, UK
e-mail: rose.fong@northumbria.ac.uk

E. Sainidis
e-mail: eustathios.sainidis@northumbria.ac.uk

H. Jahankhani
e-mail: hamid.jahankhani@northumbria.ac.uk

1   Introduction

The main aim of this research is to apply data science technologies in strategic decision-making. The strategic decision-making, here, is to select the most important technical skill modules in 'Big Data and Data Science Technology' and to find the most relevant courses to support them. A higher education system as an organisation needs to make strategic formulations to improve its performance [4].

Responding timely and appropriately to changes is always a main challenge in strategic decision-making. To manage this, first, the effective parameters should be determined, and second, they should be included in the decision-making process. In this regard, six digital age characteristics were illustrated by [40]:

1. Interconnectedness,
2. Diminishing time lag and abundance of information,
3. Increased transparency and complexity,
4. Hierarchy removal and dissolvent of personal barriers,
5. Decision enabler and integrity enhancing,
6. Humanising effect.

Among these characteristics, the 'decision enabler' hints completely at decision-making in the digital age [9, 19], and its effect on strategic decisions in companies' boards [6].

In the digital age, strategic decisions are mainly depending on the information. Some research emphasise the role of information and exhibits how executives accent using rationality methods to make decisions depending on gathering and analysing information on the internet has become the 'common practice' [20].

Higher education systems are not exceptions in the digital age. As part of strategic decision-making, course designs are changing. Higher education is under increasing social and economic pressure to provide a wider range of skills and knowledge to cope with 'super complex age' requirements [46]. Unlike traditional engineering courses such as those of civil engineering and mechanical engineering which have experienced little changes over decades, the digital age sciences such as big data and data science have just been revolutionised during the last few years, and yet the larger changes are to come every year.

To design courses, [46] investigated different gaps such as the gap between recall and understanding, the gap between understanding and having skills to practise, the gap between skills and actually wanting to use them, the gap between wanting to use and actually doing, and at last the gap between actual using the skills and changing. All these gaps are through the learning and teaching system, however, this research aim is to concentrate on the gap at a higher strategic level between job market requirements and higher education teaching materials. For this purpose, the data from job-posting websites and professional networks were used and analysed to suggest what was the domain's desired qualifications of the graduates in the data science field. This information would enable the pedagogical planners to select and adopt updated modules with course contents to train students with the actual job markets' requirements.

2 Literature Review

In the digital age, information overload is a challenge that lots of organisations are faced. What is important today is how to relate data which is close to personal desire and identify solutions based on the recommendation systems that the AI and its algorithms will produce [39]. In order to carry out strategic decision-making, today AI systems provide recommendations that can be supportive of information overload [60].

Content-Based, Knowledge-Based, Collaborative-Filtering (CF), and Hybrid are the four main classified techniques in recommendation systems. Content-based recommenders are based on users' behaviours from the past and allow them to profile the data and recommend new products depending on the similarities of the user's profile [2]. Therefore, access to users' profiles such as LinkedIn and other web pages can enhance this method. Collaborative Filtering methods are based on similarity demands among similar users. Netflix has one of the most well-known models that applies CF-based scenarios [8]. Knowledge-based recommenders are applied when the items are used rarely, or they are not related to each other. They use clear knowledge about business rules, items, and users to reach user interests and profile them. For example, they are applied to complicated scenarios like in writing policies [48]. However, today, the common use of a hybrid of the three methods above can cover the weaknesses of each technique by using of other's strengths [15, 83].

2.1 Higher Education Recommendation Systems

Recommendation systems are used in higher education for different purposes. While some research tries to use them to suggest students in university environment to select courses depends on different criteria such as time, grades, and interest scores [49], other apply a recommendation system to help students finding right universities by personal preferences and needs [28].

Guruge et al. [35] have conducted a systematic based review of articles on recommendation systems for courses in higher education. Most of them concentrate on to recommend university courses to new students. The authors demonstrate a rising trends in popularities of applying data mining in these recommendation systems. One of the challenges is using different synonyms in documents. To tackle this problem, some researchers cluster the texts by K-means and compare contents. For example, Wang et al. [78, 80] created a framework called Demandaware Collaborative Bayesian Variational Network to recommend employers different employee training packages. These views can be suggested to apply for customer focus strategy suggested in conclusion of this research for elevating student employability score.

2.2 Job Requirements and Experts' Profile Data

Social media is the main resource of text that can be extracted from profiles for analysis of data [25, 35]. For example, in LinkedIn, a 35 k skill-taxonomy has been built and used to measure the job requirement similarity of applicant profiles [44]. In business sphere, also there are Automatic ranking systems for recruiters to evaluate resumes/CVs with jobs requirements. For instance, LinkedIn using semantic matching analysis to rank applicants for advertised jobs. Skill taxonomy allows comparing applicant profiles with skills in job description [29]. However, for more complicated skills, the similarity between skills and profiles is determined by applying the node distance, such as distances among the lowest common predecessor in the skill taxonomy. New NLP techniques suggest features to improve this method: matching a CV to occupation [51], applying word embeddings (Word2Vec) [30], and integrate a graph of knowledge with BERT to know which candidates are suitable by CVs' corpus [78, 80].

The main disadvantages of building taxonomy are firstly, due to the cost implication because of human experts and time-consuming steps that it takes to create and maintain. The second, because of continuously changing in live environment, they are exposed to out-dated quickly [26]. Therefore, a lot of new attempts on analysing social media data are concentrated on other three main alternative analysis. The first category is a semantic method built on ontologies to distinguish job components such as skills [41, 68]. The second way is text mining and using machine learning to analyse online job postings to make classification for job skills by using embedding techniques such as doc2vec, and word2vec [22], or Topic Modelling techniques such as LDA [21, 22]. Also, it is possible to apply SVM, Random Forest, and Logistic Regression [12, 13]. The third one, some papers focused on applying clustering on what they mined from texts to calculate skill similarity measures in jobs [26, 81]. For building skill vectors, Bag of Words, and Embedding techniques are used. Afterwards, clustering techniques like K-Means are applied to understand the relation structure between jobs and skills [26]. As an applicable example, [14] suggested a skill scanner in order to the find common skills and missing skills among CVs, academic courses, and job posts. It is supposed these three branches are like a triangle and the common thing among them is skills (Fig. 1).

2.3 Recommendation Systems Techniques

For learning materials, content-based recommenders suggest items which have similar contents with learners' backgrounds records [47]. It has a process which firstly content profiles of items are created. Items such as learning objects and learning materials are normally unstructured data. Term Frequency-Inverse Document Frequency (TF-IDF) illustrate them by words and weighted them by vector space model [79]. On the other hand, there is structured data such as learning activities. Attributes are

Fig. 1 Skill scanner framework

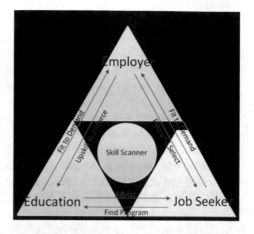

applied to illustrate these structured data. These attributes can include categories, lectures, pre-requisites and similar pedagogic methods, and in complex relations among materials, hierarchical trees or attribute vectors are applied. In the second step, profiles are made for learners as users of these recommendation systems depending on their historical record. In these records learners' educational backgrounds, their skill demands and so on are gathered in the profile. In the last step, the recommendation system calculates the similarities and matches the two category profiles of items and learners. The content-based recommendation methods contain popular techniques such as semantic-based, Attribute-based, and Query-based recommendations.

Traditional Semantic-based for extracting items, uses bag-of-words and calculate similarities by Jaccard, or cosine [57]. The advantages of these methods are their practicality, ease of deployment, and their fast output, however they cannot consider sequence relationship of words [52]. However, when talk about personalising student learning, developing techniques of word embedding enables latent vectors to represent texts. This can make items flexibly integrated into the end to end NN with binary classification to illustrate users' opinion (like/dislike) [18]. For example, to recommend learning material, [67] applied CNN for multimedia texts while Ye et al. [82] used skip-gram model to represent words and concepts in the courses as well as an encyclopaedia. Then their recommendation system calculated cosine similarity.

After building learners' profile with their historical records, both items as well as learners need to handle tree-structured data. Learner's tree is helpful to make their dynamic preference model on multiple-attributes [62]. To employ this for the job, the simple job description analysis is not precise because it has not enough information about details. Therefore, it was suggested in the conclusion of this research to use internship reports for analysis. They can be a good resource to create the similar tree-attributes for skills needed in job market and would be a basis for learning recommendations to elevate employability score of students in customer focus system.

The Query-based recommender systems are built upon users' search. As users search keywords of their interests through these webpages, recommendation systems treat them as users' profiles [79]. Then, they calculate similarities between user's profile and item profiles. In the end, the ranked item list is the output. If the system wants to personalise queries, it should consider the user's personal profile as well as queries [45].

The query-based recommendation has some advantages. First, they illustrate the current needs of the users, and secondly, they enable recommendation systems to recommend by combining the queries and the users' profiles records [16]. It should be considered that because of the lack of domain and industry's knowledge, sometimes learners use wrong keywords in their search which can lead to unrelated recommend results. This usually occur when a learner is interested in a new area. To solve this issue, a query refinement can be helpful for learners to generate more accurate query [7, 71]. Mbipom et al. [50] suggested recommendation systems first extract concepts in educational materials by the use of encyclopaedia, and then start matching the query's similarities with the concepts. At last, the created concept terms beside users' query are applied to match with educational materials and make a recommendation.

The other way to understand better what users' needs is using interact bot systems to chat with them and catch the more accurate preferences [69]. Also, [75] suggested an emotion-based recommender system in which learners can type in a chat-room and the system can detect negative emotions. For these occasions, an emotion regulation become activated to recommend depressed learners some strategies to solve their issues. These kind of usage of analysing chat box can display the importance of using information from entities like 'Ask4Help' in universities or promote them to make platforms for classmates. Students of course, are free to use other platforms such as WhatsApp or other social media platforms, however, this should be discouraged so that universities can access students' peer-query for further improvements.

The Collaborative Filtering-Based Method is the second main techniques based on past product ratings [43]. It could be an explicit score such as 1–5, or implicit feedback, such as views, and clicks on an item. These feedbacks are also applicable for eLearning materials [11]. The main task of recommendation systems in this technique is finding similar users and find what the target user did not consume while they may interest in it depending on the similar users' experience [10]. The important point of CF-based in eLearning is that the context greatly affects users' choices [63]. Two types of CF based techniques applicable in eLearning are Deep CF-based and context-aware.

Context is the situation influences in interaction the system and a user. It can be a location, atmosphere, or other users [24]. For a learner, the context information can be their background knowledge, learning goals, place, skills, emotions, and social communication and so on. Many recommendation systems are able to gather, and analyse this information to predict learners' preference [5]. Clustering learners is measured to calculate similarities by geographical information (location), mobile or laptop (device) [34], and their progress in learning [53]. Learners' emotion evolution as a context information is monitored during learning periods with brainwave, heart rate, blood pressure, and skin conductance [65].

The results show the system can recommend more precisely by being aware of learners' emotion and improve their performance. Isinkaye et al. [73] used clicks, bookmarks, views, and other browsing interactions to profile preferences of learners. To make better social relationship, skills and trust evaluation were applicable for formation of classes [23], while other research modelled social relationship by detecting learners' preferences in community structure and their influence as their closeness with other learners in the community [38]. Some eLearning recommendation systems permit learners to share their assignment and ask questions [59], augment tags [42] to use the knowledge discussions and social interactions among students and tutors to elevate the recommendations' performance.

On the other hand, deep learning has outstanding effect on the CF-based recommendation system [84]. CNN's performances were excellent to detect emotions from learners' facial expression. This can show their potential for applying in eLearning recommendation systems [72]. Also, RNNs in sequential interactions among items and learners are suitable as well as arranging pedagogical relations among items. For example, recommending learning problem step sequences from the basic levels to advance to extract learning path is applicable by RNN. It uses a trial-and-error in the process of problem-solving for each clustered learners' group. Created learning path is helpful for recommending learning resources [85]. It seems for developing smart eLearning, deep learning methods plays a key role [17].

Knowledge-based recommenders are used where there are not enough users' rating and items contain complex knowledge. They are applicable in eLearning as the pedagogical relationship complexity [74]. The most advantages of knowledge-based recommenders are lacking cold-start, or data sparsity, however, they need pre-defined structures of knowledge like ontology. To enrich ontologies and make the recommendation systems more practical, new concepts which were unavailable previously in the ontology would be added by modelling users' queries [33].

Concepts of linguistic terms have sometimes uncertain relationship; to deal with this uncertainty, fuzzy ontology is suggested. For example, it is proposed, in that learner profiling describes their relationship with concepts [31]. As the limitation of pre-defining ontology, it can substitute with self-organisation theory to formalise the relation of learners or items. For example, [77] modelled learning objects (LO), with LO attribute similarity, LO state, LO quality and learners' preferences. Moreover, the other research calculated the relationship of learners by similarity in their profiles, knowledge credits, and followers [76]. In later attempts, a multidimensional graph for knowledge with six relations of learner need's kinds was substituted for ontology of LOs [66].

3 Research Methodology

The research philosophy applied in this research is positivism. In this research the aim is to gather a large amount of data from social media about real job postings and then, by comparing the words with a taxonomy of technical skills, make insight for further decisions by the statistical results. In the second part of the research using NLP analysis, containing vectorising words and finding the similarities and sorting depending on scores, the recommended courses are suggested. With this in mind the research approach is inductive. The most important difference between inductive and deductive research is the starting point. While inductive research starts with empirical observation, the deductive approach starts with theory. In this research, at the first step, data gathering from social media was conducted. After analysing data, some were reached some patterns, and by progressing tentative hypothesis, the result as the theory was drawn.

The strategy for this research is a case study of a data science course at a UK University. By narrowing it down, it is possible to formulate a prototype of a decision enabler and in further research use this as a pilot.

In this problem-solving study, some important parts of the domain needs to make strategic decision making. Also, the key element of making a good decision is possessing high-quality information. Therefore, this research aim to apply new technology of data science to enhance management decisions. A combination of primary and secondary data was used, and quantitative data was extracted from primary, qualitative, and unstructured data to create recommendations to use in domain strategic decision-making.

The methods is to collect large sampling data from social media, and NLP analysis.

3.1 Data Science Model

The Cross Industry Standard Process for Data Mining (CRISP_DM) is a method for applying data science technology in domains and industries. This model suggests six phases to apply data science projects in any domain [37].

3.1.1 Business Understanding

Universities and higher education systems were dedicated domains in this research. It was supposed that universities' vision was to qualify students for highly disciplined related jobs. To get a strategic decision making, different strategic planning analyses were applied such as SWOT, issue-based, Balanced Scorecards etc. to get a comprehensive perspective. Balanced Scorecard (BSC) is one of the popular and up to date using a strategy which just google scholar showed 9440 articles in 2022.

BSC was selected as a basis for this research because it provides transparency indicates the domain's value-added, and displays its performance for four main customers, internal process, finance, and learning and growth perspectives [32].

What was focused on in this chapter is the internal process perspective. It is assumed that customer focus can be a part of the leadership transformation programme to bring universities to the core of the digital age. Customer perspective can apply recommendation systems widely to personalise teaching to students and control their development depending on their score on employability.

This research aim to improve universities' internal processes to service students to be qualified. By narrowing down, education systems should take towards their customer-oriented decision making which is supposed 'do right things right' [55, 58]. To get effective success in projects, not only projects should be conducted in the right way, but also, they should align with the right strategic direction.

3.1.2 Data Understanding

Data understanding is the second phase of CRSP-DM which discusses the initiative data.

The first data related to the first objective was about job posts on a professional network website. LinkedIn was called 'the most widely used professional SNW' [3].

The starting point was an initiative dataset gathered by using Octaparse website (https://www.octoparse.com/) from LinkedIn. The reason for using this website was the rules it obeyed to scrape data. For example, it gets time spent for each scrape to avoid over-pressure on the target website. It could help to gather the links to job posts.

The only applicable data from this gathered dataset was the job description links. In this stage, data gathering mainly depended on scraping data from the links. By using python libraries and scraping techniques it is possible to extract data from the internet. There was a trial and failed attempts to reach the purpose.

The second part of the gathering date was related to the second objective of this research which aimed to obtain data from a professional network. Stack Overflow, which is 'one of the most popular' communities named as the 'primary source' for data scientists and developers [54, 64]. This was selected as a reference of a professional network. Stack [70] has surveyed over 70,000 responses from experts and investigated which skills were used and desired for them.

Although this survey was not dedicated to data scientists, it was a good reference to have an expanded taxonomy of technical skills. The gross 184-word list of keywords was extracted from this survey, and the dictionary was completed with miscellaneous resources.

The last data initiative used in this research is to gather a dataset related to elearning data science courses. What was used in this part was related to a public domain dataset in Kaggle [61]. This could be considered as a complete dataset from all Udemy courses from the first until to date of publication. It possesses a 2790 Course dataset containing titles, descriptions, and URLs, its rating, reviews, duration, lecturers, course level, and instructors. The most important features considered were the popularity of Udemy as the largest market for e-learning [27], and it is 'the most popular online course' according to the Stack Overflow survey (2022). An acceptable volume of eLearning data science courses containing data description and rating for recommendation systems contained-based and collaborative filtering respectively.

3.1.3 Data Preparation

For the first stage of data preparation following points were observed:

1. Omitting any duplication of elements in the list.
2. Lowercase all words.
3. Select the bullet points of the job description to reduce the volume of unnecessary data for analysis.
4. NLP preparation for job bullets: NLP pipeline is designed to tokenise, lowercase, remove duplicates, and clean ineffective words in job bullets such as stop words, numbers, punctuations and so on.

In the second analysis stage, job descriptions depending on the most popular skills and course recommendations were categorise as follow:

1. Categorising job posts and extracting all job description bullets containing special technology.
2. Put the categorised jobs' description bullets as a cell in the list of course descriptions.
3. NLP pipeline was used for categorised job description bullets and course descriptions.
4. In this set of analyses as it is necessary for NLP analysis, words were converted to vectors by TF-IDF methods.
5. For the further step in the collaborative filtering recommendation system, the rating and review attributes of the eLearning dataset were used.

After completing all parts, the hybrid recommendation system was tested.

3.1.4 Modelling

To find the most popular techniques, it is necessary to weigh skills depending on job posts for further processing. For this, keywords were weighted by counting their repetition among jobs, and then, their percentages are calculated as an explanatory factor to help decision-makers. Analysing data creates quantitative data from the first qualitative extracted data, and it helps to understand more about the importance of each technology.

Among the different methods for recommendation discussed in the literature review, a hybrid recommendation system of content-based and collaborative filtering (CF) was applied. In this research, the focus will be on understanding the market demands by analysing data from job posts (content-based); however, it enhanced by CF for selecting its final top ranking. It could help decision-makers to consider the satisfaction of users of learning materials.

For the content-based, the TF-IDF mentioned in the literature review was selected because it is a fast method. Also, it was not necessary to use other complicated vectorising word methods, as in this project the taxonomy of skills was used. The vectorised words were used to create cosine similarities, and the similarity score of course descriptions with categorised job description bullets were calculated and sorted descending. The top ten courses with the highest similarity scores were selected for collaborative filtering.

In collaborative filtering, there are three main factors of similarity of users, the average rate, and the number of reviewers. As all courses related to data science, it can be assumed that all users were interested in the same subject, and therefore this factor was omitted. The other two important parameters of rating (score from 1 to five) and the number of people who voted (reviews) were combined depending on the normalised formulation and were used to resort to the top ten high-scored courses in the prior stage.

It is not difficult to realise the fact that to rank social media content neither only user rating is enough nor only the count of views or reviews because a high rating based on few rates may be unreliable or even fake, and also a high number of counts can be a result of advertisements and being seen while the content may not have been liked. Therefore, a wise combination of these two important categories is necessary. One scientific approach in mathematics and statistics to achieve the goal is to normalise the numerical features of elements of these different categories whose values can differ from one another by many orders of magnitude. For example, the ratings are commonly between 1 and 5 while the number of views or reviews can be different from zero for unseen content to thousands for viral content on the most popular social media. By normalising the values of each category, all numbers are adjusted and translated to a value between zero and one. Then, these different categories can be compared and/or combined. For example, to define a rational score including both important factors of rates and counts to rank the contents, one can easily make a (weighted) average of the normalised values of rates and counts and have a fair ranking. Then, for industries and businesses in which the best ranking is vital, more advanced personalised experimental formulas may be devised by professional experts who work in the company and have a practical insight into the data of the company.

As part of the evaluation stage, we investigated whether the model met the criteria for business success. Then the evaluation was used in determining future steps or new projects depending on what was conducted in this research. Evaluation is described further in this chapter.

4 Data Processing and Analysis

The first step for this research was to gather primary data from social media. Although the Requests in python is faster, as it does not need to open and browse the web page for extracting web source, due to trial and error, the codes could not get a response from the URL [1]. There were several attempts to use Insomnia to get a response, and the necessary headers tried to extract from chrome by checking the inspection of the websites. However, requests did not respond and at last, by using Selenium it was possible to extract data. Selenium is an automotive system which uses web browsing [1, 36].

For finding related information, at first in the job search on LinkedIn the word 'data science' was searched. Then, job description links of found jobs were extracted by Octaparse website. By applying BeautifulSoup, the bullets of job descriptions were extracted from them and put in the dataset. 1000 data science and 155 business intelligence jobs information were obtained. After gathering job description sources, by parsing data, all bullets were separated and saved in a new column. As a result, a dataset containing unstructured data about the bullet points of job posts was gathered.

4.1 NLP Data Pre-processing

Before any data analysis, it is necessary to pre-process the dataset and ensure there is high-quality data to process. In this research, as the data was words, the NLP pre-processing was applied to refine data and make its perform better by omitting ineffective words.

- The first step is investigating the missing values in the dataset.
- In the second step, the NLP pre-processing was executed. Omitting punctuations such as '!', '.', and '?', as part of data cleansing in NLP.
- tokenising words created a list of words instead of a long string for each job description and make it possible to analyse words.
- Stop words are common words in English such as 'the', 'a', and 'is' and they have no effect on NLP analysis. Therefore, as part of data cleansing, they were omitted.
- Stemming is used to omit prefixes and suffixes. However, after using it, some words became incorrect. Therefore, it was rejected to apply.
- Lemmatising is another part of data pre-processing to change different kinds of words to their roots. For example, different tenses of verbs become the root mode. and
- at last, all words should have lowercase letters for further analysis.

Through this data cleansing, the volume of processing data decreased by huge amounts without losing any useful and effective information.

4.2 Data Analysis

To conduct a meaningful taxonomy analysis, keywords play an important role. This was the reason that making a good taxonomy was valuable to spend a lot of investment in companies such as LinkedIn [44]. The important characteristic of data science technology is its dynamics skills, and the new technologies coming to the market every year. It means that the up-to-date taxonomy is vital to possess an acceptable result for this analysis. In this article, keywords are extracted from one of the most famous developers' communities. Stack [70] has conducted a survey in which over 70,000 developers contributed to give an insight into skills, attitudes and environment. By using this information, it is possible to guarantee the keywords are accurate and up to date. 184 keywords were gathered by this mean.

By possessing a clean dataset, and taxonomy of keywords, the analysing of data was possible. all keywords were counted on how many times were applied in job posts, and to have more meaningful information, their percentages were calculated. The index is changed to a count column to make it more organised and resorted.

By using seaborn and matplotlib libraries, it is possible to provide visualisation for results.

The result of the data analysis is in Fig. 2.

The question may be asked, what was the benefit of the taxonomies, while recommendations were applied? Due to expansion and large changes in data and technologies, it is inevitable to use artificial intelligence and machine learning to analyse much more amount of data and get better results. However, the problem with these technologies is lack of explanatory, accountability, and finally trust, as the ML is complex algorithms. These ambiguities make strategic decisions for manager more comples. One way that can help to understand more about the outputs of recommendation systems and machine learning is to use taxonomy [56].

The first concept for creating a taxonomy was to scrape and use a dataset of data scientists' profiles. It aimed to extract experience, knowledge, and skills that data scientists apply more in the real world. The problem to reach this purpose was that

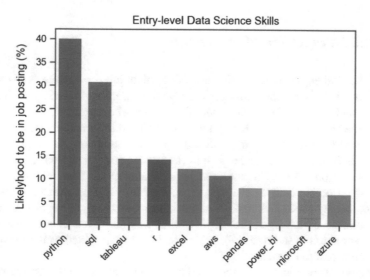

Fig. 2 Diagram of the most popular skills

LinkedIn strongly against scraping its users' profiles, and access to the profiles it is necessary to sign into the website. As signing into the website means accepting their terms and conditions and they have prohibited scraping their users' profiles, it would ethically incorrect. Therefore, by changing the methodology, and using Stack Overflow survey the primary taxonomy was gained.

This prototype project just weighted the taxonomy of technologies depending on their frequency of application in different job posts, and it could not distinguish the items. For example, Python and R, both are programming languages; Tableau and Power Bi are visualisation skills; and Azure and AWS are both cloud platforms.

On the other hand, other parameters affect universities to select technologies. For example, for cloud platforms, maybe universities can compromise with a company to give better services to their students or give some services free of charge.

When the result of this analysis is compared with some other University for example, packages like Python and Pandas, besides SQL are taught in the Applied Data Science Modules; AWS and Tableau are covered by Machine Learning on Cloud, and Big Data Analytics. However, there is a blank space for Microsoft features, especially Excel, which is the domain's interest.

There are some correlations between job posts and developers' interests survey. For example, depending to Stack [70] Python and SQL were the most popular data science professionals and AWS were nearly double in popularity as Microsoft Azure in the top two cloud platforms. However, in libraries, the developers voted more for NumPy, rather than Pandas.

To put it in context, this data analysis could help curriculum planners to be aware of job market demands on time, and depending on this vision, they could step firmly into the university's strategic vision of being 'business oriented'.

4.3 Analytics Review of the Results

One of the challenges in academic curriculum planning for modern fields such as data science is not only their changes but also their learning materials. Universities are interested in maintaining the academic theoretical disciplines besides teaching students the applications which help them be qualified for domain needs.

The second step of cooperating with strategic decision-making in this research was to build a hybrid recommendation system to recommend courses which were more like what the job market demands and popular among the learners. For example, Udemy is an online course reference of 66% of 29,389 respondents in the Stack Overflow survey (2022). A dataset of all data science online courses of Udemy was introduced as the input. To display what was the result of recommendation systems, some of the selected skills which had the top weighted were examined by this recommendation system (Fig. 3).

All results were related to Python in data science and machine learning context. This can be the ideal result, as the job bullet related to data science occupations, was filtered by Python skills.

Python course title	similarity_scores	CF-score-norms
Python-Introduction to Data Science and Machine learning A-Z	0.706119	4.375000
Data Science: Python for Data Analysis 2022 Full Bootcamp	0.639396	3.251090
Machine Learning and Deep Learning A-Z: Hands-On Python	0.681719	2.546454
Python 3 and Data Science Mastery - Practical Python 3	0.568075	2.500000
Python Programming: Machine Learning, Deep Learning | Python	0.595882	1.961272
Data Science with R and Python | R Programming	0.581646	1.932831
Learn Python - Data Analysis From Beginner To Advanced	0.628215	1.899649
Learn Python From Scratch With Lots of Examples and Projects	0.576947	1.275597
Python: Python Basics Bootcamp for Beginners in Data Science	0.615663	1.118458
Python for Data Science and Machine Learning Bootcamp	0.652691	0.018961

Fig. 3 Python recommended courses

For Tableau (Fig. 4), the recommendation could find five courses that match with Tableau course.

Five results are named SQL and MySQL in their title (Fig. 5). The other five courses possess SQL in their course descriptions.

Good results were owed to the changes in NLP pre-processing and new parsing. They are not only caused more accurate results in recommended courses but also considerably decreased computational volume. For example, the new parsing caused the length of filtered job bullets for Tableau reduced from 333,307 to 24,124.

Tableau course title	similarity_scores	CF-score-norms
Data Analysis Masterclass (4 courses in 1)	0.517176	5.000000
DATA SCIENCE with MACHINE LEARNING and DATA ANALYTICS	0.389970	2.720588
Data Visualization using Tableau	0.399482	2.515604
Big Data Analytics with PySpark + Tableau Desktop + MongoDB	0.469836	2.498611
Tableau 2021 A-Z : Master Tableau for Data Science and BI	0.571923	2.397508
Fundamentals of Statistics and Visualization in Python	0.460341	2.218494
Jupyter Notebook - Big Data Visualization Tool	0.395866	2.106810
Learn Basic Data Visualization with R	0.385514	1.955369
Getting started with Tableau	0.452296	0.000000
Data Visualization With Tableau	0.402916	0.000000

Fig. 4 Tableau recommended courses

sql course title	similarity_scores	CF-score-norms
MySQL - Statistics for Data Science & Business Analytics	0.473837	4.981618
Data Analysis Masterclass (4 courses in 1)	0.582495	4.943182
SQL and Data Visualization - The Complete Bootcamp	0.627153	4.040775
Apprendre la data science par la pratique avec Python !	0.532218	3.910846
Python for Data Science Master Course (2022)	0.516529	3.734124
Getting Started with Data Management	0.522789	3.527741
Advanced SQL Bootcamp	0.493440	2.746073
DATA SCIENCE with MACHINE LEARNING and DATA ANALYTICS	0.556558	2.663770
Azure Data Engineer Workshop In A Weekend	0.472963	2.479529
Migrating DB2 Databases to SQL Server (DB2ToSQL)	0.515572	0.000000

Fig. 5 SQL recommended courses

Also, Lemmatising and other NLP attempts such as omitting non-English courses decreased the similarity matrix size from 2791 * 8398 to 1950 * 3200.

5 Conclusion

This research is a good example of a strategic decision-making enabler in the digital age. It is a case study of curriculum planning for 'Big Data and Data Science Technology' at any given University using an NLP data analysis to achieve the business insight and prototype hybrid recommendation system to suggest supportive online courses related to modern popular skills. Although the context is strategic management under whose umbrella the strategic planning, vision, and project strategic views such as 'doing right things right', Balanced Scored Strategy, gap analysis, finding alternatives and creating quantitative criteria to making decisions were used. The methodology and tools mainly include data science technologies such as social media data scraping, NLP analysis, and recommendation systems.

Data scraping, dataset creation, data analysis and building a hybrid recommendation system were applied to assist the university in its internal processes (curriculum planning) based on the internal process aspect of the Balanced Scored Strategy.

References

1. Aahnik (2020) Answer to "comparing request module vs selenium in python." Stack Overflow
2. Adomavicius G, Tuzhilin A (2005) Toward the next generation of recommender systems: a survey of the state-of-the-art and possible extensions. IEEE Trans Knowl Data Eng 17:734–749. https://doi.org/10.1109/TKDE.2005.99
3. Aguado D, Andrés JC, García-Izquierdo AL, Rodríguez J (2019) LinkedIn "big four": job performance validation in the ICT sector. Rev Psicol Trab Las Organ 35:53–64. https://doi.org/10.5093/jwop2019a7
4. Aldhaheri F, Ameen A, Isaac O (2020) The influence of strategy formulation (vision, mission, and goals) on the organizational operations. J Crit Rev 7:1932–1941. https://doi.org/10.31838/jcr.07.17.240
5. Amasha MA, Areed MF, Alkhalaf S, Abougalala RA, Elatawy SM, Khairy D (2020) The future of using internet of things (IoTs) and context-aware technology in e-learning. In: Proceedings of the 2020 9th international conference on educational and information technology, pp 114–123
6. Andervin M, Jansson J (2016) Att leda digital transformation. Hoi Förlag
7. Baizal ZA, Widyantoro DH, Maulidevi NU (2016) Query refinement in a recommender system based on product functional requirements. In: 2016 international conference on advanced computer science and information systems (ICACSIS). IEEE, pp 309–314
8. Bennett J, Lanning S (2007) The Netflix prize. In: Proceedings of KDD cup and workshop 2007. San Jose
9. Berman S, Marshall A (2014) The next digital transformation: from an individual-centered to an everyone-to-everyone economy. Strategy Leadership
10. Bobadilla J, Ortega F, Hernando A, Gutiérrez A (2013) Recommender systems survey. Knowl-Based Syst 46:109–132
11. Bobadilla J, Serradilla F, Hernando A (2009) Collaborative filtering adapted to recommender systems of e-learning. Knowl-Based Syst 22:261–265
12. Boselli R, Cesarini M, Marrara S, Mercorio F, Mezzanzanica M, Pasi G, Viviani M (2018) WoLMIS: a labor market intelligence system for classifying web job vacancies. J Intell Inf Syst 51:477–502
13. Boselli R, Cesarini M, Mercorio F, Mezzanzanica M (2018) Classifying online job advertisements through machine learning. Futur Gener Comput Syst 86:319–328
14. Bothmer K, Schlippe T (2023) Skill scanner: connecting and supporting employers, job seekers and educational institutions with an AI-based recommendation system. In The learning ideas conference. Springer, pp 69–80
15. Burke R (2002) Hybrid recommender systems: survey and experiments. User Model User-Adapt Interact 12:331–370
16. Cai X, Han J, Li W, Zhang R, Pan S, Yang L (2018) A three-layered mutually reinforced model for personalized citation recommendation. IEEE Trans Neural Netw Learn Syst 29:6026–6037
17. Chanaa A (2018) Deep learning for a smart e-learning system. In: 2018 4th international conference on cloud computing technologies and applications (Cloudtech). IEEE, pp 1–8
18. Chen T, Hong L, Shi Y, Sun Y (2017) Joint text embedding for personalized content-based recommendation. https://arxiv.org/abs/1706.01084
19. Chew E, Semmelrock-Picej MT, Novak A (2013) Value co-creation in the organizations of the future. In: Proceedings of the European conference on management, leadership & governance, pp 16–23
20. Citroen CL (2011) The role of information in strategic decision-making. Int J Inf Manag 31:493–501. https://doi.org/10.1016/j.ijinfomgt.2011.02.005
21. Colace F, De Santo M, Lombardi M, Mercorio F, Mezzanzanica M, Pascale F (2019) Towards labour market intelligence through topic modelling
22. Colombo E, Mercorio F, Mezzanzanica M (2018) Applying machine learning tools on web vacancies for labour market and skill analysis. Terminator or the Jetsons
23. De Meo P, Messina F, Rosaci D, Sarné GM (2017) Combining trust and skills evaluation to form e-Learning classes in online social networks. Inf Sci 405:107–122

24. Dey AK, Abowd GD, Salber D (2001) A conceptual framework and a skillkit for supporting the rapid prototyping of context-aware applications. Human-Comput Interact 16:97–166
25. Diaby M, Viennet E, Launay T (2013) Toward the next generation of recruitment skills: an online social network-based job recommender system. In: 2013 IEEE/ACM international conference on advances in social networks analysis and mining (ASONAM 2013). IEEE, pp 821–828
26. Djumalieva J, Sleeman C (2018, July) An open and data-driven taxonomy of skills extracted from online job adverts. In: Developing skills in a changing world of work. Rainer Hampp Verlag, pp 425–454
27. Ederle R (2020) Udemy ranked on the annual 'change the world' list by fortune magazine—about Udemy [WWW Document]. https://about.udemy.com/press-releases/udemy-ranked-on-the-annual-change-the-world-list-by-fortune-magazine/. Accessed 31 Dec 22
28. Elahi M, Starke A, El Ioini N, Lambrix AA, Trattner C (2022) Developing and evaluating a university recommender system. Front Artif Intell 4
29. Faliagka E, Iliadis L, Karydis I, Rigou M, Sioutas S, Tsakalidis A, Tzimas G (2014) On-line consistent ranking on e-recruitment: seeking the truth behind a well-formed CV. Artif Intell Rev 42:515–528
30. Fernández-Reyes FC, Shinde S (2019) CV retrieval system based on job description matching using hybrid word embeddings. Comput Speech Lang 56:73–79
31. Ferreira-Satler M, Romero FP, Menendez-Dominguez VH, Zapata A, Prieto ME (2012) Fuzzy ontologies-based user profiles applied to enhance e-learning activities. Soft Comput 16:1129–1141
32. Fijałkowska J, Oliveira C (2018) Balanced scorecard in universities. J Intercult Manag 10:57–83
33. Fraihat S, Shambour Q (2015) A framework of semantic recommender system for e-learning. J Softw 10:317–330
34. Gallego D, Barra E, Aguirre S, Huecas G (2012) A model for generating proactive context-aware recommendations in e-learning systems. In: 2012 frontiers in education conference proceedings. IEEE, pp 1–6
35. Guruge DB, Kadel R, Halder SJ (2021) The state of the art in methodologies of course recommender systems—a review of recent research. Data 6:18
36. Hajba G (2018) Website scraping with python: using BeautifulSoup. O'Reilly Media, USA
37. Hotz N (2022) What is CRISP DM? Data Science Process Alliance. https://www.datascience-pm.com/crisp-dm-2/. Accessed 12 Aug 22
38. Hu Y, Koren Y, Volinsky C (2008) Collaborative filtering for implicit feedback datasets. In: 2008 eighth IEEE international conference on data mining. IEEE, pp 263–272
39. Isinkaye FO, Folajimi YO, Ojokoh BA (2015) Recommendation systems: principles, methods and evaluation. Egypt Inform J 16:261–273. https://doi.org/10.1016/j.eij.2015.06.005
40. Khan S (2016) Leadership in the digital age: a study on the effects of digitalisation on top management leadership
41. Khobreh M, Ansari F, Fathi M, Vas R, Mol ST, Berkers HA, Varga K (2015) An ontology-based approach for the semantic representation of job knowledge. IEEE Trans Emerg Top Comput 4(3):462–473
42. Klašnja-Milićević A, Vesin B, Ivanović M (2018) Social tagging strategy for enhancing e-learning experience. Comput Educ 118:166–181
43. Koren Y, Bell R, Volinsky C (2009) Matrix factorization techniques for recommender systems. Computer 42:30–37
44. Li J, Arya D, Ha-Thuc V, Sinha S (2016) How to get them a dream job? Entity-aware features for personalized job search ranking. In: Proceedings of the 22nd ACM SIGKDD international conference on knowledge discovery and data mining, pp 501–510
45. Li L, Yang Z, Liu L, Kitsuregawa M (2008) Query-URL bipartite based approach to personalized query recommendation. AAAI, pp 1189–1194
46. Light G, Calkins S, Cox R (2009) Learning and teaching in higher education: the reflective professional. SAGE

47. Lops P, Jannach D, Musto C, Bogers T, Koolen M (2019) Trends in content-based recommendation. User Model User-Adapt Interact 29:239–249
48. Lu J, Zhang Q, Zhang G (2020) Recommender systems: advanced developments. World Scientific
49. Ma B, Taniguchi Y, Konomi S (2020) Course recommendation for university environments 7
50. Mbipom B, Massie S, Craw S (2018) An e-learning recommender that helps learners find the right materials. In: Proceedings of the AAAI conference on artificial intelligence
51. Mikolov T, Chen K, Corrado G, Dean J (2013a) Efficient estimation of word representations in vector space. https://arxiv.org/abs/1301.3781
52. Mikolov T, Sutskever I, Chen K, Corrado GS, Dean J (2013b) Distributed representations of words and phrases and their compositionality. Adv Neural Inf Process Syst 26
53. Moore P, Zhao Z, Pham HV (2019) Towards cloud-based personalised student-centric context-aware e-learning pedagogic systems. In: Conference on complex, intelligent, and software intensive systems. Springer, pp 331–342
54. Moutidis I, Williams HTP (2021) Community evolution on stack overflow. PLoS ONE 16:e0253010. https://doi.org/10.1371/journal.pone.0253010
55. Mullins K (2022) Balanced scorecard: a model for improving government performance [WWW Document]. https://www.bpminstitute.org/resources/articles/balanced-scorecard-model-improving-government-performance#comment-form. Accessed 24 Dec 22
56. Nunes I, Jannach D (2017) A systematic review and taxonomy of explanations in decision support and recommender systems. User Model User-Adapt Interact 27:393–444
57. Pazzani MJ, Billsus D (2007) Content-based recommendation systems. In: The adaptive web. Springer, pp 325–341
58. PMI (2017) Project management body of knowledge (PMBOK® guide). Project Management Institute Inc., Newtown Sq. PA USA
59. Rafaeli S, Dan-Gur Y, Barak M (2005) Social recommender systems: recommendations in support of e-learning. Int J Distance Educ Technol IJDET 3:30–47
60. Rashid AM, Albert I, Cosley D, Lam SK, McNee SM, Konstan JA, Riedl J (2002) Getting to know you: learning new user preferences in recommender systems. In: Proceedings of the 7th international conference on intelligent user interfaces, pp 127–134
61. RAZA Y (2022) Udemy data science courses dataset [WWW Document]. https://www.kaggle.com/datasets/0e4623205a5afabb8261a1d1b9a0e4d6fea83663f73fae8f4af447ae49c923c8. Accessed 31 Dec 22
62. Salehi M (2013) Application of implicit and explicit attribute based collaborative filtering and BIDE for learning resource recommendation. Data Knowl Eng 87:130–145
63. Segal A, Katzir Z, Gal K, Shani G, Shapira B (2014) Edurank: a collaborative filtering approach to personalization in e-learning. In: Educational data mining 2014. Citeseer
64. Sengupta S, Haythornthwaite C (2020) Learning with comments: an analysis of comments and community on stack overflow
65. Shen L, Wang M, Shen R (2009) Affective e-learning: using "emotional" data to improve learning in pervasive learning environment. J Educ Technol Soc 12:176–189
66. Shi D, Wang T, Xing H, Xu H (2020) A learning path recommendation model based on a multidimensional knowledge graph framework for e-learning. Knowl-Based Syst 195:105618
67. Shu J, Shen X, Liu H, Yi B, Zhang Z (2018) A content-based recommendation algorithm for learning resources. Multimed Syst 24:163–173
68. Sibarani EM, Scerri S, Morales C, Auer S, Collarana D (2017, Sept) Ontology-guided job market demand analysis: a cross-sectional study for the data science field. In: Proceedings of the 13th international conference on semantic systems, pp 25–32
69. Souali K, Rahmaoui O, Ouzzif M (2018) Introducing a traceability based recommendation approach using chatbot for e-learning platforms. In: International conference on advanced intelligent systems for sustainable development. Springer, pp 346–357
70. Stack Overflow (2022) Stack overflow developer survey 2022 [WWW Document]. Stack Overflow. https://survey.stackoverflow.co/2022/?utm_source=social-share&utm_medium=social&utm_campaign=dev-survey-2022. Accessed 13 Dec 22

71. Su J-H, Hong T-P, Li J-Y, Su J-J (2018) Personalized content-based music retrieval by user-Filtering and query-refinement. In: 2018 conference on technologies and applications of artificial intelligence (TAAI). IEEE, pp 177–180
72. Sun A, Li Y-J, Huang Y-M, Li Q (2017) Using facial expression to detect emotion in e-learning system: a deep learning method. In: International symposium on emerging technologies for education. Springer, pp 446–455
73. Takano K, Li KF (2010) An adaptive e-learning recommender based on user's web-browsing behaviour. In: 2010 international conference on P2P, parallel, grid, cloud and internet computing. IEEE, pp 123–131
74. Tarus JK, Niu Z, Mustafa G (2018) Knowledge-based recommendation: a review of ontology-based recommender systems for e-learning. Artif Intell Rev 50:21–48
75. Tian F, Gao P, Li L, Zhang W, Liang H, Qian Y, Zhao R (2014) Recognizing and regulating e-learners' emotions based on interactive Chinese texts in e-learning systems. Knowl-Based Syst 55:148–164
76. Wan S, Niu Z (2019) A hybrid e-learning recommendation approach based on learners' influence propagation. IEEE Trans Knowl Data Eng 32:827–840
77. Wan S, Niu Z (2018) An e-learning recommendation approach based on the self-organization of learning resource. Knowl-Based Syst 160:71–87
78. Wang C, Zhu H, Wang P, Zhu C, Zhang X, Chen E, Xiong H (2021) Personalized and explainable employee training course recommendations: a Bayesian variational approach. ACM Trans Inf Syst TOIS 40:1–32
79. Wang D, Liang Y, Xu D, Feng X, Guan R (2018) A content-based recommender system for computer science publications. Knowl-Based Syst 157:1–9
80. Wang Y, Allouache Y, Joubert C (2021) Analysing CV corpus for finding suitable candidates using knowledge graph and BERT. In: DBKDA 2021, the thirteenth international conference on advances in databases, knowledge, and data applications
81. Wowczko IA (2015, Nov) Skills and vacancy analysis with data mining techniques. Informatics 2(4):31–49
82. Ye M, Tang Z, Xu J, Jin L (2015) Recommender system for e-learning based on semantic relatedness of concepts. Information 6:443–453
83. Zhang Q, Lu J, Zhang G (2021) Recommender systems in e-learning. J Smart Environ Green Comput 1:76–89. https://doi.org/10.20517/jsegc.2020.06
84. Zhang S, Yao L, Sun A, Tay Y (2019) Deep learning based recommender system: a survey and new perspectives. ACM Comput Surv CSUR 52:1–38
85. Zhou Y, Huang C, Hu Q, Zhu J, Tang Y (2018) Personalized learning full-path recommendation model based on LSTM neural networks. Inf Sci 444:135–152

The Use of Virtual Learning Environments in Higher Education—Content, Community and Connectivism—Learning from Student Users

Guy Brown and Carly Foster

Abstract Whilst technology enhanced learning has been commonplace in Higher Education for many years, from January 2020 Higher Education Institutions (HEIs) were forced to rethink their delivery models as a result of the global Covid pandemic. Campuses closed and learners were channelled into existing remote learning technologies. HEIs who had invested in Virtual Learning Environments (VLEs) were well positioned to deliver high quality on-line education, however, what emerged was mixed practice and evidence many academic teams had under-utilised their VLE platforms and used them as little more than resource repositories. Those HEIs who had developed a clear technology enhanced learning strategy were better able to engage their leaners in immersive and social learning environments and indeed are now more likely better placed to progress towards greater use of artificial intelligence, machine learning and virtual reality. This chapter summarises key findings of a post Covid study to ascertain learner requirements of a virtual learning environment, and how such a learning platform can be best utilised to move from a content repository, to a structured ecosystem which provides learners with a central curriculum content, interactivity, collaboration, scaffold support and an opportunity to build a connected and engaged learning community. The findings of a small scale study of a single HEI suggests there are fourteen basic principles to encourage ongoing learner engagement and immersion with a VL primarily relating to scaffolding, communication, relationship building and providing ease of access to wider learning resources and technologies.

Keywords Covid-19 · VLE · AI · Machine learning · Augmented reality · Virtual reality · Immersive VLE

G. Brown (✉) · C. Foster
Northumbria University, Surtherland Building, Newcastle Upon Tyne NE1 8ST, UK
e-mail: guy2.brown@northumbria.ac.uk

C. Foster
e-mail: carly.foster@northumbria.ac.uk

1   Introduction

Learners today are surrounded by computers, mobile devices and by the applications installed on them. As such these technologies and applications are shaping the ways learners think and behave [29]. In response, Higher Education Institutions (HEIs) are developing associated policies, pedagogy and practices which utilise digital connective technologies that support learner capabilities in the digital age [41].

Aşkar [10] suggests key digital advancements forcing HEIs to transform and adopt to the twenty-first century include the advancement of digital platforms enabling increased interaction and collaboration between and among instructors and learners of which Virtual Learning Environments (VLE) are one example.

Virtual Learning Environments (VLE) are now commonplace across education environments providing access to education material and delivery on-line as and when learners need it. Indeed, Ferriman [21] defined a VLE as a flexible, effective, and inspiring way to deliver learning content that best suits the needs of students. Alves et al. [8] note such web based educational systems based are being used by an increasing number of universities, schools and companies, not only to incorporate web technology into their courses, but also to complement their traditional face-to-face courses. They further suggest VLEs provide a set of tools which support the production and distribution of contents, communication, and the assessment of the teaching and learning process. Mogus et al. [36] expand the description of a VLE commenting they provide an on-line environment where students can review lecture notes, exercise notes, assignments, quizzes, questionnaires and other learning materials and prepare themselves for revision tests and examinations or develop project on certain subjects. Dale and Lane [19] also discuss the important role of online discussion within a VLE, allowing learners to engage in individual and group communication, with subsequent opportunity for lecturer or peer feedback.

Molotsi [37] further notes in adopting a VLE, institutions are increasingly searching for a better means of delivering education for their students and provides the opportunity to assess, promote, and support new teaching and learning processes. Adding to the debate, Saykili [41] considers VLEs enable students to access learning through informal and enriched online learning platforms.

Goldie [30] further consider VLEs can create an environment of interactive learning where learners can immerse themselves in a range of tutor provided resources and technologies in a single location which subsequently better connects them to their own learning and create opportunities for communities of practice with fellow learners and members of the teaching team.

Kristóf and Tóth [33] provided a useful summary of key VLE benefits, including:

- access to course work from anywhere, at any time;
- effective time management;
- expanded worldview;
- asynchronous discussion with classmates;
- immediate feedback on tests, and

- shopping digital skills.

Furthermore, making the link between VLE engagement and student performance, Boulton et al. [12] additionally found that engagement with VLE activity is associated with high grades, albeit low activity does not necessarily imply low grades.

Alves et al. [8], however, recognise VLEs have primarily been used for distribution of content, messages and notices, with some online communication through discussion forums and chats. This suggests little progress has been made since earlier studies by Cosgrave et al. [16] and Risquez et al. [40] who concluded in their study of Irish learners, VLEs were most commonly used for content delivery, student communication, and enabling more flexible forms of learning access further noting it is widely considered academic staff do not use VLEs to their full potential citing issues of impact on classroom attendance as a key drivers for limited use.

2 VLEs Types

VLEs are online platforms which support the creation, delivery, and management of educational resources and activities. Indeed there are many VLE providers with the most common being Blackboard (BB), Moodle, Canvas, and Sakai, each with their unique features and capabilities [22]. Blackboard is one of the most widely used VLEs and provides a range of tools for course management, content delivery, and communication, including features such as gradebook, discussion forums, online assessments, and multimedia support. Similarly, Moodle is another popular VLE, which is an open-source platform that provides customizable features such as content management, course administration, and social networking tools. Canvas, is a cloud-based VLE that offers a range of features such as course content management, learning analytics, and mobile accessibility. Sakai is another open-source VLE that offers features such as group collaboration, assessment tools, and content authoring [6].

Within Higher Education VLE adoption has become a strategic priority for institutions looking to improve their online teaching and learning capabilities. Furthermore, with the increasing use of artificial intelligence (AI) in education, institutions are exploring ways to integrate AI into their VLEs to enhance the student learning experience. Indeed, AI can play a crucial role in VLEs by providing personalized learning pathways, identifying areas of weakness, and offering recommendations for improvement. Additionally, AI can be used to dynamically link knowledge assessments to VLEs, enabling students to receive immediate feedback on their learning progress and helping instructors to adapt their teaching strategies based on individual student needs.

The pandemic has accelerated the adoption of VLEs, with institutions forced to shift to online teaching and learning almost overnight. The lessons learned from this experience are shaping the future development of VLEs, with institutions recognizing the need for more flexible and adaptive learning environments.

VLEs of the future will likely feature enhanced AI capabilities, allowing for personalized learning experiences that are tailored to the needs of individual students. These VLEs may also integrate social learning tools, enabling students to collaborate and engage in group work online. Additionally, VLEs may offer more immersive learning experiences through the use of augmented reality (AR) and virtual reality (VR) technologies such as the Metaverse. However, to ensure the successful adoption of VLEs, institutions must address several key challenges, including providing adequate training for tutors and students, ensuring the quality of online learning experiences, and ensuring that VLEs are accessible to all students, including those with disabilities.

3   AI and Analytics Driven Student Support and Teaching

AI plays a vital part in VLEs and both AI and analytics are increasingly being integrated into different teaching and student support practices. These tools provide an opportunity for institutions to improve their teaching and learning processes, enhance student engagement and performance, and provide personalized support to students [7], an example of this is how AI and analytics can also be used to enhance the teaching and learning experience. Indeed, the educational analytics framework [26] highlights the various ways that data can provide different roles within a university with insights into how students are engaging. For course instructors, academic analytics facilitates an immersive personalised learning environment with insights into how students are engaging with course materials and assessments, enabling them to identify areas where students may be struggling and adjust their teaching approach accordingly (ibid). Furthermore, analytics can identify patterns in student behaviour such as low engagement with course content or repeated attempts at assessment questions, indicating a need for additional support or revision [27]. This additional targeted support can be provided by academic staff or central support teams however, whilst an systematic review found it to be successful in improving student outcomes, the underlying theory of change remains elusive [24].

AI can also be used to personalize the learning experience for individual students. As an example, Adaptive learning platforms can adjust the pace and difficulty of course content based on a student's performance, enabling them to progress at a pace that is appropriate for their level of understanding. Additionally, AI can analyse student data such as their learning preferences and performance history to recommend personalized resources and activities that are tailored to their needs [7].

Institutions can also use AI and analytics to identify and support at-risk students. By analyzing data such as attendance records, course engagement, and assessment performance, institutions can identify students who may be struggling academically or socially [25]. This enables tutors and support staff to provide targeted support to these students, such as additional tutoring or counselling services. Another notable use is how AI and analytics can be used to dynamically link VLEs to knowledge assessments. For example, institutions can use AI to analyze student data and generate personalized feedback on their performance, highlighting areas where they may need additional support or revision. This can help to enhance the learning experience by providing students with immediate feedback on their progress and enabling them to identify areas where they may need to focus their attention [35].

Not only do analytics insights feed into the design and delivery of content via the VLE, defined as 'embedded analytics' [49], but data extracted from the VLE can also be used in third party apps, known as 'extracted analytics' (ibid.). Extracted analytics uses student-level data including those derived from granular VLE logins to play back meta information about students' comparative engagement. Studies show that VLE data is useful to improve students' engagement and enjoyment with their course by encouraging self-regulated learning although this can vary by subject and personality type with adoption ultimately far from being ubiquitous [23].

4 Machine Learning, SMS Messaging, and AI to Optimise Student Services and Support

The use of machine learning, SMS messaging, and AI is also becoming increasingly prevalent in optimising student services and support [15, 51]. Indeed, HEIs are leveraging these technologies to develop personalised and efficient ways of communicating with students, monitoring their progress, and providing support as such SMS messaging has been found to be an effective tool in student engagement and retention, and by integrating machine learning algorithms and AI chatbots, institutions can automate responses to frequently asked questions, such as enrolment deadlines or course schedules [15, 51]. Additionally, AI-powered virtual assistants can provide students with personalised support, such as academic advising or mental health counselling, without the need for face-to-face interactions. Machine learning algorithms can also be used to analyse student data, such as attendance records, assignment submissions, and exam results, to predict their performance and identify potential areas of improvement. These insights can be used by institutions to provide targeted interventions and support to students who are at risk of falling behind or dropping out. Moreover, AI-driven student support can be extended beyond academic matters to include career counselling and job placement services. Institutions can use machine learning algorithms to analyse job market trends and match students with job opportunities that fit their skills and career aspirations [15, 51].

Many HEIs, like commercial businesses are beginning to deploy blended and fully AI-based chatbots to support students by integrating with their VLEs.

Indeed, the deployment of chatbots in HEIs has become increasingly popular in recent years. These chatbots, which use natural language processing and machine learning algorithms, can provide a range of services to students, such as answering frequently asked questions, helping with course registration, providing reminders about assignments and deadlines, and connecting students with appropriate support services [17, 42].

In addition to providing general student support, chatbots can also integrate with VLEs to provide personalized learning experiences. One major advantage of using chatbots in student support and teaching is that they can provide immediate responses to student inquiries, reducing the need for students to wait for a response from a human support staff. This can lead to increased student satisfaction and engagement [42, 50]. However, it is important for institutions to ensure that the chatbots are designed and implemented with student privacy and security in mind. Additionally, chatbots should be regularly evaluated and updated to ensure that they are providing accurate and helpful responses to students.

Some institutions have even taken the use of chatbots a step further by integrating them with virtual assistants such as Amazon's Alexa or Google Home, allowing students to access information hands-free through voice commands [50].

In addition to the use of AI-based chatbots, HEIs are also exploring other ways to use AI and machine learning to optimize student services and support. One such way is by enabling blended use cases that empower student service personnel with data and/or use pattern recognition to help students navigate key admissions, enrolment, and course deadlines. Through the use of machine learning algorithms, student service personnel can gain insights into student behaviours and patterns, such as the times of day students are most likely to engage with course material or the types of support services they are most likely to use [34]. This data can then be used to develop more targeted and effective outreach and support strategies for individual students or groups of students. For example, AI-powered systems can identify students who are at risk of missing a deadline and proactively send them reminders or offer additional support resources to ensure they stay on track [5].

By combining the power of machine learning and human expertise, HEIs can create a more streamlined and efficient support system for students, ensuring they have the resources they need to succeed in their academic pursuits. Moreover, such initiatives can also help institutions to better manage resources and staff time, by using AI-based systems to handle routine tasks, allowing staff to focus on more complex or strategic initiatives [15].

In addition to the various AI-driven student support tools discussed previously, there is a growing trend in higher education to extend digital transformation to campus services through the use of smart speakers [14], the adoption of smart speakers in higher education represents a new frontier in digital transformation, enabling universities to leverage the power of AI and voice recognition technologies to deliver a more personalized and engaging campus experience [15], and since smart speakers have became ubiquitous in many homes, some HEIs are now exploring their potential as a tool for campus communication and service delivery [42].

For example, universities are deploying smart speakers in student accommodations to provide access to important information and services via voice commands [15]. Students can also ask it questions about campus events, class schedules, and other information, as well as control their smart home devices with voice commands, [43]. This approach is not only convenient for students, but it also enables universities to better communicate with students and provide them with personalized assistance in real-time [42]. Furthermore, smart speakers can also be used to facilitate learning through voice-activated learning and interactive exercises [39]. For instance, tutors can create interactive quizzes and flashcards that can be accessed through smart speakers, allowing students to test their knowledge and reinforce their learning through a new medium [1].

Furthermore, self-service innovations are also emerging as an effective way to make the HE experience more customer-centric [46]. These innovations, such as self-service portals, allow students to easily access the information and services they need without the need for human intervention [45]. This not only streamlines the student experience but also frees up staff time for more complex issues [2, 3]. In addition to portals, self-service kiosks are also becoming popular on campuses, allowing students to access information and services at their convenience [2, 3]. With the growing adoption of self-service innovations, HEIs are not only increasing student satisfaction but also reducing costs and increasing operational efficiency. However, it is important to note that while self-service innovations are effective in certain areas, there will always be a need for human support and interaction in many aspects of the HE experiences.

Predictive analytics has also emerged as a valuable tool in higher education for improving student outcomes. By analysing large amounts of data generated by online learning activities, institutions can identify patterns and predict student behaviour, such as which students are at risk of dropping out or struggling in a particular course [4, 20]. These insights can then be used to develop targeted interventions, such as personalized learning plans or proactive outreach from student support services, that can help students succeed. Machine learning algorithms are often used in predictive analytics to help institutions make sense of the vast amounts of data generated by online learning activities. These algorithms can identify patterns in the data that are not immediately apparent to human analysts, providing insights into student behaviour that would be difficult to obtain through manual analysis [13]. For example, machine learning algorithms can identify subtle changes in a student's engagement with a course over time, such as declining participation in online discussions or a decrease in the frequency of logins, that may signal the need for intervention [44].

5 Using VLEs to Drive Connected Learning Communities

Whilst there is much innovation emerging in Higher Education, the COVID-19 pandemic has particularly highlighted the importance and challenges of virtual learning environments (VLEs) for education and training. Indeed, VLEs have provided flexible, personalized, and interactive learning experiences that can overcome the limitations of physical classrooms and laboratories. However, VLEs also require effective design, development, and evaluation to ensure their quality, usability, and effectiveness.

Connectivism is a learning approach which considers the extent to which internet technologies such as VLEs have created opportunities for people to learn and share knowledge amongst themselves, creating a learning community [30]. Learning communities can subsequently be created when a VLE is designed to create multiple opportunities for learners to interact using online communication and collaboration tools. Adding to the debate Thomas [47] discusses the link between engagement in learning and subsequent sense of community and belonging. Indeed, Molotsi [37] notes VLEs are often being used to facilitate pedagogical approaches that create improved student engagement.

Connectivism is an emergent learning theory that proposes learners should integrate diverse thoughts, theories, and information in a meaningful way. It acknowledges that technology is an integral part of the learning process and that the constant connectivity enabled by technology affords learners opportunities to exercise agency over their learning. It also advocates for group collaboration and dialogue, enabling learners to encounter multiple viewpoints and perspectives in the processes of decision-making, problem-solving, and sense-making. Connectivism posits that learning does not occur solely within an individual, but within and across the networks of people and resources that are accessible through technology. Connectivism conceptualizes knowledge as a network and learning as a process of pattern recognition.

According to connectivism, learning and knowledge depend on the diversity of opinions, and sustaining and nurturing connections is essential to facilitate continual learning. Connectivism also asserts that learning may reside in non-human appliances, such as databases or artificial intelligence systems, and that learners can tap into these sources of information to augment their own knowledge. Therefore, connectivism challenges conventional notions of teaching and learning by emphasizing the role of technology as an enabler and mediator of learning in a digital age.

6 Creating Connected Learning Communities Through a VLE

Good and consistent educational design when creating VLE content is considered essential as a driver of creating an immersive and connected learning community and ensuing subsequent student satisfaction [8, 28, 41].

Weaver et al. [48] suggest engagement is linked to the quality of materials within the VLE and the quality of communications guiding learners to the content. Preidys and Sakalauskas [38] further highlight the importance of making content accessible, logical and easy to navigate. Heaton-Shrestha et al. [31] also discuss the importance of consistency, with programme teams working together to design and adopt an agreed template and series of VLE tools.

With regards to VLE tools, Mogus et al. [36] suggest learners are more motivated to connect and engage when there are a range of materials and activities including lecture notes, additional learning materials, quizzes, assessment guidance, video and opportunities to collaborate with teaching teams and fellow learners.

Kristóf and Tóth [33] further associate VLE connection and engagement through the opportunity of activities which allow for timely tutor and peer feedback, and embedded digital skills support.

Thomas et al. [47] also notes the need for a rational approach to using VLE tools. The use of a small number of tools which leaners become familiar is more likely to drive engagement and community than trying to use everything available from within the VLE armoury.

Ashby and Broughan [9] also discuss the importance of regular tutor–student communication to encourage engagement with VLE content and activity. This includes in class activity demonstrating use of the VLE, and regular on-line messaging to give meaning and build a sense of cohort community. Activities to encourage peer to peer communication and knowledge sharing via the VLE also develops digital fluency, networks and community.

7 Immersive VLE

VLEs have evolved considerably since their beginnings, and due to the emergence of new technology, have grown into more realistic and dynamic environments for learning. The newest development in educational technology is immersive VLEs, which integrate Virtual Reality (VR) and Augmented Reality (AR). By providing students with a more engaging and interactive learning environment, these innovations have the ability to completely change the way individuals learn.

The metaverse is a novel invention that has a significant connection with immersive VLEs. The term "metaverse" describes a shared virtual environment that is accessible through a variety of resources, such as VR headsets, desktop PCs, and mobile devices. It is a completely immersive shared virtual world where users may communicate with one another in real time, fostering a highly social and collaborative setting. Indeed, the metaverse has the ability to completely transform how individuals study, work, and communicate in the future, for instance, instructors may replicate complicated situations and establish incredibly engaging and collaborative learning environments for their students. Medical students, for instance, may utilise VR to model operations and develop their abilities in a secure setting without the usage of actual patients. Similar to this, architecture students may utilise virtual reality (VR) to develop and visualise intricate ideas in 3D, enabling them to explore and test out various materials and structures within an extremely realistic setting. Also, students may collaborate in real-time and learn from one another in a highly collaborative and social learning environment thanks to immersive VLEs and the metaverse. This can enable students from all over the world to meet within the metaverse to work on a project collaboratively, exchange ideas, and gain insight from one another's viewpoints. Collaborative learning such as these can aid in removing pre-existing obstacles and fostering a more welcoming and varied learning environment.

Yet, there are still obstacles to overcome before immersive VLEs and the metaverse can become commonplace in education. One of the most significant obstacles is the expense of integrating these technologies, which might be prohibitively expensive for some educational institutions. Furthermore, there are worries about the potential for addiction and distraction that immersive technology might produce, as well as data privacy and security problems, other than these obstacles, the possible advantages of immersive VLEs and the metaverse in education cannot be overlooked. Immersive VLEs and the metaverse are going to become more accessible and inexpensive as technology advances, and more educational institutions will incorporate these technologies into their programs. It is critical that educational institutions begin to investigate the possibilities of new technologies and devise ways for effectively integrating them into their teaching and learning activities.

Finally, immersive VLEs and the metaverse provide educational institutions a significant opportunity for developing highly engaging and dynamic educational environments for pupils. These technologies have great potential advantages, and they are anticipated to be incorporate by HEIs in the coming years. As researchers continue to investigate the possibilities of new technologies, it is critical that they tackle the issues and concerns that arise with their deployment, ensuring that they are utilised responsibly and ethically.

8 Research into Practice

Recognising the importance of consistent educational design and significant learning during the Covid pandemic, an evaluation of the key content requirements of a VLE was undertaken in 2021.

150 students from a range of undergraduate and postgraduate programmes from a single UK HEI, with an overall student population of c36000 were formed into focus groups. All participants had used a VLE for a minimum of 9 months across a minimum of 3 modules or courses. Participants were drawn from a range of subject areas and modes of delivery (full time and part time).

The overall purpose of the study was to design a set of VLE design principles which would facilitate learner engagement and create opportunities for tutor, learner and peer connectivity outside of the classroom.

Key findings suggested the following elements were essential when building an immersive VLE:

- an outline of the module or course
- an introduction to the teaching team
- contact details and 'office hours' of the teaching team
- an online guide outlining the learning activities which make up the module or course.
- session materials
- video and audio recordings of delivered sessions, or summary recordings
- access to core reading, including an online reading list
- details of summative and formative assessment

- learning checks
- on-line submission points for summative and formative assessment
- opportunities to interact with tutors
- opportunities to interact with fellow learners.
- academic skills support materials
- digital literacy skills support materials.

- *An outline of the module or course*

Participants emphasised the importance of a welcoming and detailed introduction to the module or course of study, ideally available in video format designed to provide the learner with information around content to be covered, learning objectives, assessment mechanisms, how the content will be delivered, typical learning activities, and how to access further support from the tutor. A video walk-through of the VLE site was also deemed an effective way of encouraging early engagement. Such content should be available at the beginning of a module or course and will typically form a welcome message or activity from the lead tutor.

- *An introduction to the teaching team*

The relationship between learner and members of the teaching team is considered a key driver of learner engagement and subsequent connectivism. In enabling such a connection between learner and the teaching team, participants noted the importance of a welcome video or audio recording of the lead tutor/members of the teaching team, introducing themselves, their background, their research or practice expertise, and how they will support learners. Whilst such an introduction can be presented in written format, the power of the spoken word in building a rapport was considered a critical success factor. As with the module or course introduction, this content should be available at the beginning of the module course and typically form part of the welcome message.

- *Contact details and 'office hours' of the teaching team*

Participants did not associate the use of a VLE with the withdrawal from attendance at in person classes or tutorials. Indeed, there was an association between early engagement with VLE materials and the subsequent likelihood of such engagement leading to a stronger connection with the teaching team. This connection was more likely to drive opportunities for one-to-one interaction. As such, presentation of teaching team contact details and office hours was considered an essential element of the VLE content. This should include physical and online contact details and protocols.

- *An online guide outlining the learning activities which make up the module or course*

For many study participants the most essential VLE content was the provision of an online study guide which provides granular detail of the module or course delivery. This guide acts as a scaffold to direct learner's, session by session, to what they will be studying, how they should prepare, what will happen in each learning session, opportunities for subsequent poster session learning activity, and how the learning from each session contributes to learning outcomes, and formative/summative assessment. Ideally such a guide should also include single click links to key learning resources for each session and navigation or signposting to the specific session content within the VLE site.

- *Session materials*

Providing a carefully designed and structured series of folders containing session learning materials, available at the beginning of a module or course was also considered an essential element of VLE content. Such content could include pre-reading, materials used in on-campus or online learning sessions and post session content.

- *Video and audio recordings of delivered sessions, or summary recordings*

Further housed within the session materials folders, recordings or summary recordings of delivered sessions were cited as an effective method of re-capping on core learning content, access missed class materials and enable better preparation for assessment. Interestingly, whilst participants noted the importance of such content being legible, the need for finely crafted performances were not deemed essential. Of greater importance was the natural rapport and storytelling from the deliverer. Welcome video content was deemed the most beneficial, participants also welcomed audio content, which was often more accessible and enabled re-of learning on the move.

- *Access to core reading, including an online reading list*

VLEs provide a scaffold and structured learning space and participants benefited greatly when core reading could be accessed directly from the site. Engagement with such directed reading was more likely when links were placed in the online study guide and within the session materials folders.

- *Details of summative and formative assessment*

It is without doubt assessment which creates the highest level of student anxiety. Providing detailed information and guidance around any formative also that of assessment tasks associated with the module or course within the VLE is essential. Participants particularly noted the need for clear assessment briefs, grading criteria, the summary video and audio recording outlining the key requirements of any assessment, where opportunities for feedback can be sought, and details of how assessment should be submitted. Communication tools, such as discussion forum, where key assessment related questions can be posted also considered beneficial, as long as replies were timely.

- *Learning checks*

One of the key deficiencies many participants cited within VLE use was part of formative assessment tools such as quizzes and self check activity. Where such approaches were provided participants considered these were excellent way of building connection with a module course and creating opportunities for subsequent engagement with their tutors. Consistency was considered a key design future when using such formative assessment tools, and caution was noted around teaching teams using too many different learning check approaches. Simple post session quizzes were considered the most beneficial way of students sense checking the extent to which they had understood key session content.

- *On-line submission points for summative and formative assessment*

Further creating connection with the VLE was to embed assessment submission tools enabling learners to submit formative and summative assessment within the single site. Opportunities for learners to submit draft work for review was also considered an ideal way of building engagement with the VLA and connection to their teaching team.

- *Opportunities to interact with tutors*

Where VLEs created a immersive learning platform enabling learners to engage with a range of content and activity participants noted greater weekly or daily time would be afforded in engaging, and subsequently this would lead to more desire to connect with tutors, asking questions, seeking clarity, and wishing to deepen knowledge. As such, the utilisation of interaction and communication tools such as embedded messaging and discussion forum was an essential element of a VLE.

- *Opportunities to interact with fellow learners*

Similarly, opportunities to interact with fellow learners via communication tools such as discussion boards, chat rooms and more traditional e-mail from within the VLE were considered particularly beneficial. However, participants noted the need for careful instruction of how to use such tools, and the programme level a coordinated approach to the interactivity tools teaching team would use. Whereupon water lake approach was adopted learners became familiar with a small set of communication tools and therefore use the more regularly and meaningfully.

- *Academic skills support materials*

Where VLEs were used as a immersive learning experience learners prefer to remain within this online environment while studying remotely. As such, it was important to create a single click access to a wider academic skill and learning resources without the need for learners to remove themselves from the VLE. Specifically, participants noted the importance of access to academic skills, library skills and wider library resources from within individual module or course sites.

- *Digital literacy skills support materials*

Using VLEs as an immersive and connected learning tool is a significant shift from the traditional materials repository used in many HEIs. Due to their, participants noted they were more likely to engage with new technological approaches from within a VLE environment, than outside. Furthermore they suggested this was a key element of their digital skills development. However, the need for pre-and post-enrolment training on using a VLE was considered essential. Embedding, text and video based help guides was also considered useful, although in-class introductions to individual VLE sites and walkthroughs were considered most beneficial.

9 Conclusions

Whilst VLEs have become an expectation across Higher Education, it is acknowledged that only some teaching professionals use these tools in a proactive and interactive manner. However, evidence indicates those who create a structured and connected on-line environment for their learners are likely to see increased immersion an into and engagement with the content and subsequent sense of community and enhanced performance. Furthermore, arguments which suggest increased use of VLEs beyond that of a materials repository will detract learners from engaging in classroom activity appears dated.

However, critical to the success of a VLE is the creation of a consistent template which is universally adopted, at the very least a programme level, which provides scaffolding and familiarity for learners.

Careful consideration must be given to developing learners digital literacy skills not only in how to navigate the VLE, but also how to use the various tools. To encourage regular immersion into VLE content and activity, teaching teams should also develop strategies to routinely embed VLE use into their teaching sessions, and use communication technologies routinely to direct learners to VLE content and activity.

Learning communities can be accelerated through carefully crafted module and teaching team introductions posted within the VLE. It is further recognised use of human voice, whether through video or audio content is more likely to develop connectivity between teaching team and learner.

A detailed and consistent learning plan design, used across all modules courses delivered within a programme, provides an effective and necessary scaffold, which learners will use to plan their learning activities, both within and outside of the VLE.

Immersion into the VLE is also more likely to be achieved when all necessary learning materials and resources can be sourced with minimal click within the VLE. This includes access to key reading and external online content.

Early release of learning materials onto the VLE, also helps learners prepare for classroom activity and engage in early wider independent research. Similarly, using the VLE to outline formative and summative assessment tasks, and provide clarity of assessment expectations and grading, will attract learners.

Video and audio content which catches summarises key learning delivered in classroom environments also acts as an aide memoir and draws learners into the VLE.

However, it is the use of interactive tools which is most likely to differentiate a good VLE from the VLE which immerses and builds a networked community of engaged learners. Indeed, it is the use of embedded communication technologies such as discussion forum/email and blogs, and self/collaborative assessment tasks such as quizzes which learners suggest develop an enhanced level of understanding, confidence and desire to engage.

In summary, as blended learning becomes a mainstream approach to the delivery of higher education and VLE use continues to be an expectation of learners, strategies must be adopted an institution and programme level to support teaching teams build and use such technologies to not only provide learners with a essential information, but also create connectedness and community.

References

1. Alfoudari AM, Durugbo CM, Aldhmour FM (2023) Exploring quality attributes of smart classrooms from the perspectives of academics. Educ Inf Technol. https://doi.org/10.1007/s10639-022-11452-3
2. Al-Emran A et al (2018) Artificial Intelligence impacts on higher education. Int J Emerging Techn Learn (iJET) 13(5):252–267
3. Al-Emran A et al (2018) Innovative higher education teaching and learning techniques: implementation trends and assessment approaches. Int J Emerging Tech Learn (iJET) 13(2):4–19
4. Al-Tameemi G, Xue J, Ajit S, Kanakis T, Hadi I (2020). Predictive learning analytics in higher education: Factors, methods and challenges. In: 2020 International Conference on Advances in Computing and Communication Engineering (ICACCE), June, pp 1–9. IEEE
5. Albayrak N, Özdemir A, Zeydan E (2018) An overview of artificial intelligence based chatbots and an example chatbot application. In: 2018 26th signal processing and communications applications conference (SIU), May, pp 1–4. IEEE

6. Aldulaimi SH, Abdeldayem MM, Jumaa HT, Mohamed HM, Abdulrazaq ML (2022) Critical challenges of virtual learning environments (VLEs) and learning theories. In: 2022 ASU International Conference in Emerging Technologies for Sustainability and Intelligent Systems (ICETSIS), Manama, Bahrain, pp 29–36. https://doi.org/10.1109/ICETSIS55481.2022.9888945

7. Alonso JM, Casalino G (2019) Explainable artificial intelligence for human-centric data analysis in virtual learning environments. In: International Workshop on Higher Education Learning Methodologies and Technologies Online

8. Alves P, Miranda L, Morais C (2017) The influence of virtual learning environments in students' performance. Univ J Educ Res 5(3):517–527

9. Ashby R, Broughan C (2002) Factors affecting students' usage of virtual learning environments. Psychol Learn Teach 2(2):140–141

10. Askar A (2014) Interactive ebooks as a tool of mobile learning for digital-natives in higher education: Interactivity, preferences, and ownership. Education Tech Research Dev 60:7–13

11. Bilal HE, Akbar A, Yasmin F, Rahman AU, Li S (2022) Virtual learning during the COVID-19 pandemic: a bibliometric review and future research agenda. Risk Manag Healthc Policy 15:1353–1368. https://doi.org/10.2147/RMHP.S355895. PMID: 35873112; PMCID: PMC9304638

12. Boulton CA, Kent C, Williams HT (2018) Virtual learning environment engagement and learning outcomes at a 'bricks-and-mortar' university. Comput Educ 126:129–142

13. Bujang SDA et al (2021) Multiclass prediction model for student grade prediction using machine learning. IEEE Access 9:95608–95621. https://doi.org/10.1109/ACCESS.2021.3093563

14. Ciolacu M, Tehrani AF, Binder L, Svasta PM (2018) Education 4.0—Artificial intelligence assisted higher education: early recognition system with machine learning to support students' success. In: 2018 IEEE 24th International Symposium for Design and Technology in Electronic Packaging (SIITME). Iasi, Romania 2018:23–30. https://doi.org/10.1109/SIITME.2018.8599203

15. Chen l, Chen P, Lin Z (2020) Artificial intelligence in education: a review. IEEE Access 8:75264–75278. https://doi.org/10.1109/ACCESS.2020.2988510

16. Cosgrave R, Risquez A, Logan-Phelan T, Farrelly T, Costello E, McAvinia C, Palmer M, Harding N, Vaughan N (2011) Usage and uptake of virtual learning environments and technology assisted learning. Findings from a multi institutional, multi year comparative study. The All Ireland J Teach Learn Higher Education (AISHE-J) 3(1)

17. Cordero J, Toledo A, Guamán F, Barba-Guamán F (2020) Use of chatbots for user service in higher education institutions. In :2020 15th Iberian Conference on Information Systems and Technologies (CISTI), Seville, Spain, pp 1–6. https://doi.org/10.23919/CISTI49556.2020.9141108

18. Dahlstrom E, Brooks C, Bichsel J (2014) The current ecosystem of learning management systems in higher education: student, faculty, and IT perspectives. Research report. Louisville, CO: ECAR, September

19. Dale C, Lane AM (2004) Carry on talking: developing ways to enhance students' use of online discussion forums. J Hosp Leis Sport Tour Educ 3(1):53–59

20. Doleck T, Lemay DJ, Basnet RB, Bazelais P (2020) Predictive analytics in education: a comparison of deep learning frameworks. Educ Inf Technol 25:1951–1963

21. Ferriman J (2019) Characteristics of a virtual classroom. http://www.learndash.com/characteristics-of-a-virtual-classroom

22. Flavin M (2020) Virtual library environment? VLEs in practice. In: Re-imagining technology enhanced learning. Springer, pp 43–58. https://doi.org/10.1007/978-3-030-55785-0_3

23. Foster C (2020). Students' adoption of learner analytics. https://doi.org/10.1007/978-3-030-47392-1_8

24. Foster C, Francis P (2020) A systematic review on the deployment and effectiveness of data analytics in higher education to improve student outcomes. Assess Eval High Educ 45(6):822–841

25. Foster E, Siddle R (2019) The effectiveness of learning analytics for identifying at-risk students in higher education. Assess Eval High Educ 45:842–854
26. Francis P, Foster C (2018) Educational analytics: a systematic review of empirical studies. Paper presented to Advance HE Surveys Conference, Leeds, 9th May
27. Friedrich S, Antes G, Behr S et al (2022) Is there a role for statistics in artificial intelligence? Adv Data Anal Classif 16:823–846. https://doi.org/10.1007/s11634-021-00455-6
28. Gašević D, Dawson S, Rogers T, Gasevic D (2016) Learning analytics should not promote one size fits all: the effects of instructional conditions in predicting academic success. Internet Higher Educ 2016(28):68–84
29. Glenn M (2008) The future of higher education: how technology will shape learning. The New Media Consortium, pp 1–27)
30. Goldie JGS (2016) Connectivism: a knowledge learning theory for the digital age? Med Teach 38(10):1064–1069
31. Heaton-Shrestha C, Gipps C, Edirisingha P, Linsey T (2007) Learning and e-learning in HE: the relationship between student learning style and VLE use. Res Pap Educ 22(4):443–464
32. Islam MN, Inan TT, Rafi S, Akter SS, Sarker IH, Islam AKMN (2020) A Systematic Review on the Use of AI and ML for Fighting the COVID-19 Pandemic. IEEE Trans Artificial Intell 1(3):258–270, Dec. https://doi.org/10.1109/TAI.2021.3062771
33. Kristóf Z, Tóth K (2019) Developing and examining a virtual learning environment. Hungarian Educ Res J 9(3):511–526
34. Kumar JA (2021) Educational chatbots for project-based learning: investigating learning outcomes for a team-based design course. Int J Educ Technol High Educ 18(1):1–28
35. McKinsey & Company (2022) Using machine learning to improve student success in Higher Education. McKinsey & Company. Available at: https://www.mckinsey.com/industries/education/our-insights/using-machine-learning-to-improve-student-success-in-higher-education (Accessed: March 25, 2023)
36. Mogus AM, Djurdjevic I, Suvak N (2012) The impact of student activity in a virtual learning environment on their final mark. Act Learn High Educ 13(3):177–189
37. Molotsi A (2020) The university staff experience of using a virtual learning environment as a platform for e-learning. J Educ Tech Online Learn 3(2):133–151
38. Preidys S, Sakalauskas L (2010) Analysis of students' study activities in virtual learning environments using data mining methods. Technol Econ Dev Econ 16(1):94–108
39. Reina Sánchez K, Arbáizar Gómez JP, Isasi Sánchez L, Durán-Heras A (2023) Exploring a new oral presentation approach for online education through action research. In: García Márquez FP, Segovia Ramírez I, Bernalte Sánchez PJ, Muñoz del Río A (eds) IoT and data science in engineering management. CIO 2022. Lecture Notes on Data Engineering and Communications Technologies, vol 160. Springer, Cham. https://doi.org/10.1007/978-3-031-27915-7_77
40. Risquez A, McAvinia C, Raftery D, O'Riordan F, Harding N, Cosgrave R, Farrelly T, et al (2011) An investigation of students' experiences of using virtual learning environments: implications for academic professional development. In: Emerging issues in higher education III. EDIN
41. Saykili A (2019) Higher education in the digital age: The impact of digital connective technologies. J Educ Tech Online Learn 2(1):1–15
42. Sandu N, Gide E (2019) Adoption of AI-chatbots to enhance student learning experience in higher education in India. In: 2019 18th International Conference on Information Technology Based Higher Education and Training (ITHET), Magdeburg, Germany, pp 1–5. https://doi.org/10.1109/ITHET46829.2019.8937382
43. Sciarretta E, Alimenti L (2021) Smart speakers for inclusion: how can intelligent virtual assistants really assist everybody? In: Kurosu M (eds) Human-computer interaction. theory, methods and tools. HCII 2021. Lecture Notes in Computer Science, vol 12762. Springer, Cham. https://doi.org/10.1007/978-3-030-78462-1_6
44. Sghir N, Adadi A, Lahmer M (2022) Recent advances in Predictive Learning Analytics: A decade systematic review (2012–2022). Educ Inf Technol. https://doi.org/10.1007/s10639-022-11536-0

45. Sjöström J et al (2018) Designing chatbots for higher education practice. In: Proceedings of the 51st Hawaii International Conference on System Sciences (HICSS)
46. Tierney WG, Lanford M (2016) Conceptualizing innovation in higher education. In: Paulsen MB (ed) Higher education: handbook of theory and research, vol 31. Springer International Publishing, Cham, pp 1–40
47. Thomas M (ed) (2012) Design, implementation, and evaluation of virtual learning environments. IGI Global
48. Weaver D, Spratt C, Nair CS (2008) Academic and student use of a learning management system: Implications for quality. Australasian J Educ Tech 24(1)
49. Wise AF, Speer J, Marbouti F, Hsiao, Y (2013) Broadening the notion of participation in online discussions: Examining patterns in learners' online listening behaviors. Instr Sci 41:323–343
50. Yanduri V, Majid I (2022) Chatbots in education system 60:15–18
51. Zawacki-Richter O, Marín VI, Bond M et al (2019) Systematic review of research on artificial intelligence applications in higher education—where are the educators? Int J Educ Technol High Educ 16:39. https://doi.org/10.1186/s41239-019-0171-0

Influence of Artificial Intelligence in Higher Education; Impact, Risk and Counter Measure

Musarrat Saberin Nipun, Md.Simul Hasan Talukder, Usman Javed Butt, and Rejwan Bin Sulaiman ⓘ

Abstract Artificial Intelligence (AI) is an emerging field that seeks to replicate or emulate human-like cognitive abilities using artificial means. As the world changes, the development and application of AI tools and technologies in areas such as agriculture, medicine, healthcare, and education are growing at an unprecedented pace. This chapter presents a review study on the impact, risks, and countermeasures of artificial intelligence in higher education (AIHE). The chapter begins by discussing the journey of AI in education from its beginning to the present day. It then examines the existing AI tools and technologies in education and explores their potential applications. The chapter goes on to analyze the influences of these tools in education and the challenges and risks they face in higher education. Additionally, it highlights the limitations of AI tools and proposes ways to overcome these gaps. The purpose of this study is to provide updated information to students, teachers, professors, national policymakers, and researchers, as well as to explore the scope of research on AI in higher education. By offering a comprehensive analysis of the impact of AI on higher education (HE), this chapter aims to inform and inspire the academic community to embrace AI as a transformative technology in education.

M. S. Nipun (✉) · U. J. Butt
Brunel University, London, UK
e-mail: musarrat.nipun@brunel.ac.uk

U. J. Butt
e-mail: usman.butt@brunel.ac.uk

M. H. Talukder
Nuclear Safety, Security and Safeguard Division, Bangladesh Atomic Energy Regulatory Authority, Dhaka, Bangladesh

R. B. Sulaiman
University of Bedfordshire, Bedfordshire, UK

© The Author(s), under exclusive license to Springer Nature Switzerland AG 2023
H. Jahankhani et al. (eds.), *AI, Blockchain and Self-Sovereign Identity in Higher Education*, Advanced Sciences and Technologies for Security Applications,
https://doi.org/10.1007/978-3-031-33627-0_7

1 Introduction

The world has already experienced three industrial revolutions and has recently entered the fourth industrial revolution (4IR), which comprises several significant components such as Artificial Intelligence, Internet of Things, Big Data Analytics, Cloud Computing, 3D Printing/Additive Manufacturing, Robotic Systems, Augmented Reality, and Blockchain technology [1]. AI is a rapidly growing component of 4IR and is being utilized in various sectors [2], including the education sector. Several studies have highlighted the limitations of higher education in low-income African countries, such as weak scientific competencies and a scarcity of experts in different fields [3]. In Pakistan, Iqbal and Ashraf [4] mentioned unskilled teachers who struggle to adapt to student learning styles, leading to a lack of technological support and insufficient access to online materials and libraries for students. Similarly, Parveen et al. [5] identified a lack of proficiency as the primary cause of low-quality education in Pakistan. Additionally, students with disabilities have long struggled to learn and adapt to the changing world in Bangladesh [6], with Ahmed and Hoque [6] attributing the issue to teaching incompetency, unaffordable ICT, and assistive technology devices. The COVID-19 pandemic has presented several challenges for students, including a lack of quality education and difficulties in adapting to virtual classes [7]. Research students face various challenges, such as spending significant amounts of time finding up-to-date information on research topics and scientific gaps. Additionally, evaluating dissertations and assignments can be time-consuming for teachers, leading to several challenges in higher education. AI is one of the most effective solutions to address these challenges. By creating personalized learning pathways for students based on their individual needs, strengths, and weaknesses, AI can recommend specific learning materials and resources that are most appropriate for each student. AI tools can analyze student performance and behavior, identifying knowledge gaps and providing personalized support and feedback to improve learning outcomes.

AI researchers are continuously developing new techniques, algorithms, tools, and technologies to make education easier. From literature reviews, it is evident that artificial intelligence is transforming education by providing innovative ways to teach, learn, and assess medical students, residents, and other healthcare professionals [8–10]. AI-powered adaptive testing can assess a student's knowledge and skills in real-time and adjust the difficulty of the questions based on their responses, providing a more accurate and efficient assessment compared to traditional testing methods [11–15]. AI can automatically grade assignments, provide feedback, and even identify plagiarism, freeing up time for instructors to focus on more complex tasks such as mentoring and coaching students [16–19]. AI-powered intelligent tutoring systems can provide personalized support and feedback, helping students identify their strengths and weaknesses and improve their learning outcomes [20–22]. AI can analyze data on student performance, behavior, and attendance, providing insights that can help educators identify at-risk students and intervene before they fall behind [23, 24].

However, there are numerous existing tools in education that utilize AI, as summarized in Table 1. These tools have the potential to revolutionize the education system by improving the quality of education and making it more accessible and personalized for students. By continuing to develop new techniques and technologies, AI researchers can further enhance the role of AI in education and make learning more effective and efficient.

After conducting a thorough literature review, it is evident that AI tools are increasingly being used in higher education and have significant potential to improve the quality of education. Therefore, the main objective of this study is to analyze the

Table 1 Widely used existing AI tools in HE

Refs.	Tools	Function
[25]	Quizlet	An AI-powered platform that uses machine learning to provide personalized study recommendations to students. It can also generate flashcards, quizzes, and other study materials
[26]	Coursera	An online learning platform that offers courses from top universities and organizations. It uses AI to personalize the learning experience for each student, based on their performance and learning preferences
[27]	Smart Sparrow	An AI-powered platform that allows educators to create adaptive and interactive learning experiences. It can adjust the difficulty of the content based on student performance and provide real-time feedback
[28]	Grammarly	An AI-powered writing assistant that provides real-time feedback on grammar, spelling, and punctuation. It can also suggest improvements in writing style and vocabulary
[29]	Duolingo	An AI-powered language learning platform that uses gamification to help learners improve their language skills
[30]	IBM Watson	An AI-powered platform that provides personalized learning experiences to students. It can also help educators develop custom learning plans and assessments
[31]	Knewton	An adaptive learning platform that uses AI algorithms to personalize the learning experience for each student. It can adjust the difficulty of the content based on the student's performance and learning preferences
[32]	SMART Learning Suite	An AI-powered platform that helps educators create engaging and interactive lessons. It includes features such as handwriting recognition, text recognition, and shape recognition
[33]	Teachable Machine	An AI-powered tool that allows students to create custom machine learning models without any coding. It can be used to teach students about AI and machine learning concepts
[34]	Carnegie Speech	An AI-powered platform that provides personalized language training for non-native speakers. It uses speech recognition technology to provide feedback on pronunciation and fluency

(continued)

Table 1 (continued)

Refs.	Tools	Function
[35]	Brainly	An AI-powered platform that allows students to ask and answer homework questions. It uses machine learning algorithms to match questions with the most relevant and accurate answers
[36]	Gradescope	An AI-powered platform that automates grading for paper-based assignments. It uses machine learning algorithms to recognize handwriting and provide feedback on common errors
[37]	Zoho Notebook	An AI-powered note-taking app that can automatically categorize and organize notes based on the content. It can also search for notes based on keywords and provide related suggestions
[38]	Lingvist	An AI-powered language learning app that uses data analytics to personalize the learning experience for each student. It can adapt the difficulty of the content and provide real-time feedback on pronunciation and grammar
[39]	Top Hat	An AI-powered platform that allows educators to create interactive and engaging classroom experiences. It includes features such as real-time polls, quizzes, and discussions
[40]	Proctorio	An AI-powered proctoring tool that allows educators to monitor student activity during online exams. It uses machine learning algorithms to detect potential cheating behavior
[41]	Adaptemy	An adaptive learning platform that uses AI algorithms to personalize the learning experience for each student. It includes features such as personalized recommendations, real-time feedback, and progress tracking
[42]	Lumen5	An AI-powered video creation tool that can automatically convert text into video content. It can suggest images, music, and animation based on the content
[43]	Turnitin	An AI-powered platform that checks student work for plagiarism. It uses machine learning algorithms to detect potential instances of plagiarism and provide originality reports
[44]	Unicheck	An AI-powered plagiarism checker that uses machine learning algorithms to detect potential instances of plagiarism. It provides originality reports and feedback on potential sources of plagiarism
[45]	Calm	An AI-powered meditation app that includes features such as personalized recommendations and real-time feedback based on user behavior
[46]	Otter.ai	An AI-powered tool that provides automated transcription and captioning services. It can transcribe live lectures and meetings in real-time, and provide captions for recorded videos
[47]	Scrible	An AI-powered research tool that allows students to annotate and organize web pages. It includes features such as automatic citation generation and a research dashboard
[48]	ChatGpt	ChatGPT is a large language model developed by OpenAI that is trained on a diverse range of internet text and is capable of generating human-like responses to text-based inputs. Its main function is to understand and respond to questions and other text inputs from users in a way that is informative and engaging

effects of AI tools on education, their associated risks, and propose countermeasures to mitigate these risks. The key contributions of this study are-

- Compilation of all AI tools used in education within a single study.
- Review of the effectiveness of AI tools in specific educational fields.
- Examination of the impact of AI tool usage on education.
- Carrying a survey on the perception of students, researchers, and professor in using AI tools in education.
- Identification of the shortcomings associated with the use of AI tools in education.
- Proposing integrated framework to address these shortcomings and improve the use of AI tools in education.
- Providing recommendations to enhance the effectiveness and benefits of AI tools in the field of education.

2 Methodology

In this study, we present a comprehensive analysis of the obstacles and shortcomings faced by LDC countries in higher education during pandemics, and propose an integrated AI framework to help address these issues. Firstly, we conducted an extensive review of different research studies to identify the challenges faced by LDC countries. The workflow of our study is depicted in Fig. 1. Next, we surveyed the existing AI tools in education and evaluated their potential in addressing the identified challenges. We analyzed the role of AI tools in higher education in a step-by-step manner and assessed their capacity according to the Algorithm 1. We logged into each tool and examined various aspects to extract their pros and cons. The impacts of AI tools in higher education were analyzed, highlighting their positive and negative influences throughout the chapter. To determine the influence of AI tools in education, we employed various research methods. We conducted interviews and discussions with students, researchers, teachers, and professors to gather their perspectives on the use of AI tools in education. Additionally, we collected data from social media and LinkedIn posts of professors and other scholars, and performed sentiment analysis to gauge their opinions on the topic. By combining these various research methods, we were able to gain a well-rounded understanding of the influence of AI tools in education and gather insights from different perspectives. The whole process is shown in Algorithm 2.

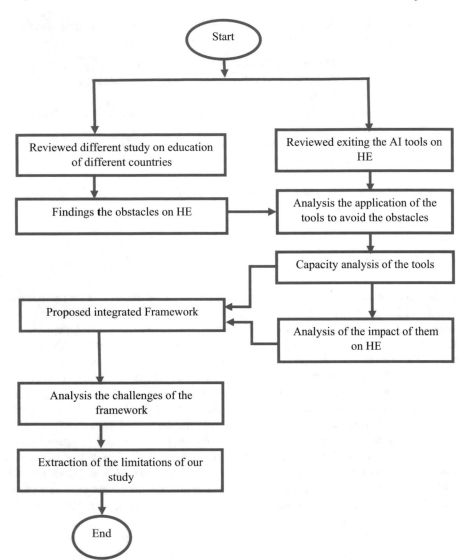

Fig. 1 Work flow of our study

Algorithm 1. Capacities analysis of the AI tools
1   Complete the registration in each tool
2   Login into the tools
3   **Loop**: counter=0; counter <No. of features of the tools; counter++
4   Command/use the tools based on their purpose and check the output
5   Diversity check of the tools
6   Beta testing of the tools
7   **End the loop**
8   Extract the pros of the tools
9   Extract the limitations of the tools
End of the algorithm.

Algorithm 2. Procedure of the analysis of the impact of the AI tools on HE
1   Select different fields: Class room, Teacher community, Research community, Professors and students post in social media and LinkedIn and so on
2   **Loop:** counter=1; counter< 100; counter++
3   Take interviews from the students, guardians' researchers and teachers
4   Analysis the sentiments of user from social media
5   Collect the post of Professor from LinkedIn
6   Collect the real incident of using AI tools
7   **End the Loop**
8   Analysed by our team to find the positive and negative impact of AI tools in HE
End of the Algorithm

Finally, we proposed an integrated AI framework that could play a positive role in higher education. However, we also explored the challenges that could arise with implementing such a framework.

3   Capacity Analysis the AI Tools

This study article looked into the benefits and drawbacks of each of the tools in order to determine how AI models influence education. This helped the research determine which AI models have a positive impact on education and at what degree.

Quizlet: As a language model, it offers multiple choice, true/false, and matching questions but not more challenging ones like fill in the blanks or essay questions.

Quizlet allows some customisation, such as background colour and text size [49], but not much. It does not integrate with other learning management systems or technologies, but it can be used alone. Quizlet provides fundamental metrics, such as study progress and performance [49], but not advanced analytics, such as learning outcomes. Quizlet supports multiple languages, but it may not contain all the features needed for non-taught languages. In conclusion, Quizlet is useful for learning vocabulary and basic concepts, but it may not be suitable for students who need higher-level information like academic research or technical instructions [49].

Coursera, Smart Sparrow, IBM Watson, Knewton, Smart Learning Suite, Zoho notebook, Lingvist , TopHat: These tools are mostly self-paced, with little instructor-student interaction. Some tools have forums or discussion boards; however, they may be inactive, making instructor response and support difficult. Some of these tools have some free courses or trial version, mostly user has to pay for whole subscription. Some of these tools provide limited courses; however, it may not cover all users' interests. Certificates gained from these tools may not be as valued by companies or academic institutions as degrees or certifications from traditional educational institutions. Some of these tools provide courses in different languages, however most are solely in English, which may deter non-English speakers. SMART Learning Suite is primarily designed for use with SMART Board interactive whiteboards [50] which may limit its compatibility with other devices or hardware. Zoho Notebook stores user data on its servers [51] which may raise privacy and security concerns for some users. TopHat is primarily used in higher education [52] it may not be accessible to students in all regions or countries. This can be a disadvantage for students who require access to a wider range of educational resources.

Grammarly: Grammarly can correct grammar and spelling, but it may not consider context. This may cause incorrect suggestions or corrections. Grammarly focuses on professional writing [53] like academic and business. Poetry and fiction may benefit less. Grammarly's free version lacks several advanced capabilities. Some consumers cannot afford it. Grammarly works online only. This can be a problem for offline or unreliable internet users. Grammarly needs user data, including personal information and writing. This can be a concern for users who value their privacy. Grammarly is best for English-language writer, sand it may not be as useful for users who write in other languages.

Duolingo: Duolingo prioritises vocabulary and sentence form over grammar [54]. This can assist beginners learn language, but it may not help advanced learners master grammar. Duolingo's language offerings may be limited compared to other language learning sites. This can hurt learners of rare languages. Duolingo is mostly self-paced. Duolingo offers many language classes, but customization is limited. For individualised learners, this can be a drawback. Its courses are useful for speaking language learning but academic writing and formal communication languages may not be possible to learn using Duolingo.

Teachable Machine: Teachable Machine lacks strong machine learning features [55]. Complex models and algorithms may not be possible. Teachable Machine has several customization options; however, it may be difficult to personalise material. For individualised learners, this can be a drawback. Teachable Machine primarily trains machine learning models for image, sound, and gesture detection. It may not be useful for learners who need other model training. For educators who desire a more complete solution, Teachable Machine may not interface effectively with other learning management systems or applications.

Carnegie Speech: Carnegie Speech primarily focuses on teaching English as a second language [56]. The language offerings may be limited in comparison to other online learning platforms, which can be a disadvantage for learners looking for courses in other languages. Carnegie Speech may not be as useful for learners who require language learning solutions for specific fields or industries. The platform's focus is on general language proficiency, and it may not offer specialized language courses.

Brainly: The accuracy of the answers on Brainly is not guaranteed [57], as anyone can answer the questions posted on the platform. Some answers may be incorrect, incomplete, or not well-explained, which can be a disadvantage for learners who rely on the platform for their studies. Brainly provides answers to specific questions but does not offer in-depth explanations or tutorials on a topic. This can be a disadvantage for learners who require a more comprehensive understanding of a subject.

Gradescope: Gradescope is primarily designed for grading assignments and exams that are in PDF or image format. It may not be as useful for grading assignments that require coding or other specialized formats [58]. Gradescope may not integrate well with other learning management systems or tools, which can be a disadvantage for instructors who require a more comprehensive solution for their grading needs.

Proctorio Proctorio demands device and data access [59], which may concern some users. Proctorio claims to offer strong security, however users should still use the software with caution. Proctorio may have technical challenges like inadequate internet connectivity or device compatibility that influence user experience. This may be a drawback for exam-challenged users. Users may feel uneasy using Proctorio's software. This may detract from the exam experience. Some educational institutions supply Proctorio, whereas others require students to buy it. This may prevent some students from enrolling.

Adaptemy: STEM-focused Adaptemy may not be suitable for students interested in other subjects. Its limited language availability may limit its accessibility for non-native English speakers [60]. Adaptemy offers personalised learning, but some educators and students may want more customization. Multiple-choice questions dominate Adaptemy's assessment tools, which may not accurately assess all aspects of student learning.

Lumen 5: Lumen5 has a simple interface, but some users may want more customization. Lumen5's 10-min video [61] limit may not meet some users' needs. Lumen5's font and colour selection may limit creativity. Lumen5's limited audio options may not suit all users.

Turnitin, Unicheck: These software's apply an algorithm to identify similarity between submitted papers [62]. and previously published content. Nevertheless, this algorithm is not always flawless and may occasionally identify non-plagiarized text as plagiarised. These applications may not be as successful at identifying plagiarism in languages except English and those for which it has extensive databases. Those might not be able to identify plagiarism in photographs or graphs, which could be a detriment for assignments that largely rely on visual resources. Both of these are a paid service; hence, certain institutions may be unable or unwilling to invest in it.

Calm: CALM may not be as effective in teaching or assessing language skills in languages other than English or those with substantial databases. CALM can offer engagement, but it may not be as successful as face-to-face interaction, limiting its language learning potential. CALM delivers automated feedback to students; however, some educators and students may prefer more thorough feedback, which may restrict its effectiveness as a learning tool. CALM may not provide enough customisation to fulfil individual learning demands.

Otter.ai: Otter.ai's transcription is accurate but not perfect [63]. Complex sentences or technical jargon may cause the software to make mistakes in the final transcript. Otter.ai can identify speakers, but if they have similar voices or speaking styles, it may not always be accurate. Otter.ai's transcription relies on audio quality. Poor audio quality or background noise may result in inaccurate or erroneous transcription. Otter.ai, like many speech recognition systems, may not recognise uncommon or specialised vocabulary, causing transcript errors. Otter.ai offers a free tier, but its advanced features and higher usage limits require a paid subscription. This may limit users who regularly transcribe large amounts of content.

Scrible: Scribble only supports a few languages [64], which can limit users who need to write in other languages. Scribble can recognise most handwriting, but it may struggle with highly stylized, artistic, or messy handwriting. Scribble is only available on Apple Pencil-equipped iPads running iPadOS 14 or later. Scribble's features may not be available to iPad users without an Apple Pencil. Scribble works with many of Apple's built-in apps, but third-party apps may not support it. This may limit non-Apple app users. Scribble is easy to use, but new users or those used to type or handwriting may need to learn.

ChatGPT: ChatGPT may not know everything despite being trained on a large corpus of text data [65]. It may be unable to answer some questions. ChatGPT may misinterpret a conversation or question and respond inappropriately. Complex or sophisticated topics require this. ChatGPT can answer questions and provide information, but it cannot offer emotional support or empathy. ChatGPT has privacy and security concerns like any online communication platform. Conversations may be recorded for analysis or training. ChatGPT can be customised based on user preferences or interactions, but it may not be as personalised as a human conversation partner. Coaching and counselling may be hampered by this.

4 Analysis of the Survey and Interview Result

After analyzing the capacity of each tool this research divides those tools in different areas of higher education which is shown in Fig. 2 to identify the impact of those in higher education.

After refining the AI tools in different learning aspects, this paper also conducted an experiment to understand the use of those tools in higher education by reading some research review, newspaper articles, and conducting interviews with a number of London, United Kingdom-based university students and teachers. This study surveyed 90 undergraduate students to determine how frequently and for what purposes they utilize AI tools. In the majority of survey questions, students were permitted to select several responses, allowing us to collect every conceivable response. We have questioned ninety students if they use any software, and one hundred per cent have responded positively. We analyze how these programs are utilized and which software is the most popular among them. The following chart in Fig. 3 illustrates their utilization for various software and purposes.

90% of students reported using Grammarly for spelling and grammar correction, as depicted in the pie chart on the left. 63% of students indicated that they utilize paraphrase tools. Only 10% of students use tools for language learning, whereas 36% of students reported using them for course-related learning, indicating that students utilize the tools mostly for coursework rather than active learning. Only 23% of undergraduate students reported using chatGPT to obtain precise responses, as it is not yet widely used among them. Five doctoral students were also given the same

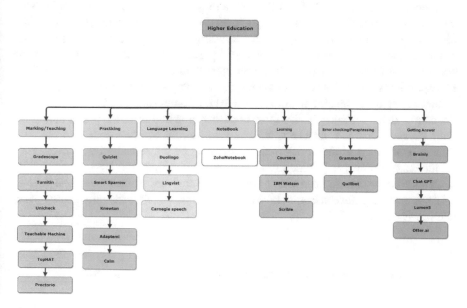

Fig. 2 Different AI tools used in different area of higher education

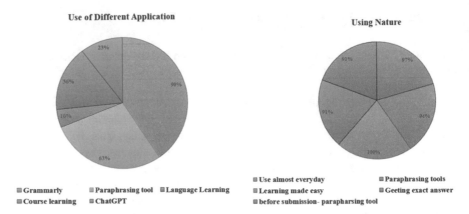

Fig. 3 A statistic of the different AI tools and their purpose used in HE

question, and they all said that they utilize chatGPT because, as research students, they find it quite useful. Additionally, Grammarly and other paraphrase programs were widely used by them. The graphic on the right depicts the frequency of usage of the tools that 97% of undergraduate students reported using almost daily. Concerned about plagiarizing, 94% of students claimed they mostly use paraphrase tools. 100% of the students reported that utilizing these tools simplified the learning process. 91% of students stated that they utilize tools such as chatGPT to find the correct answer rather than looking through several research papers. Students who answered that they mostly used the tools before submission they said mostly, they use paraphrasing tools on that time. The preceding graph in Fig. 4 illustrates student responses while discussing the benefits of using certain technologies and the classroom setting. The graph on the left demonstrates that seventy percent of students indicated that the simplicity of these tools helped them complete their assignments in less time. 20% of respondents stated that when searching for a legitimate answer, they use chatGPT to save the effort of reading many articles. 10% of them stated that having access to the course materials and practice quizzes at any time and from anywhere facilitates their learning. In the right chart, while answering about classroom environment- 70% of students said they miss student engagement while using these tools, 60% of students said they enjoy the discussion opportunities in the classroom, 40% of students said the classroom creates a competitive environment for them, and 90% of students said they have access to labs in institutions, which is actually absent when using software.

4.1 Interviewing the Professors and Doctorate Students

This study interviewed six university professors and five doctoral candidates. University Professors concurred that these technologies made it easier for students to learn,

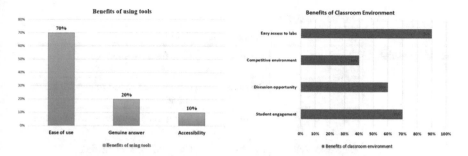

Fig. 4 Student response on the benefit of this AI tool on their HE

as they may submit their coursework through a portal and minimize plagiarism utilizing these tools. These tools also assist lecturers in grading student papers, but they are concerned about chatGPT as the number of students using it will increase day by day. Furthermore, students can acquire additional knowledge while researching a topic and reading relevant papers, as well as outside of the topic. However, by utilizing chatGPT, they will receive the desired response, which hinders their research skills and reduces their knowledge. In addition, some students may not read the answer before submitting the assignment, and even if they do, they will quickly forget it because the answer is readily available. While research helps them comprehend the idea and expand their knowledge base. While this study posed the same questions to post-doctoral students, it provides them with more space for investigation. They can generate an idea via chatGPT, but then they can access the actual resource and compare the veracity of the material. Both teachers and post-doctoral students concur that there should be a system that assists students in generating ideas, as well as a platform that requires students to generate their own understanding, so as not to hinder the actual process of acquiring knowledge. In addition, they suggested that students should have access to an online platform where they may perform practical work, as doing it on their own helped them retain the information for a longer period of time.

5 The Impact of AI Tools on Education

After analyzing the survey results this study has done a summary of the impact of using those tools in higher education which is shown in below Table 2.

Table 2 Summary of the influence of the AI tools in HE

Tools	Observation	Impact scale	Comments
Marking/teaching	Easy to use/ navigate	Positive	User friendly interface
	Easy to mark	Positive	Remove the hassle of checking paper copies
	Easy access to the resources	Positive	Can upload lectures from anywhere
	Easy feedback options	Positive	Can provide specific feedback
	Flexible work location	Positive	Can mark from anywhere, do not need to carry the physical copies
	Easy communication access	Positive	Can reply to student's query through portal or send an instant message to all students
	Online lecture facilities	Positive and Negative	Can take classes from home on emergency. However, students' engagement and participation are very less than the actual classroom environment
Practicing	Easy access	Positive	Can practice lessons form any where
	Instant Learning	Positive	Get the answers instantly
	Large number of information	Positive	Many questions to answer
	Lack of explanation	Negative	It provides the exact answer, lack of explanation
	Lack of different explanation method	Negative	It does not use several methods to explain same thing as each students have individual needs and need different explanation according to their needs
	Do not understand specific needs	Negative	It shows static answer
Language learning	Easy interfaces	Positive	Easy to navigate
	Practice platform	Positive	You can listen and speak and practice
	Vast words range	Positive	Helps increase vocabulary
	Use of words in different scenario	Negative	This software just mentions the sentence structure but not different scenarios for proper use of words
	Self-Practicing	Positive	You can practice by yourself whenever and wherever you want

(continued)

Table 2 (continued)

Tools	Observation	Impact scale	Comments
	Can loose motivation	Negative	While taking a course and practice with each other improves efficient learning and grows motivation in a social environment, which is missing in online learning
Note-Book	Instant note taking	Positive	Helps to take notes
Learning	Learn from anywhere	Positive	Takes courses and learn from anywhere anytime
	Good explanation	Positive	Videos with explanation, like real life lecture
	Good practice	Positive	Set of questionnaires to practice
	Certification	Positive	Earning certificate after completion of course
	Missing interaction	Negative	Lack of interaction with the lecturer as the lectures are video recorded
	Limited way of communication with tutor	Negative	Can only mail communication and wait for reply, two-way interaction is missing
	Lack of group discussion of seminar	Negative	Discuss only limited topic, as no relevant topic proposed by the fellow students
	Can miss something important	Negative	Lesson topics are fixed by the course instructor, cannot ask for further development in a similar topic
	Can loss interest/ motivation	Negative	Learning alone do not create a competitive environment
	Hard to access the progress	Negative	Hard to assess the actual skills of the students, as only paying the video (without watching it) and attempting quizzes multiple times can help them pass the course with certification but it can not define actual knowledge or hands on experience
Error checking and paraphrasing	Can catch spelling mistakes promptly	Positive	Easy to use and less time require
	Can suggest synonyms	Positive	Nice wordings
	Can suggest sentence structure	Positive	Provide useful sentence structure
	Cannot rely completely	Negative	While suggesting synonyms can suggest something irrelevant to the context

(continued)

Table 2 (continued)

Tools	Observation	Impact scale	Comments
	Change of sentence structure	Negative	While paraphrasing can change the actual meaning of the context
Getting answer	Very advance	Positive	Just write the question to get answer
	Nice sentence structure	Positive	Generate proper sentence structure
	Can be a barrier between learning and gaining knowledge	Negative	Students can just type and get the answer which hampers their actual learning or knowledge gaining process
	Can create dependency	Negative	Can be too dependent on the software which reduces the skills of research
	Can have invalid information	Negative	Those answers can be wrong as they are not reviewed by an expert channel/research team
	Can provide repetitive answer	Negative	For similar kind of question, it can provide the same/similar answer which hampers the originality of writing
	Can increase unethical practice	Negative	Students can just use this software to submit their coursework without having the actual knowledge

6   Proposed Integrated Framework

After analyzing the impact of these AI based tool this research found that AI-based tools have both positive and negative effects on higher education. Those apps can help users who are willing to learn on their own, even if they suffer from a lack of instruction, who want precise feedback, and who value and engage with others. Other than that, those apps can demotivate learners due to lack of engagement and participation, no specified deadline for course completion, and no learning goals like assignment submission or project production. Those can also boost unethical behavior, as university students can use them to accomplish their course work without learning it, risking a generation's education. According to Metro [66] there were 982,809 visits to the AI website from university Wi-Fi in January and 128,402 in December across eight Russell Group universities in UK, causing universities to fear a winter exam cheating epidemic. These reports show the exploitation of AI techniques that can create a generation of degree-holders without expertise.

Considering this scenario this paper come up with an idea of a framework which can be used as AI tool in terms of learning and also will have the barrier to restrict abuse. Below is the sitemap diagram in Fig. 5 for that proposed framework. This paper only showed the functional requirement of the proposed framework.

The above diagram in Fig. 5 is the initial idea of the proposed framework where purple colours indicate roles that can access what, while others indicate everyone

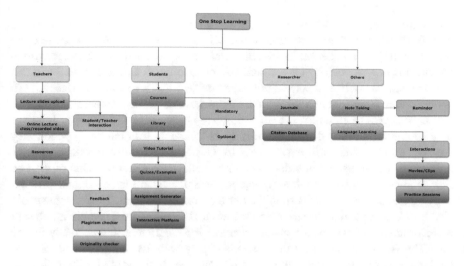

Fig. 5 Our proposed integrated framework

can access these facilities. Green blocks are role-specific facilities, blue blocks are dependent facilities. Red blocks are unique to this suggested system. Below is a summary Table 3 which includes the unique feature of this proposed system.

As you can see from the above picture- Teachers will have a system where they can post their lecture materials, as well as a community, blog, or comments feature where they can connect with students and where students can ask them any questions relating to the lecture. Even if the lecture was delivered in class, instructors' lectures should also be recorded in the system. Teachers will be able to add relevant resources to the system and share them with their group of pupils. The instructor will utilize

Table 3 Features of our proposed framework

Feature Name	Uniqueness
Originality checker	1. Checks if the answers are original 2. Checks if its not copied from other AI tools
Assignment checker	1. Own platform to provide answer 2. Do not accept copy and pasting 3. After limited number of words it will check the originality with other reports and other AI answer generated software's
Interactive platform	1. Provide interactive lab environment to the students according to their choice of department
Citation database	1. Provide list of maximum cited research paper in ascending order according to user's search
Movies/clips	1. Provide scenario-based clips to explain use of words in different scenarios
Practice sessions	1. Provide separate platform for the users who are willing to practice speaking new language together in different scenarios

the same platform to grade student copies. The current solutions provide professors with feedback and plagiarism detection services. In the suggested framework, we present an originality checker that verifies whether or not the responses were written by students or generated by other tools. To implement that a limit can be set so that this software can only accept texts published in the portal's specific interface, which is linked to another function for students known as Assignment Generator. Students will have access to all courses, even if they are not enrolled in that topic, however they should be prevented from submitting assignments for courses in which they are not enrolled. They will have access to the library, all video tutorials, practice quizzes, and prior exams in order to practice with those materials. One of the two new features described is the assignment generator. This feature should prohibit copying and pasting; students should enter their responses here. This system should also have a fast plagiarism check so that when students write a sample number of words, such as 500 words, the system checks for plagiarism instantaneously for the first 500 words and then asks the students if they want to continue or recheck. If the learner wishes to proceed, this system should verify the same for the following 500 words. Students will be compelled to read and analyse the subject on their own, rather than simply pasting text from somewhere else, as a result of this system's ongoing warnings. In addition to comparing the answers to the submitted papers, it should also compare the answers to those created by other AI systems, which would prevent plagiarism and force students to study the material. Additionally, students should have access to an interactive platform where they may observe the practical application of their work. For instance, there should be an interactive platform for all lab-required courses. Using this interactive platform, a chemical student will be able to mix the solution and view the resulting product. With a clear set of instructions, students will be able to learn the actual topic, even if they do not attend the in-class lab activity.

This integrated system should include a database of citations that is available to all researchers. It will allow users to search for a certain topic and get a list of the most cited papers for that topic, allowing them to rapidly locate relevant research. There will be some elements open to anyone who want to take notes or learn a new language, regardless of their role. In language learning features, there should be brief clips or films that explain to the learner the various uses of a single word in several contexts, hence enhancing the correct usage of words. In addition, when a user is logged into a specific language, they will be able to see other users who are there at the same time and send them a request to practice together. If the other user accepts, they will be taken to an interactive session where they can practice speaking together or solving quizzes together.

7 Challenges of This Study

While conducting the result this research faces some challenges which can have an impact on the outcome of this research.

- **Getting honest response**: When asked specific questions, such as "In their opinion, does the use of AI tools, such as chatGPT, enhance the learning experience, or are they only utilizing it to get the correct answer? ", students were unwilling to express their honest opinion. The majority of students were unable to answer the question, with some stating that it helps learning by providing the specific answer, but also makes them too lazy to explore for other viable answers. Some students acknowledge that they relied on software rather than reading the course material. It was difficult to identify the actual impact of using these tools because students are more comfortable answering yes or no questions than offering their opinions. In addition, few students believe that their freedom to use these AI technologies will be restricted if they provide honest feedback.
- **Testing all the features**: It was rather difficult to test all the features of the above-mentioned tools, but this study utilized the free versions of all of them and generate the report according to that.

8 Limitations of Our Study

The limitations observed when carrying out this study are listed below.

- **Purchasing options**: While analysing the capabilities of these AI tools, this study is unable to analyse the purchase options for all of the tools mentioned. Rather, the research was conducted using the free versions of these programs.
- **Survey result**: While conducting the survey, this study surveyed 90 undergraduate computer science students and 5 doctoral students, and interviewed 6 computing lecturers, and assessed the impact of using these tools based on their responses.
- **Research location**: This study survey was conducted just in London, United Kingdom. In terms of the use of AI tools, different scenarios may exist in various nations, which this research report does not compare.
- **Lack of analysis for primitive process of learning**: This study primarily discusses the impact of AI tools on higher education, but no research was conducted on basic learning processes, such as classroom learning, learning from books and labs, etc. Thus, it does not compare learning with AI tools to learning in a classroom setting; rather, it only discusses the impact of employing AI tools for learning.
- **Lack of analysis on course content**: This study analysed the lecture's content and delivery effectiveness by enrolling in a few of the free courses. However, not all courses were viewed; those were selected from the courses with the highest ratings, which is provided by the previous students. These lectures' content is not

approved by any appropriate board members, so this research cannot comment on the efficiency of those course material or pattern.

9   Conclusion

Twenty-four AI tools generally used in higher education were gone over the chapter. All tools are classified into seven classes based on their purposes such as marking/teaching, practicing, language learning, notebook, learning, error checking/paraphrasing, and getting answer. In the analysis of their features, it is clear that the tools are very proficient in specific task. In teaching, distance learning AI tools has added new dimensions especially during pandemic. The hassles like traffic, time of movement, writing in board, attendance and so on have been reduced. But the attention break, eye communication, understanding of student's emotion and so on are hampered. In the survey data analysis, around all the students use often Grammarly, paraphrasing tool, chatGPT in writing their assignment, thesis proposal and manuscript writing. Most of them provided positive vote. But there are some ethical issues also said by some professors and researchers. Similarly, in diversity analysis, some of shortcomings are available in each of the tools. Integrating these shortcoming and existing features, we have proposed a framework to resolve all the issues. The problems less competency in teaching in LDC countries and the learning issues about the disable students also can be solved with our proposed AI framework. However, the study is successfully completed with great effort of our team. The challenges and limitations of our study are already listed in the previous sections. In future study, the researchers can easily grasp them for further improvement. The students, researchers, teachers, professors and national education policymakers can be benefited by reading this study to adopt the positive transformation of education with the use of AI tools.

Authors Contribution Musarrat Saberin Nipun contributed prominently in capacity analysis of each AI tool, surveying students, teachers, professors and researcher's response and proposing an integrated framework. She also presented the impact of using AI tools in HE and discussed the challenges this research has faced and explained the limitation of this research work. Md. Simul Hasan Talukder performed the literature review extensively and proposed the methodology of how the research could be carried out. He planned the main scheme of the chapter framework. He also participated in writing the abstract, conclusion and formatting of the chapter. Usman Butt reviewed the full chapter and helped in surveying the response of the user also added valuable insights into the results. Finally, Rejwan Bin Sulaiman shared his valuable ideas in title selection, manuscript writing and lead the whole project.

Funding There has no funding in carrying out our study.

References

1. David LO, Nwulu NI, Aigbavboa CO, Adepoju OO (2022) Integrating fourth industrial revolution (4IR) technologies into the water, energy & food nexus for sustainable security: a bibliometric analysis. J Clean Prod 363:132522
2. Talukder MSH, Sarkar AK (2023) Nutrients deficiency diagnosis of rice crop by weighted average ensemble learning. Smart Agricultural Tech 4:100155
3. Moshtari M, Safarpour A (2023) Challenges and strategies for the internationalization of higher education in low-income East African countries. Higher Educ, 1–21.
4. Iqbal K, Ashraf S (2023) Perspective chapter: the barriers in inclusive set-up for students with visual impairment at higher education level-Pakistan scenario. In: Higher education-reflections from the field. IntechOpen
5. Parveen K, Phuc TQB, Shafiq M, Wei TX (2021) Identifying the administrative challenges encountered by the principals in low-performing public secondary schools of Faisalabad District, Pakistan. Int J Human Innov (IJHI) 4(1):5–16
6. Ahmed HU, Hoque MR (2019) Identifying and addressing the challenges faced by students with visual impairments in accessing education and learning contents in relation to ICT: the case of the tertiary education in Bangladesh. Int J Educ Knowledge Manage, 1–11
7. Sánchez AA (2023) Experiences and challenges of indigenous students in higher education during the pandemic. In: Handbook of research on revisioning and reconstructing higher education after global crises. IGI Global, pp 288–304
8. Park SH, Hwang JY, Lee JH (2021) Personalized medical education using artificial intelligence: a systematic review. BMC Med Educ 21(1):1–10. https://doi.org/10.1186/s12909-021-02684-4
9. Shariat SF, Hamdy H, Soltani Arabshahi K, Jalili M (2021) Personalized medical education: a review of the current status, opportunities, and challenges. Med Teach 43(5):499–505. https://doi.org/10.1080/0142159X.2021.1883287
10. Ahmed MA, Elsayed TS (2020) Personalized E-learning system based on adaptive educational hypermedia and artificial intelligence for medical education. J Med Syst 44(2):1–15. https://doi.org/10.1007/s10916-019-1548-9
11. Nižnanová M, Švecová L (2021) Adaptive testing in education: benefits and challenges. Education Sciences 11(2):72. https://doi.org/10.3390/educsci11020072
12. Tawfik AA, El-Said MA, Al-Mallah MH (2021) Adaptive testing with artificial intelligence: a systematic review. Educ Technol Soc 24(1):229–245
13. Zheng R, Li J, Chen C, Liao C (2021) A comparative study of three adaptive testing methods based on artificial intelligence. Front Psychol 12:709586. https://doi.org/10.3389/fpsyg.2021.709586
14. Ali A, Khan MA, Hayat M (2021) The role of artificial intelligence in adaptive testing. J Educ Comp Res 59(4):551–574. https://doi.org/10.1177/0735633120940861
15. Parra D, Rodríguez JM (2020) An artificial intelligence adaptive testing system based on fuzzy logic for mathematics education. J Educ Comp Res 57(3):652–673. https://doi.org/10.1177/0735633119888467
16. Gikas J, Grant MM (2013) Mobile computing devices in higher education: student perspectives on learning with cellphones, smartphones & social media. The Internet and Higher Education 19:18–26. https://doi.org/10.1016/j.iheduc.2013.06.002
17. Giannakos MN, Sampson DG (2016) Automated grading of programming assignments: an approach based on instructor customization and student modeling. J Educ Technol Soc 19(3):238–251
18. Hsieh CT, Yeh HT (2020) Automated scoring of Chinese writing by using deep learning. Educ Technol Soc 23(4):226–239
19. Liu R, Koedinger KR (2016) Using deep learning to generate feedback on students' rule-based problem solving. In: Proceedings of the Sixth International Conference on Learning Analytics & Knowledge, pp 143–152. ACM. https://doi.org/10.1145/2883851.2883913

20. VanLehn K (2011) The relative effectiveness of human tutoring, intelligent tutoring systems, and other tutoring systems. Educ Psychol 46(4):197–221. https://doi.org/10.1080/00461520.2011.611369
21. Baker RS (2016) The state of educational data mining in 2016: a review and future visions. J Educ Data Mining 8(1):1–18
22. Koedinger KR, Corbett AT (2006) Cognitive tutors: technology bringing learning science to the classroom. In: Handbook of Educational Psychology, Routledge, pp 645–654
23. Romero C, Ventura S (2013) Educational data mining: a review of the state of the art. IEEE Trans Syst, Man, Cybernetics: Syst 43(6):828–842. https://doi.org/10.1109/TSMCA.2013.2258018
24. Baker RS, Inventado PS (2014) Educational data mining and learning analytics. In: Handbook of research on educational communications and technology, Springer, pp 277–294. https://doi.org/10.1007/978-1-4614-3185-5_21
25. Sanosi AB (2018) The effect of Quizlet on vocabulary acquisition. Asian J Educ e-learning 6(4)
26. Korableva O, Durand T, Kalimullina O, Stepanova I (2019) Studying user satisfaction with the MOOC platform interfaces using the example of coursera and open education platforms. In: Proceedings of the 2019 International Conference on Big Data and Education, pp 26–30, March
27. Bagheri MM (2015) Intelligent and adaptive tutoring systems: How to integrate learners. Int J Educ 7(2):1–16
28. Shen L, Chen I, Grey A, Su A (2021) Teaching and learning with artificial intelligence. In: Impact of AI technologies on teaching, learning, and research in higher education. IGI Global, pp 73–98
29. Ghufron MA, Rosyida F (2018) The role of grammarly in assessing English as a Foreign Language (EFL) writing. Lingua Cultura 12(4):395–403
30. Teske K (2017) Duolingo. Calico J 34(3):393–401
31. High R (2012) The era of cognitive systems: an inside look at IBM Watson and how it works. IBM Corporation, Redbooks 1:16
32. Pisău A (2019) Smart learning suite online în procesul educațional la matematică. In: Tradiție și inovație în educație, Vol 2, pp 132–139
33. Carney M, Webster B, Alvarado I, Phillips K, Howell N, Griffith J, Chen A, et al (2020) Teachable machine: approachable web-based tool for exploring machine learning classification. In: Extended abstracts of the 2020 CHI conference on human factors in computing systems, pp 1–8, April
34. Boyd SD (1975) Insights on speech evaluation from Toastmasters and Dale Carnegie
35. Choi E, Munoz R, Mukhlas D, Balak M, Farias L, Jara D, Burkov O, et al (2016) Understanding user motivations for asking and answering a question on brainly, online social learning network. In: Conference 2016 Proceedings
36. Singh A, Karayev S, Gutowski K, Abbeel P (2017) Gradescope: a fast, flexible, and fair system for scalable assessment of handwritten work. In: Proceedings of the fourth (2017) acm conference on learning@ scale, pp 81–88, April
37. Berger P (2010) Student inquiry and Web 2.0. School Library Monthly 26(5):14–17
38. Heldner C (1989) Pippi Långstrump som lingvist. En Tvärsnitt: humanistisk och samhällsvetenskaplig forskning 11:41–49
39. Zeng M, Li J, Peng Z (2006) The design of top-hat morphological filter and application to infrared target detection. Infrared Phys Technol 48(1):67–76
40. Bergmans L, Bouali N, Luttikhuis M, Rensink A (2021) On the efficacy of online Proctoring using Proctorio. CSEDU 1:279–290
41. Ghergulescu I, Flynn C, O'Sullivan C (2015). Adaptemy science: adaptive learning for science for next generation classroom. In: E-Learn: World Conference on E-Learning in Corporate, Government, Healthcare, and Higher Education. Association for the Advancement of Computing in Education (AACE), pp 1477–1482

42. Khilnani P, Goldstein B, Todres ID (1991) Double lumen umbilical venous catheters in critically ill neonates: a randomized prospective study. Crit Care Med 19(11):1348–1351
43. Mphahlele A, McKenna S (2019) The use of turnitin in the higher education sector: decoding the myth. Assess Eval High Educ 44(7):1079–1089
44. Kolesnikov A (2019) Academic dignity in the Ukrainian educational space: problems and social threats. Regional Aspects Product Forces Develop of Ukraine 24:122–128
45. Henderson D, Woodcock H, Mehta J, Khan N, Shivji V, Richardson C, Burns A (2020) Keep calm and carry on learning: using Microsoft teams to deliver a medical education programme during the COVID-19 pandemic. Future Healthcare J 7(3):e67
46. Sterne J, Sawhney M (2022) The acousmatic question and the will to Datafy: Otter. ai, low-resource languages, and the politics of machine listening. Kalfou 9(2):288–306
47. Gautam A, Dua A (2021) Applications of artificial intelligence in open and distance learning
48. Rudolph J, Tan S, Tan S (2023) ChatGPT: Bullshit spewer or the end of traditional assessments in higher education? J Appl Learn Teach 6(1)
49. Hikmah D, Hannan A (2019) Quizlet: A digital media for learning informatics terms. Int J English Educ Linguis (IJoEEL) 1(1):1–9
50. Dron J (2018) Smart learning environments, and not so smart learning environments: a systems view. Smart Learn Environ 5(1):1–20
51. Vegesna R (2012) Collaboration in context: from the desktop to the cloud. In: 2012 45th Hawaii International Conference on System Sciences, pp 669–673, January. IEEE.
52. Ma S, Steger DG, Doolittle PE, Stewart AC (2018) Improved academic performance and student perceptions of learning through use of a cell phone-based personal response system. J Food Sci Educ 17(1):27–32
53. Zinkevich NA, Ledeneva TV (2021) Using grammarly to enhance students' academic writing skills. Professional Discour Commun 3(4):51–63
54. Su F, Zou D (2022) Learning English with the mobile language learning application 'Duolingo': the experiences of three working adults at different proficiency levels. Inter J Mobile Learn Organisation 16(4):409–428
55. Kacorri H (2017) Teachable machines for accessibility. ACM SIGACCESS Accessib Comput 119:10–18
56. Kannan J, Munday P (2018) New trends in second language learning and teaching through the lens of ICT, networked learning, and artificial intelligence
57. Le LT, Shah C, Choi E (2019) Assessing the quality of answers autonomously in community question–answering. Int J Digit Libr 20(4):351–367
58. Kumar A, Walter A, Manolios P (2023) Automated grading of automata with ACL2s. arXiv preprint arXiv:2303.05867
59. Jaggia S, Kelly A, Lertwachara K, Chen L (2020) Business analytics. McGraw-Hill US Higher Ed USE
60. Ghergulescu I, Flynn C, O'Sullivan C (2015) Adaptemy–Building the next generation classroom. In: EdMedia+ innovate learning. Association for the Advancement of Computing in Education (AACE), pp 86–95
61. Sewell C, Theobald A (2020) It's all about the timing: Developing online training resources for the post-COVID world. Online Searcher 44(6):20–23
62. Jones KO (2008). Practical issues for academics using the Turnitin plagiarism detection software. In: Proceedings of the 9th International Conference on Computer Systems and Technologies and Workshop for PhD Students in Computing, pp IV-1, June
63. Gaber M, Corpas-Pastor G (2021) Automatic speech recognition systems for interpreters: Spoken corpora exploitation by interpreter trainers and trainees
64. Yoshida N, Hu R, Neykova R, Ng N (2014) The scribble protocol language. In: Trustworthy Global Computing: 8th International Symposium, TGC 2013, Buenos Aires, Argentina, August 30–31, 2013, Revised Selected Papers 8. Springer International Publishing, pp 22–41

65. De Angelis L, Baglivo F, Arzilli G, Privitera GP, Ferragina P, Tozzi AE, Rizzo C (2023) ChatGPT and the rise of large language models: the new AI-driven infodemic threat in public health. Available at SSRN 4352931
66. Students made 1,000,000 visits to ChatGPT fuelling fears of a cheating epidemic. https://metro.co.uk/2023/03/22/universities-fear-cheating-epidemic-after-a-million-visits-to-chatgpt-18483618/

Development of a Decentralized Personal Indefinable Information (PII) Management Systems Using Blockchain dBFT Consensus Algorithm

Yunus Kareem and Hamid Jahankhani

Abstract Personal Identifiable Information (PII) management has been a major focus in data management due to the level of threat against it. Personally identifiable information is generally protected by an identity system whose roots can be traced to a centralized application whose data are saved in a database and can be retrieved through authentication using a username and password. Federated Identity management systems evolve because centralised systems get easily compromised and as a result, lots of PII data are exposed. Continuous breaches against these legacy systems have been the major concern of researchers, also the need for users to be in control of their PII data as stated in article 4 of GDPR. The aim of this research is to adopt a qualitative and design science research method to achieve the gap in the existing decentralized identity system which includes consensus algorithms, quantum-safe, compliance to GDPR policies, governance, development language, and scalability among others. This led to the use of Neo 3 blockchain in contrast to the common Ethereum and Hyperledger used by the existing system. This work has shown a new direction to safeguarding users' data considering the technological factors in decentralized Identity management and has developed a framework that future work can lean on to develop a Decentralised Application for a dBFT PII management system.

Keywords dBFT · PII · GDPR · Personal identifiable information · Blockchain · Neo 3

1 Introduction

Everyday witnesses lots of data collections out of which the most important and most targeted data by the attacker are personal data. Many recorded breaches have shown us how this data is used by criminals to either steal from the entity or pretend to be the entity while carrying out their criminal activities. Due to this, the need for information

Y. Kareem · H. Jahankhani (✉)
Northumbria University London, London, UK
e-mail: Hamid.jahankhani@northumnbria.ac.uk

confidentiality and integrity cannot be over emphasis. Research has shown most of this data got exposed because of unsecured identity and access management systems. This work focus on using delegated byzantine fault tolerance (dBFT) blockchain consensus algorithm to develop and manage personal identifiable information (PII).

Before the advent of blockchain, identity management has been the responsibility of individual organizations which is generally referred to as centralized. In a centralized identity management system, users manage their data after being granted access using a username and password. This mechanism has led to a proliferation of credentials and witnessed lots of attacks such as brute force attacks, dictionary attacks, and many others. Although much work was done to improve this system such as multifactor authentication, password manager, and setting password pattern but the technology used has called for remodification of intent which leads to the advent of federated identity. Federated Identity has given users the ability to use fewer passwords because of the single sign-on feature (SSO). Although it is built on a centralized system, the uniqueness of having a single system responsible for managing users' authentication and access to data also limit the breaches of data, as well as give small business an opportunity to leverage on high security set aside by identity providers. Federated Identity systems have been known for years as a saviour in identity and management systems, not until some of them were attacked, and the need for individuals to have control of who has access to their data arose. Decentralize identity evolve few years ago to solve the most pressing issue of an identity management system which is giving individuals control over who has access to their data, with Sovrin, MyData, Waypoint among others leading the way, the future of decentralizing identity management is promising. Just like the previous IdM systems, the technology used is important as it is responsible for its robustness, cost implication, and security of the system. Most of the known decentralized identity management systems as solved the major problem leaving behind the technology problem. A good example is Waypoint uses the Ethereum blockchain which is known for its low processing speed and requires high computing power to mine ether. This weakness calls for scalable and more efficient blockchain technology which is one of the objectives of this work.

The increasing PII data theft in cyberspace has been the motivation for this work. The internet has been filled with news on attacks of PII yearly and all the approach to curb it hasn't been successful. Just this year, companies such as Microsoft, News Corp, Red Cross, Ronin, and Flex Booker witnessed a heavy cyber-attack with millions of PII data being exposed to attackers [1]. This occurrence of exposure of PII has led to many works on PII management systems. Centralized, Federated and Decentralised Identity management system are the common means of managing and securing PII systems. The record of attacks on centralized and federated PII management system has shown that both technology is not enough to secure and protect the interest of individual PII. Decentralised Identity management has proven its efficiency with the uniqueness of users having absolute control of their PII data and can revoke access to it in case of breach or attack. Contributing to this growing technology in the area of tracking PII accesses and choosing decentralised technology with less compute power such as Decentralised Byzantine Fault Tolerance (dBFT) is the main focus of this work. This work will explain the concept of identity, why PII needs to be stored and controlled by its owner and will also guide the reader on how effective blockchain is towards providing a lasting solution for an identity management system.

2 Literature Review

In the present age, data has been the most important asset, businesses need data in the development and delivery of services. One of the major sources of data collection is the internet. As the number of internet users rises dramatically each year, so does the data gather volume. According to research, there are 4.66 million internet users, of whom 4.2 million use social media regularly. This has demonstrated that social networking sites (SNS) are used to acquire more data than any other platform. An example of data collected via the internet is personal data.

2.1 Personal Data

Personal data refers to information that reflects a user's characteristics such as age, address, name, etc. According to Information Commissioner's Office (ICO), data can be described as personal data if it has the following characteristics: "identifability, has a relationship with, Obvious data about an individual, data linked to an individual, purpose, biographical significance and concrete information about an individual" [2]. Personal data has been used as a source of wealth for some companies that focus on trading this information for marketing and another purpose without considering the privacy of the owner.

There are two main categories of this data: Non-Personal Identifiable Information (NPII) and Personal Identifiable Information (PII) [3]. Non-PII is general information also refer to as anonymous data. This data on its own cannot be used to identify an individual and can be found openly such as cookies data, device type, time zone screen size, etc. Businesses typically gather non-PII data to monitor and comprehend their customers' online activities. They can then use this to enhance the user experience and engagement of consumers online. PII is described by the Department of Homeland Security (DHS) as "any information that permits the identity of an individual to be directly or indirectly inferred, including any information which is linked or linkable to that individual".

The publication of William Prosser's seminal work classifying privacy tort law into four categories in 1960 marked a subsequent turning point in the law of privacy. Contrary to Warren and Brandeis, who based their theories of the right to privacy on ideas derived from European philosophy, Prosser was willing to create several simple classifications that, over time, were able to assume a doctrinal role. But he did not address the PII problem, unlike Warren and Brandeis. Prosser essentially thought that privacy torts only apply in cases involving an identified individual.

2.2 PII and Privacy

If Privacy is becoming more important because of the increasing number of data that businesses produce, manage, and store. The growing in complexity of computing environments more than the way they use to be, rapidly incorporating the public cloud, the company data centre, and several edge devices, such as robots, remote servers, and Internet of Things (IoT) sensors. It is more difficult to secure and monitor data due to the expanded attack surface caused by this complexity [4].

Whether PII is involved often determines the scope of privacy legislation. The fundamental premise of the applicable laws is that there cannot be privacy harm if PII is not implicated [4]. Privacy laws in their various forms typically prohibit unconstrained handling of PII, though they do not recognize sensitive versus non-sensitive PII [5]. Sensitivity often appears to depend on context, which makes it difficult to represent in a simple language analysis, yet, this does not rule out the possibility of "context-free" sensitivity as proposed by Al-Fedaghi and Al-Azmi [4]. Furthermore, establishing context-free sensitivity can deliver a preliminary categorization of data that can then be improved by a knowledge-based system, a manual method, or both. Regardless of the setting, a report about a certain person has some relevance for that person (e.g., they were talking about you). When the name of the identified individual is mentioned in connection with a behaviour, the matter is sensitive regardless of the context. Identifying sensitive data categories, particularly those that contain personally identifiable information, has proven to be challenging in practice (PII), [4]. According to Jocelyn Mackie in her article published on the TermsFeed website describe Sensitive information as a sort of personal data that can make a person susceptible to discrimination or harassment if discovered. Personal information is protected by law, but sensitive information receives additional attention due to the potential influence on an individual's livelihood, quality of life, and capacity to engage in daily, [6]. General Data Protection Regulation (GDPR) deems the following to be sensitive personal information: Racial or ethnic origin, Political opinions, Religious or philosophical beliefs, Trade union membership, Genetic data, and Biometric data [7]. According to article 6 of GDPR, this type of data can only be processed lawfully under extremely limited circumstances some of which are, when consent is given, for contract, as a compliance mechanism with a legal obligation, vital interest, public interest, and legitimate interest.

In other to further understand the rank in sensitivity, Bing suggested ranking the sensitivity of PII as follows: (1) Inherently private, sensitive information (such as medical or sexual information); (2) Judgmental information that might be harmful to the data subject, and (3) Biographical information that allows access to more private information [8]. Al-Fedaghi further improve on Bings' work by providing a semi-automated system for PII sensitivity measurement starting from basic values that can be manually and automatically improved through evaluations. The methodology is based on breaking down PII into its component parts (such as the identified person versus the action) and types (e.g., a single person vs relationship among persons). He further gives a syntactical foundation for answering the question of why some PII is more sensitive than other PII by constructing sensitivity assessments upon linguistic units. The method uses linguistic analysis to identify the "tendencies" of various forms of PII that arouse various degrees of sensitivity [4].

2.3 Information Management System

Evolution of information technology has transformed the way information are managed. The old method of information management on paper has seen a big challenge from database management and its migration to it has come with lots of challenges among which is privacy. Identity information management system evolve to solve the rising challenges in managing user data. Rosencrance and Mathias [9] define Identity management as a method of ensuring controlled access to information and also an avenue to maintain confidentiality, integrity and availability of information. Owing to the importance of Identity management systems Hansen et al. [10] explain how identity system has contributed positively to use of digital device in authentication and authorisation in their work "Identity management throughout one's whole life". They also describe identity life cycles as creation, evolution, and revocation. Identity management (IdM) is becoming increasingly popular as a medium of authentication and authorization between customers and service providers, the credit agency as It makes it easier for users to use Internet services, encourages service providers to improve their offerings, and increases internet security. The most valuable information resource an identity provider (IdP) may use to offer a variety of services is personally identifiable information (PII). Due to the users' sensitivity, it has become a severe issue that PII is leaked, loosely managed, unlawfully chosen, and unlawfully accessed [11]. Different companies (small, medium and large) manage users data including PII using the conventional database system which has diverse security level. This has contributed to loss of data before the advent of identity as a service, provided by companies such as Microsoft, Amazon, IBM etc. with the aim to centralise Identity management to a more secured infrastructure also known as federated identity. Attack on some of this infrastructure as call the attention of researcher such as Alruwies et al. [12] in their work to better improve on the services provided by Identity and Access management (IAM) service providers. They proposed an IT governance and a framework for Identity management in IT infrastructure with a privilege access management which are basically cybersecurity compliance strategies and policies. Chen et al. [11] Differentiated security levels for personal identifiable information in identity management system is another work that see to the importance of PII protection in identity management system. They develop a novel framework that uses data mining to predict future information asset value and ways it can be protected. Their work has two stages, the first stage analyses the database containing the PII with the help of the data mining tools and predict the level of security to be given to it, the higher the PII discover the more security measures to be deployed. The second stage analyses the history of illegal access and attacks and thus, use it to redevelop the decision tree and as well update the knowledge base. The need for end user given the full privilege of managing their PII are still a major concern as the goal of privacy is achieved when the control of access lies in the hand of end user not the service provider, company, or government. Developing a privacy enhanced identity management system comes with several challenges among which is getting government and private sector interest in other to create identity management solutions that preserve user privacy while striking the ideal balance between user ease and faultless data protection, [13]. An example of such enhanced identity system which gives individuals control over their data especially PII is seen in a legal framework by European Union (EU). This framework, established with the aim of giving EU citizen control over their in a project called PRIME (Privacy and Identity Management for Europe). The goal of PRIME is to give citizen the power to control the information collected from them using pseudo-identities, cryptography and certifications when interacting with vendors and service providers. Also they aim to give individuals power to have say on policies regarding their privacy with service provider on data usage and guidelines towards safeguarding it [14]. The PRIME project has been a blueprint for Identity management and privacy and as a result, many researchers have worked on similar or more advanced identity management systems using technologies such as blockchain, leveraging on its decentralized nature and high level of privacy.

2.4 Blockchain for Identity Management System

Blockchain, popularly known for its high level of privacy, integrity, and security has been seen as the most promising approach to users' control of their identity [15]. A decentralized distributed ledger technology that allows peer-to-peer communication on a distributed database has witness lots of research attention which identity and access control is among most researched topics. Blockchain consist of blocks that are linked together using cryptography. These blocks consist of records of transactions, cryptography hash of the block before it and time stamp, thus, allow it to be linked together to form a chain. These chains are hosted on a distributed network call node and a validated by hash code. Hash code creation in blockchain is through a high computation algorithm which can take main frame computer millions of years to decrypt. A transaction is said to be considered genuine when it has received the consent of every participant in the network. The approval task is accomplished by using the Consensus process. Only once the transaction has been validated does the block become an integral component of the blockchain. The network is known as a blockchain because it is continuously expanding and is connected to immutable blocks [16]. Blockchain can be of three main types, Public, consortium or federated

Table 1 Blockchain type comparison

Properties	Public	Private	Consortium
Authority	Decentralised	Not decentralized	Partially decentralized
Access	Anyone	Limited ()	Limited
Identity	Anonymous	Trusted	Trusted
Transaction speed	Low	High	High
Consensus mechanism	Open	Restricted by vote	Restricted by vote
Cost	Expensive	Cheap	Cheap
Data handling	Open	Controlled	Controlled
Immutability	Fully	Partial	Partial

and private [17]. Public blockchain are permissionless, it gives rooms to public participation with privilege to write and read access to the chain. Users have the freedom to transact freely and anonymously, a good example of this is bitcoin and Ethereum. Unlike the public blockchain, private blockchain are permission based. They are mostly used by an entity (e.g., organisation, district and association), restricted to permitted users and doesn't allow anonymity. Ripple (XRP) and Hyperledger are the common examples of private blockchain [18]. Consortium of Federated blockchain also refer to as a semi–private blockchain is a type of blockchain which are govern by multiple entities. They are like private blockchain but more robust as it contains more than one organisation. Consortium blockchain are also permission base. Table 1 shows the comparison of the common types of blockchain [16].

Blockchain adoption in several applications has grown since 2008 when it started with finance (bitcoin) and now has span through several sectors from Health, education, Internet of things, privacy and security, identity and access management, Business and Industry, data management, and entertainment. These applications are built with several blockchain framework such as Ethereum, Hyperledger fabric, Neo, R3 Corda, Hyperledger Sawtooth, Multichain, Monax, Open Blockchain etc.

Blockchain has been see to be the technology for next generation of identity management systems due to the performance of some blockchain base identity system such as uPort, Sovrin and ShoCard [19]. Some blockchain identity management system is summarised alongside other PII management works in the next section.

2.5 Related Works

Managing personal identifiable information is a domain where lots of research has been done as far back as 1995 when the internet is introduced. According to Gutierrez [20], digital identity evolve from the idea of centralise identity, then Federated identity in 2006 and presently there are ongoing research on user-centric identity,

Self-sovereign identity and decentralise identity. He further highlights some of the problem of identity which include identity theft, Fraud, impersonation, compliance and regulation, cost, complexity and unreliability, privacy and safety and acceptability [20].

Hansen et al. [10] explain how identity should be managed throughout one's live in their journal where they described the major challenges to identity as ensuring privacy and proper handling of sensitive information (PII). They lay down four mechanism which are: user-controlled privacy, under which they talked about Handling of partial identity, data minimisation, enforcing rules for data processing, and transparency functionality. Other mechanism span through all areas of life, stages of life and full life span. Their work focusses more on process and way's identity actors can ensuring identity protection throughout one's live and not technology bonded. They adopt several works theory to propose a mechanism and concluded that for security and privacy of identity, awareness of security measures and privacy issues is required by all participating bodies.

Paul De Hert [13] explains the human write view regarding managing PII with E-ID identity management. He describes the major challenge of ensuring privacy enhanced identity management to be getting government consent and support in their areas of data processing, legislator, and policies. He further explains how the sponsorship of PRIME project has shown some level of interest of EU government on self-sovereignty identity. He proposed that attaining this goal can only be possible by an anonymous credential system with an access control system base in novel paradigm, a negotiation functionality, and a reasoning system. He believes this will work together to achieve privacy and allow individuals to contribute to the effect.

One of the best technologies that has been used in the ensuring PII are secured and are managed with freedom by the owners is blockchain. A review of Identity management system using blockchain was carried out by a [15] where they search for published English based relative works using the key word "Blockchain and Identity" and a filter year of May 2017 to January 2020 on various academic databases. The aim of this research is to have a template which will highlight the research gap and benefit associated with using blockchain for Identity management system. They briefly explain the challenges of identity management system in terms of Access and resources, and trust. Also, the gave some comparison on some of the established blockchain identity management system and proposed IdM system at that time. They agreed on the fact that blockchain is the next technology for identity and proposed that future work should pay more attention to adopting unique mechanism as the primary justification for account reset.

Lim et al. [21] discuss more how self-sovereign is next level of identity, they emphasis on the role of blockchain and discuss more on some blockchain powered identity management system. Their work further highlight the open issues of this systems, challenges which include managing access key which are common attributed to server and federated environment, and also verification of users identity since there is no one responsible for the act and suggest how future work can better this work by including zero knowledge of proof as a bases of extension.

In other to safeguard identity privacy, the zero-knowledge proof (ZKP) was employed by [22], in their research of a Blockchain-and-ZKP-based digital identity management system (BZDIMS). The ZKP is one of the cryptographic approaches that allows the prover to convince the verifier that a certain claim is true without giving the verifier any more information or revealing any details about the witness. The claim could be that the prover is aware of the hash value's preimage or that they are aware of a member of a Merkle tree whose Merkle root is known. To achieve identity unlikability and behaviour privacy, their proposed BZDIMS utilises the architecture of off-chain computing and on-chain validating. This successfully prevents the exposure of the ownership between the user entity and characteristics in the distributed ledger. They suggested challenge-response protocol which can be used to produce low-cost and high-throughput authentication processes and can also be used for additional security mechanisms like access control and authorization. Their work restriction to a specific algorithm limits its diversity and functionality and inherit the problem associated with it. They can't be used in a private blockchain where some level of control is centralised.

In year 2020, Wang and Jiang propose an information authentication scheme suitable for fog computing environment using consortium blockchain technology. They use a 2-adic ring theory and other arithmetic algorithm to form a bases computation in blockchain consortium. The authors were able to create a trusted environment with high level of security as shown from their analysis. Their work focus on securing the fog computing device and the security architecture is built around this, so can't be adopted for other system. to-peer.

Bouras et al. [23] proposed a light weight architecture and the associated protocols for consortium blockchain-based identity management to address privacy, security and scalability issues in a centralized system for IOT. Using the consortium blockchain architecture will enable wider use in all domain and enhance greater degree of flexibility and resiliency. In this approach, each entity is registered to the block network only one time as the block provides a unique identifier to each entity used globally. In the same manner, revocation is an infrequent function for all entities, and an entity holder can only revoke hi identity one time. The registration phase consists of providing participants a unique identifier ID and the tools that are needed to join the consortium network. Furthermore, an entity can a request for registration, in a moment of receiving the query, the DLT platform runs the registration function that contains three main steps: checking the existence of registered entity, assigning a unique ID and communicate the ID to the register. Encryption of messages using a private key takes place in the DLT in which the DLT metadata form the unique identifier ID. Finally, as long as an entity is registered in the network, identity verification and also identity revocation can take place within the system.

Other works, [24] are among the notable blockchain identity works. Their work just like others, solve a major problem of give user control over identity (Self sovereign identity) using decentralised technology. Their major weakness lies in the technology used to solve the problem, as most of these works are built on Ethereum and Hyperledger.

This work aimed to build on the existing knowledge base of the PII management system using a scalable, robust and quantum-safe blockchain technology.

3   Research Methodology

The resent approach to developing a secured PII management system as seen from the reviewed previous work is based on self-sovereign identity (SSI) and decentralised features. The ability for user to have an absolute control and optimum privacy of their PII has been the main concern. The previous work has shown different approach to solving this problem without considering factors such as the technology robustness, speed, quantum computer proof, environment friendliness and computing power among others. This section explains the two approaches we adopted to fulfil the objectives of this work. The first part uses a qualitative research method to critically analyse previous work considering gaps identified earlier. The second part uses a design science research methods to justify our chosen consensus algorithm and to build a decentralised application model for our proposed system.

3.1   Methodology Justification

The first part of the work uses qualitative research method which is a scientific way of collecting and analysing non-numerical data. This method was used to understand and formulate a good model from the critical analyses of the previous work. The second part uses design science research methods as it is the only research methods that permit design, modelling of an application. Some of the element of it that makes it a strong choice for modelling our Decentralise PII management Application are induction and deduction of problem, design and testing and validation of research.

3.2   Approach to Critical Analysis of Previous PII Management System

After conviction that the best approach to avoid re-inventing the wheel in PII management system is to understand and deduce a new solution through critical evaluation/ analysis of previous work. This was done by sourcing for important works such as journals, articles, white papers, and conference proceeding using a strategic search approach across digital libraries (with access to up to 100 high reputable publishers including ScienceDirect, IEEE, ACM Scopus, SpringerLink and O'Reilly), google scholars and google search filter for websites articles in PII management domain. A search parameter was formulated to filter the large resources available and the work uses some know search methods to identify the high relevant work which were analysed.

3.3 Search Parameters

In other to have a broad scope of the work, keywords such as: PII management systems, Identity management system, Blockchain Identity, Blockchain technology, Decentralise Byzantine Fault Tolerance (DBFT) Identity system, Decentralised Identity management system and Decentralise PII management system were used on different occasions on the resources websites. This returned close to a thousand related works. In other to separate the work base on strength and relevant, different search method were used.

3.4 Search Methods

The work adopts different search methods at different level of the work as required. At the start of the work, quick and dirty search methods were used in other to have an idea of the scope of the research space and to formulate a concept which later leads to the research topic. In other to get a deeper understand of the literatures and previous work, a snowball method and cited reference were used interchangeably. This help reduced our workspace analysed.

3.5 Analysis Methods

The analysis was done starting from the theories proposed, evaluating each work from their root aim to the result, paying close attention to the technology used and the result. Their argument, position, recommendation, and area of improvement were also looked at. We adopt a tabulated comparison which can be found in chapter four to present the critical analysis.

3.6 Choosing Decentralise Technology

From our literatures, we could deduce that the heart of decentralise (blockchain) technology lies in its consensus algorithm. From our research we found out that the common consensus algorithms are Proof of stake (PoS), Proof of Work (PoW), Practical Byzantine Fault tolerance (PBFT), Distributed Byzantine Fault Tolerance (dBFT), Proof of Burn (PoB), Proof of Capacity (PoC) and Proof of Elapse Time

(PoET). Each of this algorithm has its pros and cons. In other to choose the best fit which in return will determine the blockchain technology to use, we analyse each algorithm strength and weakness and choose the best fit.

3.7 Modelling of Proposed DApp for PII Management System

The proposed system is model following the software development approach of a decentralised application. These features information gathering on the system requirement, block diagram, use-case diagram, data collection models, smart contract development and an infrastructure modelling for deployment.

3.8 Ethical Considerations

This research was carried out upholding the standard research ethics in other to ensure the scientific integrity is preserved, enhanced research validity and protect the participant rights where data collection is involved.

The work adopts the standard guide for research designs and practice in our methods which include confidentiality, result communication, informed consent among others.

4 Research Design and Models

This research was conducted to serve as a blueprint for future work and a guide to developing a decentralised application for managing personal identifiable Information using distributed byzantine algorithm. The previous chapter has shown the procedures and method adopted to critically review the previous work and designing a model for developing a decentralised application for our proposed system from the architecture to deployment. This chapter will present the review summary, model and a step-by-step process of setting up a neo blockchain.

4.1 Review Summary

After thorough evaluation of over hundred extracted works related to our line of research, we select some works which solve similar problem, identified their gaps and strength. These works were reviewed, and the result was presented in Table 2. Table 3 are extended works which are already in production/deployment phase. A further evaluation of common technology associated with those works were tabulated in Table 4.

From the above table we can conclude that the most used technology for identity management system is Ethereum and Hyperledger. In Table 4, we make a comparison to evaluate the technology fit for the proposed work and our findings is recorded.

We assume a best fit score of 10 for each Area of focus above and we compute for fit for purpose for each technology (Chart 1).

Where Xn is the Area of focus and n is the index of it.

$$\text{Fit for Purpose} = \sum_{0}^{n} Xn$$

4.2 Designing Dapp Models for PII Management System

4.2.1 System Requirement

System requirement were form from the core features of the existing system with new additions, paying close attention to the GDPR and ISO 27001 policies for data collections and management. The following requirements were drafted:

- Security
- Low compute and easy deployment
- Easy Node setup
- Meet up with GDPR and ISO Policies
- Easy users and organisation sign up and verification
- Every Users can participate in consensus
- Users can add, read, update, and delete their PII
- User can share and track their PII access
- Users can delete and leave the network if not interested
- Users can vote for speaker who led the consensus
- User and Organisation has equal right to be a speaker
- Block Diagram

To depict relationships between objects, entities, concepts, or different item, a diagrammatic representation of blocks that represent one or more of these things are adopted which are connected by lines, generally refer to as a block diagram.

Figure 1 shows the block diagram designed for the proposed system with some actions flow like what we have in the use case diagram.

Table 2 Review of related work

S/No	Authors	Method	Point of application	Strength	Weakness
1	[25]	Security framework that integrates the blockchain technology	PII communication in smart cities	Use of multiple blockchain application to prevent vulnerability	The develop framework lacks interoperability and scalability to be use in different platform
2	[26]	Identity blockchain system for verification and management of electronic health record and communication	Identity verification and management of patient information in health record	Encryption of patient identity information with a hash function which enhance confidentiality	The techniques need to more improvement for proper efficiency to be able address latest security concern
3	[27]	High-level framework blockchain-based identity management system named Hyperledger	Communication in PII	Utilization of plenum byzantine fault-tolerant protocol to detect malicious issues	Implementation cost of the method is high
4	[28]	Data trust framework using blockchain technology and adaptive framework	End-to-end communication in PII	Data owners can also monitor and trace access regulation and modification on their data assets	Identifying invalid access to the system remain a difficult challenge
5	[29]	Ethereum smart contract base on DecentID	Verification of personal portfolio in PII	Preserve the confidentiality of the user information and allow user to handle their attributes and identities in a single common place	The performance of the method needs to be enhance using VerifID in the blockchain
6	[30]	Blockchain technology (combination of personal health care (PHC) blockchain and external record management (ERM) blockchain)	Medical health care	Detection of any abnormalities in the data during remote monitoring	No limitation mentioned

(continued)

Table 2 (continued)

S/No	Authors	Method	Point of application	Strength	Weakness
7	[3]	Personal identifiable information management system (BCPIIMS) blockchain	Personal data sharing and tracking	User can easily predict a data breaching process and also track the exact set of breached data	No performance comparison with other existing system to ensure it efficiency
8	[31]	Conceptual model base on blockchain technology	PII data communication	Data encryption using both private key to which enhance privacy	Model evaluation against several vulnerability attacks was limited
9	[32]	Differential privacy in blockchain technology	PII	The use of Laplace and Gaussian mechanism of differential privacy can efficiently perturb specific value to ensure identity privacy	The approach has not been tested in real life application
10	[33]	Consortium blockchain base on Hybrid P2P network	PII credit card application	It enhances information control using private and public key	The research was limited to credit card application
11	[24]	Identity management protocol base on ethereum blockchain technology	Smart contract	It uses stateless server that does not overload it memory	The approach is very slow in verification because ethereum mining is not fast
12	[23]	Light weight architecture and the associated protocols for consortium blockchain-based identity management	PII registration and communication	High level of encryption which enhance privacy	Automatic user registration process and multi-factor authentication process has not been added to the technique

4.3 User-case Diagram

This diagram is a representation of the Interaction between the key entity of the system. The Fig. 2 below present use-case diagram shows three main actor and their operations on the proposed system.

Table 3 Common identity application based on blockchain

	App Name	Brief description	Blockchain technology	Network scope	GDPR compliance	Development status
1	Sovrin	A self sovereign identity for public utility	Hyperledger	Public (Permissioned)	Yes	Completed
2	Bloom	An identity management for credit scoring	Hyperledger	Limited (Permissioned)	Yes	Completed
3	ShoCard	Privacy protection identity platform	Ethereum	Public (Permissionless)	No	Completed
4	Uport	PII management on blochcain	Ethereum	Permissionless)	No	Completed
5	I/O Digital	Application based Blockchain identity	Ethereum	Permissionless	No	Completed
6	BlockAuth	Authenticate with your controlled identity in your registerar	Ethereum	Permissionless	No	Completed
7	Cambridge Blockchain	Compliance and identity management based on blockchain solutions for financial institutions	Ethereum	Permissionless	No	Completed
8	Authenteq	Electronic KYC identity verification system for crypto platform	Ethereum	Permissionless	No	Completed

The individual actor performs more activities than the other two, but its activity is subjected to the outcome of the consensus on verification of his identity and assigning of decentralised identity. Individual is privilege to create a node, perform PII Operations and act as delegate to elect speaker. The Org actor represent the organisation whose aim is to verify a claimed PII by an individual and issues a

Table 4 Blockchain technology comparison

	Area of Focus	Ethereum	Hyperledger	Neo(N3)
1	Years	2015	2017	2018
2	Network scope	Permissionless	Permissioned	Public (support all scope)
3	Consensus algorithm	PoS	PBFT	DBFT (improved PBFT)
4	GDPR compliance	No	Yes	Yes
5	Scalability	High node, less scalable	Less node, highly scalable	Less node, highly scalable
6	Speed	Low	Fast	Faster
7	Economy friendliness	Consensus is limited to stake holder	Everyone in the network take part in consensus decision	Everyone in the network take part in consensus decision
8	Governance	Carried out by developer	Linux foundation	Neo council (elected by everyone on the network)
9	Transaction currency	Ether	No specific currency	Neo gas
10	Development language	Solidity	Support common high level language e.g. C-sharp, JavaScript, Python, Go, and Java	Support common high level language e.g. C-sharp, JavaScript, Python, Go and Java
11	Quantum safe	No	No	Yes

certificate which can also be a PII. The last actor represent the consensus who are responsible for block formation and adding block to the blockchain.

4.4 Design Data Collection Models

The proposed system utilized an in-built smart contract storage made available by Neo blockchain and is private to the smart contract. This gives individual contract access to write, modify, read, and delete data. This storage allow data to be stored in a key -value pair, where key is a string, or a byte array and value is of any type. The image below shows the database relationship of some key attribute of the system (Fig. 3).

Each table are represented on Neo blockchain platform by Storage Map.

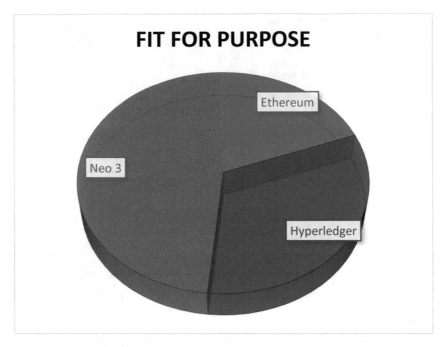

Chart 1 Technology fit for purpose

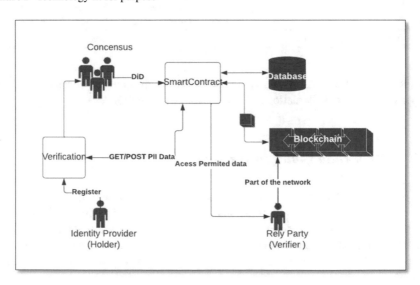

Fig. 1 Block diagram of the proposed system

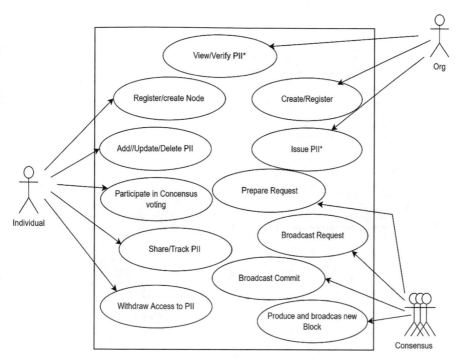

Fig. 2 PII manager D app use case diagram

4.5 *Infrastructure Design*

Figure 4 shows the system design of the infrastructure that will be needed for adequate functioning of our system. The Dapp will be built on a Linux operating system due to its efficiency, size, and ability to run both the interfaces (Frontend and the Neo Blockchain Platform) of our application. On it, is NGINX sever for running Node application (React) and Neo SDK for the blockchain. The Nginx server is configured to host the React App developed to interface with the blockchain API which are part of the flexibility Neo platform gives.

4.6 *Smart Contract*

A smart contract is a set of digitally defined promises that also specifies how participants in the contract will carry out their obligations. Smart contracts are incredibly helpful in the decentralised, un-hackable, highly trustworthy system that blockchain technology provides. One of the most significant aspects of blockchain technology and the reason why it can be referred to as a disruptive technology is smart contracts.

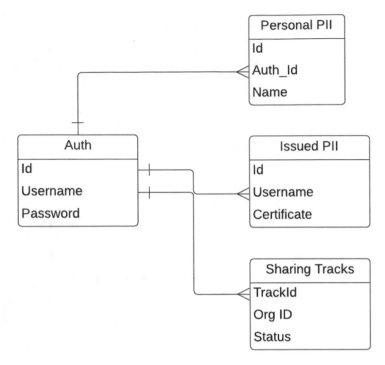

Fig. 3 Database relationship of PII manager

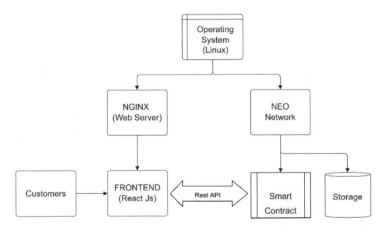

Fig. 4 System diagram of infrastructure of the PII manager

This is the also refer to the backend of a blockchain system as all actions are defined in the contract.

The proposed system smart contract was developed on Neo smart contract 2.0 written in C-sharp which is the official language of the Neo Blockchain. The contracts code can be divided into three form which are validation, functional, and application contracts. In this work a validation contract is written to validate user at every point of transaction which involve cross node transaction or within a node. Functional and Application contracts allow us to mage PII data using the contract storage. Neo smart contract 2 is run on a lightweight Neo virtual machine (VM) which makes it to start up quickly and can be used for smart contract with short procedures. Its efficacy is the main reason for choosing it as our choice of blockchain technology.

4.7 Developing dBFT App Smart Contract Using Neo 3

This section shows the steps taken to develop neo 3 private network, creating wallet and writing the smart contract for our PII management system. The first requirement is installing visual studio code Integrated development environment (IDE) which will serve as our development editor to write our code and test our network before deploying to main network. The next step is installing Neo 3 Blockchain toolkit visual studio code extension as shown in Fig. 5.

After installation we have both Neo Blockchains and Neo N3 visual devtracker added to the tool bar and a quick start guide to start development.

The setup is completed using the quick guide and the following were created: A Neo express private network with 4 nodes to allow flexible interaction between objects in different nodes, A genesis wallet with a default Neo balance of 100,000,000 NEO and a Gas Balance of 52,000,000 as seen in Fig. 6 and a smart contract default template as show in Fig. 7.

Other wallet can be created in each network node by right-clicking on the node and select create wallet then enter the name for the wallet.

Fig. 5 A screenshot of Neo blockchain toolkit

Fig. 6 Screenshot of the default wallet created for each node

Fig. 7 Screenshot of smart contract

The contract is edited to meet up with the action / activities model for our proposed system.

5   Critical Discussions

The rising needs for technologically efficient, scalable, and secure PII management system has been the inspiration of this work. Holding up our key objectives, we could see from our critical analyses that the previous work needs to be improved in area of technology and including features such as a PII tracking system so individual can be rest assured their PII data is safe. Our proposed system which is designed to be built upon the most secured (quantum-proof) blockchain technology will guarantee an efficient solution to the problem known with the previous work. Our model for the Decentralise App will serve as a blueprint for future work to build on.

6 Conclusion and Future Work

The need for secured, efficient, robust and technology friendly PII management cannot be disputed in the era of today. Fortune has been lost because of breach in PII management system and therefore many researchers tend to focus on build secured and user-controlled identity management system to secure PII and this led to the advent of a self-sovereign identity management system. Blockchain technology has proof it efficiency in this line of research with decentralised identity. This work has shown the contribution of previous works with or without blockchain technology to managing PII and has identify some gaps in the existing system which was the starting point of our objectives. Then, a secured decentralised PII management using DBFT consensus algorithm was proposed as a solution to the existing problem. This algorithm is the major power of Neo 3 blockchain which is why we adopt the blockchain platform and lastly a decentralised app was modelled in other to give a full scope of the proposed system. This work can serve as a blueprint guide to developing PII manager for government and enterprise. It can also be integrated to systems where sensitive information is to be collected, saved and tracked.

Future works are:

Developing a decentralised Applications: this work has modelled the DApp, which is a starting point for future research to build on. Different use case can be leverage such as Government Identity management system, Enterprise SSO etc.

Evaluating Security before and after data collection: One of the major problem of identify with blockchain App is usually associated to the frontend where data are inputted before been deployed to blockchain. This work couldn't look into this and can be a good area to work on for future work.

Survey to know which PII information users are most reluctant to give when asked: Since we aimed to build a user centric PII management system, The need for users to participate in the requirement definition cannot be over emphasise. Future work can incorporate this to their development.

The crypto fuel is not divisible: The work adopts Neo blockchain which used NeoGAS to fuel the transactions. NeoGAS only exist in whole number and doesn't give room for divisibility (Decimals).

References

1. Jennings M 2022 Top data breaches and cyber attacks of 2022. In: TechRadar. Retrieved from https://www.techradar.com/features/top-data-breaches-and-cyber-attacks-of-2022
2. Information Commissioner's Office (2012) Determining what is personal data. In: Information commissioner's office (ico.). Retrieved from https://ico.org.uk/media/for-organisations/documents/1554/determining-what-is-personal-data.pdf
3. Onik MMH et al (2019) Privacy-aware blockchain for personal data sharing and tracking. Open Comput Sci 9(1):80–91. https://doi.org/10.1515/comp-2019-0005
4. Al-Fedaghi S, Al-Azmi AAR (2012) Experimentation with personal identifiable information. Intell Inf Manag 4:123–133. https://doi.org/10.4236/iim.2012.44019
5. Yakowtiz J (2011) Tragedy of the data commons. Harvard J Law Technol 25(1):1–67
6. Mackie J (2022) Personal vs. Sensitive Information. In: TermsFeed. Retrieved from https://www.termsfeed.com/blog/personal-vs-sensitive-information/#The_Gdpr_And_Sensitive_Information
7. EU-GDPR (2018) EU General Data Protection Regulation (EU-GDPR). In: Official journal of the European Union. Retrieved from https://www.privacy-regulation.eu/en/index.htm
8. Bing J (1972) Classification of personal information, with respect to sensitivity aspect. In: Proceedings of the first international oslo symposium on data banks and societies, pp 98–150
9. Rosencrance L, Mathias C (2021) identity management (ID management). In: TechTarget. Retrieved from https://www.techtarget.com/searchsecurity/definition/identity-management-ID-management#:~:text=Identitymanagement(IDmanagement)is,toapplications%2Csystems ornetworks
10. Hansen M, Pfitzmann A, Steinbrecher S (2008) Identity management throughout one's whole life. Inf Secur Tech Rep 13(2):83–94. https://doi.org/10.1016/j.istr.2008.06.003
11. Chen J et al (2011) Differentiated security levels for personal identifiable information in identity management system. Expert Syst Appl 38(11):14156–14162. https://doi.org/10.1016/j.eswa.2011.04.226
12. Alruwies MH et al (2021) Identity governance framework for privileged users. Comput Syst Sci Eng 40(3):995–1005. https://doi.org/10.32604/csse.2022.019355
13. De Hert P (2008) Identity management of e-ID, privacy and security in Europe. A human rights view. Inf Secur Tech Rep 13(2):71–75. https://doi.org/10.1016/j.istr.2008.07.001
14. Camenisch J et al (2005) Privacy and identity management for everyone. In: Proceedings of the 2005 workshop on digital identity management, pp 20–27. https://doi.org/10.1145/1102486.1102491
15. Liu Y et al (2020) Blockchain-based identity management systems: a review. J Netw Comput Appl 166:102731. https://doi.org/10.1016/j.jnca.2020.102731
16. Rathee T, Singh P (2021) A systematic literature mapping on secure identity management using blockchain technology. J King Saud Univ Comput Inf Sci 34(8, Part B):5782–5796. https://doi.org/10.1016/j.jksuci.2021.03.005
17. Chang F et al (2021) A maintenance decision-making oriented collaborative cross-organization knowledge sharing blockchain network for complex multi-component systems. J Cleaner Prod 282:124541. https://doi.org/10.1016/j.jclepro.2020.124541
18. Brown RG et al (2016) Corda: an introduction, pp 1–15. https://doi.org/10.13140/RG.2.2.30487.37284
19. El Haddouti S, Ech-Cherif El Kettani MD (2019) Analysis of identity management systems using blockchain technology. In: 2019 International conference on advanced communication technologies and networking (CommNet). IEEE, pp 1–7. https://doi.org/10.1109/COMMNET.2019.8742375
20. Gutierrez C (2017) The journey to a self-sovereign digital identity built on a blockchain. Retrieved from https://www.altoros.com/blog/the-journey-to-a-self-sovereign-digital-identity-built-on-a-blockchain/

21. Lim SY et al (2018) Blockchain technology the identity management and authentication service disruptor: a survey. Int J Adv Sci Eng Inf Technol 8(4–2):1735–1745. https://doi.org/10.18517/ijaseit.8.4-2.6838
22. Yang X, Li W (2020) A zero-knowledge-proof-based digital identity management scheme in blockchain. Comput Secur 99:102050. https://doi.org/10.1016/j.cose.2020.102050
23. Bouras MA et al (2021) A lightweight blockchain-based IoT identity management approach. Future Internet 13(2):1–14. https://doi.org/10.3390/fi13020024
24. Wang S, Pei R, Zhang Y (2019) EIDM: A ethereum-based cloud user identity management protocol. IEEE Access 7:115281–115291. https://doi.org/10.1109/ACCESS.2019.2933989
25. Cai Y, Zhu D (2016) Fraud detections for online businesses: a perspective from blockchain technology. Financ Innov 2(1):1–10. https://doi.org/10.1186/s40854-016-0039-4
26. Liang Y (2019) Identity verification and management of electronic health records with blockchain technology. In: 2019 IEEE International conference on healthcare informatics (ICHI). IEEE, pp 1–3. https://doi.org/10.1109/ICHI.2019.8904712
27. Priya N, Ponnavaikko M, Aantonny R (2020) An efficient system framework for managing identity in educational system based on blockchain technology. In: 2020 International conference on emerging trends in information technology and engineering (ic-ETITE). IEEE, pp 1–5. https://doi.org/10.1109/ic-ETITE47903.2020.469
28. Rouhani S, Deters R (2021) Data trust framework using blockchain technology and adaptive transaction validation. IEEE Access 9:90379–90391. https://doi.org/10.1109/ACCESS.2021.3091327
29. Belurgikar DA et al (2019) Identity solutions for verification using blockchain technology. In: 2019 1st International conference on advanced technologies in intelligent control, environment, computing and communication engineering (ICATIECE). IEEE, pp 121–126. https://doi.org/10.1109/ICATIECE45860.2019.9063802
30. Chakraborty S, Aich S, Kim H-C (2019) A secure healthcare system design framework using blockchain technology. In: 2019 International conference on advanced communication technology (ICACT). IEEE, pp 260–264. https://doi.org/10.23919/ICACT.2019.8701983
31. Rahmadika S, Rhee K-H (2018) Blockchain technology for providing an architecture model of decentralized personal health information. Int J Eng Bus Manag 10:1–12. https://doi.org/10.1177/1847979018790589
32. Ul Hassan M, Rehmani MH, Chen J (2020) Differential privacy in blockchain: a futuristic approach. J Parallel Distrib Comput, Elsevier 145:50–74
33. Zhang J, Tan R, Yu-dong L (2020) Design of personal credit information sharing platform based on consortium blockchain. Commun Comput Inf Sci 1286:166–177. https://doi.org/10.1007/978-981-15-9739-8_14

Security Framework for Big Data Usage in Cloud-based e-Learning Application

Sree Ravali Murala and Hamid Jahankhani

Abstract A variety of businesses, academic institutions, and individual consumers have shown an interest in cloud computing since its inception in the last few years. This is due to the fact that cloud computing users are in a brand-new IT business paradigm. It holds the potential of moving away from a paradigm where businesses have to spend extensively on in-house IT resources in favour of one where they can purchase or rent services managed by a cloud provider and pay as they go for them. There is a significant shortcoming or shortage of finances among smaller educational institutions to effectively use Technology. Education, especially in outlying and impoverished areas, may benefit greatly from cloud computing's potential to improve both its quality and accessibility. It may provide improved communication and collaboration amongst educators in different places, allowing for more engaging and dynamic classroom activities. Additionally, cloud-based solutions may provide clients/academic institutions with cost savings and exposure to state-of-the-art computing. In this chapter, some of the most significant security challenges that arise when using e-learning applications in conjunction with cloud computing and big data are discussed. In addition, a greater emphasis is placed on the security of middleware applications, which are utilized to connect end-user applications and big data.

Keywords e-learning · Cloud computing · Blockchain · Big data · Hadoop · Cybersecurity

S. R. Murala · H. Jahankhani (✉)
Northumbria University, London, UK
e-mail: Hamid.jahankhani@northumbria.ac.uk

© The Author(s), under exclusive license to Springer Nature Switzerland AG 2023   193
H. Jahankhani et al. (eds.), *AI, Blockchain and Self-Sovereign Identity in Higher Education*, Advanced Sciences and Technologies for Security Applications,
https://doi.org/10.1007/978-3-031-33627-0_9

1 Introduction

Due to the rapid development of internet technology and the consistently observed improvements in network capacity and quality, real-time transmission of high-quality video and audio is currently regarded to be a practical possibility. Schools' long-held methods of teaching have evolved through time as a result of these seismic developments [1]. The meteoric ascent of e-Learning as one of the most popular forms of education is a prime example of this trend. More and more schools and businesses are using e-learning systems to better meet the demands of their students and employees.

Traditional E-leaning is still in use today after being implemented many years ago. With more and more individuals using the internet and computer networks and more and more tools available for online education, it's clear that the traditional model of e-learning is working. The efficacy of online education has been the subject of study at several universities [2]. Because of this, cloud-based learning has been growing in popularity [3], particularly when taking into account the advantages it provides within the framework of an online classroom. In most cases, organizations would rather devote their resources to creating a model that is not only useful but also cheap to maintain [2]. Indeed, these benefits have resulted from cloud-based learning, which is increasingly altering the face of online education. In contrast, the traditional method of online education has its own set of challenges. For instance, a system's development and upkeep can only be performed by employees of the company that purchased them. Fixing the traditional E-learning paradigm requires a lot of manpower and money, but it's the better option overall [4].

Students may fit their education into their busy schedules with the use of e-learning platforms, often known as Learning Management Systems (LMSs). The goals of higher education institutions as a teaching tool, the adaptability of LMSs in terms of content delivery, and the ability of users to engage with course materials regardless of their physical location are all factors that contribute to LMSs' growing popularity and acceptability [5]. The exponential growth of data has had some negative repercussions on classrooms throughout the world, despite the numerous good ones. According to [6], the vast amounts of data generated by LMSs may be analyzed to understand more about how students are learning and how well teachers are supporting student growth.

Challenges posed by the "3 V" (Volume, Variety, and Velocity) of data in e-Learning systems, already substantial due to their sheer size, are only growing in scope and complexity. The amount of data (the number of students and teachers logging in), the diversity of data (the length and format of different pieces of information), and the pace of online dialogues (the constant flow of new information) are all major obstacles. Again, it's challenging for colleges to cope with data from the many various e-learning platforms in use. Since the LMS data entries' descriptions and compositions are unique, the work proposes [7] that the systems establish a new datatype. Developing a new metric that establishes connections between different data points will allow for more extensive data collection and examination. Variety, data complexity, time, data privacy, and scalability are the most critical problems that Big Data brings to educational institutions at all levels when it comes to deriving value from data, as outlined in the work done by [8].

Sensitive information stored in Hadoop or being sent over a network may be protected using a variety of security measures. To do business across a network, it is necessary for two parties (the client and the server) to have trust in one another. Typically, the client will send its password to the server, where it will be checked for validity. Users risk having their credentials stolen if they submit sensitive information via a network that isn't properly protected. Without sending the actual credentials across the network, Kerberos provides strong authentication for client/server programs [9]. When information is being sent to Hadoop, it may be encrypted using the SASL authentication mechanism. With SASL security, a "man-in-the-middle" (MITM) cannot hijack client and server communication.

It is not sufficient to just store the data; we must also have the capacity to process it effectively. The vast majority of the time this holds true. For the time being, processing should not occur in the Hadoop encryption zone. The whole file must be decrypted if the MapReduce job is to be used on information located in an encryption zone, and only then must the decrypted data be made available for use by the MapReduce process [10]. The data must be prepared in this way before the MapReduce operation can be performed on it. To avoid slowing down Hadoop's performance, the chosen encryption and decryption system has to be able to process massive volumes of data rapidly. Hadoop encryption zone employs cypher suites like Advanced Encryption Standard (AES), known for its decent encryption performance and efficiency standards but it certainly having greater memory demand and might impact performance due to the fact that Client node has limited memory and fistulized are normally of a bigger size.

The goal of this chapter is to develop a big data security framework that will improve the performance and security of an E-learning platform hosted in the cloud.

2 Literature Review

"Big data" may be understood in a variety of ways. These descriptions often focus on the size, complexity, and diversity of the subject matter at hand. Business, medicine, and even computer science has all made use of the term "big data" as a result of the proliferation of digital technology and the increasing sophistication of data-dependent applications. Many people are interested in learning more about "big data" as a tool for teaching and learning these days [11].

According to [12] there is no one, agreed-upon definition for the term "Big Data". They went on to explain that the four pillars of the "Big Data" idea are the "Big Data", "Information Technology", "Methods", and the "Impact". Big data will be easier to grasp if these concepts are linked. "The information asset characterized by such large volume, velocity, and diversity that necessitates specialized technology and analytical procedures for its conversion into value", they write. "Big data" is the flow of data in today's world, which is networked, digitized, sensor-laden, and information-driven, according to the National Institute of Standards and Technology [13]. They emphasized that the rates of increase for big data's data speeds, volumes, and complexity are currently outpacing the traditional approaches to data management and analytics.

2.1 Big Data Attributes

Several criteria have been put forward to distinguish Big Data from traditional data. Several studies have identified 5 defining characteristics of big data, sometimes referred to as the five Vs (volume, velocity, variety, veracity, and value) [14]. But however, to label the data as Big Data, only a few of the mentioned characteristics are required. Large volumes, rapid changes, along with varied sources of information are often cited as defining Big Data. These are the vital characteristics that set Big Data apart [15].

Big Data relies on volume, a property that refers to the total amount of space required for archiving data [16]. They then go on to stress that traditional data is not analogous to Big Data because of these basic distinctions [11]. Large data sets need storage capacities of either a terabyte (240 bytes) or a petabyte (250 bytes) [17]. This data explosion may be partially attributed to the proliferation of electronic devices and the emergence of the Internet of Things (IoT). As more and more information is generated by business operations, social media platforms, machines, sensors, and network connections, it is becoming more difficult for traditional database management systems to keep up. In 2011, the worldwide output of data was estimated to reach 1.8 zettabytes, based on research by International Data Corporation (IDC). The amount of information produced by this data is predicted to double every two years [18]. In order to handle, analyse, or store Big Data on a single system, a substantial amount of computational power is required, as stated by Strom. Elgendy and Elragal [19] makes a good point regarding the limited computational power of conventional statistical and visualization methods when used with this data. NoSQL and Hadoop are only two examples of modern data storage technologies that make it possible to collect, store, and update massive volumes of data in non-Realtime. As a result, it's easier to get things done.

- Velocity: When considering velocity, it is most useful to conceive of it as the act of controlling the steady stream of information that arrives to a system every second. Before, data was often processed in batches, with samples being gathered at infrequent intervals. The real-time creation of data is the primary challenge facing modern enterprises in the era of Big Data. When considering the speed of data, it is important to take into account both the rate at which data is created and the rate at which it is subsequently processed, recorded, and disseminated [20].
- Variety: This feature of Big Data, which includes organized, semi-structured, and unstructured information, seems to be its biggest drawback [21]. Data storage in the past, including spreadsheets and databases, was organized in rows and columns

with a strict hierarchy. Today's data may be found in a wide range of file types, including audio, video, image, PDF, and document files, as well as other, less conventional forms. Unstructured data accounts for 90% of all data production [22]. The challenge comes in identifying the file formats in which these datasets are stored and developing appropriate tools and algorithms for doing so.

- Veracity: According to [23], one of the characteristics we seldom think about is the reliability of the information. The primary reason we collect data is to improve our decision-making. Therefore, reliable information that can be utilized for decision-making may be obtained by collecting the relevant information or data. Inappropriate or incorrect data may cause issues for businesses and their clients. It was [24] in the year, Ensuring the accuracy of all data and analysis is essential to the Big Data paradigm.

- Value: Value is being created by the availability of data for many different types of organisations, including schools. Research by the McKinsey Global Institute [25] estimates that public sector management in Europe might benefit annually from using Big Data to the tune of 250 billion euros. The relevance of the data refers to the potential value that may be gained through analysing the information. The value is in how data is used by educational institutions to improve instruction and learning via the application of insights gleaned through data mining. One way to do this is to cultivate a setting that encourages the pursuit of these aims.

2.2 Big Data and Cloud-based e–Learning Application

Several Big Data technologies are used in higher education for managing, storing, analysing, and visualising large datasets produced by e-learning systems. Middleware is the core component in the big data environment, where the primary role of the middleware is to increase efficiency of overall system by interconnecting various applications, tools as well as different databases to create an integrated service to user. For example, to improve the experience of both students and instructors using the e-learning application when it is hosted on the cloud-big data platform, the middleware application can assist users to search various e learning contents and well store their study materials in the cloud without any difficulty, so more positive encounter by consolidating all of the available services into a centralized point [26].

It's a system for storing and managing massive amounts of data via the use of distributed storage and parallel computing. The market for this software is expanding as more and more data analysts adopt it as the standard for working with massive data sets. Hadoop is composed of three parts: the first one is Hadoop Distributed File System (HDFS) which is the storage unit in the Hadoop environment, the second one is the processing unit called MapReduce and the third one is resource management unit called YARN [27] (Fig. 1).

Obtaining data from hundreds or thousands of servers from the cloud storage is a task that takes a lot of time and requires a lot of power consumption. The majority of the time, the middleware application needs to perform this kind of searching and

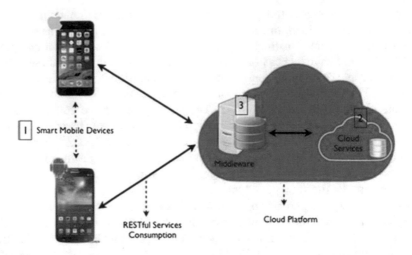

Fig. 1 An overview of the cloud-based e-learning application [28]

sorting of data from thousands of servers. When this task is performed by thousands of users again, it will create more of a burden on the middleware application [29]. To effectively manage this function google introduces a framework called MapReduce, later this is integrated into Hadoop. Map reduce refer two distinct task that performed by the middleware application: (1) map (2) reduce (Fig. 2).

Map: First, the input is segmented into manageable chunks. Thereafter, a mapper is responsible for processing each individual block. If there are 100 records in a file that need to be processed, for instance, 100 mappers may work in conjunction to handle single record each. Alternatively, fifty mappers may be able to work in

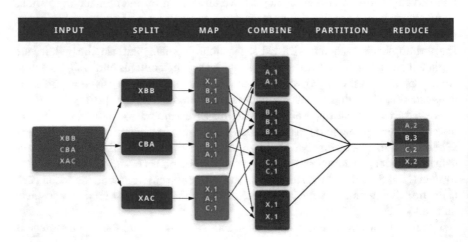

Fig. 2 Overall functioning of MapReduce framework [29]

tandem to process two records. The number of mappers used is determined by the framework according to the amount of data being handled and the size of the mapper server's memory block [30].

Reduce: When all of the mappers have finished their job, the framework will reorder and scramble the outputs before sending them to the reducers. While a mapper is running, the reducer cannot begin processing. Keyed values from the map output are aggregated into a single value by sending them to a single reducer. There are two intermediate steps between Map and Reduce [30].

Combine: The step of combining is not essential. Each mapper server has its own copy of the combiner, which operates as a reducer. Before passing on the information, it further simplifies the data on each mapper. As a result, there is less information to shuffle and sort, which speeds up those processes. In many contexts, the reducer class is used as the combiner class because of the reduce function's ability to do both cumulative and associative operations. While a distinct class isn't required, a combiner may be used if one is desired [31].

Partition: Partitioning is the process by which the "key, value" pairs produced by mappers are transformed into a different set of "key, value" pairs for use by the "reducer". The scheduler determines which reducer will receive data and how that data will be given to it. The key's hash value produced by the mapper is used by the default partitioner to identify the key's partition. Each reducer is partitioned into the same number of subsets. After the data has been partitioned, it is passed to the appropriate reducer [10].

3   Security in the Middleware Application

3.1   Security of Data in Motion

Data in the middleware application is stored in a distributed fashion across numerous Data Nodes, while metadata and an access log are kept in a separate unit called a Name Node. The Client Node and the Data Node are the two nodes that exchange data blocks with one another. The frameworks used by the middleware applications are made up of many nodes that share data with one another. Since the network is not encrypted by default, the information is sent in the clear. This leaves the sent data vulnerable to hacking attempts. Internode communication may be achieved using a variety of protocols, including Transmission Control Protocol over Internet Protocol (TCP/IP), Hypertext Transfer Protocol (HTTP), and Remote Procedure Call (RPC). Kerberos and the Simple Authentication and Security Layer are two examples of the techniques available for safeguarding communication between different nodes [32].

3.2   Security of Data at Rest

The term "data at rest" describes information that is now sitting in a non-volatile format. Lack of disk-level encryption in most of the middleware application leaves sensitive data vulnerable to security breaches. For example, the inbuilt design of hadoop worsens this problem since it distributes data over several nodes, leaving the data blocks vulnerable at each of the unprotected links. By default, these middleware applications offers a variety of options for encrypting data while it's stored in the cluster. The usage of encryption zones, an additional abstraction layer for bigdata, is one such method [33].

Some middleware software distributors, like IBM, Cloudera, and Hortonworks, promise to safeguard their customers' information. Not everyone can afford to adopt a specialised distribution system, even if their promises are correct. Information security is become a basic human right. For a safe and secure environment to be accessible to the widest possible audience, there has to be some publicly available frameworks [33]. There is still a chance for issues to arise, even for those who are using publicly accessible framework. Businesses now rely solely on remote access to their sensitive data and services through the cloud. Cloud computing presents unique security and privacy problems for businesses.

3.3   Securing the Data at Rest Using a Cryptographic Method

The majority of middleware applications use symmetric key cryptography such as AES, or Advanced Encryption Standard, which was created by the National Institute of Standards and Technology in 1997 as a result of the inadequacy of DES's 56-bit key size. The Advanced Encryption Standard (AES) algorithm is a symmetrical block cypher method that can transform 128-bit plaintext blocks into ciphertext with a corresponding key length. The AES algorithm is part of the international standard because of its reputation for security (Fig. 3).

To generate ciphertext, the AES algorithm employs a substitution-permutation (SP) network with many rounds. How many times this happens is key size dependent. Key sizes of 128 bits need 10 rounds, 192 bits require twelve rounds, and 256 bits require fourteen. In order for the algorithm to work, each of these rounds needs a round key, but the user may only enter a single key at a time [34].

3.3.1   Steps in Each Round

(1) Substitution of the bytes: S-box rules are used to make replacements in the block text's bytes as the initial stage (Fig. 4).

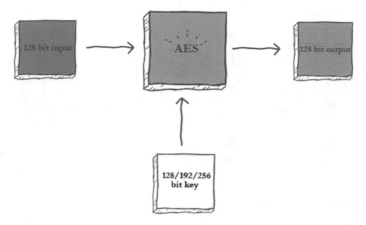

Fig. 3 Overview of the AES encryption

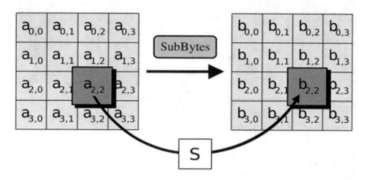

Fig. 4 Performing substitution [35]

(2) Shifting the rows: The next process is the permutation. As can be seen in the diagram below, in this phase, it moves all rows but the first by one position (Fig. 5).

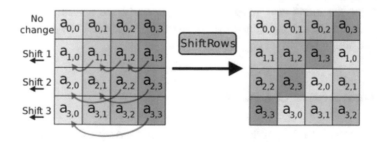

Fig. 5 Shifting the rows [35]

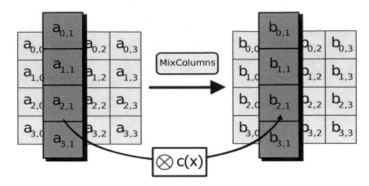

Fig. 6 Mixing the columns [35]

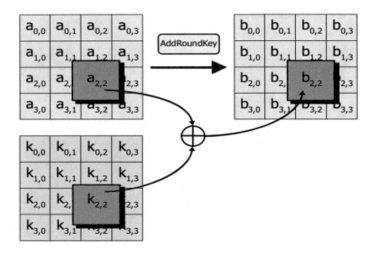

Fig. 7 Adding the round key [35]

(3) Mixing the columns: Finally, the Hill cryptography is employed to further scramble the data by rearranging the order of the block's columns (Fig. 6).
(4) Adding the round key: When everything is ready, the text is XORed with the appropriate round key. Repetition of these procedures guarantees the safety of the resulting ciphertext (Fig. 7).

3.4   Attacks on AES Cipher Suite

AES is currently widely utilized across a broad variety of devices, from 8-bit processor-equipped smart cards to massively parallel server clusters. AES has been in use for almost a decade, and several efforts have been made to completely crack it.

Nevertheless, no openly known attack exists today that can decrypt AES-encrypted ciphertexts in a practical length of time1. However, several articles have shown vulnerabilities inside the algorithm, however many of these issues need very rare occurrences to be exploited. Therefore, there is no need to abandon the usage of AES due to security concerns [36]. However, new and better attacks on AES that aim to diminish its theoretical security gap have emerged since 2008.It is feasible to launch a wide variety of attacks against the AES cypher.

Side-channel attack: Credentials may be stolen from a chip or an entire system using its security flaw known as a side-channel attack (SCA). There are a number of physical factors that may be measured or analysed to do this. Things like supply current, processing time, and electromagnetic radiation are all good examples. The modules that implement cryptographic systems are in great danger from these assaults. In fact, several methods of side-channel analysis have been shown to be effective for cracking algorithmically secure cryptographic operations and so revealing the corresponding secret keys. Attacking a programme through a side channel is called a "side-channel attack" since it does not directly affect the code. Instead, a side-channel attack is an effort to learn anything about the system or to manipulate its code by monitoring or taking advantage of unintended consequences of the software or hardware. To put it simply, a side-channel attack is any method of breaking cryptography that takes use of the information being spilled unintentionally by a system. The transient electromagnetic pulse emission standard, or van Eck phreaking assault, is one such instance. Data is seen before encryption by monitoring the electromagnetic field (EMF) radiation generated by a pc display [37].

Brute-force attack: An attacker using a brute force key guessing attack will repeatedly try every possible combination of the secret key until they succeed. This assault will succeed at some point, and it should be the quickest method to crack an encryption system. The danger posed by quantum computing to encryption has received a lot of attention. Since quantum computers operate differently from conventional ones, attacks against encryption using quantum algorithms may be significantly more effective [38].

4   Challenges in Cloud Based e-Learning Application

There are a variety of challenges associated with storing big data on the cloud, since this kind of data might include a mix of structured, unstructured, and semi-structured information. One of the biggest issues is protecting sensitive information. Keeping information safe means protecting its privacy, as well as making sure it can be accessed when needed and is in good shape. Since the cloud service provider owns and operates many data centres in different locations, the user of cloud computing has no idea where their critical data is physically stored [39]. Due to these issues, it is crucial to take precautions to protect the privacy and security of information kept in the cloud. Including, but not limited to, the inadequacy of standards in a public cloud with regards to the reporting and auditing of big data,the need to secure an extremely large amount of private or critical data of government institutes, businesses, and many organisations; and the presence of advanced threats and malicious intruders [40].

There are a number of challenges and dangers that need to be addressed in order to keep users' personal information safe and maintain the integrity of big data. With the shift toward a cloud-based model centred on the internet, stressed the need of keeping sensitive information safe from accidental disclosure or loss. Even more so as cloud computing grows in popularity [41]. Additionally, it identifies the most pressing, pressing, and least pressing issues in data security. Identity and access management, application security, vulnerability and threat management, business continuity and disaster recovery readiness, personal and physical security, incident response arrangements, data leak prevention, service and data availability, and data segregation and protection are all essential components. It also shows that avoiding data breaches and appropriately segregating and preserving data are major concerns when it comes to data security, as these problems were rated as Critical and Very Essential by 88 and 92% of respondents, respectively.

The article [42] discusses a number of problems with the data, some of which are shown in Fig. 8. Data integrity, lineage, recovery, leakage, and segregation are only a few examples of these difficulties.

The authors of the research [43] break down data security problems in the cloud into four distinct classes, each of which may have a significant effect on a company's operations in the cloud. Backup, multitenancy, and cloud storage of data may all provide new security risks, as can threats to data's confidentiality, integrity, and availability (the CIA triad). The worries regarding the network's security are shown in Fig. 9.

Each year, Cloud Security Alliance (CSA) publishes a list on their website detailing the most pressing security concerns with cloud computing. The most significant dangers are shown in [44]. In Fig. 10 below, we detail the dangers that might arise. Data breaches pose the greatest threat to security and must be handled promptly.

Fig. 8 Different challenges related to data [42]

No.	Data level challenges
1	Data integrity
2	Data recovery
3	Data lineage
4	Data backup
5	Data leakage
6	Data isolation
7	Data remanence
8	Data provenance
9	Data location
10	Data lockin
11	Data segregation

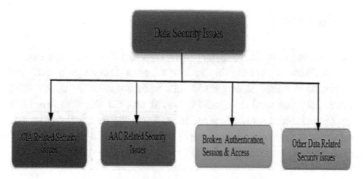

Fig. 9 Types of data security issues [43]

Top threats	2010	2013	2016	2019
1	wicked uses of cloud service	Data Breaches	Data Breaches	Data breaches
2	Insecure API	Loss of data	Inadequate credential ,identity& access management	Insufficient & misconfigure change control
3	Malicious insiders threat	hijacking of service & account	Insecure APIs	The lack of strategy and architecture of cloud security
4	The problems of Shared Technologies	Insecure APIs	Exploited Apps & sys Vulnerabilities	Inadequate credential ,key ,identity& access management
5	Data Leakage/Loss	DDoS attack	hijacking of service & account	hijacking of service & account
6	The hijacking of Service, Traffic and account	Malicious Insiders	(APTs) parasite	Internal &insider threats
7	Unknown Risk Profile	Wicked uses of Cloud Services	Malicious Insiders	Insecure APIs& interfaces
8	....	Insufficient Diligence	Loss of data	Frail &infirm control plane
9	....	The problems of Shared Technologies	Inadequate Due Diligence	Applistructure & Metastructure failures
10	....	....	wicked uses of Cloud Services	Restricted visibility of cloud usage
11	....	....	DDoS attack	wicked uses of Cloud Services
12	....	....	Shared dangers, shared technologies	....

Fig. 10 Top threats related to cloud released by CSA [44]

There are numerous open concerns, potential threats, and new avenues of research regarding the protection of individual privacy and the integrity of big data. Cutting-edge approaches and strategies should be developed to cope with the current obstacles, and future research should keep in mind the types of difficulties that may have a substantial impact on the government, corporations, and users. Here we provide an overview of some of the most significant ongoing concerns or issues issued by Cloud Security Alliance (CSA), as well as the impact these challenges and issues have on organisations [44].

4.1 Security Breach

When private or sensitive information falls into the wrong hands due to criminal activity or unauthorised access, this is known as a data breach. Any information that should not have been made public has been compromised. Information such as trade secrets, IP, financial data, and medical records fall into this category. In a nutshell, the financial and regulatory repercussions, the theft of intellectual property by competitors, and the loss of trust from business partners and customers are just a few of the devastating outcomes that may result from a data breach [45].

4.2 Misconfiguration in the Appliances

Incorrectly configured IT resources exposes them vulnerable to abuse by unauthorised users. Some examples include not changing or breaking things like default configurations, credentials, and permissions. It's the most typical cause of data loss, and it may lead to service interruption as well as the alteration or deletion of resources. The most common result is the exposure of data held in cloud repositories, which may have severe implications for the firm.

- Neither a cloud security architecture nor a cloud security strategy have been developed

  The correct security infrastructure must be in place before businesses across the globe can safely migrate portions of their IT architecture to public clouds and so reduce their vulnerability to assaults. Many corporations and organisations are still fuzzy on the details of this method. Functionality, speed of migration, and limited knowledge with the shared security responsibility paradigm all contribute to a lack of strategy and security architecture in the cloud. Cyberattacks that succeed may have far-reaching effects on businesses, including legal ramifications, brand damage, and financial loss, and they may have their roots in poor strategy and security architecture.

- Inadequacy in controlling who has access to what and who has the keys

  Organizations may protect their most precious assets via the use of rules and technologies housed in identity management systems, access management systems, and credential management systems. Inadequate safeguards against the disclosure of personal information, login passwords, and other forms of authentication data may lead to security breaches. The absence of standard automated rotation of passwords and cryptographic keys; the failure of multifactor authentication and strong passwords; the lack of scalable access management systems, identities, and credentials; and the absence of automatic password and key rotation. As a direct result, malicious actors may get unauthorized access to information, which might have disastrous results for end-users or businesses.

- Inappropriate access to an account

  Account hijacking occurs when a malicious actor acquires access to highly sensitive or privileged accounts and then abuses that access. Account takeovers result in data breaches, which in turn lead to the exposure of the sensitive company and individual data, a drop in brand value, and potential reputation damage.

- Implied danger from company insiders

  An insider may be a current or former business partner, contractor, or other trusted employee who acts in a way that has a negative influence on the firm, whether by accident or on purpose. Someone with unfettered access to a company's networks, computer systems, and sensitive data is considered an insider. The loss of proprietary and secret information might be the result of an attack from inside the company.

- Insecure application programme interfaces (APIs) and user interfaces

  When it comes to connecting to and managing their cloud services, cloud providers provide a set of APIs and UIs accessible to their customers. The integrity of these APIs determines the reliability and security of cloud services. Misuse or even data breaches may result through compromised or otherwise compromised APIs. Businesses that depend on API-disclosing services with subpar user interfaces may suffer the most severe consequences in the fields of finance and regulatory.

5 Cloud Data Security

Many experts in the field have proposed different methods over the last few years for keeping cloud data secure. Here, we'll elaborate on and provide examples of a variety of methods for keeping massive datasets secure.

A paradigm is described that allows for multilayer encryption, which may be used as an alternative to single-level encryption for the purpose of securing data stored in the cloud. The recommended model employs the utilization of RSA and AES encryption methods. The RSA technique is used to generate the first layer of encryption for every text file that is submitted [46]. The newly generated text is then subjected to the AES algorithm in order to construct a secondary layer of encryption. The encrypted text is then permanently stored in a database. Deciphering text files requires first reading ciphertext that has been stored in a database [47]. The next step in the decryption process is to use the AES algorithm. In order to create text files without encryption, the RSA technique must be implemented. Multi-level encryption makes it difficult for an unauthorized user to acquire data since he would need both the encryption key and the decryption key to access the data. This makes it difficult for an unauthorized user to proceed.

In another work [48], proposed a framework for making sure no one but authorized individuals could access stored information. This approach divided data into regular, sensitive, and critical buckets before storing it in separate cloud data centers. One option for moving log files into an AmazonS3-Bucket for processing is to use the AWS-Cloud Trail (AWS-CT), which is part of the AWS Key-Management Service (KMS). AWS-CT may remember information like the IP address of the API caller, the current time, and the parameters of the AWS service. After the datacentres have been divided up in this way, online merchants like Amazon, Salesforce, and Google will each choose their own storage service provider. Big data cryptography virtual mapping may be used with Meta Cloud Data Storage as an alternative to protecting the data itself. Instead of safeguarding the massive data, this is the better option. Multiple copies of data are stored with different cloud storage providers to ensure that data is always available, regardless of any problems that may develop with the cloud's storage capacity. The proposed design also used MapReduce to tally up the number of cloud users simultaneously signed in.

As an additional measure, [49] presented a Scheme called ENPKESS, which provides a very high degree of security to protect sensitive data in the cloud from side-channel threats like timing attacks. Efficient and Non-Shareable Public Key Exponent Secure Scheme (ENPKESS) employs RSA public keys and the Diophantine equation to encrypt and decode data over the course of three steps. To prevent the side-channel attack, the ENPKESS public key is encrypted using the Knapsack method. Therefore, one may ensure the security of their private information by picking a key size suitable for this composition.

In the research work [50] presented a model that uses two processes, such as the deterministic process and the distributed data storage process. In order to provide a high degree of security, incoming data packets are examined by a deterministic process to see whether they should be distributed over other cloud servers. In order to safeguard information from unintended use, other procedures are in charge of recombining it into its original form. If it's typical information, we don't bother encrypting it and store it all in one place. According to the proposed approach, the sensitive data was divided into segments using the Alternative Data Distribution technique, with each subset being stored on its own cloud server. Efficient Data Confliction and Secure Efficient Data Distribution is used to encrypt and decrypt data for security purposes. Both operations make use of the same algorithm. As the data is encrypted, the key is created by utilising XOR operators to determine which packets of data are being encrypted. Method of information retrieval. By combining data packets saved on many cloud servers and utilising a unique key, new information may be generated. Everything related to this will be handled remotely.

In contrast, a paradigm for protecting data from unauthorised access and maintaining its confidentiality was given in [51]. The proposed method comprises three subcomponents: user authentication on several layers, encryption, and data retrieval. Multifactor authentication is comprised of the two steps of user registration and subsequent login. A user's unique identifier and password are created once they fill out the registration form. The next step is for users to choose a picture from the available database photos. The picture is then cropped based on the pixel locations, and both the image and the user's data are stored on a cloud server. First, the user must connect in to the server by providing their username and password. Providing the data provided is accurate, the server will show related images beside the registered photo. The user may choose the image, edit it, and then upload it to the server. In order to access the data, the user must verify the information given is correct; otherwise, the server will reject the request. Within the framework of the aforementioned paradigm, the cyclic shift transposition technique, which consists of encryption and decryption operations, has been proposed as a way of protecting sensitive data. Partitioning and shifting operations, including main and secondary diagonal shifts, row and column shifts, and others, are done during encryption to conceal the original data and get the encrypted text. After that, a hash value and a timestamp are generated for the information's cloud storage. When a user makes a data request to a cloud server, the server encrypts the data and then decodes it before giving it to the user.

Furthermore, [52] proposed a parallel and multistage security system that protects against attacks like a distributed denial of service (DDoS) assault and a man in the middle (MITM) attack by using authentication, intrusion, and encryption techniques. In order to access one's account, the front end usually necessitates a user to provide their login credentials. To protect against a man-in-the-middle attack, PAP will only send this data in plain text. The CHAP protocol was used in the background of the proposed method. The user will get a challenge string; when the response has been confirmed, the server will either approve or refuse the user. If the response is correct, an incursion is found by comparing login behaviours such location and DNS, and the user is granted access to the cloud server for file downloads and uploads. There will be no indication of an incursion if the answer is declined. The proposed method of protecting sensitive information employs Advanced Encryption Standard (AES) 256-bit encryption and decoding. The proposed model's generic structure allows it to be fused with other models, including the private, public, hybrid, and community ones.

6 Research Methods

When there is any content that needs to be stored, then the encryption zone will encrypt the contents during the write process, and the encryption zone will also decrypt the data when it is being read. Where the encryption zone is a special directory in the big data environment. During the process of creating the encryption zone, a key will be generated in order to increase the level of security. In order to provide an additional layer of safety, the big data platform uses something called a Data Encryption Key, which is a one-of-a-kind key that is specific to each file that is encrypted. When a client receives the data, the client will decrypt the encrypted data encryption key, and then it will use that data encrypted key to decrypt the data. When a user sends a query to any of the big data environments, those queries are managed by some inbuilt frameworks [53]. However, before those frameworks can process the data, they must first decrypt the data that is stored in the encryption zone. Due to the fact that big data deals with very large files, this process is going to take an extremely long time, which will ultimately have an effect on the performance of the e-learning application.

Since the encryption zone uses cipher suit like Advanced Encryption Standard (AES), which require higher computation resources and by default it is designed for encrypting and decrypting in a non-big data environment. The constraints of the presently existing method for encrypting the data while it is at rest in the big data environment are the focus of the work that has been suggested as a framework with the intention of addressing such limitations. This section discusses the design and implementation of the proposed framework.

6.1 Proposed Framework

The proposed framework states that there will be no encryption or decryption operations carried out inside the big data apps, and that instead, the client applications will be responsible for carrying out the whole of the cryptographic process. When any client initiates any sort of read or write activity on a big data platform, the client is responsible for dividing the whole data set to the requested size in the middleware application. Up till now, the default block size has been 64 megabytes, but now it has been increased to 128 MB. Therefore, whenever one of the user applications sends a query to the client to get any data, the client will first receive the data from the cloud, then it will begin the process of decryption on the client side for the user, and finally, it will provide the data to the user application.

Hackers can perform a man-in-the-middle attack to tamper with the data in transit if the data is not properly encrypted with strong encryption algorithms while it is in motion. The actual communication in the big data environment takes place between the client node and the data node, where the client node represents software running on the client side and the data node represents a specific software running in the cloud. Simple authentication and security layer protocol (SASL), which is by default enabled in big data applications, is used to ensure the security of the data in motion. AN overview of the proposed framework is depicted in the Fig. 11.

6.2 Experimental Setup

To evaluate the speed and performance of the two symmetric algorithms an experimental setup is built using the oracle virtual box, an open source application used for creating virtual environments. Also, Azure portal for executing and verifying the research in a virtual machine deployed on Cloud. Inside the virtual environment multiple ubuntu desktop servers with ram size and core are configured in the virtual

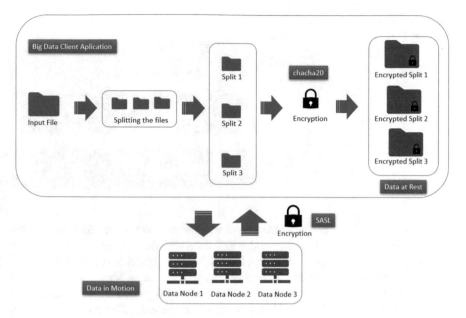

Fig. 11 The proposed framework. *Source* Author

box, this setup is used to analyse the performance of the two cipher algorithms with different hardware specifications. Different structured and unstructured files which are used in the e-learning platform will be used for testing the efficacy of the encryption as well as the decryption process. The big data file size will be ranging from 200 MB to 1 GB.

6.3 AES (Advance Encryption Algorithm)

AES consist of three block ciphers, AES-128, AES-192, AES256 which uses 128 bit key, 192 bit key as well as 256 bit key for the encryption and decryption purpose respectively. All the ciphers encrypt and decrypt the 128 bit block of data using these different keys. AES-256 is used to encrypt the confidential and top secret documents for enhanced security [54] (Fig. 12).

6.4 AES Implementation Using Python3

To implement the AES encryption, in the Linux system the python library called pycryptodome is installed using the command "pip install pycryptodome" and from the library the module is "Crypto" is imported it is because all the function related

Fig. 12 Overview of AES
algorithm [54]

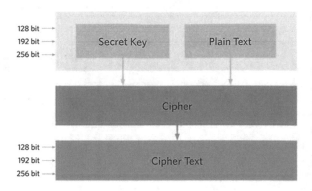

to AES algorithm is available in the crypto module and can be invoked very easily. For symmetric cryptography the sender and receiver sill uses same cryptographic keys, to generate key from a defined password "scrypt" function is used as shown in the Fig. 13. On completing the importing the modules important methods are then imported to the python file. "AES" is a method used for creating AES cipher and poly1305 is another method used to create message authentication code to verify the integrity and authentication of the message in the cipher. Here the poly1305 is used because it provides more robust authentication mechanism.

After completing the importing steps the MAC for the AES is generated and verified as shown in the Fig. 14. After generating the mac the input files are then converted using the AES function and stored in an object called encrypt as shown in Fig. 15.

To decrypt the encrypted contents with AES cipher suit, the method "AES_dec.decrypt()" is used. Initially the encrypted file is read and saved to an object "encrypted" using the method "read()" then the method "decrypt()" is used to decrypt the cipher text and saved to an object "decrypted". Finally, the decrypted contents are stored into a file, in this scenario "file_AES_decrypted" (see Fig. 16).

- Chacha20 algorithm

```
1  import secrets
2  import scrypt
3
4  password = 'password'
5  salt = secrets.token_bytes(32)
6  key = scrypt.hash(password, salt, N=2048, r=8, p=1, buflen=32)
7
8  #Encryption and MAC calculation
9  from Crypto.Cipher import AES
10 from Crypto.Hash import Poly1305
```

Fig. 13 Importing important modules and libraries. *Source* Author lab

```
def generate_Poly1305_mac(data, key, cipher=AES):
    mac = Poly1305.new(key=key, cipher=cipher, data=data)
    return (mac.hexdigest(), mac.nonce)
def verify_Poly1305_mac(data, key, nonce, mac_digest, cipher=AES):
    mac_verify = Poly1305.new(data=data, key=key, nonce=nonce,
                cipher=AES)
    try:
        mac_verify.hexverify(mac_digest)
        #print('Message Authentication Success')
    except:
        #print('Message Authentication Failed')
```

Fig. 14 Generating the mac. *Source* Author lab

```
24 cipher_text = aes_enc.encrypt(original)
25 nonce = aes_enc.nonce
26 hexdigest, poly_nonce = generate_Poly1305_mac(data=original, key=key)
```

Fig. 15 Generating the cipher text. *Source* Author lab

```
aes_dec = AES.new(key, AES.MODE_CTR, nonce=nonce)
# opening the encrypted file to decrypt
with open('fileout_aes', 'rb') as file:
    encrypted = file.read()

#performing decryption susing aes
decrypted = aes_dec.decrypt(encrypted)
'''verify_Poly1305_mac(data=decrypted, key=key, nonce=poly_nonce,
                    mac_digest=hexdigest)'''

#writting the decrupted file
with open('file_aes_decrpted', 'wb') as decrypted_file:
    decrypted_file.write(decrypted)
```

Fig. 16 Decryption script. *Source* Author

Chacha20 is stream cipher which is used to encrypt one byte at a time instead of block of 128 bit data in the block cipher like AES. Chacha20 is member of salsa20 stream cipher family and has same design as salsa20 with minor changes.it uses the 32 bytes length key (k) and nounce(r) for length 8 bytes, these parameters are inputted into the plain text to create the cipher text. The value of the nounce will be always fixed until the value of the key is changed. The 256-bit key is manipulated into 256 bit streams with 64 byte random blockes.it encrypts plain text by taking single byte from it and storing it with keystreams and then it will be authenticated with poly1305 mac (Fig. 17).

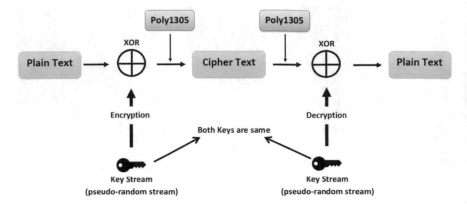

Fig. 17 Overview of chacha20. *Source* Author created

6.5 Chacha20 Implementation Using Python3

To create the cipher text using the chacha20 the crypto module is again used and the "chacha20_ploy1305" method is imported and aliases with the string cha for make the calling process more easier. then the file name that is passed as first argument is opened in the read format and the contents of the binaries are stored in the object "original" later this object encrypted using the method "chach20.encrypt_ and_digest()" and the generated cipher text is stored into the a new file "fileout_ chacha"(see Fig. 18).

To perform the decryption process at the initial stage the a encrypted opened using the "open()" function and the contents are read with "read()" method then stored into an object called "encrypted". Then this object will be passed as an argument into "decrypt_and_verify()" method to get the decrypted content and saved into "decrypted" after that a new file is created and stored all the decrypted contents into it (see Fig. 19).

```
from Crypto.Cipher import ChaCha20_Poly1305 as cha
with open(sys.argv[1], 'rb') as file:
    original = file.read()

chacha20 = cha.new(key=key)
cipher_text, mac = chacha20.encrypt_and_digest(original)
nonce = chacha20.nonce
with open('fileout_chacha', 'wb') as encrypted_file:
    encrypted_file.write(cipher_text)
```

Fig. 18 Implementation of chacha20. *Source* Author lab

```
# opening the encrypted file to decrypt
with open('fileout_chacha', 'rb') as file:
    encrypted = file.read()
#try:
chacha_poly = cha.new(key=key, nonce=nonce)
val1=datetime.now()
decrypted = chacha_poly.decrypt_and_verify(encrypted, mac)
val2=datetime.now()
difference=val2-val1

#writting the decrupted file
with open('file_chacha_decrpted', 'wb') as decrypted_file:
    decrypted_file.write(decrypted)
```

Fig. 19 Decrypting the encrypted file using chacha20. *Source* Author lab

7 Data Analysis and Critical Discussion

A Python programme is implemented and run through the command line interface of the Linux platform so that the performance of the Chacha20 as well as AES can be evaluated. The reason the Linux platform was chosen for making all of the during the experiment and evaluation stage is because these are open source and easy to install in the virtual environment, and in addition to that, there is no licencing that will be required to run these operating systems. The open-source platform has the potential to generate accurate results if Python programmes are run in an environment based on Linux. The testing is performed on fixed RAM and varying core (Scenario 1, 2, 3)and varying RAM and fixed core (Scenario 4 and 5) using different volumes of Big data files.

Scenario I: Testing the Performance of Chacha20 and AES with 1 Cores and 2 GB RAM

In this first stage of testing, the number of core of the Linux operating system is configured into one and the RAM is configured into 2 GB. A single core with 2 GB RAM is the minimum requirement needed to run a Linux OS in the virtual platform.

Then memory and CPU utilisation of the operating system before execution of the test code is depicted in the Fig. 20. After execution the of the python script, it was noted that to perform the encryption chach20 took "0.6329" seconds whereas AES took "0.8234" seconds, whereas during the decryption chacha20 took "0.6884" second and AES took "1.8606" seconds. When analysing the CPU and ram usage during both cipher's encryption and decryption process multiple peaks are visible as shown in the Fig. 20. The peaks represent the 100% utilisation of the CPU when the ciphers are executed (Fig. 21). The results are depicted in the Table 1.

When the experiment is performed with the 400 MB file with the same configuration of single core processor and 2 GB RAM ChaCha20 leads the AES. The encryption time taken by chacha20 is 1.3387 s and the decryption time is 7.691 s. Whereas the AES failed to perform the encryption and decryption, because for AES

Table 1 Test result with 200 MB file

Hardware specification	Single core with 2 GB RAM	File size: 200 MB
	Chacha20	AES
Encryption (in seconds)	0.6239	0.8234
Decryption (in seconds)	0.6884	1.8606

Source Author

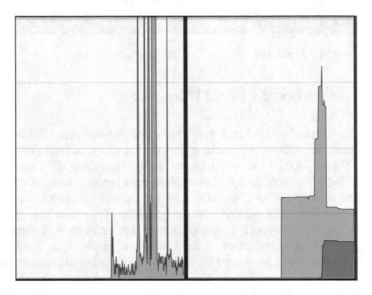

Fig. 20 Memory and CPU utilisation after testing. *Source* Author lab

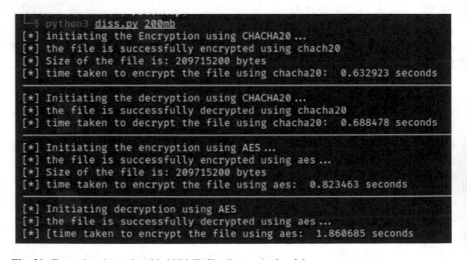

Fig. 21 Executing the code with 200 MB file. *Source* Author lab

Table 2 Test result with 400 MB file

Hardware specification	Single core with 2 GB RAM	File size: 400 MB
	Chacha20	AES
Encryption (in seconds)	1.3387	System crashed
Decryption (in seconds)	7.691	System crashed

Source Author

it demands more CPU and RAM resources from the host machine, thus the CPU usage of the host machine is reached to 100 and when it demands more than that, the system halted the encryption as well as decryption operation. The CPU utilisation of the ram and CPU is shown in the Fig. 22, and the output is depicted in the Fig. 23. The figure show the three peaks in the CPU performance it is because the test were conducted for three times and all the three times, AES crashes the system. The summary of the test is shown in the Table 2.

When the experiment is performed with the 600 MB file, chacha was able to perform the encryption but could not process with decryption, similarly the AES also failed to perform the encryption as well as decryption (see the Fig. 24).the performance of the CPU and RAM is mentioned in the Fig. 25. Also, after performing the encryption and decryption process with 800 MB file both cipher suits crashes the system (see Figs. 26, 27).

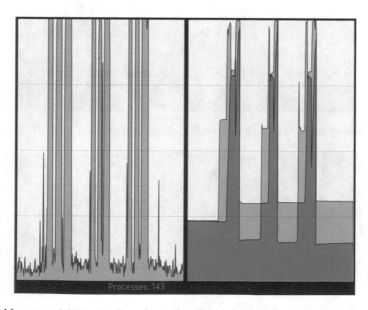

Fig. 22 Memory and CPU utilisation after testing. *Source* Author lab

```
 └$ python3 diss.py 400mb
[*] initiating the Encryption using CHACHA20 ...
[*] the file is successfully encrypted using chach20
[*] Size of the file is: 419430400 bytes
[*] time taken to encrypt the file using chacha20:  1.3387 seconds

[*] Initiating the decryption using CHACHA20 ...
[*] the file is successfully decrypted using chacha20
[*] time taken to decrypt the file using chacha20:  7.691547 seconds

[*] Initiating the encryption using AES ...
zsh: killed     python3 diss.py 400mb
```

Fig. 23 Executing the code with 400 MB file. *Source* Author lab

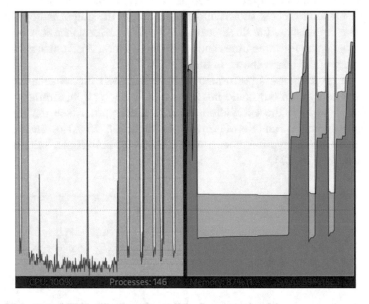

Fig. 24 Memory and CPU utilisation after testing. *Source* Author lab

```
 └$ python3 diss.py 600mb
[*] initiating the Encryption using CHACHA20 ...
[*] the file is successfully encrypted using chach20
[*] Size of the file is: 629145600 bytes
[*] time taken to encrypt the file using chacha20:  5.689486 seconds

[*] Initiating the decryption using CHACHA20 ...
zsh: killed     python3 diss.py 600mb
```

Fig. 25 Executing the code with 600 MB file. *Source* Author lab

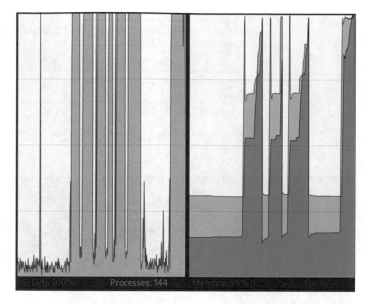

Fig. 26 Memory and CPU utilisation after testing. *Source* Author lab

```
  ⌐$ python3 diss.py 800mb
  [*] initiating the Encryption using CHACHA20 ...
  zsh: killed     python3 diss.py 800mb
Alt Text: Text
```

Fig. 27 Executing the code with 800 MB file. *Source* Author lab

Scenario II: Testing the Performance of Chacha20 and AES with 2 Cores and 2 GB RAM

With 200 MB file, Chacha20 took "0.629312" seconds to encrypt and "0.645436" seconds to decrypt. Whereas AES took "0.776672" seconds to encrypt and "1.459133" seconds to decrypt. The CPU utilisation has minor peaks but was able to complete the encryption and decryption for both algorithms. Chacha20 has quicker encryption and decryptions timings compared to AES (Table 3, Figs. 28, 29).

With 400 MB file used Chacha20 take "1.317479" seconds to encrypt and "6.798821" to decrypt. On the other hand, AES fails to encrypt and decrypt as the system crashes. Again, the resource from the host isn't enough for AES algorithm to encrypt or decrypt a 400 MB file (Table 4, Figs. 30, 31).

With 600 MB file used Chacha20 encrypts the file in "3.9002" seconds and the decryption fails. Whereas AES algorithm crashes (Encrypt/Decrypt) for 600 MB file with two core and 2 GB RAM (Table 5, Figs. 32 and 33).

Table 3 Test result with 200 MB file

Hardware specification	Two core with 2 GB RAM	File size: 200 MB
	Chacha20	AES
Encryption (in seconds)	0.6239	0.7766
Decryption (in seconds)	0.6454	1.4591

Source Author

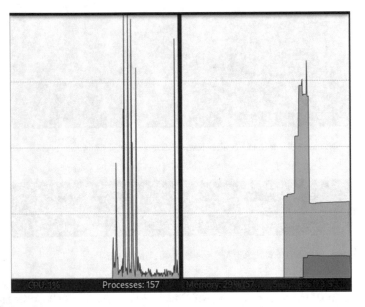

Fig. 28 Memory and CPU utilisation after testing. *Source* Author lab

With 800 MB file used Chacha20 encrypts the file in "4.515282" seconds and the decryption fails. Whereas AES algorithm crashes (Encrypt/Decrypt) for 800 MB file with two core and 2 GB RAM (Table 6, Figs. 34 and 35).

Scenario III: Testing the Performance of Chacha20 and AES with 3 cores and 2 GB RAM

With 200 MB file, Chacha20 took "0.62713" seconds to encrypt and "0.728297" seconds to decrypt. Whereas AES took "0.789645" seconds to encrypt and "1.953927" seconds to decrypt. The CPU utilisation has considerable peaks but was able to complete the encryption and decryption for both algorithms (Table 7, Figs. 36 and 37).

With 400 MB file in use Chacha20 was able to encrypt the file in "1.268901" seconds and decrypt it in "8.758214" seconds. AES encryption or decryption couldn't

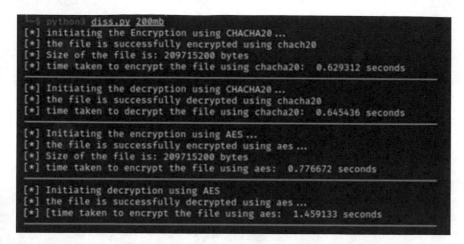

Fig. 29 Executing the code with 200 MB file. *Source* Author lab

Table 4 Test result with 400 MB file

Hardware specification	Two core with 2 GB RAM	File size: 400 MB
	Chacha20	AES
Encryption (in seconds)	1.317479	System crashed
Decryption (in seconds)	6.798821	System crashed

Source Author

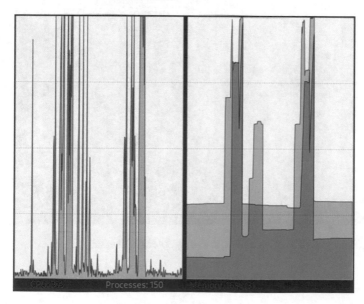

Fig. 30 Memory and CPU utilisation after testing. *Source* Author lab

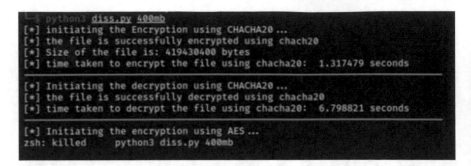

Fig. 31 Executing the code with 400 MB file. *Source* Author lab

Table 5 Test result with 600 MB file

Hardware specification	Two core with 2 GB RAM	File size: 600 MB
	Chacha20	AES
Encryption (in seconds)	3.9002	System crashed
Decryption (in seconds)	System crashed	System crashed

Source Author

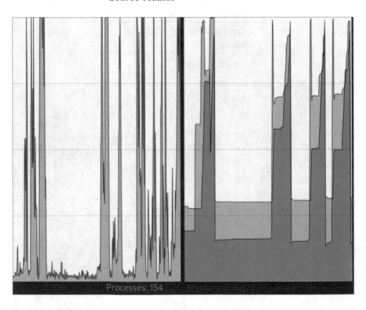

Fig. 32 Memory and CPU utilisation after testing. *Source* Author lab

```
└─$ python3 diss.py 600mb
[*] initiating the Encryption using CHACHA20 ...
[*] the file is successfully encrypted using chach20
[*] Size of the file is: 629145600 bytes
[*] time taken to encrypt the file using chacha20:   3.9002 seconds
────────────────────────────────────────────────────────────
[*] Initiating the decryption using CHACHA20 ...
zsh: killed     python3 diss.py 600mb
```

Fig. 33 Executing the code with 600 MB file. *Source* Author lab

Table 6 Test result with 800 MB file

Hardware specification	Two core with 2 GB RAM	File size: 800 MB
	Chacha20	AES
Encryption (in seconds)	4.515282	System crashed
Decryption (in seconds)	System crashed	System crashed

Source Author

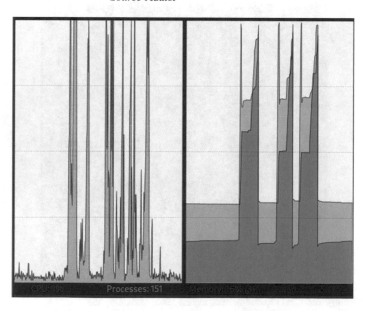

Fig. 34 Memory and CPU utilisation after testing. *Source* Author lab

Fig. 35 Executing the code
with 800 MB file. *Source*
Author lab

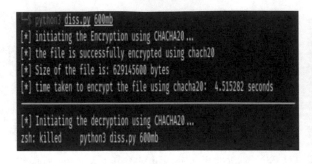

Table 7 Test result with
200 MB file

Hardware specification	Three core with 2 GB RAM	File size: 200 MB
	Chacha20s	AES
Encryption (in seconds)	0.62713	0.789645
Decryption (in seconds)	0.728297	1.953927

Source Author

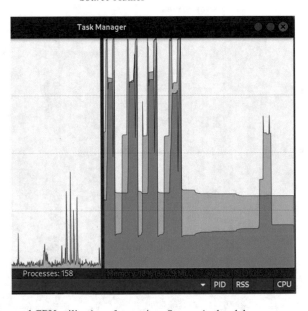

Fig. 36 Memory and CPU utilisation after testing. *Source* Author lab

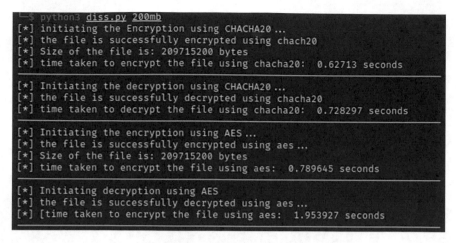

```
└─$ python3 diss.py 200mb
[*] initiating the Encryption using CHACHA20 ...
[*] the file is successfully encrypted using chach20
[*] Size of the file is: 209715200 bytes
[*] time taken to encrypt the file using chacha20:  0.62713 seconds

[*] Initiating the decryption using CHACHA20 ...
[*] the file is successfully decrypted using chacha20
[*] time taken to decrypt the file using chacha20:  0.728297 seconds

[*] Initiating the encryption using AES ...
[*] the file is successfully encrypted using aes ...
[*] Size of the file is: 209715200 bytes
[*] time taken to encrypt the file using aes:  0.789645 seconds

[*] Initiating decryption using AES
[*] the file is successfully decrypted using aes ...
[*] [time taken to encrypt the file using aes:  1.953927 seconds
```

Fig. 37 Executing the code with 200 MB file. *Source* Author lab

Table 8 Test result with 400 MB file

Hardware specification	Three core with 2 GB RAM	File size: 400 MB
	Chacha20	AES
Encryption (in seconds)	1.268901	System crashed
Decryption (in seconds)	8.758214	System crashed

Source Author

occur due to insufficient system resource leading to system crash (Table 8, Figs. 38, 39).

With 600 MB file Chacha20 encrypts in "5.662598" seconds whereas the decryption fails. In comparison, AES fails for both encryption and decryption with insufficient host resource (Table 9, Figs. 40 and 41).

After conducting the experiment with less resources Chacha20 took lesser time for encryption as well as decryption compared with AES cipher suits. Another interesting thing noted is that with lesser resources AES crashes more quickly than the chacha20.

Scenario IV: Testing the Performance of the Chacha20 and AES with 4 cores and 2 GB RAM

With 200 MB file on a host system with 4 cores and 2 GB RAM, Chacha20 took "0.617211" seconds to encrypt and "0.648423" seconds to decrypt. Whereas AES took "0.805751" seconds to encrypt and "2.005582" seconds to decrypt. The CPU utilisation has considerable peaks but was able to complete the encryption and decryption for both algorithms (Table 10, Figs. 42 and 43).

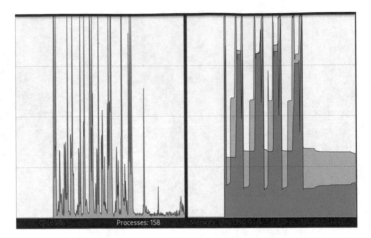

Fig. 38 Memory and CPU utilisation after testing. *Source* Author lab

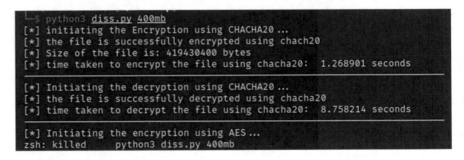

Fig. 39 Executing the code with 400 MB file. *Source* Author lab

Table 9 Test result with 600 MB file

Hardware specification	Three core with 2 GB RAM	File size: 600 MB
	Chacha20	AES
Encryption (in seconds)	5.662598	System crashed
Decryption (in seconds)	System crashed	System crashed

Source Author

With 400 MB file in use Chacha20 was able to encrypt the file in "1.296986" seconds and decrypt it in "14.419288" seconds. AES encryption or decryption couldn't occur due to insufficient system resource leading to system crash (Table 11, Figs. 44 and 45).

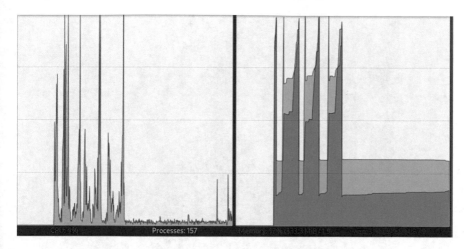

Fig. 40 Memory and CPU utilisation after testing. *Source* Author lab

Fig. 41 Executing the code with 600 MB file. *Source* Author lab

```
└$ python3 diss.py 600mb
[*] initiating the Encryption using CHACHA20...
[*] the file is successfully encrypted using chach20
[*] Size of the file is: 629145600 bytes
[*] time taken to encrypt the file using chacha20: 5.662598 seconds

[*] Initiating the decryption using CHACHA20...
zsh: killed     python3 diss.py 600mb
```

Table 10 Test result with 200 MB file

Hardware specification	Four core with 2 GB RAM	File size: 200 MB
	Chacha20	AES
Encryption (in seconds)	0.617211	0.805751
Decryption (in seconds)	0.648423	2.005582

Source Author

With 600 MB file Chacha20 encrypts in "5.230372" seconds whereas the decryption fails. In comparison, AES fails for both encryption and decryption with insufficient host resource (Table 12, Figs. 46 and 47).

Scenario V: Testing the Performance of the Chacha20 and AES with 4 cores and 4 GB RAM

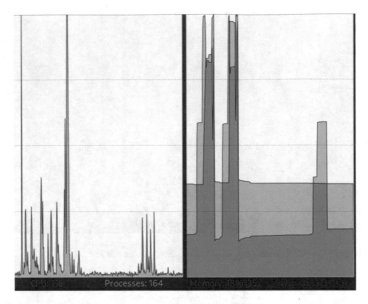

Fig. 42 Memory and CPU utilisation after testing. *Source* Author lab

Fig. 43 Executing the code with 200 MB file. *Source* Author lab

With 400 MB file in use Chacha20 was able to encrypt the file in "1.245147" seconds and decrypt it in "1.307742" seconds. AES took "1.365974" seconds for encryption and "5.061711" seconds for decryption (Table 13, Figs. 48 and 49).

With 600 MB file in use Chacha20 was able to encrypt the file in "1.914766" seconds and decrypt it in "2.838864" seconds. AES took "5.298548" seconds for encryption and "8.285469" seconds for decryption (Table 14, Figs. 50 and 51).

Table 11 Test result with 400 MB file

Hardware specification	Four core with 2 GB RAM	File size: 400 MB
	Chacha20	AES
Encryption (in seconds)	1.296986	System crashed
Decryption (in seconds)	14.419288	System crashed

Source Author

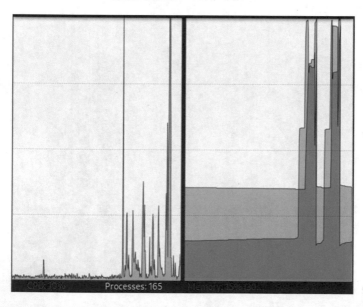

Fig. 44 Memory and CPU utilisation after testing. *Source* Author lab

```
└─$ python3 diss.py 400mb
[*] initiating the Encryption using CHACHA20 ...
[*] the file is successfully encrypted using chach20
[*] Size of the file is: 419430400 bytes
[*] time taken to encrypt the file using chacha20:  1.296986 seconds

[*] Initiating the decryption using CHACHA20 ...
[*] the file is successfully decrypted using chacha20
[*] time taken to decrypt the file using chacha20:  14.419288 seconds

[*] Initiating the encryption using AES ...
zsh: killed     python3 diss.py 400mb
```

Fig. 45 Executing the code with 400 MB file. *Source* Author lab

Table 12 Test result with 600 MB file

Hardware specification	Four core with 2 GB RAM	File size: 600 MB
	Chacha20	AES
Encryption (in seconds)	5.230372	System crashed
Decryption (in seconds)	System crashed	System crashed

Source Author

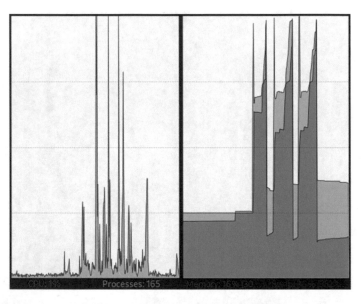

Fig. 46 Memory and CPU utilisation after testing. *Source* Author lab

Fig. 47 Executing the code with 600 MB file. *Source* Author lab

```
└─$ python3 diss.py 600mb
[*] initiating the Encryption using CHACHA20 ...
[*] the file is successfully encrypted using chach20
[*] Size of the file is: 629145600 bytes
[*] time taken to encrypt the file using chacha20:  5.230372 seconds

[*] Initiating the decryption using CHACHA20 ...
zsh: killed     python3 diss.py 600mb
```

Table 13 Test result with 400 MB file

Hardware specification	Four core with 4 GB RAM	File size: 400 MB
	Chacha20	AES
Encryption (in seconds)	1.245147	1.365974
Decryption (in seconds)	1.307742	5.061711

Source Author

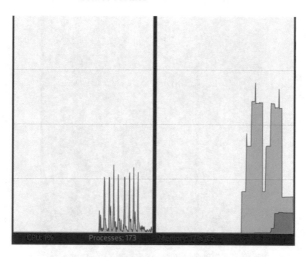

Fig. 48 Memory and CPU utilisation after testing. *Source* Author lab

```
└─$ python3 diss.py 400mb
[*] initiating the Encryption using CHACHA20 ...
[*] the file is successfully encrypted using chach20
[*] Size of the file is: 419430400 bytes
[*] time taken to encrypt the file using chacha20:  1.245147 seconds

[*] Initiating the decryption using CHACHA20 ...
[*] the file is successfully decrypted using chacha20
[*] time taken to decrypt the file using chacha20:  1.307742 seconds

[*] Initiating the encryption using AES ...
[*] the file is successfully encrypted using aes ...
[*] Size of the file is: 419430400 bytes
[*] time taken to encrypt the file using aes:  1.365974 seconds

[*] Initiating decryption using AES
[*] the file is successfully decrypted using aes ...
[*] [time taken to encrypt the file using aes:  5.061711 seconds
```

Fig. 49 Executing the code with 400 MB file. *Source* Author lab

Table 14 Test result with 600 MB file

Hardware specification	Four core with 4 GB RAM	File size: 600 MB
	Chacha2	AES
Encryption (in seconds)	1.914766	5.298548
Decryption (in seconds)	2.838864	8.285469

Source Author

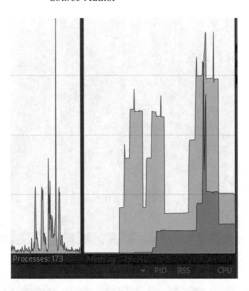

Fig. 50 Memory and CPU utilisation after testing. *Source* Author lab

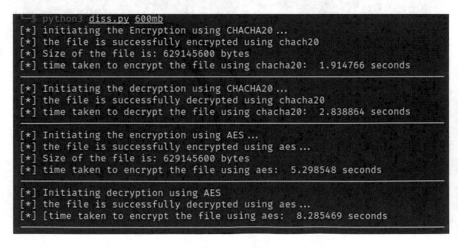

```
└─$ python3 diss.py 600mb
[*] initiating the Encryption using CHACHA20 ...
[*] the file is successfully encrypted using chach20
[*] Size of the file is: 629145600 bytes
[*] time taken to encrypt the file using chacha20:  1.914766 seconds

[*] Initiating the decryption using CHACHA20 ...
[*] the file is successfully decrypted using chacha20
[*] time taken to decrypt the file using chacha20:  2.838864 seconds

[*] Initiating the encryption using AES ...
[*] the file is successfully encrypted using aes ...
[*] Size of the file is: 629145600 bytes
[*] time taken to encrypt the file using aes:  5.298548 seconds

[*] Initiating decryption using AES
[*] the file is successfully decrypted using aes ...
[*] [time taken to encrypt the file using aes:  8.285469 seconds
```

Fig. 51 Executing the code with 600 MB file. *Source* Author lab

Table 15 Test result with 800 MB file

Hardware specification	Four core with 4 GB RAM	File size: 800 MB
	Chacha20	AES
Encryption (in seconds)	2.519731	System crashed
Decryption (in seconds)	System crashed	System crashed

Source Author

With 800 MB file in use Chacha20 was able to encrypt the file in "2.519731" seconds and decryption fails. Whereas AES encryption and decryption fails due to insufficient host system resources (Table 15, Figs. 52 and 53).

With 1 GB file in use Chacha20 was able to encrypt the file in "3.246344" seconds and decryption fails. Whereas AES encryption and decryption fails due to insufficient host system resources (Table 16, Figs. 54 and 55).

By conducting experiments with both configuration—varying core and fixed RAM/fixed core and varying RAM, the conclusion is that a minimum of 4 cores and 16 GB RAM is required to process huge big data files (say minimum 1 GB) for both encryption and decryption using both algorithms. Also it is noted, ChaCha20 is able to encrypt and decrypt with lesser resources where AES is crashing the system and halting the operation. From the results/screenshots shared above we can say Chacha20 is superlative to AES algorithm. The below graph depicts successful

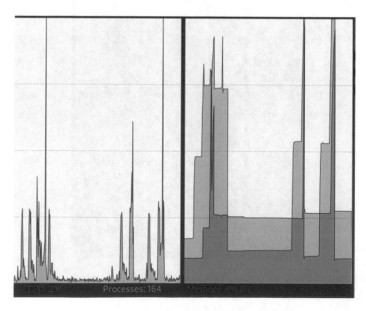

Fig. 52 Memory and CPU utilisation after testing. *Source* Author lab

Fig. 53 Executing the code with 800 MB file. *Source* Author lab

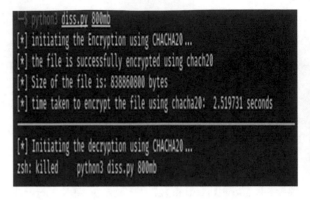

Table 16 Test result with 1 GB file

Hardware specification	Four core with 4 GB RAM	File size: 1 GB
	Chacha20	AES
Encryption (in seconds)	3.246344	System crashed
Decryption (in seconds)	System crashed	System crashed

Source Author

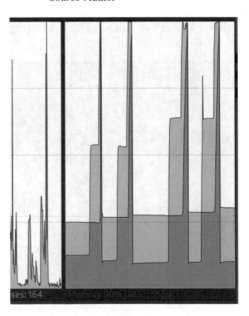

Fig. 54 Memory and CPU utilisation after testing. *Source* Author lab

```
└$ python3 diss.py 1gb
[*] initiating the Encryption using CHACHA20 ...
[*] the file is successfully encrypted using chach20
[*] Size of the file is: 1073741824 bytes
[*] time taken to encrypt the file using chacha20:  3.246344 seconds

[*] Initiating the decryption using CHACHA20 ...
zsh: killed      python3 diss.py 1gb
```

Fig. 55 Executing the code with 600 MB file. *Source* Author lab

encryption and decryption of both Chacha20 and AES on Big data file ranging from 200 MB–1 GB with 4 core and 16 GB RAM. ChaCha20 is taking lesser time to encrypt as well as decrypt compared to AES. This proves stream cipher (ChaCha20) is a best way to secure big data when it is in rest compared to traditional method of securing it using block cipher (AES) (Tables 17 and 18).

The performance of the cipher suite have been plotted in the below graph to show ChaCha20 is taking lesser time for encryption and decryption than AES (Figs. 56, 57).

Every day, people all over the world produce more than 2.5 quintillion bytes of data, which is equal to one million terabytes. Managing that data is hard, yet we frequently utilise vast portions of it in a variety of ways that are often unfathomable, despite the fact that doing so is difficult. The extraction of information from different archives and sources is what constitutes "big data", and it may lead to a greater comprehension of global events in a variety of fields, including climate change, economics, medicine, and more [17]. Researchers point out that one of the most significant challenges that are faced by those who want to collaborate with big data is that, while a portion of it may be structured, the majority of it is only semi-structured, and enormous sums of it are completely unstructured. This presents one of the most significant challenges that are faced by those who want to collaborate with big data.

The storing, managing, and analysing of all of this data is now one of the most diffi-cult tasks that the computer industry is facing today. Even though cloud computing makes available a significant number of the required tools in a decentralized fashion

Table 17 Encryption and Decryption result for file size ranging from 200 MB–1 GB

File (MB)	Encryption time		File(Mb)	Decryption time	
	Chacha20	AES		Chacha20	AES
200	1.200117	1.807391	200	1.131582	1.900241
400	2.257761	2.658602	400	2.342444	4.306854
600	3.322088	3.498764	600	3.273396	7.90117
800	4.48455	4.579377	800	4.548836	10.248254
1024	5.554087	5.759307	1024	5.677579	13.940495

Source Author

and has, to some extent, caused a revolution in information and communications technology (ICT), there is still a long way to go before we can actually deal with big data on a comprehensive level. On the other hand, cloud-based distributed storage and massively parallel processing of large amounts of data might offer the grounds upon which the future of big data and predictive modelling could be constructed.

In today's data-driven world, every company that wants to be successful must prioritise collecting and analysing large amounts of data. The movement of data through businesses has been expedited as a result of the implementation of numerous

Table 18 Code Execution proofs (4 core 16 GB RAM)

Code Execution proofs (4 core 16 GB RAM)

```
$python3 diss.py 200mb
[*] initiating the Encryption using CHACHA20...
[*] the file is successfully encrypted using chach20
[*] Size of the file is: 209715200 bytes
[*] time taken to encrypt the file using chacha20:  1.200117 seconds

[*] Initiating the decryption using CHACHA20...
[*] the file is successfully decrypted using chacha20
[*] time taken to decrypt the file using chacha20:  1.131582 seconds
----------------------------------------------------------------------
[*] Initiating the encryption using AES...
[*] the file is successfully encrypted using aes...
[*] Size of the file is: 209715200 bytes
[*] time taken to encrypt the file using aes:  1.807391 seconds
----------------------------------------------------------------------
[*] Initiating decryption using AES
[*] the file is successfully decrypted using aes...
[*] [time taken to encrypt the file using aes:  1.900241 seconds
```

```
$python3 diss.py 400mb
[*] initiating the Encryption using CHACHA20...
[*] the file is successfully encrypted using chach20
[*] Size of the file is: 419430400 bytes
[*] time taken to encrypt the file using chacha20:  2.257761 seconds

[*] Initiating the decryption using CHACHA20...
[*] the file is successfully decrypted using chacha20
[*] time taken to decrypt the file using chacha20:  2.342444 seconds
----------------------------------------------------------------------
[*] Initiating the encryption using AES...
[*] the file is successfully encrypted using aes...
[*] Size of the file is: 419430400 bytes
[*] time taken to encrypt the file using aes:  2.658602 seconds
----------------------------------------------------------------------
[*] Initiating decryption using AES
[*] the file is successfully decrypted using aes...
[*] [time taken to encrypt the file using aes:  4.306854 seconds
```

```
$python3 diss.py 600mb
[*] initiating the Encryption using CHACHA20...
[*] the file is successfully encrypted using chach20
[*] Size of the file is: 629145600 bytes
[*] time taken to encrypt the file using chacha20:  3.322088 seconds

[*] Initiating the decryption using CHACHA20...
[*] the file is successfully decrypted using chacha20
[*] time taken to decrypt the file using chacha20:  3.273396 seconds
----------------------------------------------------------------------
[*] Initiating the encryption using AES...
[*] the file is successfully encrypted using aes...
[*] Size of the file is: 629145600 bytes
[*] time taken to encrypt the file using aes:  3.498764 seconds
----------------------------------------------------------------------
[*] Initiating decryption using AES
[*] the file is successfully decrypted using aes...
[*] [time taken to encrypt the file using aes:  7.90117 seconds
```

(continued)

Table 18 (continued)

Code Execution proofs (4 core 16 GB RAM)

```
$python3 diss.py 800mb
[*] initiating the Encryption using CHACHA20...
[*] the file is successfully encrypted using chach20
[*] Size of the file is: 838860800 bytes
[*] time taken to encrypt the file using chacha20:  4.48455 seconds
----------------------------------------------------------------
[*] Initiating the decryption using CHACHA20...
[*] the file is successfully decrypted using chacha20
[*] time taken to decrypt the file using chacha20:  4.548836 seconds
----------------------------------------------------------------
[*] Initiating the encryption using AES...
[*] the file is successfully encrypted using aes...
[*] Size of the file is: 838860800 bytes
[*] time taken to encrypt the file using aes:  4.579377 seconds
----------------------------------------------------------------
[*] Initiating decryption using AES
[*] the file is successfully decrypted using aes...
[*] [time taken to encrypt the file using aes:  10.248254 seconds
----------------------------------------------------------------
```

```
$python3 diss.py 1gb
[*] initiating the Encryption using CHACHA20...
[*] the file is successfully encrypted using chach20
[*] Size of the file is: 1073741824 bytes
[*] time taken to encrypt the file using chacha20:  5.554087 seconds
----------------------------------------------------------------
[*] Initiating the decryption using CHACHA20...
[*] the file is successfully decrypted using chacha20
[*] time taken to decrypt the file using chacha20:  5.677579 seconds
----------------------------------------------------------------
[*] Initiating the encryption using AES...
[*] the file is successfully encrypted using aes...
[*] Size of the file is: 1073741824 bytes
[*] time taken to encrypt the file using aes:  5.759307 seconds
----------------------------------------------------------------
[*] Initiating decryption using AES
[*] the file is successfully decrypted using aes...
[*] [time taken to encrypt the file using aes:  13.940495 seconds
----------------------------------------------------------------
```

Source Author

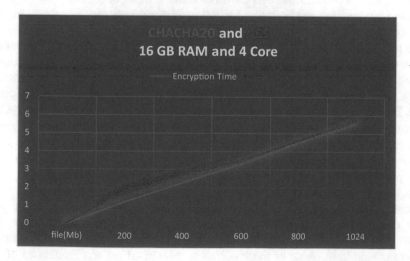

Fig. 56 4 Core 16 GB RAM encryption time of Big Data (data in rest). *Source* Author

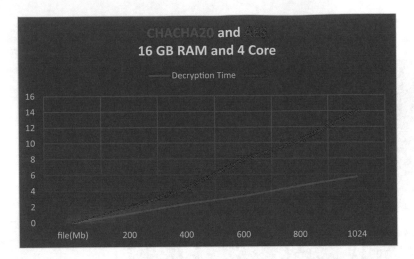

Fig. 57 4 Core 16 GB RAM decryption time of Big Data (data in rest). *Source* Author

modern infrastructures, which has enabled real-time insight delivery and improved decision-making. On the other hand, Big Data comes with a number of security threats that might have a severe effect on enterprises. Data breaches are possible outcomes of failing to implement adequate safety protocols during the storing and processing of large amounts of data. While it is important for businesses to make their data more easily accessible, it is as important for them to maintain control over their big data in order to maintain the confidence of their consumers [55].

Most middleware applications, including Hadoop, use block cyphers for the purpose of protecting the confidentiality of data while it is at rest. A number of research papers and online sources are re-examined and analysed in the course of the literature review, which focuses on the operation of big data and cloud computing. There is a variety of studies published in academic journals that highlights the risks associated with using cloud computing, when it is applied to online education. Following an examination of the research journal, it became clear that the big data and cloud environments are subject to a few threats to their data security, and it is exceedingly challenging to find a solution to all of these threats using a single piece of research. Consequently, the focus of this research paper will be on the threats to data privacy that are posed by platforms that store large amounts of data.

It was discovered after reviewing several papers that Hadoop is one of the most popular applications in the big data space, and that it makes use of AES for both encrypting and decrypting the data. This discovery was made possible by the fact that Hadoop uses AES. Even though AES is one of the best algorithms for generating cryptographic keys, some of the research articles point out the limitations of the algorithm as well as the various successful attacks that can be performed on it. These pieces of literature inspire a search for cryptographic algorithms that are both more powerful and more secure, with the end goal of encrypting and decrypting data while it is stored. There is some information in the available literature regarding the performance and indestructible nature of stream cyphers, particularly chacha20.

Conclusions and Future Work

The goal of this research is to improve the safety of an e-learning programme that makes use of cloud storage and large amounts of data. Hosting an e-learning application in the cloud raises a few security concerns, including lack of transparency into how the data is being used and the inability of corporations and individuals to take action if they have reason to suspect their information is being misused. Since there are no clear means to actively monitor the resources, this might pose a security risk. In addition, there is always the risk that their information is not deleted entirely when they stop using the service. Customers have to pool their use of physical resources and have limited access to their own data. Therefore, consumers must depend on cloud providers to utilise trust mechanisms rather than transparently handing over control of data and cloud resources [1]. Companies must have confidence that their private information is safe in the cloud and is not being accessed or sold to other parties.

Over half (54%) of UK institutions in a recent poll reported a data breach to the Information Commissioner's Office. When asked by security company Redscan under the Freedom of Information Act, 86 institutions disclosed significant weaknesses in their data leak prevention measures. Several UK institutions are among the best in the world when it comes to research, making them prime targets for cybercriminals and state-sponsored hackers. Criminals reportedly targeted institutions earlier this year in an attempt to obtain coronavirus research. As a result, the institution faces significant financial and reputational damages if the security vulnerabilities are not handled properly.

When the data is kept on the big data platform, the suggested security framework addresses all of the significant security risks that are associated to the data when it is rest. The AES block cipher is not used in the framework; instead, a stream cipher is proposed. This stream cipher has already been used by Google [56] and many other IoT giants since it provides superior security and has the potential to function even with less computing resources. The performance of the advanced encryption standard (AES) and the stream cipher chacha20 was tested in a lab environment. The results revealed that chacha20 demonstrates superior performance to AES owing to the encryption as well as the decryption [56].

The developed framework only takes into consideration one of the information security elements known as the integrity in the CIA triad. This security framework should be used to ensure that the remaining aspects of information security, such as confidentiality and availability, non-repudiation and authenticity, and so on, are appropriately addressed. The developed framework should be implemented in the form of a pure middleware application, and it should be able to integrate with any of the most commonly used middleware applications in the Hadoop ecosystem. Since Hadoop is constructed with a Java framework, the codes and frameworks should be implemented in Java. However, all of the codes in this work are implemented in Python. It should be upgraded into a flexible framework so that in the future if more efficient algorithms are discovered, it should also be possible to integrate those into the developed framework. As a starting point, the framework only focuses on the chacha20 stream cipher.

References

1. Riahi G (2015) E-learning systems based on cloud computing: a review. Procedia Comput Sci 62:352–359
2. Fernandez A, Peralta D, Herrera F, Benítez JM (2012) An overview of e-learning in cloud computing. In: Workshop on learning technology for education in cloud (LTEC'12). Springer, Berlin, Heidelberg, pp 35–46
3. Laisheng X, Zhengxia W (2011) Cloud computing: a new business paradigm for e-learning. In: 2011 Third international conference on measuring technology and mechatronics automation. IEEE, pp 716–719
4. Guoli Z, Wanjun L (2010) The applied research of cloud computing platform architecture in the E-Learning area. In: 2010 The 2nd international conference on computer and automation engineering (ICCAE). IEEE, pp 356–359
5. Chen CK, Almunawar MN (2019) Cloud learning management system in higher education. In: Opening up education for inclusivity across digital economies and societies. IGI Global, pp 29–51
6. Yi H, Nie Z, Li W (2017) Implementation of learning management system based on cloud computing. In: 2017 4th International conference on information science and control engineering (ICISCE). IEEE, pp 380–384
7. Yahfizham, Purwani F, Rukun K, Krismadinata (2017) A review of cloud learning management system (CLMS) based on software as a service (SaaS). In: 2017 International conference on electrical engineering and informatics (ICELTICs). IEEE, pp 205–210
8. Ekuase-Anwansedo A, Smith A (2019) Effect of cloud based learning management system on the learning management system implementation process. In: Proceedings of the 2019 ACM SIGUCCS annual conference, pp 176–179
9. Neuman BC, Ts'o T (1994) Kerberos: an authentication service for computer networks. IEEE Commun Mag 32(9):33–38
10. Jiang D, Ooi BC, Shi L, Wu S (2010) The performance of mapreduce: an in-depth study. Proc VLDB Endowment 3(1–2):472–483
11. Sagiroglu S, Sinanc D (2013) Big data: a review. In: 2013 International conference on collaboration technologies and systems (CTS). IEEE, pp 42–47
12. Agrawal D, Bernstein P, Bertino E, Davidson S, Dayal U, Franklin M, Gehrke J, Haas L, Halevy A, Han J, Jagadish HV et al (2011) Challenges and opportunities with Big Data 2011-1. In: Cyber center technical reports paper 1
13. Grady NW, Underwood M, Roy A, Chang WL (2014) Big data: challenges, practices and technologies: NIST big data public working group workshop at IEEE big data 2014. In: 2014 IEEE International conference on big data (Big Data). IEEE, pp 11–15
14. Kitchin R, McArdle G (2016) What makes big data, big data? Exploring the ontological characteristics of 26 datasets. Big Data Soc 3(1):1–10
15. Demchenko Y, de Laat C, Membrey P (2014) Defining architecture components of the Big Data Ecosystem. In: 2014 International conference on collaboration technologies and systems (CTS). IEEE, pp 104–112
16. Pantelis K, Aija L (2013) Understanding the value of (big) data. In: 2013 IEEE International conference on big data. IEEE, pp 38–42
17. Furht B, Villanustre F (2016) Introduction to big data. In: Big data technologies and applications. Springer, Cham, pp 3–11

18. Sawant N, Shah H (2013) Big data application architecture. In: Big data application architecture Q & A. Apress, Berkeley, CA, pp 9–28
19. Elgendy N, Elragal A (2014) Big data analytics: a literature review paper. In: Industrial conference on data mining. Springer, Cham, pp 214–227
20. Hofmann E (2017) Big data and supply chain decisions: the impact of volume, variety and velocity properties on the bullwhip effect. Int J Prod Res 55(17):5108–5126
21. Mao R, Xu H, Wu W, Li J, Li Y, Lu M (2015) Overcoming the challenge of variety: big data abstraction, the next evolution of data management for AAL communication systems. IEEE Commun Mag 53(1):42–47
22. Adnan K, Akbar R (2019) Limitations of information extraction methods and techniques for heterogeneous unstructured big data. Int J Eng Bus Manag 11:1–23
23. Grolinger K, Hayes M, Higashino WA, L'Heureux A, Allison DS, Capretz MAM (2014) Challenges for mapreduce in big data. In: 2014 IEEE World congress on services. IEEE, pp 182–189
24. Gualtieri M, Yuhanna N et al (2016) The Forrester wave: big data Hadoop distributions, Q1 2016. In: Forrester research
25. George G, Haas MR, Pentland A (2014) Big data and management. Acad Manag J 57(2):321–326
26. Tulasi B (2013) Significance of big data and analytics in higher education. Int J Comput Appl 68(14):21–23
27. Dwivedi K, Dubey SK (2014) Analytical review on Hadoop Distributed file system. In: 2014 5th International conference-confluence the next generation information technology summit (Confluence). IEEE, pp 174–181
28. Pietzuch PR, Bacon JM (2002) Hermes: a distributed event-based middleware architecture. In: Proceedings 22nd international conference on distributed computing systems workshops. IEEE, pp 611–618
29. Dean J, Ghemawat S (2008) MapReduce: simplified data processing on large clusters. Commun ACM 51(1):107–113
30. Karloff H, Suri S, Vassilvitskii S (2010) A model of computation for mapreduce. In: Proceedings of the 2010 annual ACM-SIAM symposium on Discrete Algorithms (SODA). Society for Industrial and Applied Mathematics (SIAM), pp 938–948
31. Hashem IAT, Anuar NB, Gani A, Yaqoob I, Xia F, Khan SU (2016) MapReduce: review and open challenges. Scientometrics 109(1):389–422
32. Rahul PK, GireeshKumar T (2015) A novel authentication framework for Hadoop. In: Artificial intelligence and evolutionary algorithms in engineering systems. Springer, New Delhi, pp 333–340
33. Hirzel M, Andrade H, Gedik B, Jacques-Silva G, Khandekar R, Kumar V, Mendell M, Nasgaard H, Schneider S, Soulé R, Wu K-L (2013) IBM streams processing language: analyzing big data in motion. IBM J Res Dev 57(3/4):7:1-7:11
34. Daemen J, Rijmen V (2001) Reijndael: the advanced encryption standard. Dobb's J Softw Tools Prof Prog 26(3):137–139
35. ElBadawy E-SA-M, Mokhtar A, El-Masry WA, Hafez, AE-DS (2010) A new chaos advanced encryption standard (AES) algorithm for data security. In: ICSES 2010 International conference on signals and electronic circuits. IEEE, pp 405–408
36. Schramm K, Leander G, Felke P, Paar C (2004) A collision-attack on AES. In: International workshop on cryptographic hardware and embedded systems (CHES 2004). Springer, Berlin, Heidelberg, pp 163–175
37. Standaert F-X (2010) Introduction to side-channel attacks. In: Secure integrated circuits and systems. Springer, Boston, MA, pp 27–42
38. Gautam T, Jain A (2015) Analysis of brute force attack using TG—Dataset. In: 2015 SAI Intelligent systems conference (IntelliSys). IEEE, pp 984–988
39. Yu S (2016) Big privacy: challenges and opportunities of privacy study in the age of big data. IEEE Access 4:2751–2763

40. Rubinstein I (2012) Big data: the end of privacy or a new beginning? In: International data privacy law (2013 Forthcoming), NYU School of law, public law research paper No. 12–56, pp 1–14

41. Shen W, Qin J, Yu J, Hao R, Hu J (2019) Enabling identity-based integrity auditing and data sharing with sensitive information hiding for secure cloud storage. IEEE Trans Inf Forensics Secur 14(2):331–346

42. Behl A (2011) Emerging security challenges in cloud computing: an insight to cloud security challenges and their mitigation. In: 2011 World congress on information and communication technologies. IEEE, pp 217–222

43. Rao RV, Selvamani K (2015) Data security challenges and its solutions in cloud computing. Procedia Comput Sci 48:204–209

44. Samarati P, De Capitani di Vimercati S, Murugesan S, Bojanova I (2016) Cloud security: issues and concerns. In: Encyclopedia of cloud computing, pp 1–14

45. Chou T-S (2013) Security threats on cloud computing vulnerabilities. Int J Comput Sci Inf Technol 5(3):79–88

46. Chang V, Ramachandran M (2016) Towards achieving data security with the cloud computing adoption framework. IEEE Trans Serv Comput 9(1):138–151

47. Daemen J, Knudsen L, Rijmen V (1997) The block cipher square. In: International workshop on fast software encryption. Springer, Berlin, Heidelberg, pp 149–165

48. Jouini M, Rabai LBA (2019) A security framework for secure cloud computing environments. In: Cloud security: concepts, methodologies, tools, and applications. IGI Global, pp 249–263

49. Thirumalai C, Mohan S, Srivastava G (2020) An efficient public key secure scheme for cloud and IoT security. Comput Commun 150:634–643

50. He Q, Li Z, Zhang X (2010) Study on cloud storage system based on distributed storage systems. In: 2010 International conference on computational and information sciences. IEEE, pp 1332–1335

51. Choudhury AJ, Kumar P, Sain M, Lim H, Jae-Lee H (2011) A strong user authentication framework for cloud computing. In: 2011 IEEE Asia-pacific services computing conference. IEEE, pp 110–115

52. Somani G, Gaur MS, Sanghi D (2015) DDoS protection and security assurance in cloud. In: Guide to security assurance for cloud computing. Springer, Cham, pp 171–191

53. Shetty MM, Manjaiah DH (2016) Data security in Hadoop distributed file system. In: 2016 International conference on emerging technological trends (ICETT). IEEE, pp 1–5

54. Mahajan P, Sachdeva A (2013) A study of encryption algorithms AES, DES and RSA for security. Global J Comput Sci Technol XIII(XV):15–22

55. Barona R, Anita EAM (2017) A survey on data breach challenges in cloud computing security: issues and threats. In: 2017 International conference on circuit, power and computing technologies (ICCPCT). IEEE, pp 1–8

56. Mahdi MS, Hassan NF, Abdul-Majeed GH (2021) An improved chacha algorithm for securing data on IoT devices. SN Appl Sci 3(4):1–9

A Proactive Approach to Protect Cloud Computing Environment Against a Distributed Denial of Service (DDoS) Attack

Md. Mamun Ahmed and Ayman El-Hajjar

Abstract The current range of technological and physical advances mostly rely on load dispersion as well as demand delays which modern security solutions are equipped to defend against distributed denial-of-service (DDoS) threats. Clients and website visitors consequently encounter time delays, captchas, and delayed connectivity. In this chapter, we provide a novel layered solution for cloud-based DDoS defence that makes use of Advanced Malware methods and a proactive method for identifying anomalies in traffic behaviour. The model's first level assesses the packet arrival frames' starting origin IP address, while the second level looks at request speed and forecasts the threat speed threshold. The third tier, if necessary, minimises the traffic burden by redirecting the traffic towards the proxy. In case a specific web application is the target of the assault, the fifth layer decides whether port-hopping is necessary between the gateway and the destination website. Numerous studies demonstrate how well multilayer strategy can recognise and limit threats from such a diverse variety of known and undisclosed sources.

Keywords DDoS · Cloud computing · ADDoS · IP traceback · Threat intelligence · Port-hopping · Entropy-based anomaly detection · CBF packet filtering · Intrusion detection system · Dempster Shafter theory

1 Introduction

Contemporary DDoS attacks are becoming increasingly sophisticated and destructive. During the second quarter of 2019, a most powerful attack reached speeds of up to 250 Gb/s; during the third quarter of 2019, the most powerful attack reached

Md. M. Ahmed
Northumbria University London, London, UK

A. El-Hajjar (✉)
University of Westminster, London, UK
e-mail: A.ElHajjar@westminster.ac.uk

© The Author(s), under exclusive license to Springer Nature Switzerland AG 2023   243
H. Jahankhani et al. (eds.), *AI, Blockchain and Self-Sovereign Identity in Higher
Education*, Advanced Sciences and Technologies for Security Applications,
https://doi.org/10.1007/978-3-031-33627-0_10

speeds of up to 149 Gb/s; as well as the overall amount of DDoS attacks continued to increase by 180% year-over-year [1]. Most complex attacks mimic normal "HTTP traffic" which is generated by botnets. Attackers implements some code onto malicious botnet agents, causing them to behave similarly to average consumers when they browse websites, albeit at a much faster rate. The bigger a botnet's size, the more strain it can exert on a host system [2]. By substantially delaying business processes, a DDoS attack can have a devastatingly destructive effect [3, 4]. Numerous types of businesses, including online stores, media organizations, stockbrokers, and banks, are extremely dependent on stable, uninterrupted functioning. Even a small disruption in their accessibility may result in substantial losses or even a complete shutdown of commercial services.

When a DDoS assault is launched against a cloud-based server, all traffic is dispersed throughout the cloud nodes. This eliminates a "bottleneck" in a normal system, the narrow and vulnerable spot, which is typically a way to communicate or restricted system resources. This is the usual strategy utilised by most commercial services for DDoS protection. Still, every cloud has a finite number of usable nodes and cumulative channel bandwidth. The only requirement for successfully attacking a server in the cloud is to raise the pace and volume of packets, which a larger botnet can readily achieve.

These difficulties necessitated the development of new DDoS mitigation technology. Our multi-layered system employs proactive preventive measures based on both pattern recognition and Threat Intelligence, which have a good track record of preventing attacks.

The main research question is that "What new approaches may be used to improve the present DDoS protection in the cloud?" To illustrate the concept this research analyses what approaches and procedures should be applied in a successful current DDoS prevention system. Associated questions will be addressed in order to accurately explore this "What technologies and approaches are presently available for DDoS protection and how efficient are these techniques?".

This research establishes a new sophisticated multilayer system for cloud-based DDoS prevention. It employs a very efficient approach which will have an ability to respond quickly to detect anomalous traffic behaviour. So, the basic and main objectives of this research is to design and develop, A simple and feasible multilayer security system to mitigate DDoS attack in Cloud Computing Environment.

2 Literature Review

2.1 DDoS Attack Prevention and Detection

A number of methods specifically designed to combat DDoS attacks have been investigated. These approaches are centred on both identification and avoidance, yet each system functions from a vastly distinct vantage point. This research enables a deeper comprehension of how DDoS recognition and protection might be further developed.

Cho et al. [5] offer a DDoS mitigation process which is a combination of filtering packet with two firewalls. The initial firewall employs path analysis of router, whereas the next firewall evaluates whether the data packets are normal or anomalous. This strategy is intended to avoid simple attacks, but it may generate a substantial number of errors.

Graham et al. [6] designed to identify botnet activity within such a virtualized architecture that is abstracted, such as cloud service infrastructure. They constructed a field based on the Xen hypervisor and exported NetFlow Version 9 using Open vSwitch. They acquired experimental proof that Traffic export can collect network activity variables to verify the prevalence of a controlled botnet in a virtualized environment. The conceptual architecture they describe provides a nonintrusive method for botnet prevention system identification for cloud vendors.

Karim et al. [7] also examines different approaches for detecting botnets, proposes a classification scheme for botnet detection techniques, and emphasises the qualitative study design features of such technique analysis. The authors propose potential future methods for Improving botnet detection techniques and identifying unresolved research challenges.

Mansfield-Devine [8] discusses the development of DDoS attacks and how they are used in contemporary hybrid unlawful actions. Rashmi et al. [9] elaborate on the work flow of a Distributed Denial of Service attack, and how in impacts on cloud environment, and the considerations which should be made when choosing DDoS defence mechanisms, concluding with a recommendation to select a functional, transparent, small and light, and accurate strategy to mitigate DDoS attacks.

The basis of Xiao et al. [10]'s research is the correlation analysis-aided detection of DDoS attacks. Their strategy is predicated on a classification of traffic based on its nearest neighbours and an analysis of correlation. It improves classification performance by employing specialised and efficient training examples and decreases the training data density-induced overhead.

Entropy-based anomaly detection is another way of DDoS protection [11], although, like any good theory, it can be undermined by poor implementation. For instance, a very strong algorithm for encrypting data may be undermined by flaws in its technical execution. Essentially, if at minimum a terabyte of a server's usual traffic is collected, a full analysis may be performed, and templates of permitted usage can be created, allowing for anomaly identification; however, defending against these anomalies efficiently is more challenging. Assume a regular news site provides breaking news; the piece will likely draw hundreds, if not thousands, of times as many visitors as usual. Nevertheless, this may also be an impersonating DDoS attack to increased visitor traffic. A rogue user can configure a DDoS assault to send relatively slow HTTP requests to a website's homepage or other pages, much like a typical web browser does.

Saeid et al. [12] explains how to combat both predictable and unpredictable DDoS attacks in a real-time setting. An "Artificial Neural Network" has been used to identify assaults in the basis of their unique patterns and distinguishing characteristics, which differentiate them from normal traffic patterns.

Software-Defined Networking (SDN) has gained popularity in corporate environments due to its administrative flexibility and low operating costs. However, the combination of SDN and cloud hosting has created new obstacles, notably network security concerns. Wang et al. [13] address this issue by offering a DDoS attack mitigation system that includes programmable network monitoring for DDoS attack detection. Through the implementation of a governing structure, the architecture may respond to certain attacks.

ADDoS, or application layer distributed denial-of-service attacks, target particular online services. One of the attack methods consists of sending Simple Object Access Protocol (SOAP) requests with harmful XML content, which consumes a substantial amount of server resources. Because these packets are genuine, neither the network nor transport layers detect them. Vissers et al. [14] proposes a new adaptive method for detecting assaults of this type, which functions by extracting identifying traits and using the feature extraction to model usual requests, allowing for the comparison-based detection of malicious requests.

Kijewski et al. [15] discusses a recently published ENISA report produced by CERT Polska titled "Proactive Detection of Network Security Incidents," which highlights the consequences for early warning of security incidents on a national scale. The research is primarily focused on national/government CERTs, although many of the concerns uncovered are applicable to any team entrusted with incident detection. The report gives an overview of automated incident processing and Threat Intelligence technologies, as well as an explanation of the Collective Intelligence Framework. To provide a systematic approach to evaluation, the authors present a set of criteria that are mostly based on the quality of the data.

Krylov et al. [16] provide a second strategy for preventing DDoS attacks that is based on protocol-level defence mechanisms. This approach employs IP address switching in real time. The changeover schedule is restricted to only authorised users. This schedule is not accessible to malicious users, preventing them from knowing the exact IP address to submit queries to. This eliminates server burden and decreases botnet-generated traffic.

Two strategies are utilised by Bereziski et al. [17] detection and training. In training mode, the profile of "clean" legal traffic is developed. Additionally, the categorization model is created. It will be utilised for comparative and evaluative purposes.

In detection mode, existing filtering probes are evaluated to the classification algorithm and regular traffic profile constructed in training mode. The profile of lawful traffic comprises entropy edge values (min and max values). The present entropy is computed and compared to the minimum and maximum values of the profile to determine the anomalous threshold. Detection is conducted on the present relative entropy, taking the minimum and maximum values into account. An abnormality is identified when the entropy value is near to 0. When entropy approaches 1, the detection accuracy approaches 50%, rendering it hard to discern whether or not an attack is occurring.

This approach sets the tolerance for the edge values using the coefficient to minimise false positives. If it equals 1, the rate of detection is increased. If 2 is true, false alarms are decreased. The final phase of the process, extraction, enables the system to determine the IP addresses of the frames, which have the greatest impact on the change in entropy value.

Pal et al. [18] study cloud security challenges and present a way for determining the trustworthiness of service seeking authorities using the agent-based framework WAY (Who Are You) to secure cloud nodes.

Hwang et al. [19] propose using trusted access to safeguard virtual clusters and datacentres. A datacentre may contain a huge number of resources; yet, the reputation of certain nodes on the inside of the data centre could be questionable. A hypothesized hierarchy reputation system addresses the issue of peer-to-peer connections' lack of trust.

This paper advances fuzzy-theoretic trust models of [20] in cloud security systems, which focuses on P2P cloud transactions. It compiles reputation values and makes a determination using fuzzy logic.

He et al. [21] propose a trust relationship for ubiquitous computing based on the credibility of cloud nodes with unclear trust relationships. This model proposes a way for computing both propagating and aggregating trust clouds in order to avoid ambiguous entity interactions in pervasive computing.

Effective contact between peers involves the estimation of trustworthiness; for this estimation, it is necessary to collect data. The question arises: how can the privacy of these data be protected? Ylitalo et al. [22] examines potential ways of privacy protection from a variety of perspectives, including what information can be released, how to secure the primary channels of leaking, and how to prevent personal data compromise.

Zhou et al. [23] investigates the issues of trust in peer-to-peer communications. This paper presents a gossip trustworthiness and gossip-based protocol for rapid reputation accumulation and ranking of peers, as the process of data collection for reputation estimate can be time-consuming.

Habib et al. [24] examine cloud computing difficulties. It analyses the challenge of quality management of cloud services and strategies for establishing confidence in cloud environments, as well as many aspects of trust, reputation, and their incorporation into cloud computing.

Jsang et al. [25] examines techniques for establishing trust and reputation in cloud systems. It explains current trends and methods of trust computation, as well as the estimation of the cloud nodes' reputation based on these methods.

Everett et al. introduces a third-party evaluation provider to rank the reliability of cloud services based on their reputation in a different method. It provides an overview of the Cloud Security Alliance's activities to develop cloud trust and assess the integrity of its nodes. As demonstrated by these works, the issue of trust is crucial for businesses. Trust must be built in all conversations, and identification and management control are crucial for assuring satisfaction among all parties.

2.2   IP Traceback Method

The conventional inspection of traffic and identifying of packet origins are ineffective due to the prevalence of unidentified proxies and Tor. Numerous publications describe advanced IP traceback techniques, such as "hash-based IP traceback" [26], "Probabilistic traffic marking for IP traceback on a wide scale" [27] as well as "IP traceback methos in the basis of network logging [28].

In the case of a botnet-based DDoS attack, the sources are entirely legal; they may consist of infected home computers. This indicates that the characterised methods will become more impactful when employed in tandem. If a DDoS attack is properly configured, it's really hard to differentiate between such a botnet agent as well as a genuine website visitor; as described above, malicious attackers load scripts onto botnet agents, which generate simple approaches to request Web pages of aim websites, as regular authorized customers do. Efficient identification and preventative measures can only be accomplished by combining several of these methods with new techniques.

The IP traceback issue is inherent to the IP protocol itself. It assumes that the network is trustworthy and does not validate the source IP. This design flaw enables extremely potent DDoS attacks utilising amplified methods; attacker creates a tiny number of packets with the IP address of the specific website as the source address. These packets are transmitted to the web server, which generate responses significantly larger than the initial request.

Such servers return their responses to the IP address from which the requests originated. Thus, the attack website fails because will be unable to give a response to those received packets.

Existing IP traceback solutions mainly involve updating IP headers and RFC 791; creating new smart routers that can label and trace the path of packets; or upgrading the software and hardware of Internet companies to re-route suspected packets in the event of a DoS attack detection. By investigating a larger abstraction level, existing systems permit packet tagging, logging, and rerouting. They can be tagged with hashes of their origin IPs or route edges. Re-routing enables suspect packets to be routed for in-depth examination by professionals before they reach the destination website.

Ramesh et al. [29] present a method for reconstructing DDoS attack pathways and calculating the chance of variable marking based on the difference between both the particular website and router.

The work of Saurabh et al. [30] relies on a probabilistic packet marking technique and proposes a method to improve its precision by computing the number of packets required for completing the traceback (Completion Condition Number). This technology improves accuracy to 95% and enables researchers to reconstruct attack vectors, even for distributed denial of service attacks.

Li et al. [27] offer a technique for the logging of a limited percentage of traffic (less than 5%) on routers. Then, attack pathways are reconstructed by correlating data from neighbouring routers. The research resulted in the introduction of a new sampling method that enhances the correlation and precision of traceback data.

Gong et al. [31] examines two significant IP traceback techniques: probabilistic network marking and hash-based packet logging. Through network identifying, the route of some packets can be partially preserved; however, due to the probabilistic nature of the process, packet marking is incapable of reconstructing the complete path of approach for all packets. Packet logging enables the storage of hashes of all packets routed via a particular router; however, this technique may be limited by space on routers. The authors offer a new technique that combines the advantages of packet marking with packet recording.

The research of Foroushani et al. [32] examines an approach based on packet tagging, although the approach is not probabilistic. It proposes a deterministic mechanism that enables the restitution of the complete pathway of DDoS attacks, even when the attacker is hiding behind a proxy or NAT. The approach is reportedly simple, effective, and capable of pinpointing up to 99% of attacks.

Yan et al. [33] investigate hybrid IP traceback. It was founded from both probabilistic packet marking and hash-based packet logging and utilises their benefits; nonetheless, design defects may lead to errors in tracing attack paths. The authors describe a novel strategy that avoids these problems and makes the tracing procedure more efficient and stable.

Foroushani et al. [34] evaluate deterministic packet marking (DPM) and deterministic flow marking (DFM). This study does not introduce any new methodologies; rather, it evaluates the efficacy of DPM and DFM. Even if certain packets are corrupted or faked, or if the assault originates via a NAT-protected network or proxy, the research demonstrates that DFM is capable of retrieving the complete attack path.

By filtering packets, Sung et al. [35] describe an approach for decreasing DDoS attacks. This approach checks whether the network edge is clean (legal user) or infected by tracing the origin of packets (hacker or botnet). Then, it has the option of allowing or blocking the packet. By blocking questionable traffic, potential DDoS assaults are averted.

Park et al. [36] examines methods to decrease attack path spoofing. The performance of a probabilistic packet marking method of IP traceback is examined from the perspective of a minimax optimization process, where system administrators are constantly battling attackers with multi-stage objectives: first attack, to detect all attack paths and reduce false positives; and second attack, to forge as many packets as possible.

Song et al. [37] offer an advanced marking method and an authenticated marking technique for IP traceback and defence against distributed denial of service attacks. These strategies reduce router overload and generate a small number of false positives. The authenticated technique protects the integrity of samples on routers, reducing the likelihood of forgery or spoofing during the analysis of an attack.

Evaluating a current Ip traceback approach to the proposed upgraded method employs [38]. Consider R to be the router's address, w to be the packet, and v to be the victim. Each packet includes the addresses of all gateways between the hacker and the victim. At the end of the voyage, each packet will provide comprehensive route information. If the packets' size exceeds the maximum transmission unit (MTU), they will become excessively heavy and may fracture.

To remedy this issue, the authors of [38] introduce a probability value, p. Instead of marking each packet with the addresses of all routers, they specify the chance of identifying and checking. If a randomized probability x is less than the predetermined value, the router's address is appended to the packet's reserved restricted space node. Thus, they lower the router's load and the packet size.

As a result, not all frames are marked, but the pathway could still be recovered if an assault sends enough packets. However, if the routers are positioned a sufficient distance from the victim, the likelihood of their marking is diminished, and the IPs may be destroyed.

To overcome these concerns, the authors advise writing only the route's edges as opposed to all nodes. Each packet saves room for two addresses—the beginning and ending points of the connection between routers, as well as the distance between them.

If a router marks a packet, the distance field is examined. In the absence of a value, the router writes its IP address into the beginning field and changes the distance to zero. If distance is 0, the preceding router has already tagged the packet, thus the current router puts its IP to the end field. If the router chooses not to flag the packet, it simply increases the distance by one.

When the target receives the packet, the distance field would indicate the number of routers the packet has traversed between the last edge and the victim. During the reconstruction operation, the victim constructs the graph G with edges and then enumerates all of the route's addresses R.

To boost the performance of the method, the researchers condense the designated space in packets for two IPs by writing the edge ID instead of the end address in half of the address space. The edge ID is obtained by XORing the start value with the router's current IP address. The victim's final edge's address is not changed. In the reconstruction phase, the final address is XORed with the ID of the prior edge to recover the previous edge, and so on until the initial beginning point is located.

On the basis of the preceding, we may conclude that IP traceback is a significant problem for which there are now no effective solutions. Any proposed DDoS protection strategies based purely on IP traceback will be ineffective unless leading suppliers offer robust ways for verifying source IPs.

2.3 Threat Intelligence

Appala and his colleagues have developed a comprehensive methodology for Threat Intelligence systems [39]. This system may analyse threat information from several sources to provide an in-depth report and make suggestions for the proper course of action. Cyber Threat Intelligence is expressed using the structured language called "STIX" (Structured Threat Information eXpression). Securely disseminating these recommended actions and Threat Intelligence in association with relevant information, Appala's technology determines what reaction system is best suited to carry it out. Even though the associated information provides some semi-automation strategies for better mitigation and repair, this system does not deal with specific threats or the identification and control of distributed denial-of-service (DDoS) assaults.

Girish et al. [40] offers to create a public source Advanced Threat system for small businesses with limited budgets. Data from CERT and security vendors, as well as from private feeds containing APT profiling data stored in a MySQL database, are used in the system. As an analytical tool, SpagoBI, an open software intelligence suite, was used. Due to the fact that SpagoBI isn't built for threat analysis, it may result in false positives when used. There are two applications that work every day of the week, including weekends and holidays, thanks to Girish's work. All throughout the time the computer is functioning, a number of system processes remain active. The results are simply highlighted by the fact that companies can leave applications running on the system while they have incomplete tasks or documents that must stay open.

Threat Intelligence is defined in Henry Dalziel's book but the publication does not explain analytics engine techniques and does not address threats themselves.

Ring [41] explains and examines the reasons why individuals and organisations do not exchange threat data, a crucial subject requiring examination. Companies prefer to examine cyber security incidents internally and do not tell security providers and law enforcement agencies about the incidents. Sharing as much information as possible about assaults and new threats will considerably improve the efficacy of existing analytics tools and empower defensive data security teams to participate in minimising cyber security concerns.

Thriveni et al. [42] present a real-time, adaptive system based on Threat Intelligence. Big data analytics with cloud-based Threat Intelligence identify new dangers. Prediction tools utilise international threat data to avoid assaults, as opposed to defending against those that have already occurred. These technologies expose concealed problems, allowing workers to modify the appropriate security settings. The paper covers a variety of tools for the analysis of massive data.

Adebayo et al. [43] present a technique based on intelligence that combines conventional "signature-based" identification with "next-generation-based" detection, cataloguing Threat Intelligence for future occurrence prevention. The suggested paradigm is comprised of a virtual runtime environment, identification module, and a mitigation module. The virtual runtime environment is designed to study and process a file which suspected of having malicious thing, on the other hand other modules examine, identify, and block the execution of malware in the basis of the Central Management System's intelligent data collection (CMS). This solution focuses on malware and neither detects nor handles DDoS attacks; yet, it clearly demonstrates the utility of learning algorithms in detecting system risks.

2.4 Proxy Server

Companies that have implemented Web proxy servers indicate that this proxy server technology significantly decreased network costs. Numerous companies purchased proxy servers to reduce connection delays. However, they obtained an unforeseen advantage when caching decreased Internet traffic. According to observers in the business, proxy servers frequently cut traffic to the point where additional bandwidth servers are no longer required [44]. There is a significant demand for proxy servers among businesses, organisations, the government, and academic institutions. In their different Internet server releases, Microsoft, Netscape, and Novell all include proxy-server software. Given the performance enhancements experienced by users, it is simple to understand the great demand. Generally, proxy server speed enhancements for end users vary from 20 to 25%, or a one-quarter reduction in communication cost [45, 46]. In addition, corporations have reported proxy server cache traffic rates exceeding 40%, as well as caches containing hundreds of live Web resources [44].

Very little thought has been paid to the limitations and disadvantages of proxy servers. Proxy servers typically lack the extensive data points, monitoring, alarm, and auditing capabilities of stand-alone firewalls. An elite proxy server costs approximately $1000. The price range for firewalls is between $5000 and $50,000 [2]. In addition, industry professionals warn that proxy servers cannot replace a second high-speed Internet connection if the main connection is overburdened. Reports indicate that proxy servers have few disadvantages beyond these characteristics.

Given the numerous favourable outcomes, it is not surprising that proxy servers remain an important topic of study. In contrast to their filtering capabilities, the majority of proxy server research focuses on strategies to improve their performance. Jeffery et al. [47] investigated the architecture and consequences of an enlarged proxy server that shares cache assets with both itself and its immediate neighbours. As a result of this proxy sharing, they noticed a significant decline in network demand. This shared cache also contributed to the enhanced performance. The maximum performance was achieved with a basic, non-hierarchical deployment strategy; proxies interact utilising the Web's natural structure. In place of cache swapping, Law and Nandy [48] investigated a distributed proxy server design that can improve availability and reliability, permit system scalability, and spread load. A TCP-based switching device with more granular session control and dynamic resource allocation is utilised by the system.

2.5 Port Hopping Technique

Sattar et al. and Lee et al. [49, 50], increase the likelihood of DDoS detection and prevention by using random port hopping technique, but none of these methods is more effective. However, by combining the port-hopping strategy proposed in this study with some of these methods, as explained the efficiency of DDoS detection increases considerably.

Each server service utilises a unique port number. For example, HTTP utilizes port 80, FTP utilizes channel 21, Telnet utilises channel 23, SMTP utilizes port 25, etc. In total there are 65,536 port numbers. If a hacker wishes to exploit servers, the initial stages of research often involve port scanning. This provides the hacker with knowledge of the services and programmes operating on the targeted system and the port numbers used by those services and applications. Then, a database of vulnerabilities can be utilised to determine what system vulnerabilities for these services, allowing the hacker to exploit them.

Port hopping is indeed an appropriate defence mechanism that prevents server services from being mapped to its port numbers [51]. It is used to defend against a variety of possible server service assaults (applications, daemons). The port hopping method functions by considerably in different the port numbers delegated to correlating server services; nevertheless, the effectiveness of this method based on a variety of variables, including the volume of the serial port pool, the frequency of port number hopping, the method of port number hopping, and the approach of port number synchronisation among server and the client [52, 53].

Ideally, port hopping must occur arbitrarily for each connection the user requests to the server, however there are synchronisation problems in practise. Client and server must be using the same sequence number for the target service; otherwise, the host will reject a request made with the incorrect port number.

Using such a Pseudo-Random Number Generator (PRNG) that is synchronised on both ends and a function of time to change port numbers with the correct frequency can resolve these concerns.

3 Research Methodology

The proposed strategy is predicated on integrating many protection systems and including IP traceback, proxy server and port hopping technique. This begins by implementing five levels of protection for all incoming packets. The below Figure will depict the diagram of logic (Fig. 1).

3.1 Layer 1 Logic and Concept

In the first layer, IP sources are analysed. The IPs are checked to a record to determine if they are botnet IPs if an abnormally a massive amount of traffic originates from a specific range of IPs. The data of botnet IPs will be attached to the Thresholds system on layer two. Since the levels are interconnected, the IP is passed through a code to be compared with entries in the database of botnet IPs. To obtain the originating IP address, the TCP header of each packet is analysed in accordance with its standard structure. In a single database, the IP addresses of botnets are maintained in a source IP address table.

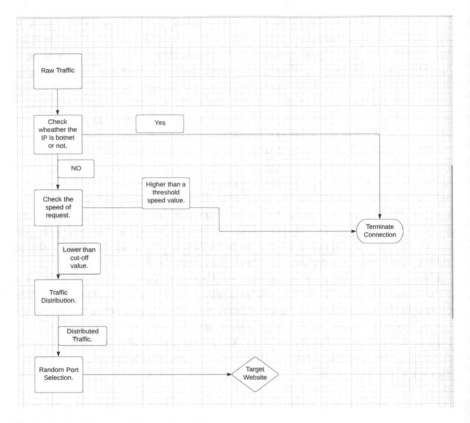

Fig. 1 Logic diagram of proposed method

The simple evaluation (checking for duplicate entries) of this table's contents reveals whether or not the source IPs are unique. DoS (the IPs are from the same source) or DDoS attacks can be identified in the event of an assault (all IPs are different). Whether arriving packets originate from a single source or multiple sources, the system derives the right conclusion. The source IP address is then passed as an argument to a function that sends a request to the database. This function queries the database of botnet IP addresses associated with the Threat Intelligence engine. If a botnet IP is found, the method returns TRUE; otherwise, FALSE is returned.

On Internet traffic, NAT and encapsulating are two examples of packet-forwarding methods that can be used on Internet traffic; however, these techniques obscure the packets' actual origin. The traceback method is used to analyse the source IP address and check the information against the botnet database. If entries are matched to botnet IPs, the IP is not obscured and can be banned effectively.

There is no realistic commercial deployment of IP traceback that functions successfully with the current Internet infrastructure. This fact has necessitated the consideration of various necessary changes to existing hardware, IP protocol standard, and ISP equipment. While maintaining the protocol, one of the objectives of this research is to reduce the number of essential adjustments.

The suggested method improves prior research [27, 29–38] and offers an approach that 'Improved Deterministic Packet Marking (iDPM)' is what we refer to as having the ideal efficiency and implementation ease ratio.

3.2 Layer 2 Logic and Concept

The second layer examines the request response time. Because the primary function of layer one is to pass the raw traffic and the functioning of layer two relies on that values, layers one and two are generalised and integrated in a block. A C function can create for blocking or transmitting the traffic to a firewall if it is judged that the frequency of incoming traffic exceeds a maximum speed threshold, S, which will be defined in the section that follows. Otherwise, layer three simply receives the traffic.

Calculations where the speed S is established can be used to determine the rate at which we regard traffic to be harmful. Web analytics software is used to gather data on average traffic rates for various website kinds, including promotional campaigns and regular users. The computation of this cut-off speed is straightforward. Starting out, we will gather a variety of monthly visitors according to the highest value for that range for the previous three months. This data will be extremely helpful in determining the likely attack speed threshold. Using Eq. (1), the speed of attack, S, can be computed for HTTP traffic given the number of visitors triggering the attack.

$$S = (A/86400) * \text{size of (packet)} \tag{1}$$

Equation (1) Cut-off Speed Calculation

where S is the rate of traffic which can be considered to the target website and A is the level of attack formula which will be calculated average visor per day and value of peak traffic.

For instance, if a 100 Gb/s request is made to an e-checkout store's page, the assault may be detected. Users can be redirected to the homepage in this situation by adding RewriteCond and RewriteRule to the target website's.http file, reducing database load to prevent a successful DDoS attack while avoiding the use of inefficient scripts and other potential target points that attackers may find, or users can be required to complete a CAPTCHA on the target website to confirm they are not bots.

3.3 Layer 3 Logic and Concept

If necessary, the third layer will direct the activity to the proxy server to alleviate the stress on the network.

The dispatcher's job is to take all traffic and send it to the proxy. Since significant traffic may cause the proxy to shut down and result in a denial of service to the target

website, not all traffic is immediately routed through the proxy. There are two or
more examples of proxy, at least. The precise number of occurrences depends on
the popularity of the website for example the volume of visits; the more visitors we
have, the more well-liked the website is). The master proxy is one. They are copied
instantly, enabling proxies to access the same data on all instances simultaneously.
Since the information is reserved, another instance will be used automatically without
generating outages if one instance goes offline. This has no impact on the system's
performance. A straightforward C script written by Dispatcher pings the master
proxy and computes the average response time from the response times by parsing
them. Let's presume this script's measurement of the average response time, N ms,
is accurate. The second proxy instance is designated as the master proxy when the
dispatcher notices that the response time has increased to N*3 ms.

This enables the provision of proxy reservation and ongoing operation. A cloud
service's hardware abstraction infrastructure also reserves the dispatcher itself.
Because the internal addresses of the servers and instances are only known to the
dispatcher, the attacker is only able to learn how many physical or logical servers or
instances are located behind the dispatcher's IP address through this design.

3.4 Layer 4 Logic and Concept

If the assault is intended to specifically target a certain online application, port
hopping will be implemented in the fifth layer which will decide the port numberbe-
tween the gateway and the destination website is necessary.

Port hopping is a method for preventing direct access to the target website by an
attacker by changing the port number between predetermined time frames [69, 70].
The system proxy and the target website are the only ones who are aware of the port-
changing algorithm. The target website rejects packets that arrive with the incorrect
port number for the current time period. If a specific web application is the target of
the attack, layer five port hopping is carried out between the proxy and the destination
website. We create a pseudo-random mechanism for port number switching that is
only known to the proxy and the target website. Services on the target website use
various port numbers across various time periods. When combined with the other
levels in the suggested method, this technique offers a useful additional benefit of
attack avoidance. When speed > S but A == 0, or when traffic speed is high but the
attack was not discovered on layer three, port hopping is defined as being necessary.

The layer three proxy uses port hopping to prevent an attacker from directly
accessing the destination website; as the attacker won't be aware of the current
port. Port numbers are changed using a pseudo-random technique (Eq. 2) that is only
known by the proxy and the target website. A port's numbers Port change as a function
of time t, where PRND0 is synchronised between the proxy and the target website's
pseudo-random number generator. Services on the target website use various port
numbers across various time periods. The key is calculated by the algorithm using
time t. The target website rejects packets with the incorrect port number for the

current time period without even inspecting their contents. The formulation of the pseudo-random formula was based on earlier publications [69–71].

$$Port(t) = (PRNDO \oplus t)mod\ 65535 \qquad (2)$$

Equation (2) Pseudo-Random Port Hopping Algorithm

where t = current time, 65,535 = highest allowable port number, and PRND0 = coordinated pseudo-random number generator used by the proxies and also the destination website.

4 Results and Analysis

In this work, a prototype system is set up and real-world tests are carried out to validate the theories and strategies for assault detection and avoidance. The experiment's goal is to demonstrate the viability, accuracy, and superiority of the created strategy for preventing DDoS attacks in a cloud environment.

A virtual cloud is created in the test lab using virtual machine images. Various scripts inserted into the cloud platform networks simulate the four tiers of the defence system. The program is then linked to sources of external danger data.

A virtual botnet is built up on several virtual machines, and a target website is set up on a different virtual machine. The dispatcher and proxies are hosted by two more virtual machines. Deploying Kali Linux tools and outside web applications like vThreat Apps, DDoS assaults are mimicked by using botnets to attack the target website. Attacks occur through cloud servers that are organised as a multilevel system, allowing the effectiveness of the layers in attack mitigation to be examined. Browser add-ons that monitor the target website's speed prior, during, and after an attack are used to determine effectiveness.

4.1 Virtual Environment Configuration

OpenStack software was used to build a virtual cloud for our tests. Ten virtual computers were set up, as shown in Table 1.

4.2 Layer One Implementation

A variety of studies involving the IP traceback technique must be done to evaluate the layer 1 operation.

Table 1 Virtual lab configuration

Virtual machine name	OS version	Purpose
Virtual machine 1	Ubuntu 16.08	Target website
Virtual machine 2	Ubuntu 16.08	Traffic dispatcher
Virtual machine 3	Ubuntu 16.08	Master proxy
Virtual machine 4	Ubuntu 16.08	Proxy
Virtual machine 5	Ubuntu 16.08	Proxy
Virtual machine 6	Kali GNU	Client
Virtual machine 7	Kali GNU	Client
Virtual machine 8	Kali GNU	Client
Virtual machine 9	CentsOS 7	Client
Virtual machine 10	CentsOS 7	Client

Fig. 2 IP traceback experiment results

Routeriptb.php is loaded from the command prompt of VM6 to verify IP traceback, while targetrt.php is installed on VM2 to check IP traceback. The below Figure shows there is no output from it (Fig. 2).

4.2.1 IP Traceback Implementation

The below command is performed from VM6 while the code routeriptb.php is open and running in the background (Fig. 3).

Then targetrt.php script will be run on virtual Machine 2 (Fig. 4).

The actual source IP is determined by the program from the Options field.

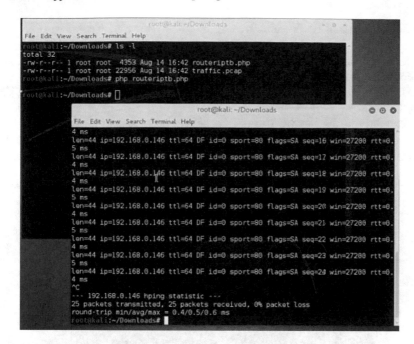

Fig. 3 hping3 command result

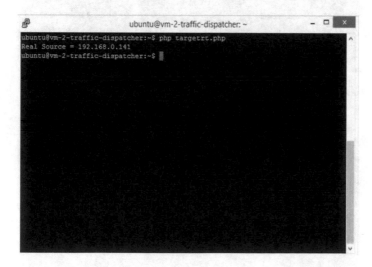

Fig. 4 targetrt command results

4.2.2 Obfuscated IP Traceback

Now, the very same check is performed on the simulated IP with obfuscation. In this section, the actual source IP is disguised using the command below (Fig. 5).

After the IP has now been impersonated, targetrt.php is executed again on VM2 (Fig. 6).

According to the Figure. The option field is still used to identify the genuine source, which still points to the actual IP address 192.168.0.141. It may be concluded that this method is effective because the real IP is noted by VM6 and restored on

Fig. 5 Command to obfuscate IP

Fig. 6 targetrt command on obfuscated IP

VM2. Once IP traceback has been established, traffic variable generation needs to be examined. On VM2, the trafficvars.php script is active.

4.3 Layer Two Implementation

To effectively test the second layer, two extra PHP scripts are required. With various delays, trafficgenerate.php will produce TCP packets and requests. The speed of queries will be determined via speedcalc.php.

The subsequent experiments' goal is to determine the traffic speed under both high and low request counts. When there are many requests, the traffic speed is calculated to be high, and when there are few requests, the traffic speed is calculated to be low. Although peaks in increased traffic should be carefully noted and recorded in order to later use them in assessing new attacks in the future, heavy traffic speed does not always signal an assault.

4.3.1 10 Ips at Low Speed

From the client side IP the following command will be executed:
'php trafficgenerate.php 10 10000'.

The requests are made to the specific website once per N seconds, where N is equivalent to a sequence of random values selected from the range of 1 to 10,000 ms. This command produces 10 IPs. The sent server executes speedcalc.php, gathering information from the initial fifty requests made. The outcomes of the executed command are depicted in the graph below, in which the number of responses is plotted against the speed of traffic in megabits per second (Fig. 7).

4.3.2 100 IPs at Low Speed

From the client side, the following command will be executed:
php trafficgenerate.php 100 10000.

This command creates 100 IPs and the target website receives requests from this command once every N seconds, where N is a sequence of random numbers drawn from the range of 1 to 10,000 ms. The sent server executes speedcalc.php, gathering information from the initial fifty requests made. Figure 8.18: speedcalc Command Results for 100 IPs at Low Speed displays the results of the command ran and plots the quantity of requests against the Mb/s of traffic (Fig. 8).

This result depicts that the higher number of requests create a higher number of traffic speed, which also validate that our method of calculation is working in a right way.

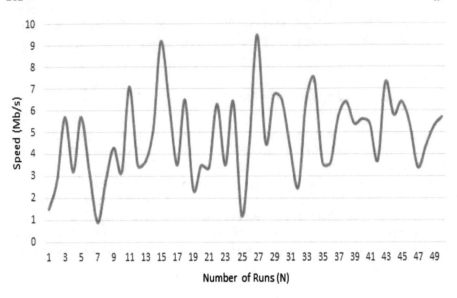

Fig. 7 speedcalc command results for 10 IPs at low speed

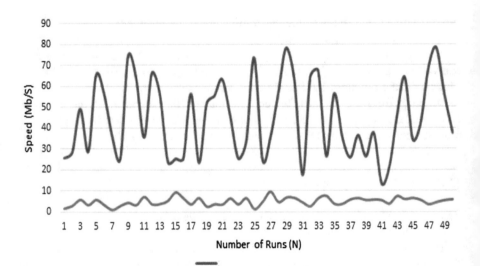

Fig. 8 speedcalc command results for 100 IPs at low speed

4.3.3   10 IPs at High Speed

Now the following command executed from every client-side virtual machine.

php trafficgenerate.php 10 10.

This command sends 10 requests from each client-side IP address to the specified website once in every N seconds, wherein N is a series of random values between 1

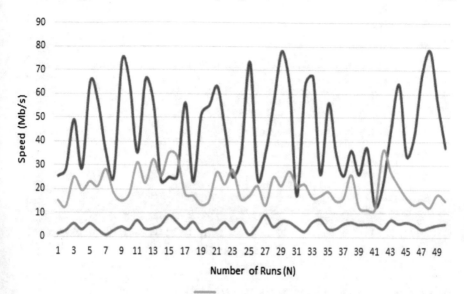

Fig. 9 Speedcalc command results for 10 IPs at high speed

and 10 ms. The sent server launches speedcalc.php and collects data from the first fifty requests. The consequences of the program run are depicted in the grey graph in the picture below (Fig. 9).

4.3.4 100 IPs at High Speed

Again, executing the following command from every client-side virtual machine.

php trafficgenerate.php 100 10.

This command generates 100 requests that are sent to the target website from the client-side IPs once every N seconds, where N is a series of random numbers between 1 and 10 ms. speedcalc.php is performed on the remote server using the results of the initial fifty responses. The outputs of the program run are graphed in orange in the figure that follows (Fig. 10).

All this graphical experiments are carried out to provide evidence that an attack does not always signal high traffic speeds. However, as explained in methodology, the computed S value is used in subsequent tests, along with other variables, to ascertain whether the target website is under assault.

4.3.5 Amplification Co-efficient Selection

The system is run at its top speed to choose the amplification coefficient M, which is utilised to modify the threshold of attack:

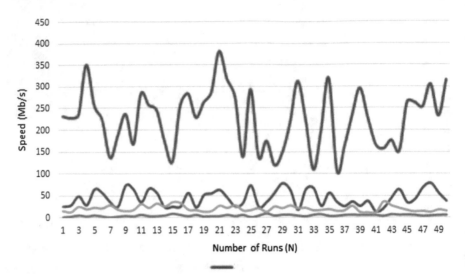

Fig. 10 speedcalc command results for 100 IPs at high speed

php trafficgenerate.php 100 10.

This command produces 100 IPs, and the requests are made to the target website once per N seconds, where N is equal to a sequence of random numbers drawn from the range of 1 to 10,000 ms. The first fifty requests that are received are used to run speedcalc.php on the dispatched server (Fig. 11).

The picture above depicts the initial results, whereas the figures below depict the effects of varying the amplification coefficient (Figs. 12, 13, 14, 15 and 16).

Indicated in the graphics above are several significant facts. When M = 2, the peak speed chart almost approaches the attack threshold trend line, which could lead to false alerts if there is an unexpected rise in genuine traffic. The threshold is too high in the circumstances of M = 4 and M = 5, which could lead to valid attacks going undetected. With M = 3, the trend line is in the best possible position to be utilised as an attack threshold, lowering the possibility of false alarms while maintaining a level that will detect many attacks.

4.4 Layer Three Implementation

The layer two data show that there is no attack but high speed at the target point. The high speed should be resolved by layer four. In comparison to the highest numbers from Experiment 12, the system can generate the following speed values using a C application on the Dispatcher side: 100 IPs at High Speed (Fig. 17).

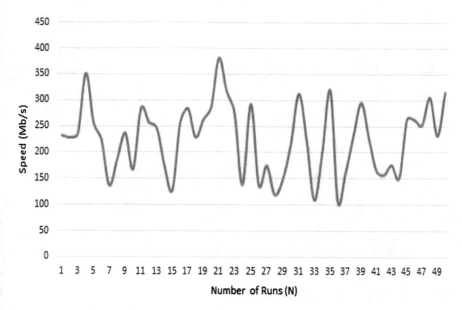

Fig. 11 Initial results of amplification coefficient

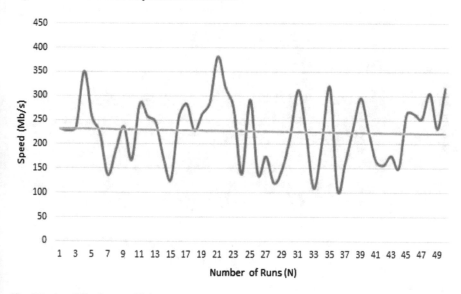

Fig. 12 Amplification coefficient (M) equals one

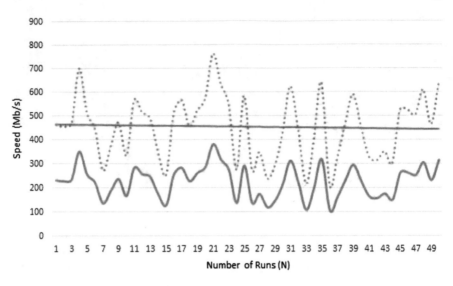

Fig. 13 Amplification coefficient (M) equals two

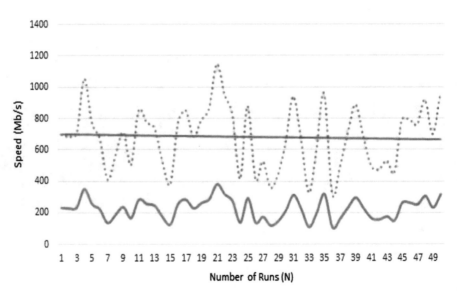

Fig. 14 Amplification coefficient (M) equals three

Figure 18 is a graphical representation of the outcomes of experiments 4.4.4 (shown in blue) and 4.5 (represented in red). The image clearly demonstrates that the speed reduced when the traffic dispatcher was in operation.

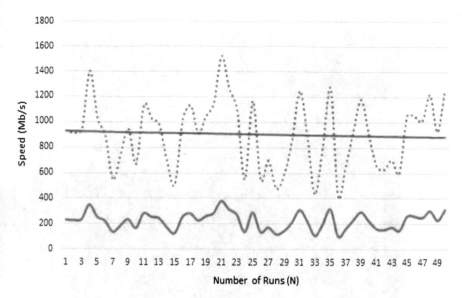

Fig. 15 Amplification coefficient (M) equals four

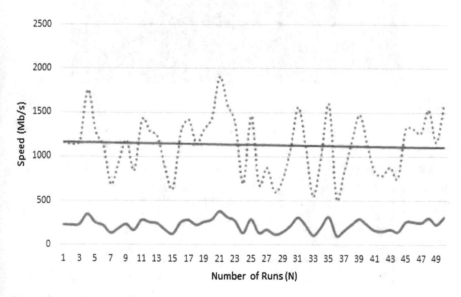

Fig. 16 Amplification coefficient (M) equals five

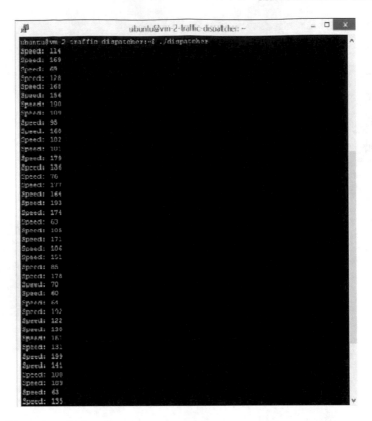

Fig. 17 Dispatcher speed results

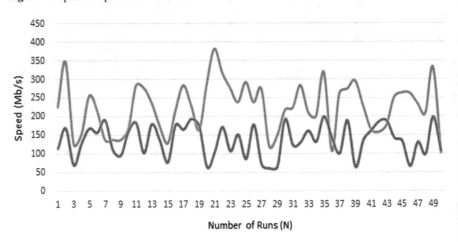

Fig. 18 Speed comparative between experiment 4.4.4 and 4.5

Fig. 19 Port-hopping calculation results

4.5 Layer Four Implementation

The system runs the script for five rounds on the Dispatcher side using the first 25 results, making sure the values do not duplicate and are difficult for an evil user to retrieve (Fig. 19).

4.6 Overall Operation Implementation

4.6.1 DDoS Attack Detection and Prevention at Low-Speed Traffic

Virtual machine name	Loaded script
Virtual machine 6	routeriptb.php trafficgenerate.php 10 10000
Virtual machine 2	.dispatcher .porthop php ti.php

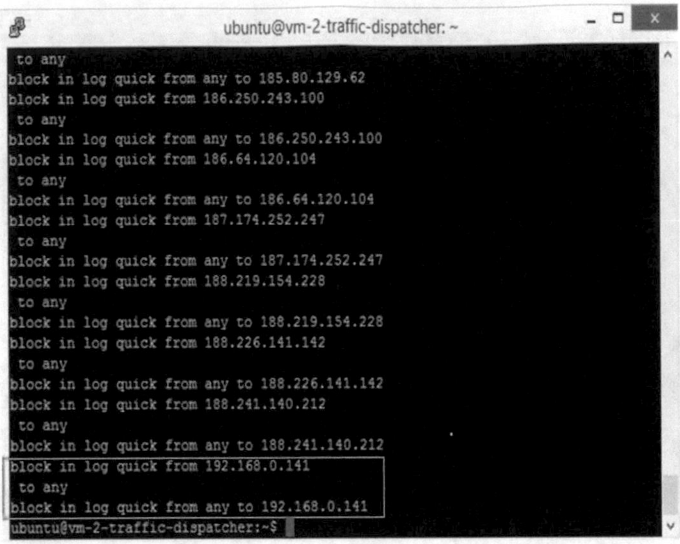

Fig. 20 Low speed firewall rules verification

As a consequence of attack identification and control, firewall rules are generated to stop incoming assaults. Initially, the ipfw.rules document should be empty, as must be confirmed (Fig. 20).

The initial portion of the instructions are derived from the attack rules feed. The rules shown in Fig. 8.33 are the ones added to block VM6. This verifies the anticipated outcome, and the threat is effectively identified and thwarted.

4.6.2 DDoS Attack Detection and Prevention at Normal-Speed Traffic

Virtual machine name	Loaded script
Virtual machine 6	routeriptb.php trafficgenerate.php 10 1000
Virtual machine 7	trafficgenerate.php 10 1000
Virtual machine 2	.dispatcher .porthop php ti.php

Rules are added using the attack rules feed. As depicted in Fig. 8.34, only the final results remain. We retain only the final findings associated with VM6 and VM7. This verifies the anticipated outcome, and the threat is effectively identified and thwarted (Fig. 21).

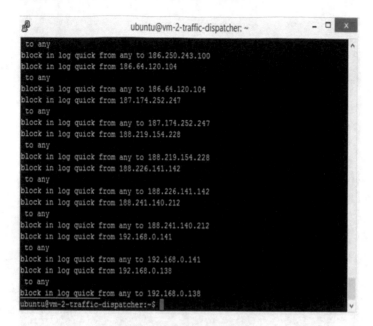

Fig. 21 Normal speed firewall rules verification

4.6.3 DDoS Attack Identification and Mitigation at High Traffic

Virtual machine name	Loaded script
Virtual machine 6	routeriptb.php trafficgenerate.php 100 10
Virtual machine 7	trafficgenerate.php 100 10
Virtual machine 8	trafficgenerate.php 100 10
Virtual machine 9	trafficgenerate.php 100 10
Virtual machine 10	trafficgenerate.php 100 10
Virtual machine 2	.dispatcher .porthop php ti.php

Fig. 22 High speed firewall rules verification

This verifies the anticipated outcome, and the threat is effectively identified and thwarted (Fig. 22).

4.7 Method Comparison

The comparative criteria and parameters are detailed in the following table (Table 2):

Conclusion, Limitations and Future Work

The basic hypothesis of this study is that, while recognising how the risk environment is changing, a cloud-based DDoS defence system may be constructed. The limitations of the existing approaches are demonstrated throughout this study and series of experiments, demonstrating that they could not support this theory. At the very same time, the suggested solution included improvements to already-used methods including reputation management, port-hopping, and IP traceback. The research also offers a brand-new definition and methodology for threat intelligence and validates with experimental findings that it is essential to the proposed protection technique

Table 2 Method comparison

Parameter	Proposed method	IP traceback method	Port hopping method	Entropy-based anomaly detection
Utilization of numerous methods	Yes	No	No	No
Number of techniques utilized	4	1	1	1
Requesting of client response	No	Yes	No	No
Capability to identify unidentified threats	Yes	Yes	Yes	Yes
Implemented	Yes	Yes	Yes	Yes
Resource or frequency band depletion	Both	Band	Band	Band
IN CLOUD SECURITY	Yes	No	No	No
SOFTWARE/ HARDWARE	Software	Software/ Hardware	Hardware	Hardware
INLINE/EXTERNAL FILTRATION	Both	Inline	Inline	Inline
OVERALL PERFORMANCE	Excellent	Good	Good	Good

and to proactively halt complicated DDoS attacks without the need for human intervention. The main hypothesis is proven to be true by the suggested method's demonstration of zero false-positive, the quickest responsiveness on destination under load, the capacity to identify emerging risks, and a high degree of implement ability.

Various IP Traceback implementations, such as hash-based IP Traceback, probabilistic packet marking, deterministic packet marking, packet recording, and others, are among the known approaches and methodologies for DDoS defence. Port-hopping, entropy-based anomaly detection, packet monitoring TTL approach, CBF packet filtering method, and intrusion detection systems based on the Dempster Shafter theory are a few further protective strategies. The research examined these techniques.

The majority of the methods mentioned above are theoretical and would be challenging to apply in real life. IP traceback is a very helpful tool for identifying the true attack source, but its execution would require either a change to the TCP/IP specification, which would have an impact on how the Internet functions as a whole, or significant firmware updates for routers as well as other productive network equipment from any vendor in the world.

Any one of the currently used techniques can be strengthened to increase security and possibly thwart more sophisticated attacks. The protection is now more pertinent and efficient because to enhancements made to IP traceback, port-hopping, and reputation management. Défense's against NAT, Tor, and hidden proxies were implemented, as well as protections against port number calculation, reputation calculation, and IP traceback.

These advancements raised a crucial query; "what tactics and methods ought to be implemented in a successful contemporary DDoS defence system?".

No one strategy will work since DDoS attacks are a growing danger to the entire Internet infrastructure. The goal of this research is to create a sophisticated multilayer system with a sophisticated and automated Threat Intelligence engine at its core. The proposed solution is simple to put into reality, and since the bits of code were created throughout the study process, developers and suppliers can use them.

The study suggests using a multi-technology strategy to mitigate DDoS attacks, which is a widespread issue. The majority of other research focus on a single technology.

This study combines many existing technologies, examines their shortcomings, strengthens the techniques, and makes them work together as a single system. Following is a list of all the technologies used, along with their actual effects and improvements during the conduct of this research.

IP traceback is a technique in the realm of scientific information security that has undergone thorough study and analysis. There are still numerous open issues. One of the main issues is how to safely and without loss save IPs in traffic packets. It is also unclear how to put this strategy into practise without modifying the whole TCP/IP standards. At stage one of the suggested protection solution, IP Traceback is utilised.

Study Effects:

This chapter introduces a straightforward and trustworthy technique for deterministic packet marking utilising the description field of the TCP/IP protocol.

This technique is easier to apply in practise because suppliers simply need to update the routers' software to accept the new technology.

All current networking hardware is capable of managing traffic peaks and offering thorough monitoring and statistics for all traffic kinds. It is frequently challenging to examine large amounts of data while calling for a clear approach to establish the attack threshold. The suggested protection system's second layer is where the threat threshold is determined.

Study Effects:

1. To determine the current mean traffic speed, the target website's access log is processed. Experiments were used to calculate the multiplier coefficient, which is used to modify the results. The attack threshold is shown by the end results.
2. The threshold is employed as a crucial component along with other elements to determine if an attack has occurred rather than just as a standalone indicator of an attack.

By dividing the traffic between proxies, traffic routing is used to slow down attacks. In the suggested system, layer four is where it is used.

Study Impact: This method was entirely created from start in this study, and it was put to the test through experiments.

4.7.1 Port Hopping

A well-known attack mitigation technique called port-hopping uses completely random port numbers both on the origin and destination sides. The fifth layer of the suggested system makes use of this method.

Study Effects: The study offers a novel method for calculating port numbers based on some other system factors, allowing the calculations to be integrated into other system layers. The source is layer four, the destination is the target website, and the creation of random port numbers is coordinated between these two points.

- Limitations

There are several restrictions on the research design this study used. First off, there are restrictions due to the topic matter itself. DDoS assaults originate from a variety of places on the Internet. At same time, these attacks are typically directed by one or more members of a hacking gang. In reality, they are also constrained by IP range and attack methods.

An attack's IP range is determined by the botnets that the hackers use. Most antivirus and security companies regularly monitor network activities. All shady behaviour is tracked and investigated. Network sensors can stop attacks of any strength, regardless of how damaging they might be to servers. Major botnets' IP addresses are known and stored in security databases. Such databases are employed as an additional source of attack information in this work.

The fact that DDoS attacks draw a lot of resources is another issue. This study might have trouble simulating actual attacks inside the test lab if it also utilised computation power or bandwidth to thwart these attempts. The algorithms are clever and do not rely on the scale of the attack. They do a behaviour analysis and employ a pro-active strategy for attack mitigation. This means that the size of an attack is less significant in this study, allowing for successful local modelling of potential scenarios in the lab.

It was said before in this document that it can be difficult to identify an attack since the same IP may be used for both malicious and lawful traffic. Our approach is specifically designed to identify the harmful behaviour included within traffic packets. The test findings show that reputation management and a variety of other criteria are successfully used to address this issue.

To sum up, the techniques and strategies used in this study enable the system to simulate real-world attacks in a testing environment without compromising the accuracy of the findings.

- Future Work

Despite the fact that the findings of this study stand on their own, additional research might be conducted as a direct result of this study, such as studies examining the effects of combining many DDoS defence methods into a single complicated multilayer system. There are numerous conceivable protocols for their interaction and enhancement that might be used to integrate the existing and newly created approaches into a single system.

Users and system administrators, in order to stay one step ahead of today's dangers, must be cognizant of the repercussions of an attack and constantly adapt. In response, we can no longer afford to rely solely on technological procedures to counter our enemies, and instead must adopt novel, sophisticated techniques of doing so. To date, there is no stand-alone system capable of mitigating a DDoS reflection assault with a throughput of more than 500 Gb/s. The only way to win the fight against cybercriminals is for scientists and security providers to work together to develop comprehensive solutions that can prevent and respond to attacks of any kind. We also suggest focusing further on tests at maximum speeds of tens and hundreds of Gb/s, as our study only considers a modest traffic volume. To do this, a DNS reflection attack or another sort of DDoS simulation can be used to mimic a real-world DDoS attack from outside the test lab, with an increase in its force.

References

1. Akamai. State of the internet report, December 2019
2. Caglayan A, Toothaker M, Drapeau D, Burke D, Eaton G (2012) Behavioral analysis of botnets for threat intelligence. IseB 10(4):491–519
3. Arbor Networks. Worldwide Infrastructure Security Report (2016) DDoS threat landscape. APNIC conference
4. Riverhead Networks. DDoS mitigation: maintaining business continuity in the face of malicious attacks
5. Cho JH, Shin JY, Lee H, Kim JM, Lee G (2015) DDoS prevention system using multi-filtering method
6. Graham M, Winckles A, Sanchez-Velazquez E (2015, July) Botnet detection within cloud service provider networks using flow protocols. In: 2015 IEEE 13th international conference on Industrial informatics (INDIN). IEEE, pp 1614–1619
7. Karim A, Salleh RB, Shiraz M, Shah SAA, Awan I, Anuar NB (2014) Botnet detection techniques: review, future trends, and issues. J Zhejiang Univ Sci C 15(11):943–983
8. Mansfield-Devine S (2014) The evolution of DDoS. Comput Fraud Secur 2014(10):15–20
9. Deshmukh RV, Devadkar KK (2015) Understanding DDoS attack & its effect in cloud environment. Procedia Comput Sci 49:202
10. Xiao P, Qu W, Qi H, Li Z (2015) Detecting DDoS attacks against data center with correlation analysis. Comput Commun 67:66–74
11. Navaz AS, Sangeetha V, Prabhadevi C (2013) Entropy based anomaly detection system to prevent DDoS attacks in cloud. arXiv preprint arXiv:1308.6745
12. Saied A, Overill RE, Radzik T (2016) Detection of known and unknown DDoS attacks using artificial neural networks. Neurocomputing 172:385–393
13. Wang B, Zheng Y, Lou W, Hou YT (2015) DDoS attack protection in the era of cloud computing and software-defined networking. Comput Netw 81:308–319
14. Vissers T, Somasundaram TS, Pieters L, Govindarajan K, Hellinckx P (2014) DDoS defense system for web services in a cloud environment. Futur Gener Comput Syst 37:37–45
15. Kijewski P, Pawliński P (2014) Proactive detection and automated exchange of network security incidents. Abgerufen am, 20

16. Krylov V, Kravtsov K (2014) DDoS attack and interception resistance IP fast hopping based protocol. arXiv preprint arXiv:1403.7371
17. Bereziński P, Jasiul B, Szpyrka M (2015) An entropy-based network anomaly detection method. Entropy 17(4):2367–2408
18. Hwang K, Kulkareni S, Hu Y (2009, Dec) Cloud security with virtualized defence and reputation-based trust management. In: 2009. DASC'09. Eighth IEEE international conference on dependable, autonomic and secure computing. IEEE, pp 717–722
19. Song S, Hwang K, Zhou R, Kwok YK (2005) Trusted P2P transactions with fuzzy reputation aggregation. Internet Comput, IEEE 9(6):24–34
20. He R, Niu J, Yuan M, Hu J (2004, Sept) A novel cloud-based trust model for pervasive computing. In: Null. IEEE, pp 693–700
21. Ylitalo K, Kortesniemi Y (2005, Sept) Privacy in distributed reputation management. In: Workshop of the 1st international conference on security and privacy for emerging areas in communication networks, pp 63–71
22. Zhou R, Hwang K, Cai M (2008) Gossiptrust for fast reputation aggregation in peer-to-peer networks. IEEE Trans Knowl Data Eng 20(9):1282–1295
23. Habib SM, Ries S, Mühlhäuser M (2010, Oct) Cloud computing landscape and research challenges regarding trust and reputation. In: 2010 7th international conference on ubiquitous intelligence & computing and 7th international conference on autonomic & trusted computing (UIC/ATC). IEEE, pp 410–415
24. Jøsang A, Ismail R, Boyd C (2007) A survey of trust and reputation systems for online service provision. Decis Support Syst 43(2):618–644
25. Snoeren AC, Partridge C, Sanchez LA, Jones CE, Tchakountio F, Kent ST, Strayer WT (2001, Aug) Hash-based IP traceback. ACM SIGCOMM Comput Commun Rev 31(4):3–14. ACM
26. Goodrich MT (2007) Probabilistic packet marking for large-scale IP traceback
27. Gong C, Sarac K (2005, May) IP traceback based on packet marking and logging. In: ICC 2005. 2005 IEEE international conference on communications, 2005, vol 2. IEEE, pp 1043–1047
28. Ramesh S, Pichumani S, Chakravarthy V. Improving the efficiency of IP traceback at the DoS victim
29. Saurabh S, Sairam AS Increasing accuracy and reliability of IP traceback for DDoS attack using completion condition
30. Li J, Sung M, Xu J, Li L (2004, May) Large-scale IP traceback in high-speed Internet: Practical techniques and theoretical foundation. In: Proceedings. 2004 IEEE symposium on security and privacy, 2004. IEEE, pp 115–129
31. Foroushani VA, Zincir-Heywood AN (2013, March) Deterministic and authenticated flow marking for IP traceback. In: 2013 IEEE 27th international conference on advanced information networking and applications (AINA). IEEE, pp 397–404
32. Yan D, Wang Y, Su S, Yang F (2012) A precise and practical IP traceback technique based on packet marking and logging. J Inf Sci Eng 28(3):453–470
33. Aghaei-Foroushani V, Zincir-Heywood AN (2013, May) On evaluating IP traceback schemes: a practical perspective. In: Security and privacy workshops (SPW), 2013 IEEE. IEEE, pp 127–134
34. Sung M, Xu J (2003) IP traceback-based intelligent packet filtering: a novel technique for defending against internet DDoS attacks. IEEE Trans Parallel Distrib Syst 14(9):861–872
35. Park K, Lee H (2001) On the effectiveness of probabilistic packet marking for IP traceback under denial of service attack. In: INFOCOM 2001. Twentieth annual joint conference of the IEEE computer and communications societies. Proceedings. IEEE, vol 1. IEEE, pp 338–347
36. Song DX, Perrig A (2001) Advanced and authenticated marking schemes for IP traceback. In: INFOCOM 2001. Twentieth annual joint conference of the IEEE computer and communications societies. Proceedings. IEEE, vol 2. IEEE, pp 878–886
37. Savage S, Wetherall D, Karlin A, Anderson T (2000, Aug) Practical network support for IP traceback. ACM SIGCOMM Comput Commun Rev 30(4):295–306. ACM
38. Appala S, Cam-Winget N, McGrew D, Verma J (2015, Oct) An actionable threat intelligence system using a publish-subscribe communications model. In: Proceedings of the 2nd ACM workshop on information sharing and collaborative security. ACM, pp 61–70

39. Nair SG, Puri P (2015) Open-source threat intelligence system. Int J Res 2(4):360–364
40. Ring T (2014) Threat intelligence: why people don't share. Comput Fraud Secur 2014(3):5–9. https://doi.org/10.1016/s1361-3723(14)70469-5
41. Thriveni TK, Prashanth CSR (2015) Real-time threat prediction for cloud based assets using big-data analytics
42. Adebayo OS, AbdulAziz N (2014, Nov) An intelligence-based model for the prevention of advanced cyber-attacks. In: 2014 the 5th international conference on information and communication technology for the muslim world (ICT4M). IEEE, pp 1–5
43. Computerworld, April 21, 1997 v31 n16 p16 (1) Proxy servers gain user appeal Laura DiDio
44. Jeffery CL, Das SR, Bernal GS. Proxy-sharing proxy servers. 7–10 May 1996. Proceedings of COM'96. First annual conference on emerging technologies and applications in communications
45. Computerworld, Nov 17, 1997 v31 n46 p6 (1) Planning blunts web traffic spikes. Sharon Machlis
46. Computerworld, Jan 26, 1998 v32 n4 p47 (2) Web-caching servers cut network costs. Bob Wallace
47. Nam KD, Lee HT. Design of a virtual server for service interworking over heterogeneous networks. 20–22 Aug. 1997. In: 1997 IEEE pacific rim conference on communications, computers and signal processing, PACRIM. 10 years networking the Pacific
48. Sattar I, Shahid M, Abbas Y (2015) A review of techniques to detect and prevent distributed denial of service (DDoS) attack in cloud computing environment. Int J Comput Appl 115(8)
49. Lee HC, Thing VL (2004, Sept) Port hopping for resilient networks. In: Vehicular technology conference, 2004. VTC2004-Fall. 2004 IEEE 60th, vol 5. IEEE, pp 3291–3295
50. Chawla I, Kaur D, Luthra P. DDoS attacks in cloud and mitigation techniques
51. Luo YB, Wang BS, Cai GL (2015) Analysis of port hopping for proactive cyber défense. Int J Secur Appl 9(2):123–134
52. Shi F (2013) U.S. patent no. 8,434,140. Washington, DC: U.S. Patent and Trademark Office
53. Source code of the entropy-based network traffic anomaly detector, https://github.com/anacristina/entropy-based-anomaly-detector

Ransomware Attack on the Educational Sector

Usman Butt, Yusuf Dauda, and Baba Shaheer

Abstract The world today is confronted with the challenging task of juggling the adoption of innovative technology with securing information systems and data that enables essential everyday operations. In recent years, spectacular breaches of numerous computer systems, including those of airlines, health organizations, credit agencies, governments, financial institutions, telecoms, education sectors, and many others, have made cybersecurity an increasingly prominent news topic (Blazic in EDULEARN21 Proceedings, 2021, pp. 6619–6626, [1]). Due to the expansion of the internet, people now enjoy different realms of both the existing reality and the digital reality (Rahman et al. in Int J Inf Educ Technol 10:378–382, [2]). With the advent of search engines like Yahoo, and Google as well as video-sharing platforms like YouTube, everyone can access any information easily.

Keywords Ransomware · Cyber physical system · Malware · Phishing · Educational tools · Cybersecurity

1 Introduction

The combination of "real world" (physical), "virtual" (cyber), and "social" (human) elements in order to produce a comprehensive and safe infrastructure refers to as Physical Cyber Social Systems [3]. These systems are taking on an ever-growing amount of significance in the modern world as an expanding number of vital services and infrastructures are getting connected to the internet. The importance of PCSS can be seen in several areas such as the Internet of Things (IoT), Critical Infrastructure Protection, Smart Cities, etc.

Unfortunately, users may experience negative repercussions from this expanding cyberspace through threat actors exploiting system vulnerabilities. Password compromise, ransomware attacks, and stolen databases are just a few examples of

U. Butt (✉) · Y. Dauda · B. Shaheer
Northumbria University, London, UK
e-mail: usman.butt@northumbria.ac.uk

© The Author(s), under exclusive license to Springer Nature Switzerland AG 2023
H. Jahankhani et al. (eds.), *AI, Blockchain and Self-Sovereign Identity in Higher Education*, Advanced Sciences and Technologies for Security Applications,
https://doi.org/10.1007/978-3-031-33627-0_11

security issues. Human is regarded as the most vulnerable asset in the information security standard due to their nature [4]. Threats can take many different forms, including advanced persistent threats (APT), malware, ransomware, phishing, social engineering, distributed denial of service (DDoS) attacks, among others. Depending on the attack, there may be a variety of negative effects, such as operational disaster, data breaches that result in the loss of sensitive information or financial loss and damaged reputations [5].

The need to build global cybersecurity capacity, which includes improvements in cybersecurity education, awareness campaigns, and training at multiple levels, from regions to organizations to individuals, is one major counter to these risks that raise concerns about how to improve digital security [6]. Recently, the cybersecurity landscape has benefitted a complex and dynamic increase due to technological improvements and the growing interconnection of computer systems and networks. Most institutions in charge of sensitive data, such as financial information, have heavily invested in cybersecurity by hiring information security professionals, creating comprehensive security policies, incorporating high-end security technologies, and continuously training their security personnel. This has helped to protect the data and reduce the number of potential cybercrimes [7].

Organizations and governments have put in place a variety of traditional cybersecurity measures, such as firewalls, intrusion detection systems, encryption, and incident response plans, to defend against these threats [8]. To find and fix vulnerabilities in their systems, they frequently turn to threat intelligence, incident response teams, and penetration testing.

Furthermore, Artificial Intelligence (AI) and Machine Learning (ML) technologies are being more frequently used in security solutions. These technologies are employed to analyze big data sets and spot trends that can allude to a security incident. A few security procedures, like threat detection systems and incident response, can also be automated using them.

In conclusion, the cybersecurity landscape is constantly evolving, and organizations must stay up-to-date with the latest threats and security measures to effectively protect against cyberattacks. In order to mitigate the risk, organizations should conduct regular security assessments, employee education and awareness, implement security protocols and regulations, and have incident response plans in place. This combined approach will allow organizations to effectively protect their assets and mitigate the risks associated with cyber-attacks.

2 Cybersecurity Threats and Challenges

2.1 Cybersecurity Definition

To safeguard computer systems, networks, and data against unauthorized access, use, disclosure, interruption, modification, or destruction, there are many distinct aspects of cybersecurity that must be considered. National Cyber Security Center defined "Cyber security as how individuals and organizations reduce the risk of cyber attack, and its' core function is to protect the devices we all use (smartphones, laptops, tablets, and computers), and the services we access—both online and at work—from theft or damage".

One of the generally accepted definitions of cybersecurity is from the ISO/IEC 27032, which defines "Cybersecurity as the "preservation of the confidentiality, integrity, and availability of information in Cyberspace".

Although different academic journals and sources may provide slightly varying definitions of cybersecurity, in general, it is thought to be the protection and defense of digital assets. In addition, it is important to keep in mind that, depending on the context, the terms "cybersecurity" and "information security" or "computer security" may occasionally be used interchangeably; these concepts are similar but have slightly distinct meanings and applications depending on the context of implementation. Taherdoost [9] in his research considered "Cybersecurity" to defend the internet from cyberattacks while "Information security" examines defending data from any threat, whether it be physical or digital, highlighting Cybersecurity as a scope of information security as seen in the figure below.

2.2 Pillars of Cybersecurity—The CIA Triad

In the context of all definitions of cybersecurity above, the protection of information from unauthorized access is the main objective of cybersecurity. The CIA triad is seen as the primary model of a security system that sets the foundation for a comprehensive strategy for securing information systems [10].

Confidentiality deals with the idea that valuable information should be shielded from unapproved access or exposure. Several technical and administrative restrictions, including encryption, access controls, and data classification, can be used to achieve this [11]. It is crucial for safeguarding confidential information, including financial and personal information.

Integrity is the concept of making sure the data is complete, accurate, and authorized [11]. Controls like data validation, input validation, and digital signing can be used to accomplish this. Integrity is essential to preserving information's accuracy and reliability and preventing unauthorized parties from manipulating or modifying it.

Availability is the principle that information should be easily accessible to authorized users when they need it [10]. Planning for disaster recovery and business continuity, load balancing, failover, and redundant systems and networks can all help with this. For systems to continue to operate and function properly and for users to have access to the data they require to do their jobs, availability is crucial.

For any security posture infrastructure to be compliant with the principles of confidentiality, integrity, and availability, organizations must implement several layers of security controls and conduct regular reviews of their security plan.

2.3   The Challenges of Cyber Attacks

In Cybersecurity, cyberattacks are activities taken against computer systems, networks, and digital infrastructure with the intent to interfere with equipment performance, alter processing, obtain unauthorized access, or tamper with stored data [12]. The information transmitted via computers is disrupted by computer-to-computer and computer-to-network attacks that compromise their availability, confidentiality, and integrity. Criminals launch cyberattacks with social, political, and financial objectives. Cybercrime activities have been growing exponentially along with the exponential growth in the use of cyberspace. These cyberattacks pose different challenges to their victim organization, some of these include:

Financial & Reputation Loss: Cyberattacks can result in financial losses for organizations, including the cost of recovering from the attack, lost revenue, and potential fines for data breaches [13].

Loss of Confidential Information: Cyberattacks can result in the theft or compromise of sensitive and confidential information, such as personal data, financial information, and trade secrets [14]. This can have significant legal and reputational consequences for organizations.

Disruption of Operations: Cyberattacks can disrupt operations, causing delays, outages, and lost productivity [15]. This can be particularly damaging for organizations that rely heavily on technology and online systems.

Difficulty in Detection and Attribution: It can be difficult to detect, and attribute cyberattacks, making it challenging to identify the source of an attack and hold the attackers accountable.

Difficulty in responding and recovering: Developing and implementing an incident response plan can be challenging and it is difficult to predict how an attack will unfold and how to respond to it [16]. Furthermore, recovering from an attack can be time-consuming and expensive, and it's not always possible to fully restore systems and data to the pre-attack state.

Cyberattacks can have both short-term and long-term effects [17], it's important for organizations to understand the potential impact and have a plan in place to mitigate it.

Cyber threats have become a major challenge of cybersecurity. They now occur in everyday business activities; these threats are of different forms and exist at different stages of information security [18]. The common threats are;

Phishing: Phishing is a type of fraud in which phony emails that appear to be from reliable sources are sent; nonetheless, the purpose of these emails is to obtain sensitive data, such as login or credit card information [19].

Ransomware: A form of malware that encrypts a victim's files and demands payment in return for the decryption key. Organizations suffer large financial losses as a result of ransomware attacks.

Malware: Malware is any malicious software that is designed to cause harm or damage to an organization's information systems and data [20]. Malware can take many forms, including viruses, worms, Trojans, and adware).

Advanced Persistent Threats (APTs): APTs are a specific kind of cyber-attack distinguished by their persistence, sophistication, and anonymity. APTs are frequently employed to rob critical data, sabotage operations, and obtain unauthorized access to an industry's networks and systems.

Denial of Service/Distributed DOS (/DOS/DDoS): The goal of a DOS/DDoS attack is to flood organizations' networks and computers so that authorized users cannot access the systems. Operations are severely disrupted by these types of attacks, which can be challenging to mitigate.

IoT and Mobile threats: Mobile and Internet of Things (IoT) devices are increasingly the targets of sophisticated and regular cyberattacks. These tools can be used to break into a network and steal or encrypt private information.

Cloud Security threats: New security threats like Insecure interfaces and APIs, improperly configured cloud storage services, and data leaks driven by third-party service providers have developed as more businesses employ cloud-based infrastructure.

Social Engineering: In the cybercrime realm, social engineering refers to a variety of techniques used to trick victims into divulging private information or taking other unwanted acts.

Insiders' threats: The acts of past or current employees, contractors, or other insiders having authorized access to an organization's systems and data can be considered an insider threat. These actions can be malevolent or careless in nature [21].

Supply Chain Attacks: Attacks against a company's supply chain take place when a malicious actor targets the company by compromising a third-party vendor, supplier, or other external entity that has access to the company's systems and data [22].

2.3.1   Understanding Malware

Malware as a programme that is secretly placed into another programme with the purpose of deleting data, running invasive or harmful programmes, or otherwise jeopardising the victim's data, programs, or operating system, sometimes known as

Fig. 1 Information security
and cybersecurity difference

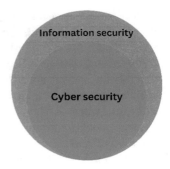

malicious code [23]. The majority of hosts are often threatened by malware, which disrupts operations and causes substantial damage, demanding extensive recovery efforts inside most businesses. Reference [24] defines malware as malicious software, is a programme or piece of code that interferes and disrupts with a computer's regular operation.

Malware is mostly used nowadays to steal sensitive financial, personal, or corporate data for the advantage of others. Malware can occasionally be deployed against business or governmental websites to acquire sensitive data or generally impede their operation. But malware is frequently used against people to steal their personal data, such social security numbers, banking, or credit card details, and so on [25].

Malware has become the greatest external threat to most hosts, causing damage and requiring extensive recovery efforts within most organizations. The following are the classic categories of malware:

Types of malwares [26].

By definition, Malicious software known as malware targets and compromises other computer programmes for illicit purposes by covertly inserting itself into other programmes with the goal to harm or interfere with them [27] and there are five distinct varieties of malwares, as depicted in Fig. 1. These include.

- **Virus**: Viruses are programmes that can attach themselves to other programmes and cause them to become viruses as well, if we take programmes to be sequences of symbols and computer systems to be habitats [28].
- **Worm**: A harmful software that duplicates itself, autonomously spreading through a network and disseminating copies of itself from computer to computer is referred to as a worm virus [29].
- **Trojan**: Trojan is a harmful application that impersonates trustworthy software. Unlike certain other forms of malware like viruses or worms, Trojan horse programmes cannot reproduce themselves. A Trojan horse can be purposefully added by a programmer to other useful software, or it can spread by deceiving users into thinking it is a helpful application [30].
- **Rootkit**: A Rootkit is a programme that modify or replace the system's preexisting code execution routes (Trojan). Modifies or hooks into the processes of running crucial OS operations [31].

- **Ransomware**: A type of malicious software that when used inhibits a computer's operation in some way. A notice requesting payment is displayed by the ransomware application in order to unlock functionality. The PC is effectively held ransom by the malware [32].

2.4 Ransomware

Ransomware attacks are the most significant of the top developments affecting the cyber security sector, according to [33]. Despite technological advancements that allow threat actors to grow more sophisticated, tried and established ransomware strategies continue to pose ongoing and developing hazards. And the top targeted industries have remained consistent during the third quarter of calendar year 2021 [34], with ransomware threat actors proving most successful against the manufacturing industry, followed by financial services, Education, healthcare, construction and technology.

The United States [35], Australia [36], and the United Kingdom [37] issued a joint alert underlining the globalised danger of ransomware. The alert contained data on attacker behaviour, trends, and mitigating advice.

2.5 History of Ransomware

According to [38] Ransomware was characterised as a sort of attack in which threat actors take control of a target's assets and demand a ransom in exchange for the assets' availability being restored. The work focuses on the three main components of every ransomware attack: assets, activities, and blackmail. This action-agnostic definition was required to account for the evolving ransomware threat landscape, the prevalence of many extortion strategies, and the various purposes other than monetary gain. The study also discusses the four high-level activities employed by ransomware to affect the availability, confidentiality, and integrity of assets (lock, encrypt, destroy, and steal). It can be used as a guide to better comprehend this threat. The evolution of ransomware from the aids trojan in 1989 to the latest, well-publicized attack on the ICS colonial pipeline is seen in the Fig. 2.

2.5.1 General Classification of Ransomware

Ransomware is a type of malware that encrypts the victim's files and demands a ransom payment in order to provide the decryption key. Ransomware can be classified into several different categories based on the method of distribution, the type of encryption used, and the behaviour of the malware [39].

Fig. 2 The CIA triad

2.5.2   Ransomware Methodology

The way ransomware is delivered to the victim is through phishing emails, which trick the victim into clicking on a link or attachment that downloads the malware [40] or Ransomware is delivered through a software exploit that takes advantage of a vulnerability in a program to install the malware on the victim's computer [41] and sometimes Ransomware is delivered through a drive-by-download, which happens when the victim visits a compromised website and the malware is automatically downloaded without the victim's knowledge [42].

When a user clicks on a link that has been provided by the attackers, malware will automatically begin searching for system vulnerabilities in order to break into the device of the victim and encrypt their data using a public key. Now, in order for us to be able to decrypt the data, we need a private key, which the cybercriminals will only provide us after they have been paid the ransom [43, 44, 45].

2.5.3   Types of Ransomwares

There are several types of ransomwares that have emerged over the years as shown in Fig. 3, each with their own unique characteristics. Some of the most common types of ransomwares include:

Crypto-ransomware is the most common type of ransomware and it encrypts the victim's files and demands a ransom payment in exchange for the decryption key. Examples of crypto-ransomware include WannaCry, Petya, and Cerber. Lock-screen ransomware locks the victim's screen, making it impossible for them to access their files or use their computer. It often displays a message demanding a ransom payment in order to unlock the screen. Examples of lock-screen ransomware include Revenge Ransomware, Guster and Xpan. Scareware ransomware does not actually encrypt the victim's files, but instead uses social engineering tactics to convince the victim to pay a ransom. This type of malware typically displays a fake error message or warning claiming that the victim's computer is infected with a virus and demands payment in exchange for a "fix." Examples of Scareware include "Computer locked" or "Your PC is blocked" [46, 47, 48].

Fig. 3 Types of malwares

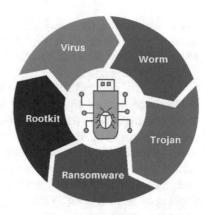

Ransomware-as-a-service (RaaS): Ransomware-as-a-service (RaaS) is a type of malware that is offered as a service to cybercriminals. This type of malware is typically rented or purchased by cybercriminals and then distributed using a variety of methods to infect victims' systems [44].

3 Most Common Attacks of Ransomware on Individuals and Organisations

Individuals and organizations are common targets for ransomware attacks because they often have valuable data that they need access to and may be willing to pay to regain access. Additionally, organizations may have more resources to pay the ransom, making them more attractive targets for attackers. It's important for individuals and organizations to take steps to protect themselves from ransomware attacks, such as keeping their software and systems updated, regularly backing up important data, and being cautious when clicking on links or opening attachments in emails [49, 50].

3.1 Individuals

One reason is that individuals often have valuable personal data, such as family photos, financial information, and other sensitive information, that they may be willing to pay to regain access to. Additionally, individuals may not have the technical expertise or resources to defend against ransomware attacks, making them more vulnerable to these types of attacks.

Another reason why individuals are targeted is that attackers can use social engineering tactics to trick individuals into downloading malware or giving away sensitive information. For example, attackers may send phishing emails that appear to be from a legitimate source, such as a bank or government agency, and ask the recipient to click on a link or download an attachment. When the individual does so, they unknowingly install malware on their computer that encrypts their files and demands a ransom payment [51].

A recent study by [52] found that individuals accounted for more than half of all ransomware victims, with many of these attacks being launched through phishing emails or malicious websites. Moreover, according to the same study, the most common types of files targeted by ransomware attacks on individuals include documents, photos, and videos. It is important for individuals to take proactive steps to protect themselves from ransomware attacks, such as keeping their software and systems updated, regularly backing up important data, and being cautious when clicking on links or opening attachments in emails. Additionally, individuals should be aware of the common tactics used by attackers and avoid falling for social engineering scams [53].

3.2 Organisations

Ransomware is a significant threat to organizations, with attackers targeting them as a prime target for several reasons. One reason is that organizations often have valuable data, such as financial records, customer information, and other sensitive information, that they may be willing to pay to regain access to [54]. Additionally, organizations may have more resources to pay the ransom, making them more attractive targets for attackers. Another reason why organizations are targeted is that they often have more complex systems and networks, which can make them more vulnerable to attacks. For example, an attacker may be able to gain access to an organization's network through a vulnerability in an outdated software or by exploiting a weak password. Once inside the network, the attacker can spread the ransomware to multiple systems, making it more difficult for the organization to recover from the attack [55].

According to a recent report by [56], it is estimated that ransomware has targeted 92,863 corporate users which includes 12,699 small scale business users and Fig. 4 represents the total number of corporate users affected due to ransomware attacks.

It's important for organizations to take steps to protect themselves from ransomware attacks, such as keeping their software and systems updated, regularly backing up important data, and implementing security best practices, such as multi-factor authentication and network segmentation. Additionally, organizations should have incident response plans in place in case of a ransomware attack and should also educate their employees on how to identify and avoid phishing and other types of social engineering attacks.

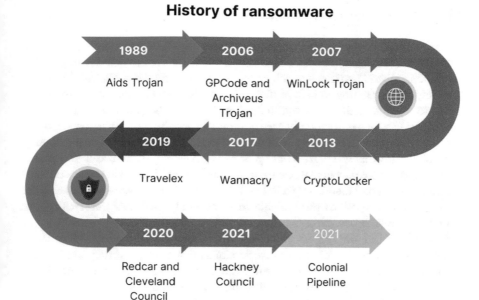

Fig. 4 Ransomware history. *Source* [57]

3.3 There Are Several Common Methods Used to Distribute and Spread Ransomware to End-Users, Some of the Most Common Include

As per [58] ransomware is often distributed through phishing emails that contain a malicious link or attachment. The victim is tricked into clicking on the link or attachment, which then downloads the ransomware onto their computer and Ransomware can also be distributed through drive-by downloads from malicious websites. Visiting such a website can cause the malware to automatically download on the user's computer. Cybercriminals can also use exploit kits, which are toolkits that automate the process of finding and exploiting vulnerabilities in software. When a user visits a compromised website that is running an exploit kit, the kit can use any vulnerabilities in the user's software to download malware, including ransomware, onto the user's computer [59]. Social engineering tactics, such as disguising the malware as a legitimate software update or a document that users are prompted to open or making the user to click on any spam link will also be used to spread the ransomware [60]. It's important to note that these methods can also be combined, making it more difficult for users to protect themselves from ransomware attacks. Keeping software and operating system up to date, as well as being aware of common attack methods, and having proper backup, can greatly reduce the risk of falling victim to ransomware.

3.3.1 Most Common Attacks of Ransomware on Organisations

As per [61] annual survey 66% of the organisations were hit by ransomware. The techniques used by attacks to compromise the Organizations are targeted with phishing emails that contain malicious attachments or links, which when clicked, install the ransomware. Exploiting vulnerabilities in outdated software and systems to gain access to an organization's network [62]. Attackers can take the advantage of protocols like RDP which is commonly used to remotely access an organisation's network to deploy the ransomware if the protocol is not secure [63]. According to the findings of a global study that was carried out by BCI [64], ransomware attacks are becoming a significantly more prevalent threat for major businesses. The impact of ransomware is created by a combination of technical and social characteristics, and one of the reasons that organisations were unable to successfully protect themselves against ransomware assaults was either a lack of security policies or a failure to comply with such standards [65, 66]. Ransomware can also spread via third-party software and hardware, for example, when a software vendor's update server is compromised, and the malware is spread via the software updates. Some ransomware attacks are highly targeted and carefully planned, with the attackers spending weeks or even months studying their target, looking for weaknesses in their defences and identifying valuable data that they can encrypt and hold for ransom. It is important for organizations to have robust security measures in place, such as regular security updates and patching, employee security training, and use of anti-virus and anti-malware software. Additionally, regular backups can help organizations recover their files in case of a ransomware attack [67].

Nevertheless, phishing and ransomware are currently the two most common types of cyber threats that affect both humans and cyber-physical systems.

3.4 Impact on Cyber Physical Systems

Cyber-physical system development presented new difficulties. One of the trickiest issues with a variety of cyber-attack defences is ensuring the information security of cyber-physical systems [68]. Numerous increasingly diverse and intricately interconnected sets of technologies are in daily use in a variety of industries, like pharmaceuticals, the power grids, oil rigs, nuclear reactors, Transport, food manufacturing units and modern transportation systems for logistics and public transportation, to control significant portions of the global process. Industrial Control Systems is the organisation that represents all these sectors of sophisticated control technology [69]. Because of the volume, variety, and intensity of cyberattacks on industrial control systems (ICS) that are rising quickly, the cyber risks that operators of these systems must deal with today are more difficult than ever [70].

According to [38] Out of the total of 18, three new activity groups have been found to have the capacity or intent to target OT networks.

Table 1 Reported ransomware attacks

Government		News media and security companies		Ransomware groups on their web	
Year	Complaints	Year	Complaints	Year	Complaints
2021	3729	2021–22	3696	2021–22	4110

Source [58]

Which threats are impacting cyber physical systems?

- Ransomware
- Spear phishing
- Phishing
- Social Engineering
- Malwares
- Dos attacks.

According to [58], there have been 623 ransomware instances globally, with a particular concentration on Europe, the United Kingdom, and the United States. The actual number of ransomware attacks Reported publicly (Table 1).

3.5 Most Popular Cyber-Attacks on Industrial Control Systems

Industrial control systems (ICSs) are cyber-enabled embedded devices that run vital infrastructure (e.g., Water, power, Energy, Transport). ICS devices are less well-known and are usually specific to the cyber operational technology (OT) framework, which differs from business information technology (IT) [71]. There are various popular ransomware attacks happened on ICS as represented in Fig. 5.

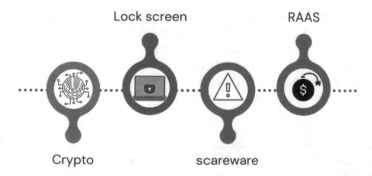

Fig. 5 Types of ransomwares

1. Stuxnet

Stuxnet targets industrial control systems, which are frequently utilised in power grids, oil refineries, and nuclear power stations, in contrast to the majority of malware. It targets Windows PCs used to programme particular Siemens programmable logic controllers, which are specialist computers used in typical industrial control systems to control automated physical operations like robot arms [72].

Stuxnet was signed using certificates taken from Realtek and JMicron, and it used four "zero day" Windows vulnerabilities to spread and acquire administrator rights once inside a computer. Most intriguingly, analysts found code that modifies Siemens SCADA systems, which are used in some centrifuges. Many believe Stuxnet was created specifically to destroy the centrifuges used by Iran's nuclear programme to enrich uranium, and the Iranian government claimed the virus at least partially succeeded in this [73].

2. Gas Pipeline cyber intrusion campaign

A sophisticated threat actor launched an ongoing series of cyber-intrusions against businesses in the natural gas pipeline sector starting in late December 2011, according to ICS-CERT. ICS-CERT received information from several sources revealing targeted efforts and intrusions into numerous enterprises involved in the natural gas pipeline sector [74].

3. Shamoon

Another malware, Shamoon, hit Saudi Arabia's state oil corporation Aramco, the world's largest oil producer company, in August 2012, wiping out data from 30,000 client PCs in the company [75].

4. New York DAM

Iranian hackers allegedly gained access to a small dam close to Rye Brook, New York, in 2013. This is according to the U.S. Justice Department. The attack was not sophisticated, but the Iranian attackers believed it to be a test to see what they could gain access to.

The Bowman Dam, a modest utility, is used to regulate storm surges. A cellular modem was used to connect the SCADA system at Bowman Dam to the Internet. At the time of the attack, the SCADA system was undergoing maintenance, making control impossible; only status monitoring was possible. The majority of people believe that the dam was attacked due to its weak Internet connection and a lack of security measures rather than a deliberate cyberattack [76].

5. Notpetya

It is said to have started in Russia and the Ukraine before spreading to the United States, the United Kingdom, India, Italy, Germany, poland and France. In other words, it is practically universal. The "NotPetya" attacks are comparable to the extremely recent WannaCry ransomware, which spreads through networks by using the NSA hack EternalBlue. In addition, NotPetya spreads over computers through a variety of propagation methods. It comprises Credential stealer, which can steal credentials, and PsExec, which can access other systems linked to that domain on the same network using the usernames and passwords that have been acquired [77].

6. Solarwinds

The SolarWinds Attack was a component of a large-scale, highly technical cyber espionage operation carried out by Russian Foreign Intelligence Service actors under the aliases "APT 29" and/or "Cozy Bear," with an emphasis on stealth and the appropriation of confidential data. Even though the majority of Orion's customers were not the target of a subsequent infiltration, at least nine federal agencies and almost 100 businesses were affected [78].

7. Colonial pipeline

The Colonial Pipeline Company made the announcement on May 8, 2021, that it had stopped its pipeline operations owing to a ransomware assault. This caused essential supply of gasoline as well as other refined fuels to be disrupted all along the East Coast. This attack was quite similar to a ransomware attack that was carried out on a pipeline in the year 2020, which similarly resulted in the pipeline being shut down [79].

3.6 Impact of Ransomware on Education Sector

The incorporation of technology in education has been increasing globally over the past few years. The collection of technologies that are used in educational sector play an important part in the teaching and learning process. The manner in which instruction and the distribution of material are taking place through online learning applications and learning management systems is the aspect of the learning process that is currently considered to be the most essential. In addition, training systems are beginning to include predictive learning analytics in order to boost the efficiency of the training process [80]. Higher education institutions in 188 nations were impacted by the Covid-19 virus as of April 6, 2020 [81].

The National Cyber Security Centre (NCSC) in the United Kingdom issued a warning that the education sector was being specially targeted for ransomware attacks. This warning was made in response to the increase in the number of assaults [82, 83]. The school system was severely impacted as a result of the pandemic. Systems such as e-learning activities, online teaching tools, and learner management systems were important in order to maintain students' access to the core curriculum and tests. However, this change to total dependence on technology means that the cyber-attack area got extended, meaning that a growing number of e-institutions were made exposed as a result of employing new technologies throughout the course of the school day.

This is mirrored by [84], which, based on worldwide threat activity, positions the education sector solidly in top place. According to [84], the education sector is the industry that has been the most affected by reported business malware incidents in the last 30 days. The educational industry is being challenged by ransomware as a result of several vulnerabilities that are specifically targeted on remote access methods such as VPN and RDP. And even carrying out phishing operations with the intention of deploying ransomware, which, in the event that it is successful in doing so, will exploit susceptible applications and networks [85].

4 Education Sector

4.1 The Role of the Education Sector in an Economy

The goal of education under the human capital theory is to increase labor productivity, which will increase the output of products and services. The right to education was listed as one of the fundamental human rights in the Universal Declaration of Human Rights more than 50 years ago. The primary human resource development component is provided by the higher education system. Traditionally, a person's professional and academic credentials have been referred to as their education capital. It comprises of corporate and professional attributes as well as information, skills, and abilities learned in educational institutions.

The scientific and educational systems are undergoing developments aimed at tightening the standards for the caliber of specialized training and the certification of higher education institutions. At the same time, control over the efficiency of scientific research institutes is gaining strength, and institutions of higher education are forming new connections with government and corporate structures. Higher education institutions now develop their own scientific-innovative policies, the commercialization of scientific-technical inventions, and drawing all teaching staff of the education organizations to participate in the scientific process in order to achieve the strategic goals of innovative development [86]

Economic growth, employment, and income are all significantly influenced by education. Ignoring the economic value of education would jeopardize the prosperity of future generations and have significant negative effects on poverty, social exclusion, and the viability of social security systems [87] Innovation and productivity of a country's economy are thought to be significantly influenced by education. Education increases a person's likelihood of starting a business and creating new technology, which can create new goods, services, and industries and boost the economy. The education sector is crucial in the economy through the provision of a skilled and educated workforce that can spur economic growth and development.

According to Barro [88] and Gyimah-Brempong et al. [89], the major impact of the education sector on an economy includes:

1. Poverty Eradication: Education can help to reduce poverty by providing individuals with the skills and knowledge needed to find better-paying jobs and improve their economic situation.

2. Human capital development: Education helps to develop the knowledge, skills, and abilities of individuals, which can increase their productivity and earning potential. This, in turn, can lead to higher economic growth and development.
3. Innovation and entrepreneurship: Education can help to foster innovation and entrepreneurship by providing individuals with the knowledge and skills needed to start and grow new businesses.
4. Labor force: A well-educated workforce is considered as a source of competitive advantage for countries, as it increases the productivity and earning potential of individuals, as well as the overall competitiveness of the economy.

The education sector contributes to the growth of entrepreneurship and innovation, social mobility, increase in government revenue, economic diversification, and improved living standards which give a country the liberty to compete at the global economic level.

4.2 Technology in Education Sector

The development of the internet and mobile technology has had a significant impact on education in the twenty-first century, offering new and creative ways for teachers to impart knowledge and for students to learn. Students nowadays can access educational materials and attend classes online giving them more flexibility and convenience during learning. Students also use devices such as smartphones and tablets to access instructional content from any location made possible by mobile technology [90].

Technology has been an important contributor to the field of education, helping to pave the way for innovative and forward-thinking approaches to teaching as well as learning for both students and teachers. The following are some of the ways in which technology has influenced educational practices:

- Online learning: Internet and digital platforms have made it feasible for students to access educational resources and take courses online, providing convenience and flexibility in learning.
- Virtual and Augmented Reality: Technologies are being utilized to develop immersive learning environments for students, enabling them to interact and explore difficult ideas in ways that would be impossible using conventional teaching techniques.
- Adaptive learning: By giving students tools and content that are specifically tailored to their needs and aptitudes, technology is being used to personalize their educational experiences.
- Collaborative learning: Students are now able to remotely interact and communicate with one another thanks to technology, which has also made it possible for them to work together on projects and tasks in real-time.

- Artificial Intelligence: AI-powered technologies such as natural language processing, machine learning, and computer vision are being used to create personalized learning experiences, assessments, and formative feedback.
- Automated administrative tasks: Automation of administrative activities, such as record keeping, scheduling, and contact with students and parents, has been made possible by technological advancements in educational institutions like schools and colleges.

Ultimately, technological improvements have provided education stakeholders with new tools and resources to better student learning, increase the sector's general performance and effectiveness, and make it more accessible to a larger population.

4.3   Cybersecurity Challenges in the Education Sector

As more and more educational institutions rely solemnly on technology to assist the delivery of education and the administration of students' data, the challenge of cybersecurity has become an increasingly critical one in the education industry. The incorporation of new technologies into educational settings has resulted in a plethora of positive outcomes, the most notable of which are an expansion of educational opportunities, exploring new digital courses, and easy accessibility to studies, However, this has resulted in the introduction of new cybersecurity threats and risks that need to be addressed in order to preserve the integrity and confidentiality of student data.

Cybercriminals are able to steal sensitive information from institution servers, including that pertaining to individuals, companies, and students, because there are not enough mitigation measures and adequate resources available for the education sector. Ansari and Khan [91] evaluated the cybersecurity concerns that institutions and students encountered during online learning while the education industry struggled with COVID-19, these threats included DDoS assaults and malicious domains, mobile learning apps, websites, and social media posts.

The research by Filipczuk et al. [92] showed evidence that there is a shortage of cybersecurity expertise, which has led to an increased risk of cyberattacks. They discovered that hackers targeted school and student information by taking advantage of the vulnerabilities due to limited resources. Similar findings were revealed by Oyedotun [93], who discovered that the shift toward remote learning enhanced students' susceptibility to phishing and social engineering attacks. This result was based on the author's observation that these types of attacks became more prevalent. When the COVID-19 outbreak occurred, many educational institutions lacked the necessary security technologies and expertise to provide students and educators with hands-on training on technology and the dangers posed by cyberattacks.

4.4   Why the Education Sector is a Target of Ransomware

For the past few years, ransomware attacks have been creating chaos both in private and public organizations around the world, affecting sectors as diverse as financial services, manufacturing, telecommunications, and IT, as well as healthcare. Cybercriminals target more gullible targets like the education sector as these sectors continue to boost their cybersecurity investment and seek ways to defend against ransomware threats.

The recent exponential increase in ransomware attacks has affected every part of the educational institution from institutions' websites to third-party applications, databases, and so on. This has caused abrupt damage to the reputation of the sector whereby some schools and education centers have closed or reduced their technological dependence. These cyber attackers have subjected many educational institutions to double-extortion schemes, in which hackers not only deny them access to their information systems but also steal their data and threaten to post it online if the ransom is not paid [94]. Some attackers even go as far as selling this information on the dark web to other potential threat actors.

This stolen data can contain personally identifying information such as a passport number, a Social Security number, information on a guardian or parent, tax records, or financial transactions. Health information such as COVID-19 test data, disability reports, reports on past convictions, and psychological evaluations of students may also be included. It may also contain contracts and other legal documents, financial reports containing details about bank accounts, health information such as COVID-19 test data, and reports on previous convictions.

Several issues, including a lack of adequate cybersecurity resources, the usage of general populace portals, and third-party applications access to the community, parents, and students, have led to an increase in ransomware attackers targeting educational institutions in recent years. These ransomware attacks on schools and colleges are quite destructive because they interfere with crucial information systems, computer devices, educational processes, administrative operations and most importantly put both students' and staff's information and safety at risk [95].

In response to ransomware attacks, UK educational institutions spend an average of £2 million, according to Jisc's Cyber Impact Report 2022 topping the list of Education sector cyber security risk involving more than 100 institutions as victims [96]. Supporting this evidence is the Endsleigh Insurance report, which claimed that over the past two years, 41% of elementary schools and 70% of high schools experienced some form of cyber-attack.

UK GDPR reported that the implementation of remote work practises and COVID-19 are to blame for the rise in attacks against the education sector. Nowadays, there are more and more devices outside of campuses that hold personal data and information. Protecting that data, wherever it is located, has increased security issues and unintentionally resulted in some significant security incidents. Additionally, they highlighted that vulnerable RDP settings had given ransomware perpetrators access to victims' PCs.

Generally, the education sector may be a popular target for ransomware attack for several reasons such as;

- **Sensitive data**: educational institutions gather and keep a lot of private information about students and employees, including names, grades, and financial data. Attackers may find this information valuable and utilize this information for financial gain or reconnaissance.
- **Limited IT resources**: Due to their constrained IT budgets and resources, many educational institutions find it challenging to adequately adopt and maintain effective cybersecurity protocols and strategies making them more susceptible to ransomware attacks.
- **Limited cybersecurity preparedness**: many personnel and students in the education sector have a limited understanding of cybersecurity policies, standards, and methods making them more susceptible to phishing schemes and other social engineering attacks that might result in ransomware infestations.
- **Reputation**: Educational institutions have a lot to lose in terms of reputation if they are targeted by a ransomware attack. This can lead them to pay the ransom as a means of preserving their reputation and avoiding negative publicity.

It's critical for educational institutions to be aware of these causes and to take precautions against ransomware attacks by putting in place a thorough cybersecurity strategy, implementing information standards and being up to date on the most recent threats and best practices, and maintaining effective incidence response plans.

4.5   Popular Ransomware Attacks on the Educational Sector

There have been several high-profile ransomware attacks on the educational sector in recent years, few of them are;

- **Petya**: Several institutions were impacted by the massive attack that Petya launched against organizations in 2017 across the globe. Due to the use of the "EternalBlue" attack method, which took advantage of a flaw in Microsoft Windows, the attack was able to spread quickly over networks. Attacks by Petya on the University of the Witwatersrand in South Africa [97] and the University of Calgary in Canada [98] are examples of attacks in the educational sector. The attack in 2017 disrupted university operations and resulted in some systems and data becoming inaccessible. To prevent the malware from spreading, the University had to cut off its networks and computer systems. It was reported that major institutions had to pay the ransom before the encryption keys were released.
- **Ryuk**: In 2019, the deployment of Ryuk in a deliberate attack on the District of Lodi School, Wisconsin. A number of the district's systems, including those that contained student and employee data, were encrypted as a result of the attack, which also seriously disrupted business as usual. For access to its systems to be restored, the school district was forced to pay a ransom. Another illustration is

the 2020 Ryuk ransomware attack on the Universities of California, Los Angeles (UCLA) (UCSF) [99]. The attack resulted in the encryption of numerous of the university's systems and caused severe interruption to its operations. The university made the decision not to pay the ransom, therefore in order to regain access to its systems, it was forced to rely on backups.

- **REvil/Sodinokibi**: In 2020 and 2021, REvil/Sodinokibi ransomware attacks affected several educational institutions, encrypting files and demanding payment in Bitcoin in order to restore access. The University of California, San Francisco (UCSF) disclosed that they had experienced a REvil ransomware in 2020. Some of the university's files were encrypted as a result of the attack, and the attackers wanted a $1.14 million ransom to decrypt the data [99]. The St. John the Baptist Parish School Board in Louisiana was attacked by REvil ransomware in 2021. The school district was compelled to pay the $250,000 ransom requested by the attackers to recover access to their systems.
- **Maze**: In 2020, Maze ransomware attacks affected several educational institutions, encrypting files and demanding payment in Bitcoin to restore access. It is also unique in that it exfiltrates data before encryption, threatening to publish the stolen data if the ransom is not paid. UC Berkeley announced a Maze ransomware attack in 2020 and to decrypt some university files, the attackers requested $1.4 million [99]. Pelham City School District in Alabama was infected by Maze ransomware in 2020, in order to regain access to their systems, the school district had to pay a $150,000 ransom to the hackers. The Torrance Unified School District in California was infected by Maze ransomware in 2020, though the attackers demanded $1.5 million, but the school district did not pay and had to restore data from backups [100].

These instances highlight how crucial it is to put in place appropriate security safeguards, such as consistent backups, upgrades, and personnel training, to prevent and lessen the effects of a ransomware assault. It is also crucial to keep in mind that paying the ransom can encourage the attackers to carry out more nefarious actions because there is no guarantee that they will provide the decryption key.

5   Mitigation Strategy

It's the general belief of cybersecurity professionals that cyber-attacks on the education sector will likely rise in frequency and sophistication as technology progresses and more educational institutions are expected to transition into digital systems and online platforms and also upgrade their existing technologies to fit with the evolution. Here are a few ways that cyber-attack may span on the education sector in the future:

Increased focus on ransomware attacks: Ransomware attacks, which involve encrypting a victim's files and demanding a ransom in exchange for the decryption key, has already been a major threat to the education sector. As this type of attack proves to be successful, it is likely that attackers will continue to focus on targeting educational institutions with ransomware.

More advanced phishing attacks: Phishing attacks, which involve tricking victims into providing sensitive information or clicking on malicious links, are also likely to become more sophisticated. Attackers may use more personalized and convincing tactics, such as using the name of a specific person or department within an educational institution.

Ransomware-as-a-Service (RaaS): "RaaS is a "subscription-based business model" that enables affiliates to carry out ransomware attacks using premade ransomware tools. Then, a portion of each successful ransom payment goes to these affiliates. When ransomware operators give clients ready-to-use ransomware tools to begin ransomware attacks. Anyone can buy and use pre-made malware using this technique, even those with little or no programming knowledge. A would-be criminal only needs access to the dark web and evil intent now that a plethora of RaaS alternatives are available in the market.

Artificial intelligence Expansion: Artificial intelligence is required for any autonomous creation, including robotics, smart cities, smart grids, smart cars, and smart buildings. AI expansion is necessary to meet the exponential for smart innovation. It will cause numerous ethical and societal issues. The machine will converse with people in a human-like manner. If the control of the human-like machine is lost due to a security breach, it will be very difficult.

Blockchain Revolution: Global monetary system faces numerous difficulties because of the growing need for blockchain technology. Numerous cryptocurrencies are produced using blockchain technology. Without appropriate security measures to protect every product and service that the blockchain revolution has inspired. The blockchain revolution has several securities challenges and fixing them all is exceedingly difficult.

Establishing a culture of cybersecurity awareness regarding all network devices and digital services is an essential step. Implementing robust security standards, policies and comprehensive digital event documentation can help mitigate any potential system risk from ransomware attacks. Usman et al. advise adopting the best cyber hygiene practices like Storage Backup, regular Risk Assessment analysis, Employee Training, Preparing and practicing incident response plans, installation, and regularly updating anti-virus and anti-malware, among other traditional measures as necessary actions to secure vulnerable networks.

However, the current evolution in technology offers sophisticated security measures that can be used to prevent, minimize, and respond to cybersecurity threats. Kok et al. [47, 101] studied different research on ransomware detection and mitigation methods such as Machine Learning, Honeypot, Artificial Intelligence as advanced measures that can be implemented.

Cybersecurity professionals everyday research different models, and frameworks, creating enhanced security policies, standards, and procedures in a way to bridge the gap between cyberattacks and the information system.

5.1 Future Adoptions

Future trends suggest that the adoption of technology and cybersecurity in the educational sector will continue to expand. Here are a few explanations:

- Virtual Reality: Virtual reality contributes to education by enabling immersive teachings that have a lasting impression on learners. These VR learning opportunities help students develop crucial interpersonal abilities like empathy, teamwork, and social skills they will need in the future.
- Internet of Things (IoT): IoT will enable schools to automate classroom processes, improve campus safety, cater to students with special needs, and expand students' access to relevant information. "Smart lesson plans," as opposed to the more static plans of yore, can be developed by educators with the use of this technology.
- Artificial intelligence (AI) and machine learning (ML): AI offers solutions to several issues in contemporary education, including bridging the technological divide between students and teachers, maintaining the integrity and authenticity of the educational process, enabling remote learning, and creating high-quality data and information solutions for the current educational process. ML is helping teachers/educators identify at-risk pupils earlier and intervene to increase achievement and retention.
- Blockchain technology: The education sector is expected to use blockchain technology to manage and secure staff and student data and create digital credentials like degrees and certificates.
- Cloud-based solutions: Cloud-based solutions are expected to be increasingly adopted in the education sector to store and manage student data, and to enable remote access and collaboration.
- 5G Computing: The development of edge and 5G computing technologies makes it possible to give high-speed internet connectivity to remote and rural locations, bridging the digital divide and expanding access to technology in education.

In conclusion, the education sector will continue to adopt and invest in cybersecurity and technology in the future, driven by the increasing reliance on technology to support remote learning, the adoption of IoT devices, the use of AI and ML, the implementation of blockchain technology, and the use of cloud-based solutions. Educational institutions should anticipate these developments and take steps to protect themselves by implementing a comprehensive cybersecurity strategy, staying informed about the latest threats and best practices, and having incident response plans in place.

5.2 The Exponential Growth of Dependency of the Educational Sector on Technologies, Potential Benefits, Potential Drawbacks, Concerns, and Ethical Issues in Education

Easy access to a larger variety of resources and educational materials is one big advantage of technology in education. The learning process can be improved and made more interesting for students by using online lessons, films, interactive simulations, and virtual reality experiences [101].

The use of digital devices and online resources in the classroom is one part of the exponential growth and dependency on technology in education. For instance, a study by the National Center for Education Statistics (NCES) found that in the United States, the proportion of classrooms with internet connection climbed from 35% in 2000 to 99% in 2015 [102]. The rapidly increasing use of technology for online and remote learning has been fueled by the development of online learning platforms like Blackboard, Moodle, Microsoft Teams, etc., and the broad availability of the internet. According to a study by the Babson Survey Group, 6.7 million students were enrolled in at least one online course in 2016 from 1.6 million in 2002 [103].

The emergence of Artificial Intelligence (AI) technology like an AI-based chatbot can be used to help teachers grade assignments and give feedback to students as well as to offer personalized support and coaching to students [104]. Machine learning (ML) makes it possible to analyze student data and provide insights into student learning patterns and progress. To forecast student performance, spot at-risk students, and modify lesson plans to each student's requirements, ML algorithms can be utilized. Also, through gamification, teachers can now use game-based activities and simulations to teach complex and complicated concepts, and can use points, badges, and leaderboards to motivate students [104].

Overall, the educational sector's dependence on the exponential rise of technology has created several opportunities that have improved communication and collaboration in the sector's development. However, there have been challenges, potential drawbacks, and ethical concerns related to the use of technology in education. When integrating technology into education, there are ethical concerns about the security and privacy of student data as well as the preservation of intellectual property. The fear of the data collected by tech companies being sold or shared with third parties without the prior knowledge or consent of students or parents [105].

The digital divide, which refers to the unequal distribution of access to technology and the internet among various socioeconomic levels, is one of the key issues. Due to this, students from underprivileged backgrounds may not have access to the same technological resources as their more favored peers, which may cause inconsistencies in their educational achievement [106]. Using technology in education has the potential to reinforce or even amplify preexisting biases and discrimination [107]. An AI-based system, for instance, might make discriminating conclusions if it was trained on data that is not representative of the population [108].

Another typical drawback is that these technologies can be expensive, both in terms of the necessary hardware and software and in terms of the support and training that students and educators required to utilize them effectively, moreover, the adoption and efficiency of these technologies in the classroom may be hampered by educators' and students' lack of digital literacy abilities [109].

Other major concerns include over-reliance on technology which may have a negative effect on students' capacity for concentration and retentive memory, also the role of teachers in human interaction being replaced by technology in education could have a negative impact on socializing and learning.

In addition to highlighting the necessity for educators and researchers to be aware of these ethical concerns and to take action to solve them when integrating technology in the classroom, it's critical to note that these drawbacks are not permanent and can vary depending on how the technology is implemented. This can be accomplished by creating moral standards and norms as well as continuous assessment and evaluation of how technology is used in education [110, 111].

6 Digital and Modern Education

The modern digital educational environment has a significant impact on the transformation of the entire system of digitalization, causing, at the same time, often not quite sufficient change in the Outlook of prospective customers of services using these innovations, which necessitated a close study and study of the problem [112]. This necessitated a close study and study of the problem has necessitated a close study and study of the problem. People's whole value systems as well as their entire ways of life are being profoundly reshaped as a result of the widespread adoption of new digital resources and technology. The advancement of informatization, which later provided the foundation for the digitalization of modern society, has brought about substantial changes in the methods by which students are educated and trained [113].

Because of the significant influence that digitization has had on many different aspects of society, as well as the intricate and multi-tiered educational system, a fundamental revaluation of the educational process's goals and its subject matter has become essential [114]. The employment of cloud computing technologies in educational settings, as stated by Ref. [115], "will allow science to overcome all current barriers: geographical, technological, and social". The authors note that the use of cloud technology by educators significantly improves their capacities, particularly in regard to the creation of group projects that include collaboration.

6.1 Edtech

According to [116] about two-thirds of educators (65%) report that they make daily use of digital learning tools in the classroom; 22% use them a few times a week, and 13% utilize them once a week or less frequently. A little more than half of all instructors (53%) say that their pupils make daily use of digital learning tools to further their education. Seven out of ten students say that they do coursework using digital learning tools outside of the classroom on at least a couple days each week on average.

7 Educational Tools by Category

In this day and age, providing and administering education requires the use of cutting-edge educational resources. Some examples of these cutting-edge tools are learning management systems and online learning platforms as shown in Fig. 6. However, if an appropriate security measures safeguard against cyber assaults like ransomware, but they also no guarantee that educational services will continue without interruption. The absence of appropriate security measures can, in the event of an attack, result in disruptions in the delivery of educational services, which in turn can cause severe harm to both students and instructors [117] (Figs. 7 and 8).

A data breach known as the Blackbaud hack took place at Blackbaud Inc., which is a supplier of cloud-based software solutions for the not-for-profit, educational, and healthcare industries. It wasn't until May of 2020 that the attack was uncovered, although investigators suspect it occurred earlier in the year. Blackbaud is one of the major producers of CRM (customer relationship management) software to non-profit

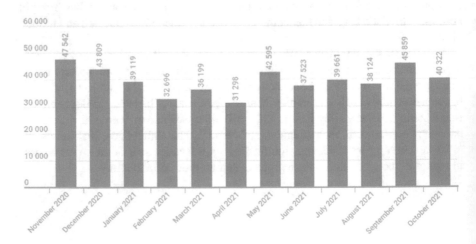

Fig. 6 Number of corporate users affected due to ransomware

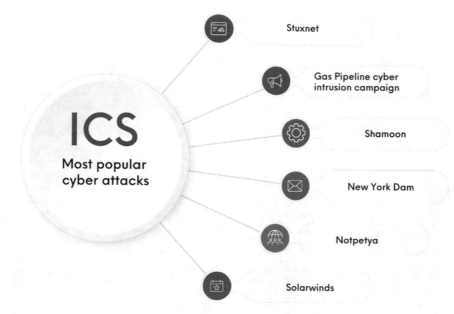

Fig. 7 Popular cyber-attacks on ICS

organisations, educational institutions, and healthcare providers [119]. This type of software helps organisations better manage their relationships with their customers. The company's platform is used to store sensitive personal information of individuals, such as names, addresses, phone numbers, email addresses, and financial information. Examples of this type of information include names, addresses, and email addresses.

The cybercriminals were able to get access to a portion of the data stored for a variety of Blackbaud customers, including information from educational institutions, medical facilities, and charitable organisations [120]. According to the company's statement, the data that was accessed did not contain any Social Security numbers, information on credit cards, or details about bank accounts. However, it's possible that some of the material obtained contained contact information, and in certain instances, details about an individual's affiliation with the group. The first notification from Blackbaud said that the hackers had been removed from their systems and that the company had adopted security steps to prevent further unwanted access. In spite of this, it was later revealed that the hackers had made off with a copy of the data, and that Blackbaud had paid the hackers a ransom in order to get them to destroy the data that they had taken. This event underscores both the need of safeguarding sensitive data in the cloud as well as the necessity for enterprises to develop comprehensive security policies in order to defend themselves from cyber-attacks [121].

It is necessary for educational institutions to employ security measures such as routine backups, software updates and patches, user education and awareness, and incident response plans in order to reduce the danger of these sorts of attacks.

LEARNING TOOLS & PLATFORMS	
Edu learning platforms	Google, Classroom | Moodle | Canvas
Edu content	Wordwall | Live Worksheets
Edu quizzes/tests	Quizizz | Quizlet
Corporate learning platforms	Moodle | a NewSpring
Online course platforms	LinkedIn Learning | Udemy | Coursera
Language learning apps	Duolingo
Authoring	Articulate | Camtasia | Easygenerator
CONTENT DEVELOPMENT	
Screenshots	Snagit
Screencasts	Camtasia | Screencast-O-matic | Loom | Screencastify
Graphics:	Canva | Genially | Adobe Photoshop
Animation	Vyond | Powtoon
Video	Biteable | Adobe Premiere Pro | Panopto
Audio	Audacity
Live video streaming	OBS Studio | MS Stream
Interactive content	hihaho | H5P | Thinglink
Forms and surveys	Google Forms | Survey Monkey | MS Forms
Blogs and websites	WordPress | Google Sites
OFFICE TOOLS	
Docuemntation	Google docs, MS word
Presentation	Powerpoint, google slide, prezi
Spreadsheet	Google sheets, MS Excel
File sharing	Google Drive | Dropbox | OneDrive
Email	Gmail | Outlook
Digital notebooks	OneNote | Evernote
SOCIAL & COLLABORATION PLATFORMS	
Video meeting	Microsoft Teams | Zoom | Google Meet | Whereby | Flipgrid
Messaging apps	WhatsApp | Telegram| Discord
Live Engagement	Kahoot | Mentimeter
Social networks	LinkedIn | Twitter |Instagram | Facebook | TikTok

Fig. 8 Educational tools. *Source* [118]

7.1 Business Continuity

In this day and age, the provision of education and its administration are dependent upon the utilisation of various educational instruments, such as learning management systems (LMS) and online learning platforms. However, because these gadgets are connected to the internet and contain sensitive information, they leave themselves open to the possibility of being attacked via the internet. Because of this, maintaining the continued operation of educational tools' businesses is absolutely necessary [122]. The capacity of a company to sustain its operations and services during and after a disruptive event, such as the occurrence of a natural catastrophe or a cyber assault, is what is meant by the term "business continuity." When it comes to educational tools, maintaining business continuity is absolutely necessary to guarantee that both students and teachers will continue to have access to and be able to make use of the resources as required [123].

The provision of educational services is susceptible to being disrupted in the event that a cyber attack, such as one using ransomware, takes place when the organization's educational tools do not have the appropriate level of protection in place. This interruption may result in inconvenient circumstances and the loss of vital data, both of which may have a detrimental influence not only on the educational experience of the students but also on the reputation of the organisation [124]. In addition, as a result of the present pandemic scenario, a large number of educational institutions have been compelled to transition to the use of remote learning, which has led to an increasing reliance on educational technologies as well as the necessity of ensuring business continuity.

8 Conclusion

Ransomware attacks on the educational sector have become a growing concern in recent years. These attacks target schools, universities, and other educational institutions, with the goal of encrypting sensitive data and demanding a ransom payment in exchange for the decryption key. The attacks can cause significant disruptions to the educational process and can lead to financial losses for the affected institutions. One of the reasons why educational institutions are particularly vulnerable to ransomware attacks is that they often have limited resources and budget to invest in cybersecurity. Additionally, many educational institutions have a large number of employees and students who may not be properly trained in cybersecurity best practices, making it easier for attackers to exploit vulnerabilities.

To protect against ransomware attacks, educational institutions should invest in robust cybersecurity measures such as regular software updates, firewalls, and anti-virus software. They should also provide cybersecurity training to all employees and students to raise awareness of the risks and teach them how to identify and avoid potential threats. Additionally, institutions should regularly back up their data to minimize the impact of a successful attack, and they should have incident response plans in place to quickly respond to and mitigate a ransomware incident. It's also important to note that, paying the ransom is not a solution and it doesn't guarantee that the attackers will decrypt the files, and in some cases, the attackers may demand additional payments. Moreover, paying the ransom could also encourage attackers to target more educational institutions.

Another important aspect is for the educational institutions to have a clear incident response plan in place, which should include steps to be taken in the event of a ransomware attack, procedures for communicating with employees and students, and procedures for reporting and responding to the attack. This will help the institution to minimize the damage, and to minimize the disruption caused by the attack. Furthermore, educational institutions should have a well-defined data governance policy in place, which defines the responsibilities of employees and students, and outlines the measures that should be taken to protect sensitive data. This policy should be reviewed and updated regularly to ensure that it remains up-to-date.

In addition, educational institutions should have a robust incident detection and response mechanism in place, which should include monitoring tools and incident response procedures. This will help the institution to detect a ransomware attack at an early stage, and to respond quickly and effectively. Finally, educational institutions should establish effective communication channels with the relevant authorities, such as the Cybercrime Unit, in order to get the necessary support in case of a ransomware attack. This will help the institution to minimize the impact of the attack, and to recover from the attack as quickly as possible.

9 Summary

Ransomware attacks on the educational sector can cause significant disruptions and financial losses. Educational institutions should invest in robust cybersecurity measures, provide regular training to employees and students, have a clear incident response plan, data governance policy, incident detection and response mechanism and establish effective communication with authorities to reduce their vulnerability to these attacks. By taking these steps, institutions can better protect themselves against ransomware and minimize the impact of a successful attack.

References

1. Blazic AJ (2021) New approach in cybersecurity education–introducing new practices and innovations. In: EDULEARN21 proceedings, pp 6619–6626
2. Rahman N, Sairi I, Zizi NAM, Khalid F (2020) The importance of cybersecurity education in school. Int J Inf Educ Technol 10(5):378–382
3. Khang A, Hahanov V, Abbas GL, Hajimahmud VA (2022) Cyber-physical-social system and incident management. In: AI-centric smart city ecosystems. CRC Press, pp 21–35
4. Jalkanen J (2019) Is human the weakest link in information security?. Systematic literature review
5. Meisner M (2017) Financial consequences of cyber attacks leading to data breaches in healthcare sector. Copernican J Finan Account 6(3):63–73
6. Shillair R, Esteve-González P, Dutton WH, Creese S, Nagyfejeo E, von Solms B (2022) National level evidence-based results, challenges, and promise. Comput Secur 102756
7. Khader M, Karam M, Fares H (2021) Cybersecurity awareness framework for academia. Information 12(10):417
8. Butt UJ, Abbod M, Lors A, Jahankhani H, Jamal A, Kumar A (2019) Ransomware threat and its impact on SCADA. In: 2019 IEEE 12th international conference on global security, safety and sustainability (ICGS3), pp 205–212
9. Taherdoost H (2022) Understanding cybersecurity frameworks and information security standards—a review and comprehensive overview. Electron (Basel) 11(14):2181
10. Stallings W, Brown L, Bauer MD, Howard M (2012) Computer security: principles and practice, vol 2. Pearson Upper Saddle River
11. Samonas S, Coss D (2014) The CIA strikes back: redefining confidentiality, integrity and availability in security. J Inf Syst Secur 10(3)

12. Sajal SZ, Jahan I, Nygard KE (2019) A survey on cyber security threats and challenges in modem society. In: 2019 IEEE international conference on electro information technology (EIT), pp 525–528
13. Furnell S, Heyburn H, Whitehead A, Shah JN (2020) Understanding the full cost of cyber security breaches. Comput Fraud Secur 2020(12):6–12
14. Pastore J (2016) Practical approaches to cybersecurity in arbitration. Fordham Int'l LJ 40:1023
15. Jawad A, Jaskolka J (2021) Analyzing the impact of cyberattacks on industrial control systems using timed automata. In: 2021 IEEE 21st international conference on software quality, reliability and security (QRS), pp 966–977
16. Lis P, Mendel J (2019) Cyberattacks on critical infrastructure: an economic perspective 1. Econ Bus Rev 5(2):24–47
17. Huang K, Ye R, Madnick S (2019) Both sides of the coin: the impact of cyber attacks on business value
18. Choo K-KR (2011) The cyber threat landscape: challenges and future research directions. Comput Secur 30(8):719–731
19. Seemma SP, Nandhini S, Sowmiya M (2018) Overview of cyber security. Int J Adv Res Comput Commun Eng 7(11):125–128
20. Nagahawatta RTS, Warren M, Yeoh W (2018) A study of cybersecurity awareness in Sri Lanka. In: 17th Australian cyber warfare conference (CWAR), October 10–11th, 2018, Melbourne, Victoria, Australia, p 45
21. Steele S, Wargo C (2007) An introduction to insider threat management. Inf Syst Secur 16(1):23–33
22. Livingston S, Sanborn S, Slaughter A, Zonneveld P (2019) Managing cyber risk in the electric power sector. Deloitte. As of 17
23. Souppaya M, Scarfone K (2013, July) Guide to malware incident prevention and handling for desktops and laptops. NIST Special Publication, pp 800–83
24. ciso.uw.edu (2015) Things to know about malware
25. FTMS (2019) Computing basics, CSCA0101 ed
26. Pachhala N, Jothilakshmi S, Battula BP (2021) A comprehensive survey on identification of malware types and malware classification using machine learning techniques. In: Proceedings—2nd international conference on smart electronics and communication, ICOSEC 2021, pp 1207–1214. https://doi.org/10.1109/ICOSEC51865.2021.9591763
27. Souppaya M, Scarfone K (2013) NIST special publication 800-83 revision 1 guide to malware incident prevention and handling for desktops and laptops. NISThttps://doi.org/10.6028/NIST.SP.800-83r1
28. Cohen F (1985) Computer viruses
29. Toutonji O, Yoo S-M (2009) An approach against a computer worm attack
30. Haagman D, Ghavalas B (2005) Trojan defence: a forensic view. Digit Investig 2(1):23–30. https://doi.org/10.1016/j.diin.2005.01.010
31. Butler J, Silberman P (2006) Raide: rootkit analysis identification elimination. Black Hat USA, vol 47
32. O'Gorman G, McDonald G (2012) Ransomware: a growing menace. Symantec Security Response
33. Accenture (2021) Threats unmasked cyber threat intelligence report
34. IBM (2022) X-force threat intelligence index 2022. IBM
35. cisa.gov (2022, Feb) 2021 trends show increased globalized threat of ransomware, cisa.gov
36. cyber.gov.au (2022) 2021 trends show increased globalized threat of ransomware, cyber.gov.au
37. ncsc.gov.uk (2022, Feb) Joint advisory highlights increased globalised threat of ransomware, ncsc.gov.uk
38. ENISA (2022, Oct) ENISA threat landscape 2022 about ENISA, ENISA, pp 24–25. https://doi.org/10.2824/764318
39. Gazet A (2010) Comparative analysis of various ransomware virii. J Comput Virol 6(1):77–90. https://doi.org/10.1007/s11416-008-0092-2

40. Thomas JE (2018) Individual cyber security: empowering employees to resist spear phishing to prevent identity theft and ransomware attacks. Int J Bus Manage 13(6):1. https://doi.org/10.5539/IJBM.V13N6P1

41. Reshmi TR (2021) Information security breaches due to ransomware attacks—a systematic literature review. Int J Inf Manage Data Insights 1(2):100013. https://doi.org/10.1016/J.JJIMEI.2021.100013

42. Rapid7 (2020) Ransomware playbook, Rapid7

43. Komatwar R, Kokare M (2021) Retracted article: a survey on malware detection and classification. J Appl Secur Res 16(3):390–420

44. Meland PH, Bayoumy YFF, Sindre G (2020) The ransomware-as-a-service economy within the darknet. Comput Secur 92:101762

45. Khammas BM (2020) Ransomware detection using random forest technique. ICT Express 6(4):325–331

46. Andronio N, Zanero S, Maggi F (2015) Heldroid: dissecting and detecting mobile ransomware. In: International symposium on recent advances in intrusion detection, pp 382–404

47. Kok SH, Abdullah A, Jhanjhi NZ, Supramaniam M (2019) Prevention of crypto-ransomware using a pre-encryption detection algorithm. https://doi.org/10.3390/computers8040079

48. Beaman C, Barkworth A, Akande TD, Hakak S, Khan MK (2021) Ransomware: recent advances, analysis, challenges and future research directions. Comput Secur 111:102490. https://doi.org/10.1016/J.COSE.2021.102490

49. Brewer R (2016) Ransomware attacks: detection, prevention and cure. Netw Secur 2016(9):5–9. https://doi.org/10.1016/S1353-4858(16)30086-1

50. Thomas JE (2018) Individual cyber security: empowering employees to resist spear phishing to prevent identity theft and ransomware attacks. Int J Bus Manage 13(6). https://doi.org/10.5539/ijbm.v13n6p1

51. Levesque FL, Fernandez JM, Somayaji A (2014, Dec) Risk prediction of malware victimization based on user behavior. In: Proceedings of the 9th IEEE international conference on malicious and unwanted software, MALCON 2014, pp 128–134. https://doi.org/10.1109/MALWARE.2014.6999412

52. kaspersky (2021) Over half of ransomware victims pay the ransom, but only a quarter see their full data returned|Kaspersky, kaspersky. https://www.kaspersky.com/about/press-releases/2021_over-half-of-ransomware-victims-pay-the-ransom-but-only-a-quarter-see-their-full-data-returned. Accessed 20 Jan 2023

53. Jansen J, Leukfeldt R (2016) Phishing and malware attacks on online banking customers in the Netherlands: a qualitative analysis of factors leading to victimization. Int J Cyber Criminol 10(1):79

54. Mansfield-Devine S (2016) Ransomware: taking businesses hostage. Netw Secur 2016(10):8–17. https://doi.org/10.1016/S1353-4858(16)30096-4

55. Furnell S, Emm D (2017) The ABC of ransomware protection. Comput Fraud Secur 2017(10):5–11. https://doi.org/10.1016/S1361-3723(17)30089-1

56. Kaspersky (2021) Kaspersky security bulletin 2021. Statistics, kaspersky

57. Ministry of Justice UK (2022) Cyber and technical security guidance, ministry of justice UK

58. ENISA (2022) ENISA threat landscape for ransomware attacks july 2022, European Union Agency for cyber security. https://doi.org/10.2824/456263

59. Trendmicro (2020, Nov) Ryuk 2020: distributing ransomware via trickbot and bazarLoader, Trendmico

60. Hoseini A (2022) Ransomware and phishing cyberattacks: analyzing the public's perception of these attacks in Sweden. Accessed: 21 Jan 2023. [Online]. Available: http://www.teknat.uu.se/student

61. Sophos (2022, April) Ransomware hit 66% of organizations surveyed for Sophos annual state of ransomware 2022, Sophos

62. Thomas J (2018) Individual cyber security: Empowering employees to resist spear phishing to prevent identity theft and ransomware attacks. Int J Bus Manage 12(3):1–23

63. Wang ZH, Liu CG, Qiu J, Tian ZH, Cui X, Su S (2018) Automatically traceback RDP-based targeted ransomware attacks. Wirel Commun Mob Comput 2018. https://doi.org/10.1155/2018/7943586
64. thebci.org (2018) BCI contInuIty and ResIIIenCe RePoRt 2018 raising the impact of business continuity
65. Hull G, John H, Arief B (2019) Ransomware deployment methods and analysis: views from a predictive model and human responses. Crime Sci 8(1):1–22
66. Choi K, Scott TM, LeClair DP (2016) Ransomware against police: diagnosis of risk factors via application of cyber-routine activities theory. Int J Forensic Sci Pathol
67. Connolly LY, Wall DS, Lang M, Oddson B (2020, Jan) An empirical study of ransomware attacks on organizations: an assessment of severity and salient factors affecting vulnerability. J Cybersecur 6(1). https://doi.org/10.1093/CYBSEC/TYAA023
68. Alguliyev R, Imamverdiyev Y, Sukhostat L (2018, Sept 1) Cyber-physical systems and their security issues. Computers in industry, vol 100. Elsevier B.V., pp 212–223. https://doi.org/10.1016/j.compind.2018.04.017
69. Butt UJ, Jahankhani H, Abbod M, Jamal A, Lors A, Kumar A (2019) Ransomware threat and its impact on SCADA; ransomware threat and its impact on SCADA
70. Peterson D (2016) Ransomware in ICS/SCADA. It's happening and predictions. Dale Peterson
71. Hemsley KE, Fisher RE (2018) History of industrial control system cyber incidents. [Online]. Available: http://www.inl.gov
72. Chen TM, Abu-Nimeh S (2011) Lessons from Stuxnet. Comput (Long Beach Calif) 44(4):91–93. https://doi.org/10.1109/MC.2011.115
73. Russinovich M (2019, June) Analyzing a stuxnet infection with the sysinternals tools, part 1', microsoft
74. ICS-CERT (2012) ICS-CERT monitor, cisa
75. Alelyani S, Kumar HGR (2018) Overview of cyberattack on Saudi organizations. J Inf Secur Cybercrimes Res. https://doi.org/10.26735/16587790.2018.004
76. U.S. Attorney's Office (2016, March) Manhattan U.S. attorney announces charges against seven iranians for conducting coordinated campaign of cyber attacks against U.S. financial sector on behalf of islamic revolutionary guard corps-sponsored entities
77. Lakshmi R, Prasanna S, Pavan Kumar T (2019) Reverse engineering the behaviour of NotPetya ransomware. Int J Recent Technol Eng (IJRTE) 7(6S)
78. Neuberger A (2021, Feb) Press briefing by press secretary Jen Psaki and deputy national security advisor for cyber and emerging technology
79. CRS INSIGHT (May 2021) Colonial pipeline: the darkside strikes, Congressional research service
80. Ng W (2015) New digital technology in education. Springer
81. Toquero CM (2020) Challenges and opportunities for higher education amid the COVID-19 pandemic: the Philippine context. Pedagogical Res 5(4):2468–4929. https://doi.org/10.29333/pr/7947
82. ncsc.gov.uk (2020, Sept) Cyber security alert issued following rising attacks on UK academia. NCSC
83. Koomson JG (2021, Oct) Rise of ransomware attacks on the education sector during the COVID-19 pandemic, isaca.org
84. Microsoft (2023) Global threat activity, Microsoft
85. ncsc.gov.uk (2021, June) Alert: further ransomware attacks on the UK education sector by cyber criminals, NCSC
86. Gretchenko AI, Nikitskaya EF, Valishvili MA, Gretchenko AA (2018) Role of higher education institutions in developing hr potential in a forming innovation economy. Revista Espacios 39(21):13
87. Woessmann L (2016) The economic case for education. Educ Econ 24(1):3–32
88. Barro RJ (2001) Education and economic growth, The contribution of human and social capital to sustained economic growth and well-being. 79:13–41

89. Gyimah-Brempong K, Paddison O, Mitiku W (2006) Higher education and economic growth in Africa. J Dev Stud 42(3):509–529
90. Qureshi MI, Khan N, Raza H, Imran A, Ismail F (2021) Digital technologies in education 4.0. Does it enhance the effectiveness of learning?
91. Ansari JAN, Khan NA (2020) Exploring the role of social media in collaborative learning the new domain of learning. Smart Learn Environ 7(9)
92. Filipczuk D, Mason C, Snow S (2019) Using a game to explore notions of responsibility for cyber security in organisations. In: Extended abstracts of the 2019 CHI conference on human factors in computing systems, pp 1–6
93. Oyedotun TD (2020) Sudden change of pedagogy in education driven by COVID-19: perspectives and evaluation from a developing country. Res Globalization 2:100029
94. Alawida M, Omolara AE, Abiodun OI, Al-Rajab M (2022) A deeper look into cybersecurity issues in the wake of Covid-19: a survey. J King Saud Univ-Comput Inf Sci
95. Levin DA (2021) The state of K-12 cybersecurity: 2020 year in review. K-12 cybersecurity resource center
96. Jisc (2022) The impact of cyber security incidents on the UK' s further and higher education and research sectors observations, advice and questions to ask
97. Schell B, Passi K, Roy L (2019) How US and Canadian universities and colleges dealt with malware and ransomware attacks in 2016–2017. J Inf Syst Secur 15(2)
98. Connolly AY, Borrion H (2022) Reducing ransomware crime: analysis of victims payment decisions. Comput Secur 119:102760. https://doi.org/10.1016/j.cose.2022.102760
99. State of ransomware 2021 compiled by HG threat hunters Q1-Q2
100. Kok S, Abdullah A, Jhanjhi N, Supramaniam M (2019) Ransomware, threat and detection techniques: a review. Int J Comput Sci Netw Secur 19(2):136
101. Martín-Gutiérrez J, Mora CE, Añorbe-Díaz B, González-Marrero A (2017) Virtual technologies trends in education. Eurasia J Math, Sci Technol Educ 13(2):469–486
102. KewalRamani A et al. Student access to digital learning resources outside of the classroom
103. Solmon MA (2018) Promoting academic integrity in the context of 21st century technology. Kinesiol Rev 7(4):314–320
104. Okonkwo CW, Ade-Ibijola A (2021) Chatbots applications in education: a systematic review. Comput Educ: Artif Intell 2:100033
105. Sabourin J, Kosturko L, FitzGerald C, McQuiggan S (2015) Student privacy and educational data mining: perspectives from industry
106. Yang SC, Chen Y-J (2007) Technology-enhanced language learning: a case study. Comput Human Behav 23(1):860–879
107. Kizilcec RF, Lee H (2020) Algorithmic fairness in education. arXiv preprint arXiv:2007.05443
108. Mirbabaie M, Stieglitz S, Frick NRJ (2021) Artificial intelligence in disease diagnostics: a critical review and classification on the current state of research guiding future direction. Health Technol (Berl) 11(4):693–731
109. Al-Qallaf CL, Al-Mutairi ASR (2016) Digital literacy and digital content supports learning: the impact of blogs on teaching English as a foreign language. Electron Libr
110. Catota FE, Morgan MG, Sicker DC (2019, Jan) Cybersecurity education in a developing nation: the Ecuadorian environment. J Cybersecur 5(1). https://doi.org/10.1093/CYBSEC/TYZ001
111. Sen R (2018) Challenges to cybersecurity: current state of affairs. Commun Assoc Inf Syst 43(1):2
112. Dmitrievich AN, Nickolaevna SO, Nickolaevna SZ (2019) Preliminary results of the university participation in the project modern digital educational environment. Азимут научных исследований: педагогика и психология 8(1–26):16–19
113. Morozov AV, Kozlov OA (2019) Information and communication technologies in modern digital educational environment. In: CEUR workshop proceedings. 2. Cep. InnoCSE 2019—proceedings of the 2nd workshop on inovative approaches in computer science within higher education, p 211

114. Savotina NA (2020) Digital technology in modern education: risks and resources. https://doi. org/10.1088/1742-6596/1691/1/012095
115. Petrovych OB, Vinnichuk AP, Poida OA, Tkachenko VI, Vakaliuk TA, Kuzminska OH (2022) The didactic potential of cloud technologies in professional training of future teachers of Ukrainian language and literature. Accessed 21 Jan, 2023. [Online]. Available: https://library. vspu.edu.ua/inform/nauk_profil.htm#tkachenko_viktoria
116. newschools.org (March 2020) Education technology use in schools, newschools
117. Chapman J, Chinnaswamy A, Garcia-Perez A (2018) The severity of cyber attacks on education and research institutions: a function of their security posture. In: Proceedings of ICCWS 2018 13th international conference on cyber warfare and security. Academic Conferences and Publishing Limited, pp 111–119
118. Hart J (2022) Top 100 tools for learning 2022
119. Anders SB (2020) Nonprofit accounting resources. CPA J 90(4):64–65
120. ncsc.gov.in (2023, Jan) Cyber threat report: UK charity sector, ncsc
121. labour.org.uk (2021) Blackbaud data breach, labour.org.uk
122. Phillips R, Tanner B (2019) Breaking down silos between business continuity and cyber security. J Bus Contin Emer Plan 12(3):224–232
123. IFTODE D (2020) Business continuity management in higher education institutions. European finance, business and regulation EUFIRE 2020, p 195
124. ncsc.gov.uk (March 2021) Support for UK education sector after growth in cyber attacks, ncsc.gov.uk

Printed in the United States
by Baker & Taylor Publisher Services